Full Stack Web Development with React, Angular, Node.js, and DevOps

Build scalable frontend architectures using React hooks and Angular services while integrating Node.js backends and RESTful API communication layers

Rupesh Kumar Tipu

Pankaj Agarwal

www.bpbonline.com

First Edition 2026

ISBN: 978-93-65891-249

LIMITS OF LIABILITY AND DISCLAIMER OF WARRANTY

The information contained in this book is true and correct to the best of author's and publisher's knowledge. The author has made every effort to ensure the accuracy of these publications, but the publisher cannot be held responsible for any loss or damage arising from any information in this book.

All trademarks referred to in the book are acknowledged as properties of their respective owners but BPB Publications cannot guarantee the accuracy of this information.

Distributors:

BPB PUBLICATIONS
20, Ansari Road, Darya Ganj
New Delhi-110002
Ph: 23254990/23254991

DECCAN AGENCIES
4-3-329, Bank Street,
Hyderabad-500195
Ph: 24756967/24756400

MICRO MEDIA
Shop No. 5, Mahendra Chambers,
150 DN Rd. Next to Capital Cinema,
V.T. (C.S.T.) Station, MUMBAI-400 001
Ph: 22078296/22078297

Published by Manish Jain for BPB Publications, 20 Ansari Road, Darya Ganj, New Delhi-110002 and Printed by him at Repro India Ltd., Rewari.

www.bpbonline.com

Dedicated to

My beloved wife, Yamini, and my son, Aarav

-Rupesh Kumar Tipu

My father, S.K Agarwal

-Pankaj Agarwal

About the Authors

- **Dr. Rupesh Kumar Tipu** is an assistant professor at K.R. Mangalam University, Gurugram, with more than 12 years of teaching experience and over 6 years of research experience. His work spans web development, machine learning, deep learning, computer vision, optimization, and AI-driven engineering applications. He regularly designs application-oriented courses, mentors student projects, and develops practical learning resources that connect strong fundamentals with hands-on implementation.

- **Dr. Pankaj Agarwal** is professor and dean, School of Engineering and Technology, K.R. Mangalam University, Gurugram, India. He holds a Ph.D. in computer science from Jamia Millia Islamia and brings more than 21 years of teaching experience and over 15 years of research experience. His work focuses on data science, machine learning, deep learning, computer vision, natural language processing, data analytics, and algorithms. He has published more than 60 research papers, holds 12 patents, and has authored books in important areas of computer science and software development.

About the Reviewers

- **Poornakumar Rasiraju** is a senior software engineer with over a decade of experience designing and building large-scale enterprise applications. He specializes in modern web technologies, microservices architecture, artificial intelligence-enabled systems, and cloud-native application development. His work spans high-impact enterprise domains, where he has contributed to scalable, secure, and performance-critical solutions.

  Poornakumar holds bachelor's and master's degrees in computer science, with a strong academic foundation in software engineering, distributed systems, artificial intelligence, and applied computing. His professional interests include enterprise system design, intelligent automation, observability, and the application of AI techniques to improve software quality and operational efficiency.

  He also actively contributes to the software engineering community through technical reviewing and knowledge sharing via technical articles, with a focus on advancing best practices in enterprise soft ware development.

- **Roman Fedytskyi** is a senior frontend engineering leader specializing in scalable, secure, and compliance-driven user interface platforms for fintech and large-scale digital systems. He began his career as a frontend software engineer at Datamart Inc., where he developed production-grade web applications and established a strong foundation in modern frontend architecture.

  From 2016 to 2024, he held senior engineering and leadership roles at international software companies, including N-iX, JetSoftPro, Valtech, and American Eagle Outfitters. During this period, he led the development of enterprise-scale UI platforms, design systems, and high-performing frontend teams supporting complex fintech and global e-commerce products.

  Since 2024, he has been with ORSNN, a U.S.based institutional fintech company, where he serves as vice president of user experience and frontend engineering. In this role, he leads the architecture and delivery of secure, scalable, and regulatory-compliant user interfaces for institutional loan trading and financial data platforms. His professional interests include micro-frontend architecture, real-time UI systems, frontend performance optimization, developer platform design, and compliance-aware user experience engineering in regulated financial environments.

Acknowledgements

This book has taken shape through the support, encouragement, and contributions of many people. Deep gratitude goes to family members for their patience, motivation, and understanding throughout the writing process.

A sincere thanks to BPB Publications for their guidance, editorial support, and professional assistance in bringing this book to completion. Appreciation is also due to the reviewers, editors, and technical experts whose suggestions helped improve the structure, clarity, and practical value of the manuscript.

Gratitude is extended to colleagues, collaborators, and students whose discussions, questions, and feedback helped refine many of the ideas presented in this book. Their engagement with modern web technologies, application development, and software engineering practices helped shape the hands-on approach followed throughout these chapters.

Finally, heartfelt thanks go to every reader who chooses this book as part of a learning journey in full stack web development. That trust and interest give this work its real purpose.

Preface

Web development has changed dramatically over the last few years. What once focused mainly on static web pages now includes responsive user interfaces, component-based frontend frameworks, scalable backend services, secure APIs, database integration, cloud deployment, and automated DevOps workflows. Modern developers are expected to understand not only how to build applications, but also how to test, secure, deploy, and maintain them effectively. This book is designed to support that complete journey.

This book presents a practical and structured pathway for learning modern full stack development. It starts with the foundations of HTML, CSS, JavaScript, and web technologies, then moves into modern frontend development with React and Angular. The later chapters focus on backend development with Node.js and Express.js, database integration, web services, APIs, and DevOps practices such as containerization, CI/CD, orchestration, monitoring, and deployment. The book follows a hands-on style with examples, projects, exercises, and real-world application scenarios throughout.

This book is written for students, beginners, aspiring full stack developers, and working professionals who want to strengthen practical skills across the full web development lifecycle. It aims to help readers move from basic markup and styling to building secure, database-driven, production-ready applications with modern deployment practices.

Chapter 1: HTML – This chapter introduces the structure of web pages and explains essential HTML elements such as headings, paragraphs, lists, links, tables, forms, media, semantic structure, and basic page creation.

Chapter 2: Styling HTML with CSS – This chapter explains how to style web pages using CSS, including selectors, cascade, specificity, box model, colors, typography, layouts, forms, tables, and responsive presentation.

Chapter 3: Advanced CSS Concepts – This chapter explores responsive design, layout systems, media queries, Bootstrap, Tailwind, advanced selectors, transitions, transforms, animations, and modern CSS techniques for real projects.

Chapter 4: JavaScript Fundamentals – This chapter builds a solid foundation in JavaScript, covering syntax, variables, data types, operators, browser interaction, development setup, and core concepts needed for dynamic web applications.

Chapter 5: JavaScript and DOM Manipulation – This chapter focuses on interacting with the browser through the DOM, handling events, updating page content dynamically, and building interactive client-side behavior.

Chapter 6: Web Technology Fundamentals – This chapter explains HTTP, HTTPS, request-response flow, cookies, sessions, headers, CORS, REST concepts, and the client-server model that supports modern web systems.

Chapter 7: React – This chapter introduces component-based frontend development with React, including JSX, props, state, hooks, routing, forms, state handling, testing, and deployment-oriented practices.

Chapter 8: Angular Framework – This chapter presents Angular's modular structure, templates, data binding, components, services, forms, routing, guards, HTTP communication, and enterprise-oriented frontend development practices.

Chapter 9: Hands-on Projects and Frameworks Comparison – This chapter gives practical exposure through React and Angular projects and helps readers compare both frameworks in terms of structure, flexibility, tooling, and use cases.

Chapter 10: Backend Development with Express.js – This chapter explains Node.js and Express.js, middleware, routing, RESTful APIs, authentication, authorization, backend architecture, and production-ready server development.

Chapter 11: Databases and Integration – This chapter covers working with databases in full stack applications, including SQL and NoSQL integration, data models, backend connectivity, and persistence workflows.

Chapter 12: Web Services and APIs – This chapter explains API design, third-party API consumption, service communication, and techniques for building connected and extensible applications.

Chapter 13: DevOps for Web Development – This chapter concludes the book with practical DevOps coverage, including Git-based workflows, CI/CD, Docker, Docker Compose, Kubernetes, Jenkins, GitHub Actions, deployment, monitoring, and logging.

By the end of this book, readers will be able to design, build, secure, deploy, and maintain modern full stack web applications with greater confidence. The knowledge and practical exposure gained through these chapters will help them work more effectively in academic, project, and professional software development environments.

Code Bundle and Coloured Images

Please follow the link to download the
Code Bundle and the ***Coloured Images*** of the book:

https://rebrand.ly/4abb3c

The code bundle for the book is also hosted on GitHub at **https://github.com/bpbpublications/Full-Stack-Web-Development-with-React-Angular-Node.js-and-DevOps.** In case there's an update to the code, it will be updated on the existing GitHub repository.

We have code bundles from our rich catalogue of books and videos available at **https://github.com/bpbpublications**. Check them out!

Errata

We take immense pride in our work at BPB Publications and follow best practices to ensure the accuracy of our content to provide an indulging reading experience to our subscribers. Our readers are our mirrors, and we use their inputs to reflect and improve upon human errors, if any, that may have occurred during the publishing processes involved. To let us maintain the quality and help us reach out to any readers who might be having difficulties due to any unforeseen errors, please write to us at: **errata@bpbonline.com**

Your support, suggestions and feedback are highly appreciated by the BPB Publications' Family.

Piracy

If you come across any illegal copies of our works in any form on the internet, we would be grateful if you would provide us with the location address or website name. Please contact us at **business@bpbonline.com** with a link to the material.

If you are interested in becoming an author

If there is a topic that you have expertise in, and you are interested in either writing or contributing to a book, please visit **www.bpbonline.com**. We have worked with thousands of developers and tech professionals, just like you, to help them share their insights with the global tech community. You can make a general application, apply for a specific hot topic that we are recruiting an author for, or submit your own idea.

Reviews

Please leave a review. Once you have read and used this book, why not leave a review on the site that you purchased it from? Potential readers can then see and use your unbiased opinion to make purchase decisions. We at BPB can understand what you think about our products, and our authors can see your feedback on their book. Thank you!

For more information about BPB, please visit **www.bpbonline.com**.

Join our Discord space

Join our Discord workspace for latest updates, offers, tech happenings around the world, new releases, and sessions with the authors:

https://discord.bpbonline.com

Table of Contents

1. HTML ... 1
Introduction ... 1
Structure ... 1
Objectives ... 1
Basic structure of an HTML document ... 1
HTML headings ... 3
Hierarchy of headings ... 3
Output ... 4
HTML paragraphs ... 5
Other related tags ... 5
Example usage ... 5
Output ... 6
Best practices for using paragraphs ... 6
Lists in HTML ... 7
Attributes of HTML lists ... 7
Example usage ... 7
Output ... 8
Best practices for using lists ... 9
HTML links ... 9
Attributes of the <a> tag ... 10
Example usage ... 10
Output ... 11
Best practices for using links ... 11
Images and videos in HTML ... 12
Images in HTML ... 12
Attributes of the <img> tag ... 12
Example usage of <img> ... 12
Videos in HTML ... 13
Attributes of the <video> tag ... 13
Example usage of <video> ... 13
Best practices for using images and videos ... 14
HTML tables ... 15
Elements and attributes of tables ... 15
Example usage of <table> ... 15
Output ... 16
Advanced table styling with CSS ... 17
HTML forms ... 17

Attributes of the <form> tag 18
Common form elements 18
Example usage of <form> 19
Best practices for forms 20
Markup in HTML 20
Understanding <!DOCTYPE> in HTML 21
HTML comments 21
ID and class attributes 21
Block vs. inline elements 22
The <section> tag 22
Embedding external content using <iframe> 23
Understanding the meta tag in HTML 23
Escape characters in HTML 23
Hands-on building a static website 24
Homepage 24
About page 24
Contact page 25
CSS stylesheet 26
Output 26
Case study on the evolution of a web page 26
Conclusion 27
Exercises 27

2. Styling HTML with CSS 29
Introduction 29
Structure 29
Objectives 29
Types of CSS 29
External CSS 30
Internal CSS 30
Inline CSS 31
CSS cascade order 31
Order of CSS rule application 31
Example of CSS cascade order 31
CSS specificity 32
Example of CSS specificity 32
CSS inheritance 32
Example of CSS inheritance 33
Example of external stylesheet usage 33
CSS selectors 33
Commonly used CSS selectors 34

Additional CSS selectors ... 35
Best practices for using CSS selectors ... 35
Example of CSS selectors in action ... 36
CSS selectors and styles ... 36
CSS Box Model ... 37
Components of the CSS Box Model ... 37
Example of CSS Box Model properties ... 38
Box sizing property ... 38
Collapsing margins ... 38
Best practices for using the Box Model ... 39
CSS Flexbox for layouts ... 39
Application of flexbox ... 39
Understanding the Flexbox Model ... 40
Basic Flexbox properties ... 40
Centering content using Flexbox ... 40
Creating a navigation bar with Flexbox ... 41
Responsive layout with Flexbox ... 41
Best practices for using Flexbox ... 41
CSS Grid for layouts ... 42
Application of CSS Grid ... 42
Understanding the CSS Grid model ... 42
Basic CSS Grid properties ... 42
Creating a simple Grid layout ... 43
Creating a responsive Grid layout ... 43
Grid layout for a web page ... 44
Best practices for using CSS Grid ... 45
CSS colors and transparency ... 45
Foreground and background colors ... 46
CSS color formats ... 46
CSS3 opacity and transparency ... 48
Opacity property ... 48
RGBA and HSLA colors ... 48
CSS typography and text styling ... 49
Techniques for choosing typefaces ... 49
Specifying Typefaces in CSS ... 50
Font size, type scales, and units ... 50
Using custom fonts with @font-face ... 51
Font weight, uppercase, lowercase, underline, and strike-through ... 52
Line spacing, letter spacing, and word spacing ... 52
Text alignment, indenting, and shadow ... 53

Styling first letter or first line 53
Styling links 53
CSS attribute selectors 54
Styling lists, tables, and forms with CSS 55
Styling lists in CSS 55
Different bullet point styles in CSS 55
Adding images as bullet points in lists 56
Controlling the position of list markers 56
List styling shorthand 56
Styling tables in CSS 57
Basic table styling 57
Border on empty cells 57
Gaps between cells 57
Styling forms in CSS 58
Styling text inputs 58
Styling submit buttons 58
Styling fieldsets and legends 58
Aligning form controls 59
Misaligned form controls 59
Using Flexbox for alignment 59
Cursor styles in CSS 59
Hands-on project 60
Project overview 60
Project requirements 60
Project steps 60
Conclusion 61
Exercises 61
3. Advanced CSS Concepts **63**
Introduction 63
Structure 63
Objectives 63
Web developer toolbar 63
Inspecting and debugging a simple form 64
CSS Layout and positioning techniques 65
Containing elements 65
Normal flow 65
Relative positioning 66
Absolute positioning 66
Fixed positioning 66
Overlapping elements 67

Floating elements 67
Elements side-by-side 68
Clearing floats 68
Parents of floated elements 68
Multi-column layouts with floats 68
Screen sizes, resolutions, and page sizes 69
Device pixels vs. CSS pixels 69
Responsive units 69
Media queries and breakpoints 69
Layout grids 70
Grid system 70
Popular column grid 70
Implementing a basic grid 71
Responsive grid adjustments 72
Common layout patterns 72
Best practices 72
CSS frameworks for layouts 72
Using a CSS framework effectively 72
Popular frameworks 73
Quick start with Bootstrap 73
Bootstrap grid layouts 73
Core grid components 74
Two-column layout 74
Responsive breakpoints 74
Tailwind CSS for layouts 75
Utility-first philosophy 75
Responsive grid utilities 75
Flexbox utilities 76
Configuration and customization 76
Bootstrap vs. Tailwind 76
Foundation grids 76
Grid setup 76
Responsive cells 77
Offsets and order 77
Nested grids 77
Choosing a CSS framework 78
Framework criteria 78
Ease of use 79
Customization 79
Performance 79

Style ... *80*
Comparison example ... *80*
Media queries ... 81
Approach ... *81*
Standard breakpoints ... *81*
Orientation ... *82*
High-density ... *82*
Combined conditions ... *82*
Scalable units ... *82*
Root em ... *82*
Element em ... *83*
Grid and flexbox layouts ... 83
Grid layout ... *83*
Flexbox layout ... *84*
Combined layout ... *84*
Responsive visibility ... *84*
Auto grid ... *84*
Advanced CSS techniques ... 85
Transitions ... *85*
Transformations ... *85*
Animations ... *86*
Performance tips ... *86*
CSS variables and selectors ... 86
Defining variables ... *86*
Variable scope ... *87*
Dynamic updates ... *87*
Variables in media queries ... *87*
Advanced selectors ... *88*
Pseudo-classes and pseudo-elements ... 88
Pseudo-classes ... *88*
Pseudo-elements ... *89*
Combinators ... *89*
Negation ... *89*
Variables ... *90*
Responsive webpage design with CSS ... 90
Project requirements ... *90*
Step 1: HTML structure ... *90*
Step 2: Styling with CSS ... *91*
Project output ... *93*
Conclusion ... 94

Exercises 94

4. JavaScript Fundamentals 95
Introduction 95
Structure 95
Objectives 95
JavaScript overview 96
Language characteristics 96
Basic syntax 96
Browser API 96
Server environment 97
Ecosystem and tooling 97
Polyfills and transpilation 97
JavaScript history 98
Origins 98
ES5 standard 99
Strict mode 99
ES6 standard 100
Modules 100
Modern updates 101
Modern ES features 102
JavaScript and the browser 103
DOM 103
Events 103
Fetch API 103
Timers 104
Storage 104
DevTools 104
Performance 104
JavaScript vs. other languages 105
Feature comparison 105
Typing model 106
Concurrency 106
Ecosystem 107
Performance 107
Security fundamentals 107
CSRF mitigation 108
Content Security Policy reporting hooks 108
Web Workers 109
Memory and closures 109
Choosing the right tool 110

Development environment 111

VS Code setup 111

Node.js setup 111

Browser console 112

Debugging 112

Testing basics 113

Package management and scripts 113

Key points to remember 114

Dynamic web applications 114

Modern features 114

DOM interactions 114

Tooling 115

Statements and expressions 115

Statements 115

Expressions 116

Comparison 116

Comments in JavaScript 116

Purpose 117

Types 117

Single-line 117

Multi-line 117

Documentation 118

Best practices 118

Variables 118

Declaration 118

Scope 119

Hoisting 119

Comparison 119

Data types in JavaScript 119

Primitive types 120

Reference types 120

Date and time 120

Type checking 121

Regular expressions 122

Type conversion and coercion 122

Explicit conversion 123

Implicit coercion 123

Falsy values 124

JavaScript operators 124

Arithmetic operators 124

Comparison operators......125
Logical operators......125
Assignment operators......125
Bitwise operators......126
Conditional statements......126
If statement......126
If else statement......126
If else if statement......127
Switch statement......127
Loops in JavaScript......127
For loop......128
While loop......128
Do while loop......128
Iteration protocols......129
Loop control......130
break statement......130
continue statement......131
Functions......131
Definition and invocation......131
Declaration and expression......131
Arrow functions......132
Parameters......132
Closures......133
Recursion......133
Methods and bind......134
IIFE......134
Generators......134
Hoisting......134
Error handling......135
throw and try catch finally......135
Custom error types......135
Propagation and logging......136
Objects prototypes classes......136
Object basics......137
Prototype chain......137
Constructor functions......138
Classes......138
Arrays and array methods......139
Array basics......139
Adding and removing elements......139

Iteration techniques ... 140
Transform filter reduce ... 141
Finding and sorting ... 141
Destructuring ... 142
Multidimensional arrays ... 142
Object methods ... 143
Array methods beyond map, filter, and reduce ... 143
Destructuring in practice ... 144
Spread and rest operators with destructuring ... 145
Spread and rest ... 145
Destructuring ... 146
Asynchronous JavaScript ... 147
Event loop and task queues ... 147
Callback patterns ... 147
Promises and chaining ... 148
Async await ... 148
Microtasks vs. macrotasks ... 149
Conclusion ... 149
Exercises ... 149

5. JavaScript and DOM Manipulation ... 151
Introduction ... 151
Structure ... 151
Objectives ... 152
DOM overview ... 152
Selecting elements ... 152
Query selector ... 153
All selectors ... 153
Method comparison ... 154
Modifying HTML and CSS dynamically ... 154
Content updates ... 154
Attribute updates ... 154
Style updates ... 155
Class manipulation ... 155
Element creation ... 155
Element removal ... 156
Event listeners and event delegation ... 156
Adding event listeners ... 156
Event delegation ... 157
Handling form input and validation ... 157
Validation overview ... 157

Basic validation ... 158
Custom validation ... 158
Live feedback ... 158
Web storage ... 159
Local storage ... 159
Session storage ... 159
DOM traversal and update ... 159
DOM traversal ... 160
DOM update ... 160
Interactive todo app ... 160
HTML structure ... 160
Script logic ... 161
Data persistence ... 161
User interactions ... 162
Click events ... 162
Keypress events ... 163
Scroll events ... 163
Error handling and debugging ... 164
Common errors ... 164
Try catch finally ... 164
Custom errors ... 165
DevTools ... 165
Console methods ... 166
Logging basics ... 166
Table output ... 166
Grouped logs ... 166
JavaScript modules ... 166
Module basics ... 166
Named exports ... 167
Default export ... 167
Combined exports ... 167
Practical example ... 168
Template literals ... 168
Destructuring objects ... 169
Destructuring arrays ... 169
Symbols and BigInt ... 169
Symbols ... 169
BigInt ... 170
Optional chaining ... 170
Nullish coalescing ... 170

Event-driven programming....171
Event bubbling and capturing....171
Bubbling....171
Capturing....171
Event delegation....172
Custom events....172
Throttling and debouncing....172
Throttling....172
Debouncing....173
JavaScript and the Web API....173
Fetch API....173
XHR basics....174
Handling JSON data....175
WebSockets....176
States....176
Usage....176
Geolocation API....177
Methods....177
Errors....177
Examples....178
Canvas API....178
Drawing....178
Animation....178
Drag and Drop API....179
Events....179
Data transfer....179
Example....180
Notification API....180
Permissions....180
Creating notifications....181
Notification options....181
Notification events....181
Best practices....182
Hands-on project interactive calculator....182
Implementation....182
HTML structure....182
CSS styling....184
Calculator logic....185
Error handling....186
Keyboard support....186

Project output *186*
Conclusion 187
Exercises 187

6. Web Technology Fundamentals **189**
Introduction 189
Structure 189
Objectives 189
Understanding HTTP 190
Key HTTP features *190*
Request methods *190*
Request-response cycle 191
Process steps *191*
Request structure *191*
Response structure *192*
Status code classes *192*
Secure HTTP 192
Benefits *192*
TLS handshake *193*
Certificate chain *193*
Redirect example *193*
Server setup *193*
Cookies and sessions 194
Cookies *194*
Sessions *194*
Cycle steps *195*
HTTP example *195*
HTTP headers and cookies 195
Header overview *195*
Header examples *196*
Cookie mechanics *196*
Common HTTP request and response headers 197
Request headers *197*
Response headers *197*
Custom headers 198
Understanding cookies 198
Cookie types *198*
Cookie attributes *199*
Setting cookies *199*
Accessing and deleting cookies *199*
Cookie management with JavaScript 200

Set cookie 200
Read cookie 200
Delete cookie 200
Cookie security 200
Client-server model 201
Client and server roles 201
Request example 201
Response example 202
Communication examples 202
Advantages and limitations 202
CORS mechanism 202
Need for CORS 203
CORS error handling 203
Server CORS setup 203
REST APIs 204
Server and client roles 204
REST principles 205
REST API example 205
HTTP methods 205
Building a simple web server with Node.js 206
Project setup 206
Implementation of the web server 206
Running the server 206
Testing the web server 206
Extending the project 207
Conclusion 207
Exercises 207

7. React 209
Introduction 209
Structure 209
Objectives 209
Getting started 210
Environment setup 210
Project creation 210
Folder structure 211
JavaScript XML basics 211
JSX syntax 212
Expressions in JSX 212
JSX and Babel 213
Components 213

Function components 213
Class components 215
Component properties 216
Children prop 216
Default props 217
State management 217
useState hook 217
useReducer hook 218
Lifting state 220
Effect hook 221
useEffect usage 222
Dependency array 222
Cleanup functions 223
Event handling 223
Handling events 223
Synthetic events 224
Binding context 225
Routing 225
Router setup 226
Route parameters 226
Nested routes 227
Context API 228
When to use context or props 228
Creating context 229
Providing context 229
Consuming context 229
Example 1: Common UI setting theme 231
Example 2: Authentication, user session across the app 232
Custom hooks 233
Creating hooks 233
Reusing logic 234
Performance 234
Memoization 234
useMemo hook 234
useCallback hook 236
React.memo 236
Forms 237
Controlled forms 237
Uncontrolled forms 239
Form validation 240

Testing 240
Jest setup 241
Testing library 241
Async testing and mocking API calls 242
Snapshot testing 244
Styling 244
Tailwind CSS 244
CSS Modules 245
Styled components 246
CSS in JS 246
State libraries 247
Redux basics 247
Redux Toolkit 248
MobX overview 249
Build and deploy 250
Production build 250
Deployment options 251
Ecosystem 251
Tooling overview 252
Popular libraries 252
Community resources 252
Advanced patterns 253
Higher order components 253
Render props 254
Portals 254
Best practices 255
Folder structure 255
Code organization 256
Performance tips 256
Hands-on project 257
Overview 257
Setup 257
Folder structure 258
Implementation 258
Demo 265
Summary 266
Conclusion 266
Exercises 266

8. Angular Framework 269

Introduction 269

Structure 269

Objectives 269

Getting started 270

Environment setup 270

Project creation 270

Folder layout 271

Architecture 271

NgModules 271

Components 272

Templates 273

Data binding 274

Interpolation 274

Property binding 274

Event binding 275

Two-way binding 276

Directives 276

Component directives 276

Attribute directives 277

Structural directives 277

Services 278

Creating services 278

Dependency injection 279

Injector hierarchy 280

Routing 280

Router setup 280

Route parameters 281

Nested routes 282

Guards and resolvers 282

Forms 283

Template driven 283

Reactive forms 284

Validation 285

HTTP client 286

Setup 286

CRUD operations 287

Interceptors 287

Pipes 288

Built-in pipes 288

Custom pipes 289
Lifecycle 289
Lifecycle hooks 289
Change detection 290
Testing 291
Unit testing 291
End-to-end testing 292
Performance 292
Lazy loading 293
Ahead Of Time 293
Deployment 294
Build configuration 294
Hosting options 295
Hands-on project 296
Conclusion 296
Exercises 296

9. Hands-on Projects and Frameworks Comparison 297
Introduction 297
Structure 297
Objectives 297
Hands-on React project 297
Project overview 298
Technologies and tools 298
Directory structure 298
Learning outcomes 299
Todo list application with React 299
Application requirements 299
Component structure 299
Functional goals 300
Tools required 300
Initial setup preview 300
Project setup 301
Install Node and npm 301
Create React App 301
Review folder layout 301
Start the development server 302
Clean up boilerplate 302
Organize the source folder 302
Component development 303
TodoInput 303

TodoItem......304
TodoList......304
Integrate in app......304
Styling components......305
Managing state and events......306
State hook......306
Event handling......307
Parent state updates......307
Deploying a React application......308
GitHub Pages......308
Netlify hosting......308
Vercel hosting......309
Firebase hosting......309
Deployment practices......309
Hands-on Angular project......310
Project overview......310
Technologies used......310
Functional requirements......310
Application structure......311
Development steps......311
Expected output......312
React vs Angular comparison......312
Learning curve......312
Performance efficiency......313
Scalability practices......314
Case studies......315
Facebook platform......315
Gmail clone......316
Netflix UI......316
Forbes migration......316
Summary and practices......317
React practices......317
Angular practices......317
Framework selection......318
Further resources......318
Conclusion......318
Exercises......319

10. Backend Development with Express.js......321
Introduction......321
Structure......321

Objectives 321
Introduction to Node.js 322
Node.js features 322
Event-driven I/O 322
Environment setup 323
First application 323
Express.js framework 323
Express overview 324
Installing express 324
Basic server 324
Middleware usage 325
Project structure 325
E-commerce API example 325
Express use cases 326
Middleware and routing 327
Middleware functions 327
Route handlers 327
Dynamic segments 327
Router modules 328
Protected API example 328
Express routing 329
Basic routing 329
Route parameters 330
Query parameters 330
Multiple handlers 330
Router modules 330
Product routes example 331
RESTful APIs 332
Principles 332
Endpoints 333
Server start 334
API testing 334
Authentication and authorization 335
Authentication versus authorization 335
Authentication 335
Authorization 335
Implementation overview 336
JWT workflow 336
Auth routes example 337
Testing auth 338

JSON Web Token 339
JWT overview 339
Installation and setup 340
Login and token creation 340
Token verification 341
Protecting routes 341
Best practices 341
OAuth integration 341
OAuth overview 341
Core terminology 342
Auth code flow 342
Google OAuth setup 343
Advanced topics 344
Best practices in backend development 344
Project structure 344
Environment variables 345
Error handling 345
Input validation 345
Asynchronous code 346
Logging and monitoring 346
Security 346
Database practices 346
Version control and documentation 347
Testing 347
Security considerations 347
Input sanitization 348
HTTPS enforcement 348
Dependency hygiene 348
Code organization 349
Creating a RESTful API server 349
Overview and requirements 349
Structure and initialization 350
CRUD implementation 350
JWT authentication 352
Testing and deployment 353
Conclusion 353
Exercises 354
11. Databases and Integration 355
Introduction 355
Structure 355

Objectives 355
Database fundamentals SQL vs. NoSQL 355
SQL relational 356
NoSQL non-relational 356
Document stores 356
Key-value stores 357
Wide-column stores 357
Graph databases 357
Choosing between SQL and NoSQL 358
Scalability and performance 358
NoSQL databases 359
Document stores 359
Key-value stores 360
Column-family stores 360
Graph databases 360
Comparing NoSQL models 361
Choosing a NoSQL database 361
Comparison of SQL vs. NoSQL 361
Introduction to MongoDB 362
Connecting and CRUD basics 363
Indexing for performance 364
Replication architecture 364
Sharding for scale 364
Aggregation framework 365
Backup and monitoring 365
PostgreSQL overview 365
Defining tables 365
Advanced data types 366
Index strategies 366
Querying JSON data 366
Transactions and concurrency 367
Replication setup 367
Extensibility with extensions 367
Backup and monitoring 367
Database integration with Node.js 368
Connecting with Mongoose 368
Defining schemas and models 369
Basic CRUD operations 369
Advanced queries 370
Aggregation and indexing 370

CRUD with Mongoose 371
PostgreSQL with Sequelize 372
Configuring Sequelize 373
Defining models 373
Model associations 374
CRUD operations 374
Managing transactions 374
Indexing and query optimization 375
Transactions and consistency 375
Security best practices 376
Building a data-driven application 377
Requirements overview 377
Backend setup and database connection 377
API development and CRUD logic 378
Sync database and create tables 380
Build API routes 380
Register API routes in the main app 381
Authentication and protected routes 382
Deployment and testing 384
Local testing 384
Environment configuration 384
Production deployment options 384
Testing in production 385
Monitoring and logging 385
Conclusion 385
Exercises 385

12. Web Services and APIs 387
Introduction 387
Structure 387
Objectives 387
JSON and AJAX 388
JSON structure 388
AJAX requests 388
Fetch API usage 389
XHR usage 389
Dynamic user loading 389
AJAX use cases 390
Consuming third-party APIs 391
Integration techniques 391
Frontend with Fetch 391

Frontend/Backend with Axios 392
Backend with Node.js 392
Authentication methods 392
API keys 392
OAuth 2.0 392
Bearer tokens with JSON Web Tokens 393
Basic authentication 393
Best practices 394
Version control with Git and collaboration with GitHub 394
Git fundamentals 394
Branching strategies 395
GitHub collaboration 396
Deployment strategies 397
Cloud deployment platforms 397
Environment configuration 397
Monitoring and logging 398
Web application security fundamentals 399
Common security threats 399
Securing web applications 399
Hands-on API integration and deployment 400
Project overview and tools 400
Fetching and displaying data 400
Securing API credentials 401
Deployment and monitoring 401
Netlify deployment 401
Vercel deployment 402
Monitoring recommendations 402
Real-world API integration and security practices 402
Secure integration of a payment gateway 402
Conclusion 404
Exercises 404

13. DevOps for Web Development 407
Introduction 407
Structure 407
Objectives 407
CI/CD pipeline and containerization 408
Introduction to CI/CD and DevOps culture 408
Introduction to Docker and containerization 409
Docker architecture and components 409
Creating and managing Docker containers 409

Docker Compose for multi-container applications....410
Kubernetes overview....410
Cluster components....410
Control plane components....410
Worker node components....411
Workload resources....411
Deploying Kubernetes....411
Create a deployment....411
Expose via service....412
CI/CD with Jenkins....412
Installation and setup....412
Defining a pipeline....413
GitHub integration....414
Managing credentials securely....414
Pipeline as code benefits....414
CI/CD with GitHub Actions....415
Workflow triggers....415
Sample workflow....415
Workflow components....416
Secrets and variables....416
Cloud deployment....416
Advantages of actions....416
Comparison table....416
Monitoring and logging....417
Application monitoring....417
Logging fundamentals....417
Structured logging in Node.js....418
Setup and configuration....418
Metrics collection with Prometheus....418
Node.js exporter integration....418
Grafana dashboard setup....419
Best practices for monitoring and logging....419
CI/CD containerization project....420
Project overview....420
Simple Node.js API....420
Dockerfile setup....421
GitHub setup....421
GitHub Actions CI/CD....421
Jenkins CI/CD....422
Cloud deployment....423

Project summary 423
Company case study 423
Conclusion 424
Exercises 424

Appendix A: Resources for Further Reading **427**
Books and documentation 427
Online courses and tutorials 427
Communities and forums 427
Tooling and hosting platforms 428

Appendix B: Glossary of Terms **429**

Index **431-438**

Chapter 1
HTML

Introduction

HyperText Markup Language (**HTML**) forms the backbone of every web page. It defines a set of elements and rules for structuring content so that browsers can render text, images, links, tables, forms, and multimedia. This chapter introduces the basic syntax and elements of HTML5. It explains how to create headings, paragraphs, lists, hyperlinks, images, videos, tables, and forms. It also covers semantic markup, accessibility considerations, and best practices for search engine optimization. By the end of this chapter, you will be able to build a simple static website and understand how HTML interacts with **Cascading Style Sheets** (**CSS**) and JavaScript to create modern, responsive web pages.

Structure

This chapter covers the following topics:

- Basic structure of an HTML document
- HTML headings
- HTML paragraphs
- Lists in HTML
- HTML links
- Images and videos in HTML
- HTML tables
- HTML forms
- Markup in HTML
- Hands-on building a static website

Objectives

By the end of this chapter, the reader will be able to explain the purpose and syntax of HTML5 and construct the basic structure of a valid HTML document. The reader will identify and apply semantic elements like headings, paragraphs, lists, tables, and forms to organize content meaningfully. They will learn to embed hyperlinks, images, and video with the correct attributes, and implement accessibility features such as alternative text for images, href values for links, and controls for media playback. The reader will also apply best practices for search engine optimization by using descriptive tags and meta information, and ensure responsive design through flexible layouts and viewport settings. These learning outcomes lay the groundwork for creating accessible, well-structured, and modern web pages.

Basic structure of an HTML document

An HTML document follows a predefined structure that includes essential elements to ensure proper display and functionality.

The minimal skeleton of an HTML5 page is as follows:

```
<!DOCTYPE html>
<html lang="en">
<head>
<meta charset="UTF-8">
```

```
<meta name="viewport" content="width=device-width, initial-scale=1.0">
<title>Basic HTML Page</title>
</head>
<body>
<h1>Welcome to HTML</h1>
<p>This is a simple HTML page demonstrating basic structure.</p>
</body>
</html>
```

The structure of an HTML document is hierarchical, where elements are nested within each other. Understanding the purpose of each element is crucial for effective web development.

The elements nest hierarchically, where **<!DOCTYPE>** declares HTML5, **<html>** is the root, **<head>** holds metadata and title, **<body>** contains visible content.

The following figure visually represents the hierarchical structure of a basic HTML document, illustrating the relationship between **<!DOCTYPE>**, **<html>**, **<head>**, and **<body>** elements:

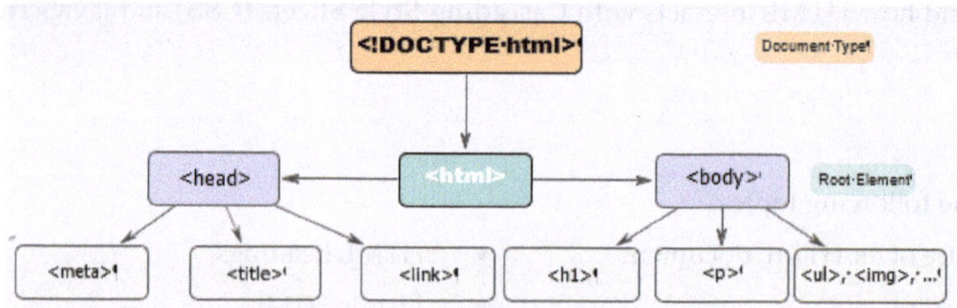

***Figure 1.1:** Structure of an HTML document*

The key features of HTML are as follows:

- **Platform independent**: HTML can be viewed on any web browser, regardless of the **operating system** (**OS**).
- **Simple and easy to learn**: The syntax is straightforward, making it accessible for beginners.
- **Structured content**: HTML elements provide a clear and well-organized layout for web pages.
- **Integration with other technologies**: HTML seamlessly works with CSS for styling and JavaScript for dynamic behavior.
- **Semantic markup**: HTML5 introduces elements such as **<header>**, **<article>**, and **<section>** to improve SEO and accessibility.

HTML has evolved significantly, with new versions introducing enhanced features and improvements. The versions of HTML are as follows:

- **HTML 4.01**: Introduced structural improvements but lacked modern multimedia support.
- **XHTML**: A stricter version of HTML that enforces proper syntax and formatting rules.
- **HTML5**: This is the latest version, and it provides better multimedia support, improved semantic elements, and enhanced mobile compatibility.

> **Note: Understanding the differences between HTML versions is essential for web developers, as older versions may lack the capabilities required for modern web applications.**

HTML is the foundation of web development, allowing content to be structured in a standardized manner. As we progress in this chapter, we will explore various HTML elements, attributes, and best practices to create efficient and accessible web pages.

Refer to the following wireframe which visually demonstrates a typical HTML5 page structure, highlighting the semantic layout regions: **<header>**, **<nav>**, **<main>**, **<aside>**, and **<footer>**:

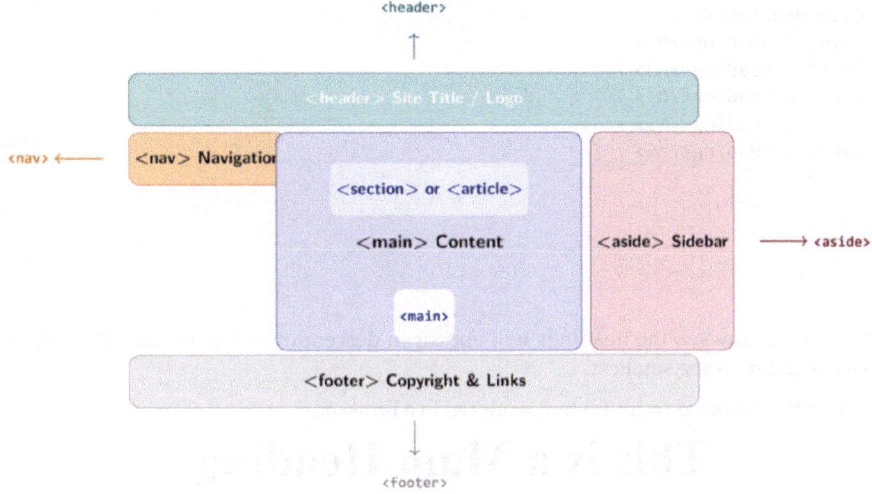

Figure 1.2: *HTML5 semantic layout*

HTML headings

Headings in HTML define the structure of a webpage, improving readability and organization. The **<h1>** tag represents the most important heading, while the **<h6>** tag represents the least important heading. Search engines and accessibility tools rely on heading structures to interpret content hierarchy.

Web browsers automatically display heading text in different sizes. Typically, **<h1>** appears in the largest font, and **<h6>** in the smallest. However, these sizes can be modified using CSS.

Hierarchy of headings

Using headings correctly enhances webpage structure, **Search Engine Optimization** (**SEO**), and accessibility. Search engines use headings to understand content importance, and assistive technologies rely on them for navigation.

The following list outlines a structured approach to using headings:

- **<h1>**: The main title of the page (used only once per page)
- **<h2>**: Major sections under the main title.
- **<h3>**: Subsections under <h2>.
- **<h4>**: Detailed subsections under <h3>.
- **<h5> and <h6>**: Used for minor headings or highly specific subsections.

The following HTML example demonstrates the way to use all six levels of headings:

```
<!DOCTYPE html>
<html lang= " en " >
<head>
<meta charset=" UTF-8">
<meta name="viewport" content="width=device-width, initial-scale=1.0">
<title>HTML Headings Example</title>
```

```
</head>
<body>

<h1>This is a Main Heading</h1>
<h2>This is a Level 2 Heading</h2>
<h3>This is a Level 3 Heading</h3>
<h4>This is a Level 4 Heading</h4>
<h5>This is a Level 5 Heading</h5>
<h6>This is a Level 6 Heading</h6>

</body>
</html>
```

Output

When displayed in a web browser, the headings will appear in descending order of size. The **<h1>** heading is the largest, and the **<h6>** heading is the smallest.

The following figure is the expected output when rendered in a browser:

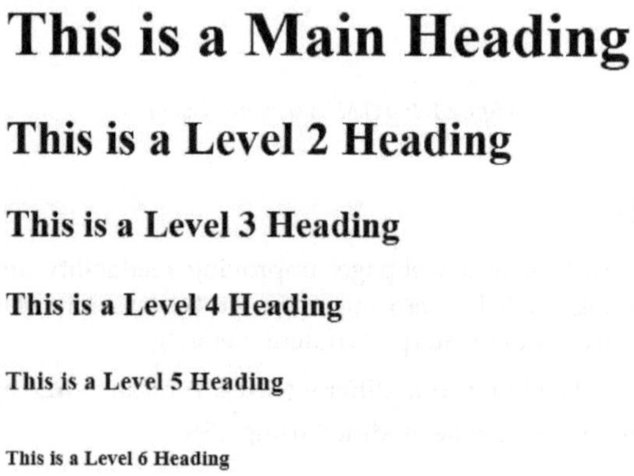

This is a Main Heading

This is a Level 2 Heading

This is a Level 3 Heading

This is a Level 4 Heading

This is a Level 5 Heading

This is a Level 6 Heading

Figure 1.3: *Rendered HTML headings*

Key points to remember are as follows:

- Use only one **<h1>** per page for better SEO and content clarity.
- Maintain a logical hierarchy (e.g., do not skip directly from **<h1>** to **<h3>**).
- CSS can be used to customize heading styles.

This section provided a foundational understanding of HTML headings and their significance in structuring web content. The key takeaways are as follows:

- **HTML structure**: HTML organizes web content using elements such as headings, paragraphs, images, and links.
- **Headings in HTML**: Six levels of headings (**<h1>** to **<h6>**) define the content hierarchy.
- **SEO and accessibility**: Proper heading usage improves search engine rankings and enhances accessibility for assistive technologies.
- **Best practices**: Use only one **<h1>** per page, maintain a logical heading structure, and avoid skipping levels.

- **Customization with CSS**: Headings can be visually styled using CSS.

Understanding these principles ensures that web pages are not only well-structured but also accessible, user-friendly, and optimized for search engines.

HTML paragraphs

In HTML, the **<p>** tag is used to define paragraphs. It automatically adds space before and after the text to separate blocks of content, improving readability and organization.

Paragraphs are essential for structuring text content on a webpage. Without them, text would appear as a continuous block, making it difficult to read. The use of paragraphs enhances the presentation of information by breaking it into meaningful sections.

Note: Proper use of paragraphs improves the clarity and visual organization of web content.

The benefits of well-structured paragraphs are as follows:

- Enhance readability and user experience.
- Make content more accessible for screen readers.
- Help search engines better understand the webpage structure.
- Improve maintainability by making code more organized.

Other related tags

Besides the **<p>** tag, HTML provides several other tags that influence text formatting. The details are as follows:

- **
**: Inserts a line break within text, forcing content onto a new line without starting a new paragraph.
- **<hr>**: Creates a horizontal line (divider), often used to separate sections.
- **<pre>**: Preserves whitespace, line breaks, and formatting, making it useful for code snippets or preformatted text.

Example usage

The following example demonstrates how to use paragraphs and related tags in an HTML document:

```
<!DOCTYPE html>
<html lang="en">
<head>
<meta charset="UTF-8">
<meta name="viewport" content="width=device-width, initial-scale=1.0">
<title>HTML Paragraph Example</title>
</head>
<body>

<p>This is a paragraph. HTML automatically adds space before and after paragraphs.</p>

<p>This is another paragraph. <br> This sentence is in the same paragraph, but after a      \
\  line break.</p>

<hr>
```

```
<p>The following text is preformatted:</p>
<pre>
This is an example of preformatted text. The spaces and line breaks are preserved.
</pre>

</body>
</html>
```

Output

When the preceding code is rendered in a web browser, it displays properly formatted paragraphs, line breaks, and a horizontal rule.

The following is the expected output when rendered in a browser:

This is a paragraph. HTML automatically adds space before and after paragraphs.

This is another paragraph.
This sentence is in the same paragraph, but after a line break.

The following text is preformatted:

```
This is an example of preformatted text.
The spaces and line breaks are preserved.
```

***Figure 1.4:** Rendered HTML paragraphs and related tags*

Best practices for using paragraphs

Using paragraphs correctly is crucial for structuring web content effectively. Some essential best practices are as follows:

- **Use <p> tags for blocks of text**: This ensures logical separation and improves readability.
- **Avoid using <br> excessively**: Line breaks should only be used when necessary, such as for addresses or poetry.
- **Use <hr> for section dividers**: This helps visually separate content without introducing excessive whitespace.
- **Use <pre> for preserving formatting**: Ideal for displaying code snippets or **American Standard Code for Information Interchange** (**ASCII**) diagrams.
- **Write short, meaningful paragraphs**: Each paragraph should focus on a single idea to improve clarity.

Key points to remember are as follows

- Paragraphs (`<p>`) structure text content and ensure readability by automatically adding spacing before and after.
- Line breaks (`<br>`) should be used sparingly; prefer paragraph separation instead.
- The `<hr>` tag creates horizontal dividers and is commonly used for section breaks.
- The `<pre>` tag preserves original formatting, making it useful for displaying code, ASCII art, or structured text.
- Semantic content improves web accessibility and SEO, making webpages easier to navigate and index by search engines.

This section provided a comprehensive understanding of HTML paragraphs and related text formatting elements. The key takeaways include:

- Paragraphs (`<p>`) organize content logically and should be used instead of excessive line breaks.
- The `<br>` tag should be used sparingly—prefer paragraph separation for better readability.
- Horizontal rules (`<hr>`) help separate sections, making content visually appealing.
- Preformatted text (`<pre>`) is useful for preserving whitespace and indentation, making it ideal for displaying code.
- Structuring content properly improves web accessibility and SEO, making pages easier to read and navigate.

Mastering these elements ensures that web pages are well-structured, visually organized, and accessible to a broad audience. In the next section, we will explore how to create lists in HTML to further improve content organization.

Lists in HTML

HTML provides different types of lists to structure and present information effectively. Lists help organize content, improve readability, and enhance the user experience. The three main types of lists in HTML include:

- **Ordered lists (<ol>)**: Used for numbered lists where sequence matters.
- **Unordered lists (<ul>)**: Used for bulleted lists where order is not important.
- **Definition lists (<dl>)**: Used for presenting term-definition pairs, commonly used for glossaries or explanations.

Lists are widely used in webpages for navigation menus, displaying instructions, organizing content, and creating structured data representations.

Proper use of lists enhances the following:

- **Readability**: Organizing content into lists makes it easier for users to scan and process information.
- **Navigation**: Lists are frequently used for menus and links.
- **SEO**: Well-structured lists can help search engines understand content better.
- **Accessibility**: Screen readers can navigate through lists more effectively, improving web accessibility.

Attributes of HTML lists

HTML lists support several attributes that modify their behavior and appearance:

- **Type**: Specifies the bullet style for `<ul>` (e.g., circle, square) and numbering style for `<ol>` (e.g., 1, A, i).
- **Start**: Defines the starting number for ordered lists.
- **Reversed**: Displays the list in descending order.
- **Compact (deprecated)**: Used in older versions of HTML to reduce spacing between list items.

Example usage

The following example demonstrates the use of ordered, unordered, and definition lists in HTML:

```
<!DOCTYPE html>
<html lang="en">
<head>
<meta charset="UTF-8">
<meta name="viewport" content="width=device-width, initial-scale=1.0">
<title>HTML Lists Example</title>
```

```
</head>
<body>

<h2>Ordered List</h2>
<ol type="A" start="3" reversed>
<li>First item</li>
<li>Second item</li>
<li>Third item</li>
</ol>

<h2>Unordered List</h2>
<ul type="square">
<li>Item One</li>
<li>Item Two</li>
<li>Item Three</li>
</ul>

<h2>Definition List</h2>
<dl>
<dt>HTML</dt>
<dd>Hypertext Markup Language</dd>
<dt>CSS</dt>
<dd>Cascading Style Sheets</dd>
</dl>

</body>
</html>
```

Output

When the preceding code is rendered in a web browser, it displays properly formatted ordered, unordered, and definition lists.

The following is the expected output when rendered in a browser:

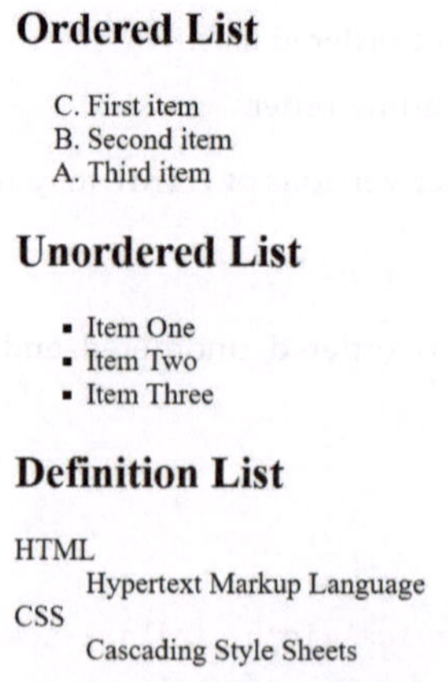

Ordered List

C. First item
B. Second item
A. Third item

Unordered List

- Item One
- Item Two
- Item Three

Definition List

HTML
    Hypertext Markup Language
CSS
    Cascading Style Sheets

Figure 1.5: Rendered HTML lists

Best practices for using lists

Using lists effectively enhances web content structure and clarity. The following list outlines the best practices:

- Use ordered lists (`<ol>`) when sequences matter, such as for steps in a tutorial or ranked items.
- Use unordered lists (`<ul>`) for grouping related items, such as navigation menus, grocery lists, or feature listings.
- Use definition lists (`<dl>`) for presenting term-definition pairs, such as glossaries or **Frequently Asked Questions** (**FAQs**).
- Keep list items short and concise to improve readability and usability.
- Customize list appearance using CSS to match the website's design (covered in the next chapter).

The key points to remember are as follows:

- Ordered lists (`<ol>`) are useful for sequences and ranking.
- Unordered lists (`<ul>`) are best for general item grouping.
- Definition lists (`<dl>`) should be used for presenting definitions.
- Attributes like type, start, and reversed control list appearance.
- Lists can be styled and customized using CSS for better aesthetics and usability.

This section provided a comprehensive understanding of lists in HTML and their significance in web development. The key takeaways include:

- Lists improve content organization, readability, and accessibility.
- Ordered lists (`<ol>`) are ideal for sequences and rankings.
- Unordered lists (`<ul>`) are best for general item grouping.
- Definition lists (`<dl>`) are useful for term-definition relationships.
- Styling lists with CSS enhances their visual appeal and usability.

Mastering these elements ensures that web pages are well-structured, visually organized, and easy to navigate. In the next section, we will explore how to create hyperlinks in HTML, enabling navigation between different pages.

HTML links

The HTML `<a>` tag (anchor tag) is used to create hyperlinks. Hyperlinks allow users to navigate between different web pages, sections of the same page, email addresses, downloadable files, or external resources.

Links are one of the most fundamental elements of the web, enabling seamless navigation between different resources. Without hyperlinks, the web would be a collection of disconnected pages rather than an interconnected network of information.

Hyperlinks play a crucial role in the following aspects:

- **Navigation**: They allow users to move between different web pages.
- **SEO**: Proper linking improves website ranking and discoverability.
- **User engagement**: Links provide easy access to additional content, keeping users engaged.
- **Resource sharing**: They facilitate access to documents, files, and references.
- **Web accessibility**: Screen readers and assistive technologies use links to help users navigate efficiently.

Attributes of the <a> tag

HTML links support several attributes that control their behavior:

- **href**: Specifies the URL of the destination (external, internal, email, or file link).
- **target**: Defines how the link opens:
  - **_self (default)**: Opens in the same tab.
  - **_blank**: Opens in a new tab.
  - **_parent**: Opens in the parent frame (useful in iframes).
  - **_top**: Opens in the full body of the window.
- **rel**: Specifies the relationship between the current and linked document:
  - **nofollow**: Tells search engines not to follow the link.
  - **Noopener**: Prevents security risks when opening links in a new tab.
  - **Noreferrer**: Prevents sending referrer information to the linked site.
- **download**: Allows users to download the linked resource instead of opening it.
- **title**: Provides additional information as a tooltip when the user hovers over the link.

Example usage

The following example demonstrates different types of links in HTML:

```
<!DOCTYPE html>
<html lang="en">
<head>
<meta charset="UTF-8">
<meta name="viewport" content="width=device-width, initial-scale=1.0">
<title>HTML Links Example</title>
</head>
<body>

<!-- External Link -->
<p><a href="https://www.example.com" target="_blank" rel="noopener noreferrer">Visit      \
\  Example.com</a></p>

<!-- Internal Link -->
<p><a href="about.html">Go to About Page</a></p>

<!-- Email Link -->
<p><a href="mailto:someone@example.com">Send an Email</a></p>

<!-- Download Link -->
<p><a href="document.pdf" download>Download the PDF</a></p>

<!-- Link with Tooltip -->
<p><a href="https://www.wikipedia.org" title="Go to Wikipedia">Wikipedia</a></p>

</body>
</html>
```

Output

When the preceding code is rendered in a web browser, it displays hyperlinks with different behaviors based on their attributes.

The following is the expected output when rendered in a browser:

Visit Example.com

Go to About Page

Send an Email

Download the PDF

Wikipedia

Figure 1.6: Rendered HTML links

Best practices for using links

To ensure accessibility, security, and usability, consider the following best practices:

- **Use descriptive anchor text**: Avoid vague text like `Click Here`; instead, use meaningful labels like `Read More About HTML`.
- **Use target="_blank" only when necessary**: Opening links in new tabs should be used for external links but avoided for internal navigation to prevent user frustration.
- **Add rel="noopener noreferrer" for external links**: This enhances security when opening links in a new tab.
- **Use title attributes sparingly**: Tooltips should provide useful, non-redundant information.
- **Use email and download links properly**: Provide clear instructions when linking to downloads or email addresses.

The following are the key points to remember:

- Use href to define the destination **Uniform Resource Locator** (**URL**), which can be external, internal, email, or file download.
- Use `target="_blank"` for opening links in new tabs, enhancing user experience for external resources.
- Use download for file links, allowing users to save resources.
- Use `rel="noopener noreferrer"` when opening in new tabs to prevent security vulnerabilities.
- Ensure link accessibility by using meaningful anchor text.

This section provided a comprehensive understanding of HTML links and their attributes. The key takeaways include:

- HTML links (`<a>`) enable navigation between web pages and resources, making content interactive.
- Attributes like `href`, `target`, `rel`, `download`, and `title` control link behavior, enhancing user experience and security.
- Properly formatted links improve SEO, usability, and accessibility.

Mastering these concepts ensures efficient navigation and interactive web pages. In the next section, we will explore how to embed images and videos in HTML for enhanced visual presentation.

Images and videos in HTML

HTML allows embedding images and videos using the `<img>` and `<video>` tags, respectively. These elements enhance the visual appeal, engagement, and interactivity of web pages by providing multimedia content.

Visual content significantly improves user experience, making web pages more engaging. Images enhance information retention, while videos allow dynamic storytelling and multimedia communication.

Embedding images and videos in web pages improves:

- **User engagement**: Multimedia content makes web pages more interactive and visually appealing.
- **SEO**: Properly optimized images and videos improve rankings in search engines.
- **Accessibility**: Providing alt text and captions ensures that visually impaired users can understand content.
- **Performance**: Using the correct formats and attributes enhances page loading speed and reduces bandwidth consumption.
- **Content understanding**: Videos provide a richer way to present complex ideas compared to text alone.

Images in HTML

The `<img>` tag is used to display images on a webpage. It is a self-closing tag that does not require a closing `</img>`. The `src` attribute specifies the image's file path or URL so the browser knows where to fetch it. Including an `alt` attribute ensures a descriptive text appears when the image fails to load and assists screen readers.

Setting `width` and `height` reserves the exact space needed, preventing layout shifts as the page renders. The `title` attribute can display a tooltip when the user hovers over the image. Adding `loading="lazy"` defers offscreen images until they scroll into view, improving page load speed. The `srcset` and `sizes` attributes allow the browser to pick the best image resolution for different screen widths. Choosing formats like JPEG for photos, PNG for transparency, SVG for vectors, or WebP for reduced file size balances quality and performance.

Attributes of the <img> tag

The `<img>` tag supports several attributes to enhance image loading and accessibility, details as follows:

- **src**: Specifies the image source (URL or file path).
- **alt**: Provides alternative text for screen readers and accessibility.
- **width and height**: Control the image dimensions.
- **loading**: Defines how images are loaded (lazy for deferred loading, eager for immediate loading).
- **title**: Displays a tooltip when the user hovers over the image.

Example usage of <img>

The following example demonstrates embedding an image in HTML:

```
<!DOCTYPE html>
<html lang="en">
<head>
<meta charset="UTF-8">
<meta name="viewport" content="width=device-width, initial-scale=1.0">
<title>HTML Image Example</title>
</head>
<body>
```

```
<h2>Displaying an Image</h2>
<img src="image.jpg" alt="A beautiful scenery" width="400" height="300" loading="lazy">

</body>
</html>
```

The following output is expected when rendered in a browser:

Displaying an Image

Figure 1.7: Rendered HTML image

Videos in HTML

The **<video>** tag is used to embed videos in web pages. Unlike images, videos require a closing **</video>** tag. The **src** attribute points to the video file's URL or path, telling the browser where to load the content from. Use the **controls** attribute to display native play, pause, and volume controls without extra scripting. Including multiple **<source>** elements lets you offer different formats (e.g., MP4, WebM, Ogg) so the browser picks the best one. The **poster** attribute specifies an image to show before playback begins, improving the user's first impression. Adding **autoplay** starts the video automatically, while pairing it with **muted** avoids unexpected audio playback.

The **loop** attribute makes the video replay continuously when it reaches the end. The **preload** attribute (with values like **auto**, **metadata**, or **none**) hints to the browser how much of the video to load in advance.

Attributes of the <video> tag

The **<video>** tag supports multiple attributes to improve video playback:

- **controls**: Displays play, pause, and volume buttons.
- **autoplay**: Plays the video automatically when the page loads.
- **loop**: Repeats the video continuously.
- **muted**: Starts the video with the sound muted.
- **poster**: Displays an image before the video starts playing.
- **preload**: Defines how the browser loads the video before playback starts (auto, metadata, or none).

Example usage of <video>

The following example demonstrates embedding a video in HTML:

```
<!DOCTYPE html>
<html lang="en">
<head>
<meta charset="UTF-8">
<meta name="viewport" content="width=device-width, initial-scale=1.0">
<title>HTML Video Example</title>
</head>
<body>

<h2>Playing a Video</h2>
<video width="500" height="300" controls poster="poster.jpg">
<source src="video.mp4" type="video/mp4">
<source src="video.ogg" type="video/ogg"> Your browser does not support the video tag.
</video>

</body>
</html>
```

Best practices for using images and videos

To optimize images and videos in HTML:

- Use modern image formats like *WebP* or *SVG* for better compression and quality.
- Always provide alternative text (`alt`) for images to improve accessibility.
- Use `loading="lazy"` for images to enhance page loading speed.
- Offer multiple video formats (**MPEG-4** (**MP4**), ogg) to ensure browser compatibility.
- Use the poster aflribute for videos to provide a preview image before playback.
- Keep media files optimized and compressed to prevent slow loading times.

The following are the key points to remember:

- Use `<img>` for static images and always provide alt text for accessibility.
- Use `<video>` for embedding videos and include controls for user interaction.
- Use multiple `<source>` elements inside `<video>` to support different file formats.
- The poster aflribute provides a preview image before video playback begins.
- Optimize media for faster loading times using proper compression and modern formats.

This section provided a comprehensive understanding of embedding images and videos in HTML. The key takeaways include the following:

- Images and videos enhance user experience and engagement.
- Using proper attributes improves accessibility and performance.
- Optimizing media files ensures faster page loading.

Mastering these concepts ensures that web pages are visually appealing and interactive. In the next section, we will explore how to create tables in HTML for structured data presentation.

HTML tables

The **<table>** tag in HTML is used to present structured data in rows and columns. Tables help in organizing data efficiently, making it easy to compare information in a structured format. A table consists of multiple elements such as headers, data cells, and captions.

Tables are commonly used for displaying tabular data, such as pricing charts, schedules, comparison tables, or statistical reports.

Tables provide a structured way to represent data with:

- **Clear data organization**: Allows easy comparison and structuring of large datasets.
- **Improved readability**: Helps users understand relationships between different data points.
- **Efficient display of information**: Useful for reports, analytics, pricing plans, and schedules.
- **Befler accessibility**: Screen readers can navigate well-structured tables effectively.
- **Custom styling capabilities**: CSS can be applied to enhance table design and layout.

Elements and attributes of tables

A table consists of the following key elements:

- **<table>**: Defines the entire table structure.
- **<tr>**: It is also known as Table Row, which represents a row in the table.
- **<th>**: It is also known as Table Header, which defines header cells, typically bold and centered.
- **<td>**: It is also known as Table Data, which represents standard data cells.
- **<caption>**: Provides a title or description for the table.
- **<colgroup> and <col>**: Allow grouping and styling of table columns.
- **<thead>, <tbody>, <tfoot>**: Define different sections of the table for better organization.

Example usage of <table>

The following example demonstrates how to create a structured table in HTML:

```
<!DOCTYPE html>
<html lang="en">
<head>
<meta charset="UTF-8">
<meta name="viewport" content="width=device-width, initial-scale=1.0">
<title>HTML Table Example</title>
<style>
table {
border-collapse: collapse; width: 100%;
}
th, td {
border: 1px solid black; padding: 8px;
text-align: left;
}
th {

}
```

```
</style>
</head>
<body>
background-color: #f2f2f2;

<h2>Student Grades</h2>

<table>
<caption>Student Grade Report</caption>
<colgroup>
<col style="background-color:lightgray">
<col>
<col style="background-color:lightblue">
</colgroup>
<thead>

<tr>
<th>Student Name</th>
<th>Subject</th>
<th>Grade</th>
</tr>
</thead>
<tbody>
<tr>
<td>John Doe</td>
<td>Mathematics</td>
<td>A</td>
</tr>
<tr>
<td>Jane Smith</td>
<td>Physics</td>
<td>B</td>
</tr>
</tbody>
<tfoot>
<tr>
<td colspan="3">End of Report</td>
</tr>
</tfoot>
</table>

</body>
</html>
```

Output

When the preceding code is rendered in a web browser, it displays a structured table with headers, a caption, and formatted columns.

The following is the expected output displayed in a browser:

Student Grades

Student Grade Report

Student Name	Subject	Grade
John Doe	Mathematics	A
Jane Smith	Physics	B
End of Report		

Figure 1.8: Rendered table output

Advanced table styling with CSS

Tables can be customized using CSS for better design and readability:

- Use `border-collapse: collapse` to merge table borders for a cleaner look.
- Apply background colors to headers and alternate rows for readability.
- Use `text-align` property to control text alignment in cells.
- Set `width` and `max-width` properties to prevent tables from overflowing.
- Use hover effects (`:hover`) to enhance interactivity.

The key points to remember are as follows:

- Use `<th>` for table headers, which are bold and centered by default.
- Use `<caption>` to describe the table for better accessibility.
- Use `<colgroup>` to apply styling to specific columns.
- Use `<thead>`, `<tbody>`, and `<tfoot>` to separate table sections.
- Use border, cellpadding, and cell spacing attributes to improve table layout.
- Apply CSS to improve table appearance using background colors, borders, and spacing.

This section provided a comprehensive understanding of HTML tables and their significance in web development. The key takeaways include:

- Tables (`<table>`) are used to present structured data, making them ideal for reports, schedules, and comparisons.
- Table elements like (`<tr>`, `<th>`, `<td>`, `<caption>`, `<colgroup>`, `<thead>`, `<tbody>`, `<tfoot>`) help format and structure tables.
- CSS can be applied to improve table design, enhancing readability and user experience.
- Proper table organization improves data accessibility for all users, including those using screen readers.

Mastering these concepts ensures that web pages display structured information effectively. In the next section, we will explore how to create forms in HTML for user input and interaction.

HTML forms

The `<form>` tag in HTML is used to collect user input. Forms enable users to enter data such as text, passwords, and selections, and submit it to a server for processing.

Forms play a crucial role in web development, facilitating user interaction, authentication, and data collection. They are widely used for tasks like registration, login, feedback submission, and data retrieval.

Forms are essential in web applications because they:

- **Collect user input**: Forms allow users to submit data such as names, email addresses, and passwords.
- **Enable interactivity**: They enable user actions like signing up, logging in, and searching.
- **Facilitate secure data submission**: By using **Hypertext Transfer Protocol Secure** (**HTTPS**) and secure form methods, data can be securely transmitted.
- **Support user validation**: Forms help ensure users enter valid information through required fields, input constraints, and JavaScript validation.
- **Enhance user experience**: Well-structured forms guide users and prevent incorrect submissions.

The following figure illustrates how data flows from form fields in the browser to the server upon form submission:

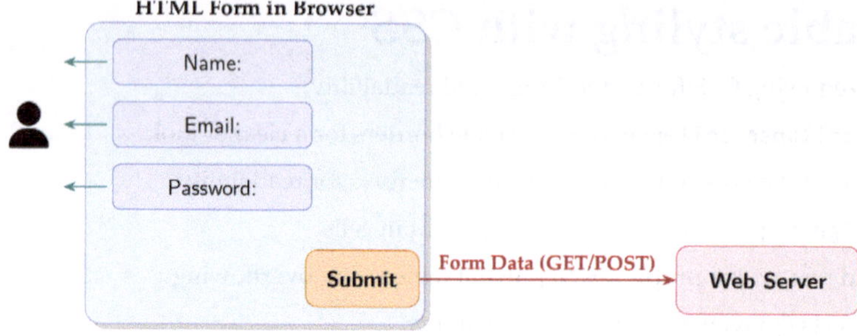

Figure 1.9: *Upon submission, the browser sends userfilled form data to the server via the <form> tag's method and action*

Attributes of the <form> tag

The `<form>` tag supports multiple attributes that control form behavior:

- **action**: Specifies the URL where form data is sent.
- **method**: Defines the HTTP method for submission:
  - **GET**: Appends form data to the URL (used for search forms).
  - **POST**: Sends data securely in the request body (used for authentication and sensitive information).
- **target**: Specifies where to open the response:
  - **_self (default)**: Opens in the same tab.
  - **_blank**: Opens in a new tab.
- **autocomplete**: Enables or disables autofill (on, off).
- **novalidate**: Prevents browser validation when submitting the form.

Common form elements

Forms consist of various elements to collect user input:

- **<input>**: Used for text fields, passwords, emails, checkboxes, radio buttons, etc.
- **<textarea>**: Creates multi-line text input fields.
- **<select> and <option>**: Used for dropdown lists.
- **<button>**: Defines a clickable button for submission or actions.
- **<label>**: Associates text descriptions with form fields for accessibility.

- **<fieldset> and <legend>**: Group related form elements for better organization.

Example usage of <form>

The following example demonstrates a basic HTML form:

```
<!DOCTYPE html>
<html lang="en">
<head>
<meta charset="UTF-8">
<meta name="viewport" content="width=device-width, initial-scale=1.0">
<title>HTML Form Example</title>
</head>
<body>

<h2>User Registration Form</h2>

<form action="submit_form.php" method="POST">

<!-- Text Input -->
<label for="name">Full Name:</label>
<input type="text" id="name" name="name" placeholder="Enter your full name" required>
<br><br>

<!-- Email Input -->
<label for="email">Email:</label>
<input type="email" id="email" name="email" required>
<br><br>
<!-- Password Input -->
<label for="password">Password:</label>
<input type="password" id="password" name="password" required>
<br><br>

<!-- Radio Buttons -->
<label>Gender:</label>
<input type="radio" name="gender" value="male"> Male
<input type="radio" name="gender" value="female"> Female
<br><br>

<!-- Dropdown List -->
<label for="country">Country:</label>
<select id="country" name="country">
<option value="usa">USA</option>
<option value="uk">UK</option>
<option value="india">India</option>
</select>
<br><br>

<!-- Checkbox -->
<input type="checkbox" id="terms" name="terms" required>
```

```
<label for="terms">I agree to the terms and conditions</label>
<br><br>

<!-- Submit Button -->
<button type="submit">Register</button>

</form>

</body>
</html>
```

Best practices for forms

To ensure usability, accessibility, and security, consider the following best practices:

- Use **<label>** elements for better accessibility and user experience.
- Use proper type attributes for inputs, such as email, password, date, etc.
- Use the placeholder aflribute to guide users in entering the correct data.
- Use client-side validation (e.g., HTML5 validation attributes and JavaScript) for better user feedback.
- Use required, pattern, and maxlength attributes to enforce input constraints.
- Ensure secure data transmission by using HTTPS and POST requests for sensitive data.

The key points to remember are as follows:

- Use the **action** aflribute to specify the form submission destination.
- Choose the correct method (GET or POST) based on data sensitivity.
- Always associate labels with input fields using the for attribute.
- Use required fields to enhance the user experience and data integrity.
- Group related inputs using **<fieldset>** and **<legend>** for better organization.

This section provided a comprehensive understanding of HTML forms and their importance in web applications. The key takeaways include the following:

- Forms collect and process user data, making websites interactive.
- Proper Attributes and validation improve usability and security.
- Best practices ensure a seamless user experience and data accuracy.

Mastering HTML forms enables developers to build efficient, user-friendly, and secure web applications. In the next section, we will explore how to enhance HTML with CSS for improved styling and design.

Markup in HTML

The **<!DOCTYPE>** declaration defines the document type and version of HTML. It ensures that the browser correctly interprets the document as an HTML page and applies the appropriate rendering mode. The **<html>** tag wraps the entire document and defines the root element.

The **<head>** section contains metadata such as **<title>**, **<meta>**, linked stylesheets, and scripts. The **<body>** tag holds all visible content like paragraphs, headings, images, and links. Most elements use opening **<tag>** and closing **</tag>** pairs, while self-closing tags like **
** or **<hr>** omit a closing tag.

Proper nesting ensures validity, and the inner tags must close before their parent tags. Semantic tags (e.g., **<header>**, **<nav>**, **<article>**, **<footer>**) convey meaning and improve accessibility, and comments (**<!-- comment -->**) let you annotate code without affecting page display.

Understanding <!DOCTYPE> in HTML

The **<!DOCTYPE>** declaration is essential because:

- It ensures the document is interpreted in standards mode instead of quirks mode.
- It helps maintain consistency across different web browsers.
- It specifies which version of HTML is being used (HTML5, XHTML, etc.).

The following example shows the correct HTML5 doctype declaration:

```
<!DOCTYPE html>
<html lang="en">
<head>
<meta charset="UTF-8">
<title>Document Title</title>
</head>
<body>
<p>Content goes here...</p>
</body>
</html>
```

HTML comments

HTML comments are written inside **<!>** and are ignored by browsers. They help developers annotate the code for better understanding and documentation.

Adding comments to an HTML document:

```
<!-- This is a comment -->
<p>This is visible content.</p>
```

Refer to the following list to understand the best practices for HTML comments:

- Use comments to explain complex sections of code.
- Avoid excessive comments that clutter the document.
- Use comments to disable sections of code temporarily for debugging.

ID and class attributes

HTML uses the **id** and **class** attributes target elements precisely: the **id** attribute assigns a unique identifier to a single element, while the **class** attribute groups multiple elements for shared styling or scripting, which are as follows.

- The **id** attribute uniquely identifies an element within a page.
- The **class** attribute groups multiple elements for CSS styling or JavaScript manipulation.

Example using **id** and **class**:

```
<p id="unique">This paragraph has a unique ID.</p>
<p class="grouped">This paragraph belongs to a class.</p>
```

Block vs. inline elements

The following list outlines how HTML distinguishes elements by how they occupy space and flow within their container:

- Block elements take up the full width of the parent container and start on a new line.
- Inline elements only take up as much width as necessary and remain within the same line.

An example of block and inline elements is as follows:

```
<!-- Block Element -->
<div>This is a block element.</div>
<!-- Inline Element -->
<span>This is an inline element.</span>
```

The following figure illustrates the way block-level and inline elements appear within a web page layout, showing their stacking and flow behavior:

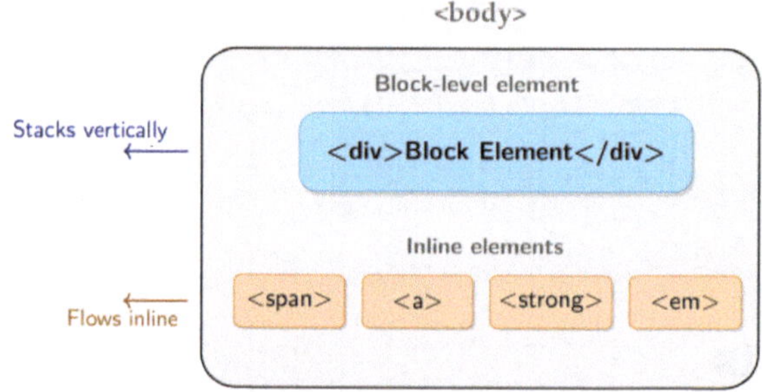

Figure 1.10: *Block elements span the full width and stack vertically, while inline elements flow within a line*

Grouping elements with **<div>** and **<span>** are as follows:

- The **<div>** tag is used to group block-level elements.
- The **<span>** tag is used to group inline elements for styling purposes.

The following is an example of using **<div>** and **<span>**:

```
<div style="background-color: lightgray;">
<h2>Grouped Content</h2>
<p>This is inside a div.</p>
</div>

<p>This is <span style="color: red;">highlighted</span> text.</p>
```

The <section> tag

The **<section>** tag in HTML is used to define thematic sections of a document, grouping related content together.

The following is an example of using the **<section>** tag:

```
<section>
<h2>Introduction</h2>
<p>This is an introductory section.</p>
</section>

<section>
```

```
<h2>Features</h2>
<ul>
<li>Feature 1</li>
<li>Feature 2</li>
<li>Feature 3</li>
</ul>
</section>
```

Embedding external content using <iframe>

The **<iframe>** tag allows embedding another webpage inside the current webpage.

An example of embedding a YouTube video using **<iframe>** is as follows:

```
<iframe width="560" height="315" src="https://www.youtube.com/embed/example">
</iframe>
```

Understanding the meta tag in HTML

Metadata provides information about the document, such as character set, viewport settings, and SEO data.

An example of commonly used **<meta>** tags is as follows:

```
<meta charset="UTF-8">
<meta name="viewport" content="width=device-width, initial-scale=1.0">
<meta name="description" content="This is a sample HTML page.">
```

Escape characters in HTML

Escape characters allow inserting reserved characters in HTML that would otherwise be interpreted as markup.

The following list outlines the common HTML escape characters:

- **< - <** (Less than)
- **> - >** (Greater than)
- **& - &** (Ampersand)
- **" - "** (Double Quote)
- **' - '** (Single Quote) Example of using escape characters:

```
<p>This is how you write &lt;div&gt; in HTML.</p>
```

The following are the key points to remember:

- Use **<!DOCTYPE>** to specify the document type.
- Use **id** for unique element identification.
- Use **class** for grouping elements together.
- Use **<div>** for grouping block elements and **<span>** for inline elements.
- Use **<iframe>** to embed external content.
- Use **<meta>** tags for document metadata.
- Use escape characters to display reserved HTML symbols.

This section provided an essential understanding of additional markup elements in HTML. Mastering these concepts will help in creating well-structured, semantically meaningful, and accessible web pages.

Hands-on building a static website

In this project, a simple static website will be created using HTML. The website will include a homepage, an about page, and a contact page. Each page will be linked through a navigation bar.

The following is the structure of the project:

```
project-folder/
|— index.html
|— about.html
|— contact.html
|— styles.css
|— images/
```

Follow these steps to complete the project:

1. Create an **index.html** file with a homepage that includes a heading, paragraph, and navigation links.
2. Add an **about.html** file with details about the project or a fictional company.
3. Add a **contact.html** file with a form for user inquiries.
4. Link all pages using a navigation bar.
5. Style the website using a **styles.css** file.

The following section provides the full solutions for each file.

Homepage

The following is the complete HTML structure for the homepage of a website:

```html
<!DOCTYPE html>
<html lang="en">
<head>
<meta charset="UTF-8">
<meta name="viewport" content="width=device-width, initial-scale=1.0">
<title>Home</title>
<link rel="stylesheet" href="styles.css">
</head>
<body>
<nav>
<a href="index.html">Home</a>
<a href="about.html">About</a>
<a href="contact.html">Contact</a>
</nav>
<h1>Welcome to My Website</h1>
<p>This is a simple static webpage created using HTML.</p>
</body>
</html>
```

About page

The following is the HTML code for the website's About page:

```html
<!DOCTYPE html>
<html lang="en">
<head>
```

```
<meta charset="UTF-8">
<meta name="viewport" content="width=device-width, initial-scale=1.0">
<title>About</title>
<link rel="stylesheet" href="styles.css">
</head>
<body>
<nav>
<a href="index.html">Home</a>
<a href="about.html">About</a>
<a href="contact.html">Contact</a>
</nav>
<h1>About Us</h1>
<p>This website is created as part of a hands-on HTML project.</p>
</body>
</html>
```

Contact page

The following is the HTML code for the website's Contact page.

```
<!DOCTYPE html>
<html lang="en">
<head>
<meta charset="UTF-8">
<meta name="viewport" content="width=device-width, initial-scale=1.0">
<title>Contact</title>
<link rel="stylesheet" href="styles.css">
</head>
<body>
<nav>
<a href="index.html">Home</a>
<a href="about.html">About</a>
<a href="contact.html">Contact</a>
</nav>
<h1>Contact Us</h1>
<form>
<label for="name">Name:</label>
<input type="text" id="name" name="name" required>
<br>
<label for="email">Email:</label>
<input type="email" id="email" name="email" required>
<br>
<label for="message">Message:</label>
<textarea id="message" name="message" rows="4" required></textarea>
<br>
<button type="submit">Submit</button>
</form>
</body>
</html>
```

CSS stylesheet

The following is the CSS code used to style the website:

```
body {
font-family: Arial, sans-serif; margin: 20px;
padding: 20px;
background-color: #f4f4f4;
}
nav {
background-color: #333;
padding: 10px;
}
nav a {
color: white; margin: 10px;
text-decoration: none;

}
h1 {
  color: #333;
}

p {
  color: #333;
  font-size: 16px;
}
form {
background-color: white; padding: 15px;
border-radius: 5px;
}
```

Output

When the preceding code is rendered in a web browser, it displays a simple static website with three pages: **Home**, **About**, and **Contact**. Each page has a navigation bar linking to the other pages.

The following is the expected output when rendered in a browser:

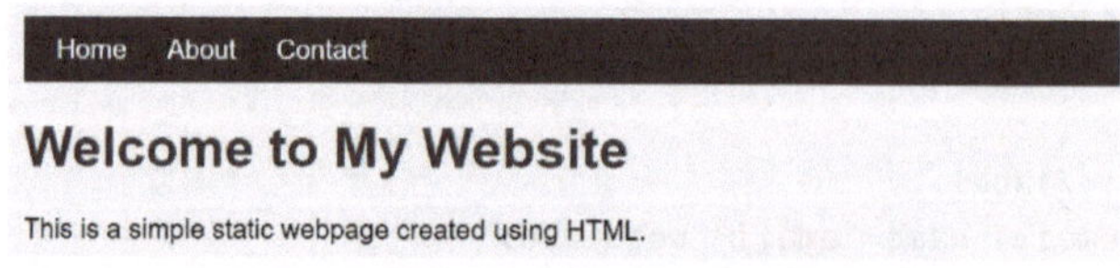

***Figure 1.11**: Rendered output of Extra Markup in HTML*

Case study on the evolution of a web page

Web development has evolved significantly over the years, moving from simple static HTML pages to dynamic and interactive web applications. This case study explores the changes in web design and functionality over different eras.

The evolution of a web page from the 1990s to modern times:

- **1990s**: Simple HTML pages with text and basic links.
- **Early 2000s**: Introduction of CSS for styling and layout.

- **2010s**: JavaScript and dynamic elements for interactivity.
- **Present**: Responsive and mobile-friendly design, progressive web apps.

This case study highlights the transformation of web development practices over time, emphasizing the importance of adapting to new technologies and trends.

Conclusion

This chapter covered the fundamentals of HTML5. It explained how to structure an HTML document, create headings, paragraphs, lists, links, tables, forms, and embed multimedia. It also introduced semantic and accessibility features that improve SEO and user experience. With these skills, you can build a static website and lay the groundwork for styling with CSS. In the next chapter, we will explore CSS, the language that defines the presentation of HTML documents. The chapter begins by distinguishing external, internal, and inline CSS, demonstrating how linked stylesheets support centralized control and maintainable designs. It then examines the cascade principle, specificity rules, and inheritance behavior, showing how conflicting declarations resolve in a browser. The discussion highlights external stylesheet benefits, including caching, consistency, and separation of concerns. Next, the overview covers CSS selectors, from basic elements, classes, and ID patterns to advanced combinators and attribute selectors, before detailing the box model that governs content, padding, border, and margin calculations. Layout techniques such as Flexbox and CSS Grid receive focus, demonstrating responsive and flexible designs without floats. A section on color management introduces named, **HEX**, **RGB(A)**, and **HSL(A)** formats along with opacity controls. Typography and custom fonts appear next, including the @font-face rule, font weights, and text decoration. The final part examines styling lists, tables, and forms for improved readability and accessibility. Practical exercises reinforce each concept through hands-on application, and the next chapter will discuss the purpose and syntax of CSS and apply selectors to target and style HTML elements.

Exercises

1. Which line puts a browser into standards mode for HTML5?
   a. <html lang="en">
   b. <meta charset="UTF-8">
   c. <!DOCTYPE html>
   d. <head>
2. Which statement about headings is correct?
   a. Use multiple <h1> tags for SEO
   b. Do not skip levels; keep a logical hierarchy
   c. <h6> is more important than <h2>
   d. Headings cannot be styled with CSS
3. Which attribute makes an image defer loading until near the viewport?
   a. defer
   b. loading="lazy"
   c. async
   d. delay="true"
4. When opening external links in a new tab, which attribute pair improves security?
   a. target="_self" rel="nofollow"
   b. target="_blank" rel="noopener noreferrer"

c. target="_parent" rel="external"

d. target="_top" rel="noreferrer"

5. In a table, header cells use the ______ element, while data cells use the ______ element
6. The form submission URL goes in the ______ attribute, and the HTTP verb goes in the ______ attribute.
7. Use the ______ attribute on <img> to provide text for screen readers and when the image fails to load.
8. To display < literally in HTML, write the escape sequence ______.
9. Explain the roles of <head> and <body> in an HTML document.
10. Differentiate between block-level and inline elements with one example each.
11. When should you use <ol> versus <ul>? Give one realistic example for each.
12. State two accessibility or usability best practices for links or media used on a page.
13. Headings hierarchy:
    a. <h1>Web Basics</h1>
    b. <h3>Document Structure</h3>
    c. <h2>Headings</h2>
    d. Identify the hierarchy issue and provide a corrected sequence.
14. Image without accessibility and performance features:
    <img src="team.jpg">
    Rewrite the tag to include appropriate attributes for accessibility and performance.
15. Table with structure issues (header cells missing, no grouping):
    <table>
     <tr><td>Name</td><td>Subject</td><td>Score</td></tr>
     <tr><td>Ava</td><td>Math</td><td>92</td></tr>
    </table>
    Rewrite to add a caption, proper header cells, and semantic sections.
16. Link that opens a new tab without security attributes:
    <a href="https://example.com" target="_blank">Docs</a>
    Rewrite with safer attributes.
17. Write the minimal, valid HTML5 skeleton that sets UTF-8 and a responsive viewport, and shows an <h1> in the page.
18. Create one ordered list that starts from 3 and counts backward using uppercase letters, with three items.
19. Embed a video with native controls, a poster image, and two <source> formats (MP4 and WebM). Include a fallback message.
20. Build a compact form fragment for "Newsletter Signup" with a labeled email and a required submit button. Use proper types and associate labels correctly.
21. What will a browser do with <pre> content compared to a normal paragraph? Answer in one or two sentences and give one suitable use case.
22. A page uses <a href="file.pdf" download>. Describe what happens when the user clicks it, and mention one scenario where this is preferable to a normal link.
23. Create a simple three-page static site (Home, About, Contact) with a shared top navigation made of links, a main <h1> on each page, and on the Contact page a short form with name, email, and message. Write only the HTML for one page in full and outline the differing parts for the other two pages.

CHAPTER 2
Styling HTML with CSS

Introduction

Cascading Style Sheets (**CSS**) is the language used to control the appearance of **Hypertext Markup Language** (**HTML**) documents. By separating content from presentation, CSS makes it easy to update fonts, colors, spacing, and layout without touching the HTML structure. In this chapter, the reader will learn how CSS selectors target elements, how the cascade and specificity rules determine the styles that are to be applied, and how the box model governs element sizing and spacing. The chapter also covers modern layout techniques, Flexbox, and CSS Grid, which enable responsive, flexible designs. Finally, the reader will explore color formats, transparency, typography, and the styling of lists, tables, and forms, then apply these skills in a hands-on project.

CSS allows developers to separate content (HTML) from presentation (CSS), making web pages easier to maintain, update, and customize. By keeping styling separate from HTML, CSS enhances the efficiency of web development.

Structure

The chapter covers the following topics:

- Types of CSS
- CSS Box Model
- CSS colors and transparency
- CSS typography and text styling
- CSS attribute selectors
- Hands-on project
- CSS selectors
- CSS Grid for layouts
- CSS3 opacity and transparency
- Text alignment, indenting, and shadow
- Styling lists, tables, and forms with CSS

Objectives

Upon completing this chapter, the reader can describe the purpose and syntax of CSS and apply selectors to target and style HTML elements. The reader will understand how the cascade, specificity, and inheritance rules work together to resolve style conflicts. They will use the box model to control element dimensions, padding, and margins. The reader will create responsive layouts using Flexbox and CSS Grid, manage colors and transparency with various formats, and apply typography rules, including custom fonts. They will also style lists, tables, and forms for clarity and accessibility, and consolidate these skills by building a styled, responsive web page in the hands-on project.

It is important to note that CSS is a language used to describe the presentation of HTML documents. CSS controls the layout, colors, fonts, and overall appearance of web pages, ensuring a visually appealing and consistent user experience.

Types of CSS

CSS can be applied in three different ways, each with specific use cases:

- **External CSS**: Uses an external `.css` file linked to the HTML document. This method is preferred for large projects because it enables centralized control of styles across multiple pages.

- **Internal CSS**: Defines styles within the **<style>** tag inside the **<head>** section of the HTML document. It is useful when styling is required only for a single page.
- **Inline CSS**: Applies styles directly to HTML elements using the **style** attribute. This method is typically used for quick fixes or when dynamic styling is needed via JavaScript.

External CSS

Using external CSS allows reusability and maintainability of styles across multiple pages. The CSS rules are written in a separate file (**styles.css**), and the HTML document links to it using the **<link>** tag.

An example of linking an external CSS file is as follows:

```
<!DOCTYPE html>
<html lang="en">
<head>
<link rel="stylesheet" href="styles.css">
<title>External CSS Example</title>
</head>
<body>
<h1>Welcome to My Website</h1>
</body>
</html>
```

The corresponding **styles.css** file is as follows:

```
/* styles.css */
h1 {
color: blue;
text-align: center;
font-family: Arial, sans-serif;
}
```

Internal CSS

Internal CSS is defined within the HTML document itself using the **<style>** tag inside the **<head>** section. It is useful when styling is required only for that particular page.

The following is an example of defining styles within the HTML document:

```
<!DOCTYPE html>
<html lang="en">
<head>
<style>
h1 {
color: green; font-size: 24px;
font-family: Verdana, sans-serif;
}
</style>
<title>Internal CSS Example</title>
</head>
<body>
<h1>Welcome to My Website</h1>
</body>
</html>
```

Inline CSS

Inline CSS is applied directly to an element using the **style** attribute. It is generally used for quick modifications or dynamic styling controlled by JavaScript.

The following is an example of applying styles directly to an element:

```
<h1 style="color: red; font-size: 30px; text-align: center;">Welcome to My Website</h1>
```

CSS cascade order

The order in which CSS rules apply follows the cascade principle, which determines which styles take precedence when multiple rules target the same element.

The cascade principle is fundamental in CSS and governs how styles are applied when multiple rules conflict. It ensures that the most relevant styles take effect while allowing flexibility in styling elements.

Order of CSS rule application

The cascade principle prioritizes styles in the following order:

- **Inline styles**: Defined within an element's **style** attribute. These have the highest priority.
- **Internal styles**: Defined within the **<style>** tag inside the HTML **<head>**.
- **External stylesheets**: Linked via **<link>** in the HTML **<head>** and usually provide global styles.
- **Browser default styles**: It is applied when no user-defined styles are available. These have the lowest priority.

Note: If multiple rules conflict, the rule defined last in the CSS file or closest to the element (e.g., inline styles) takes precedence. This is known as the last rule wins principle.

Example of CSS cascade order

Consider the following example, where an **<h1>** element is styled using different CSS methods:

```
<!DOCTYPE html>
<html lang="en">
<head>
<title>CSS Cascade Example</title>
<link rel="stylesheet" href="styles.css"> <!-- External stylesheet -->
<style>
h1 {
color: green; /* Internal CSS */
}
</style>
</head>
<body>

<h1 style="color: red;">This is a heading</h1> <!-- Inline CSS -->
</body>
</html>
```

The CSS file used in this example is named (**styles.css**):

```
h1 {
color: blue; /* External CSS */
}
```

As per the cascade order, the **<h1>** element will be displayed in red because inline styles have the highest priority, followed by internal styles, and then external styles. Since inline styles have the highest priority, the **<h1>** will be displayed in red.

CSS specificity

Specificity determines which style rule is applied when multiple rules target the same element. It follows a hierarchy where more specific selectors override less specific ones.

Specificity values are assigned based on the type of selector:

- Inline styles (`style` attribute) have the highest specificity.
- ID selectors (`#id-name`) are more specific than class or element selectors.
- Class, attribute, and pseudo-class selectors (`.class-name`, `[attribute]`, `:hover`) have lower specificity than ID selectors but are more specific than element selectors.
- Element selectors (`p`, `div`, `h1`) have the lowest specificity.

Example of CSS specificity

Consider the following CSS rules and HTML structure to illustrate specificity:

```
/* Element selector */
p {
color: blue;
}
/* Class selector */
.paragraph {
color: green;
}

/* ID selector */
#main-text {
color: red;
}
```

The following HTML code defines a paragraph element with an ID of main-text and a class named paragraph:

```
<p id="main-text" class="paragraph">This is a paragraph.</p>
```

In this example, the **<p>** element has both an ID and a class. The specificity hierarchy is as follows:

- **ID selector (#main-text)**: 100 points
- **Class selector (.paragraph)**: 10 points
- **Element selector (p)**: 1 point

The total specificity for the **<p>** element is 111 points. Therefore, the text will be displayed in red because the ID selector has the highest specificity. Since ID selectors have higher specificity than class and element selectors, the paragraph will be displayed in red.

CSS inheritance

CSS inheritance is a fundamental concept that allows certain styles to be passed from parent elements to their child elements. This behavior helps maintain consistency across a web page without requiring repeated declarations for every element. By default, text-related properties such as **color**, **font-family**, **font-size**, and **line-height** are inherited. These ensure that child elements visually align with the parent unless explicitly overridden.

However, not all CSS properties are inherited automatically. Box model properties such as **`margin`**, **`padding`**, **`border`**, **`width`**, and **`height`** must be defined individually for each element if needed, as they do not inherit by default. Developers can control inheritance using the **`inherit`**, **`initial`**, or **`unset`** values. For example, setting **`border: inherit;`** on a child element explicitly tells the browser to apply the parent's border value, even though it is not inherited by default.

Understanding how inheritance works improves code reusability and helps create more maintainable stylesheets.

Example of CSS inheritance

Consider the following example to illustrate inheritance:

```
body {
font-family: Arial, sans-serif;
color: blue; /* Inherited by child elements */
}
p {
font-size: 16px; /* Not inherited */
}
```

Since color is an inheritable property, all text inside the **`<body>`** will be blue unless overridden.

Note: External stylesheets offer several advantages:

- **Separation of content and design, making the code easier to maintain.**
- **Consistency across multiple pages, ensuring a uniform design.**
- **Improved performance, as browsers cache external stylesheets for faster loading.**
- **Reusability, reducing redundancy by applying the same styles to multiple pages.**

Example of external stylesheet usage

To link an external CSS file, use the **`<link>`** tag in the HTML **`<head>`** section. The following is an example of linking an external CSS file:

```
<head>
<link rel="stylesheet" href="styles.css">
</head>
```

This method allows you to define styles in a separate file (**`styles.css`**), which can be reused across multiple HTML documents.

The key takeaways are as follows:

- CSS rules follow a cascading order, where inline styles override internal and external styles.
- Specificity determines which rule takes precedence when multiple rules apply to an element.
- Inheritance allows certain properties to pass down from parent elements to child elements.
- External stylesheets are recommended for better organization, maintainability, and performance.

CSS selectors

CSS selectors are essential components of any stylesheet. They define how styles are applied to HTML elements by identifying which elements the rules should target. Selectors provide a powerful and flexible way to control the presentation of content on a webpage.

There are several types of selectors in CSS:

- **Basic selectors**: These include type selectors (**`p`**, **`h1`**, etc.), class selectors (**`.class-name`**), and ID selectors (**`#id-name`**). They form the foundation of most stylesheets.

- **Group selectors**: These allow multiple elements to share the same styles. For example, `h1, h2, h3 { color: navy; }` applies the same rule to all three headings.
- **Combinator selectors**: These define relationships between elements, such as parent-child (`div > p`), descendant (`div p`), adjacent sibling (`h1 + p`), and general sibling (`h1 ~ p`).
- **Attribute selectors**: These target elements are based on the presence or value of their attributes. For example, `input[type="text"]` selects all text input fields.
- **Pseudo-classes and pseudo-elements**: Pseudo-classes like `:hover` or `:nth-child()` target elements in specific states, while pseudo-elements such as `::before` and `::after` allow insertion of content.

Using selectors effectively helps create modular, maintainable, and scalable CSS. Proper structuring also minimizes code duplication and ensures consistent styling across a website. Mastery of selectors is vital for both beginner and advanced web developers aiming to build responsive and visually appealing designs.

Commonly used CSS selectors

Different types of CSS selectors exist to target elements based on various attributes and relationships. The following are some commonly used selectors:

- **Element selector**: Targets all instances of a specific HTML element. It applies the same style to every occurrence of that element.
  - **Example:**

    ```
    p {
    color: blue;
    }
    ```

    This rule applies to all `<p>` elements in the document, setting their text color to blue.
- **Class selector**: Targets elements that belong to a specific class. A class selector is prefixed with a dot (`.`).
  - **Example**:

    ```
    .highlight {
    background-color: yellow;
    }
    ```

    Any HTML element with `class="highlight"` will have a yellow background.
- **ID selector**: Targets a unique element with a specific ID. The ID selector is prefixed with a `#`.
  - **Example**:

    ```
    #main-title {
    font-size: 36px;
    }
    ```

    This rule applies only to the element with `id="main-title"`, setting its font size to 36px.
- **Group selector**: Targets multiple elements at once and applies the same styles to them.
  - **Example**:

    ```
    h1, h2, h3 {
    color: navy;
    }
    ```

    This rule sets the text color to navy for all `<h1>`, `<h2>`, and `<h3>` elements.
- **Universal selector**: Targets all elements on the page.
  - **Example**:

```
* {
margin: 0;
padding: 0;
}
```

This rule removes default margin and padding from all elements.

- **Descendant selector**: Targets elements that are inside another element, regardless of their depth.
  - **Example**:

```
div p {
color: gray;
}
```

This rule applies to all **<p>** elements that are contained within a **<div>**, setting their text color to gray.

Additional CSS selectors

Apart from the basic selectors, CSS provides additional advanced selectors that allow for greater control over styling:

- **Child selector (>)**: Targets only the immediate child elements.
  - **Example**:

```
div > p {
color: black;
}
```

This rule applies only to **<p>** elements that are direct children of a **<div>**.

- **Adjacent sibling selector** (+): Targets the next adjacent sibling element.
  - **Example**:

```
h1 + p {
font-style: italic;
}
```

This rule applies to a **<p>** element that directly follows an **<h1>**, making its text italic.

- **General sibling selector (' ')**: Targets all sibling elements of a specified element.
  - **Example**:

```
h1 ~ p {
color: green;
}
```

This rule applies to all **<p>** elements that follow an **<h1>** on the same level.

- **Attribute selector ([attribute])**: Targets elements based on their attributes.
  - **Example**:

```
input[type="text"] {
border: 2px solid black;
}
```

This rule applies only to **<input>** elements with **type="text"**, adding a black border.

Best practices for using CSS selectors

To ensure efficient and maintainable stylesheets, follow these best practices:

- Use class selectors instead of ID selectors for styling multiple elements, as IDs are unique.

- Avoid using the universal selector (*) too often, as it may negatively impact performance.
- Be specific when selecting elements to prevent unnecessary overrides and conflicts.
- Group selectors when applying the same styles to multiple elements to reduce redundancy.
- Use descendant and child selectors wisely to avoid unintended styling of deeply nested elements.

Example of CSS selectors in action

The following example demonstrates how different CSS selectors can be used to style an HTML document:

```
/* Apply styles to all paragraphs inside a div */
div p {
font-size: 14px;
line-height: 1.6;
}

/* Style only the first paragraph inside a div */
div > p:first-child {
font-weight: bold;
}

/* Apply a red border to all input fields of type text */
input[type="text"] {
border: 1px solid red;
}

/* Change background color of elements with class "highlight" */
.highlight {
background-color: yellow;
}

/* Set font size for elements with ID "main-title" */
#main-title {
font-size: 36px;
text-align: center;
}
```

CSS selectors and styles

Try creating an HTML page with:

- A `<div>` containing multiple paragraphs, with the first paragraph having bold text.
- A `<h1>` element styled using an ID selector.
- A `<p>` element styled using a class selector.
- An `<input>` field where the border changes color based on its `type` attribute.
- A group of elements sharing a common style using a group selector.

Note: Ensure the CSS is structured properly and follows best practices.

CSS Box Model

Every HTML element is treated as a rectangular box following the CSS Box Model. This model defines how elements are displayed on a web page and how space is distributed within and around them. Understanding the Box Model is essential for creating structured, visually appealing layouts.

The Box Model consists of four main areas, which are as follows:

- **Content**: The innermost part, where text or other elements appear.
- **Padding:** The space between the content and the border, used to add internal spacing.
- **Border**: A visible line surrounding the padding and content, which can be styled with different widths, colors, and patterns.
- **Margin**: The outermost layer, creating space between the element and neighboring elements.

Each of these areas contributes to the total size of an element. For example, increasing the padding or border width will expand the element's dimensions unless the **`box-sizing: border-box;`** rule is applied. This rule ensures that padding and borders are included within the defined width and height, simplifying layout design.

A solid understanding of the Box Model allows developers to align elements accurately, prevent layout issues, and design responsive web interfaces effectively.

Components of the CSS Box Model

The Box Model consists of the following four main parts:

- **Content**: The area where text, images, or other elements are placed. It is the core of the box.
- **Padding**: The space between the content and the border. Padding increases the space inside the element without affecting its outer dimensions.
- **Border**: The outline surrounding the content and padding. It can have different styles (solid, dashed, dotted) and thickness.
- **Margin**: The space outside the border that separates one element from another. It helps to position elements on the page.

  Refer to the following figure:

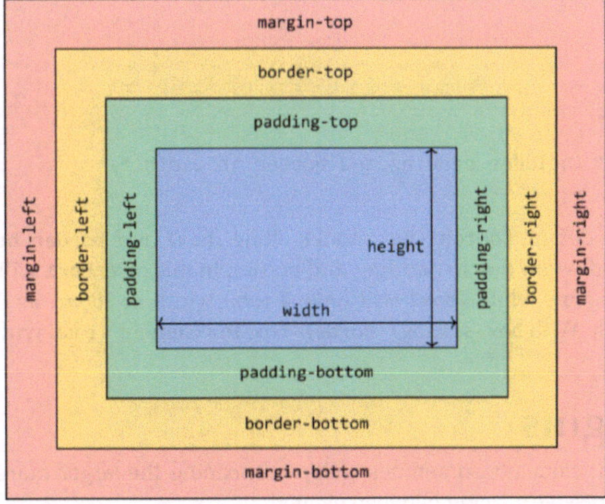

Figure 2.1: *CSS Box Model components*

Example of CSS Box Model properties

The following example demonstrates how the Box Model works by defining a styled **<div>** element:

```
div {
width: 200px;    /* Width of the content area */
padding: 20px;   /* Space between content and border */ border: 5px solid black; /* Defines the border around the element */ margin: 15px;        /* Space outside the border */
}
```

The element's total width and height are calculated using the Box Model as follows:

- *Total width = Content Width + 2 × Padding + 2 × Border*
- *Total height = Content Height + 2 × Padding + 2 × Border*

For the preceding example, the calculated dimensions are:

- *Total width = 200px + (20px × 2) + (5px × 2) = 250px*
- *Total height = Content Height + (20px × 2) + (5px × 2) = Content Height + 50px*

These represent the final computed dimensions of the element when rendered in the browser.

Box sizing property

By default, the **width** and **height** properties apply only to the content area. However, using the **box-sizing** property, we can modify how these dimensions are calculated:

- **content-box (default)**: The width and height apply only to the content, excluding padding and border.
- **border-box**: The width and height include padding and border, making layout calculations easier.

The following example of **box-sizing** property shows how it affects the box model:

```
.box1 {
width: 200px;
padding: 20px;
border: 5px solid black;
box-sizing: content-box; /* Default behavior */
}

.box2 {
width: 200px;
padding: 20px;
border: 5px solid black;
box-sizing: border-box; /* Includes padding and border in width */
}
```

In this example, **box1** uses the default **content-box** model, while **.box2** uses **border-box**. The total width of **.box1** will be larger than the specified width due to padding and border. In this case, **box1** will have a total width of *250px (200px + 20px + 20px + 5px + 5px)*, while **.box2** will have a total width of *200px*, as the padding and border are included in the specified width. With **box-sizing: border-box**, the element's total width remains *200px*, including padding and border.

Collapsing margins

Margins between two adjacent elements sometimes collapse, meaning the larger margin value is used instead of adding both. This prevents excessive spacing between elements.

For example, consider the following CSS:

```
p {
margin-bottom: 20px;
}

div {
margin-top: 30px;
}
```

When a **<p>** element is followed by a **<div>**, the margins may collapse. In this case, the bottom margin of the **<p>** and the top margin of the **<div>** will not add up. Instead of *20px + 30px = 50px* margin, the final margin between the **<p>** and **<div>** will be *30px*, as the larger value is used.

Best practices for using the Box Model

To ensure better layout consistency, follow these best practices:

- Use **box-sizing: border-box;** to simplify layout calculations.
- Use consistent margins and padding to maintain uniform spacing.
- Set **margin: auto;** for centering block elements within their parent.
- Use **overflow: hidden;** or **overflow: auto;** to handle content exceeding the box size.
- Be mindful of margin collapsing, which may affect spacing unexpectedly.

CSS Flexbox for layouts

Flexbox, or Flexible Box Layout, is a layout model designed to efficiently align and distribute elements within a container, even when their sizes are unknown or dynamic. It provides an improved way to create responsive designs without relying on float-based layouts or complex positioning techniques.

A Flexbox layout consists of a parent container with **display: flex**, and its child elements become flex items. The layout direction can be controlled using the **flex-direction** property, allowing elements to be arranged in rows (**row**) or columns (**column**).

Flexbox also offers properties like **justify-content, align-items**, and **align-content** to control the alignment and spacing of items along the main and cross axes. It supports wrapping of items with **flex-wrap** and ordering using the **order** property.

Each flex item can grow, shrink, or remain fixed using the flex shorthand, which combines **flex-grow**, **flex-shrink**, and **flex-basis**. This makes it easy to create flexible and adaptive interfaces.

Flexbox is particularly useful for building one-dimensional layouts, such as navigation bars, cards, sidebars, and centering elements both vertically and horizontally. Understanding Flexbox is essential for modern web development and crafting responsive, mobile-friendly designs.

Application of flexbox

Flexbox offers several advantages over traditional layout methods:

- Provides a flexible and efficient layout for arranging elements dynamically.
- Allows horizontal and vertical alignment without needing extra CSS hacks.
- Supports equal spacing, auto-resizing, and content wrapping based on available space.
- Works well for responsive design, adjusting content based on screen size.
- Reduces reliance on floats and positioning, simplifying CSS layout management.

Note: Flexbox is particularly useful for creating navigation bars, galleries, and responsive layouts where elements need to adapt to different screen sizes.

Understanding the Flexbox Model

A Flexbox layout consists of two main components:

- **Flex container**: The parent element that holds the flex items.
- **Flex items**: The child elements inside the flex container that will be arranged dynamically.

The flex container is defined using the `display: flex;` property, which activates the Flexbox model. The child elements (flex items) are then automatically arranged based on the properties applied to the container and items. The Flexbox model allows for flexible and responsive layouts by controlling the alignment, direction, and size of items within a container.

Basic Flexbox properties

Flexbox provides several properties to control the layout and alignment of items within a flex container. The key properties include the following:

- **Flex container properties**: The following properties are applied to the parent container:
  - **display: flex;**: Activates the flex layout.
  - **flex-direction**: Defines the main axis direction (`row`, `column`, `row-reverse`, `column- reverse`).
  - **justify-content**: Aligns items along the main axis (`flex-start`, `center`, `flex-end`, `space- between`, `space-around`, `space-evenly`).
  - **align-items**: Aligns items along the cross axis (`flex-start`, `center`, `flex-end`, `stretch`, `baseline`).
  - **align-content**: Controls spacing between flex lines in a multi-line container (`flex-start`, `center`, `flex-end`, `space-between`, `space-around`, `stretch`).
  - **flex-wrap**: Determines whether items wrap (`nowrap`, `wrap`, `wrap-reverse`).
- **Flex item properties**: The following properties are applied to child elements (flex items):
  - **flex-grow**: Defines how much a flex item should grow relative to others.
  - **flex-shrink**: Defines how much an item should shrink if needed.
  - **flex-basis**: Sets the initial size of a flex item before growing or shrinking.
  - **align-self**: Overrides the 'align-items' value for a specific item.

Centering content using Flexbox

The following example demonstrates how to use Flexbox to center items horizontally and vertically:

```
.container {
display: flex;
justify-content: center; /* Align items horizontally */ align-items: center; /* Align items
vertically */ height: 300px;
background-color: lightgray;
}
```

The following is the HTML structure:

```
<div class="container">
<p>This is a flexbox container.</p>
</div>
```

Creating a navigation bar with Flexbox

One of the most common applications of Flexbox is creating a responsive navigation bar. The following example shows how to create a simple navigation bar using Flexbox:

```
.navbar {
display: flex;
justify-content: space-between; background-color: #333; padding: 10px;
}

.navbar a {
color: white;
text-decoration: none; padding: 10px;
}
```

The following HTML code creates a navigation bar using a **<div>** element with the class **navbar**, containing four anchor links: Home, About, Services, and Contact:

```
<div class="navbar">
<a href="#">Home</a>
<a href="#">About</a>
<a href="#">Services</a>
<a href="#">Contact</a>
</div>
```

Responsive layout with Flexbox

Flexbox makes it easy to create a responsive layout where items adjust based on screen size.

The following example demonstrates a responsive layout with three boxes that adjust their size based on the available space:

```
.container {
display: flex; flex-wrap: wrap; gap: 10px;
}

.box {
background-color: lightblue; padding: 20px;
text-align: center;
flex: 1 1 200px; /* Flex-grow, flex-shrink, flex-basis */
}
```

The following HTML code defines a container **<div>** with the class **container**, which holds three child **<div>** elements, each with the class box, labeled as Box 1, Box 2, and Box 3, respectively. This structure is typically used to demonstrate layout models such as Flexbox or Grid:

```
<div class="container">
<div class="box">Box 1</div>
<div class="box">Box 2</div>
<div class="box">Box 3</div>
</div>
```

Best practices for using Flexbox

To utilize the maximum benefits of Flexbox, follow these best practices:

- Use **flex-wrap: wrap;** to allow items to flow naturally on smaller screens.

- Prefer `justify-content: space-between;` for evenly spaced navigation menus.
- Set `align-items: center;` when centering items vertically.
- Use `flex: 1;` on items when equal distribution of space is needed.
- Combine Flexbox with media queries for better responsiveness.

CSS Grid for layouts

CSS Grid is a powerful two-dimensional layout system that allows precise control over the placement and alignment of elements within rows and columns. Unlike Flexbox, which is primarily one-dimensional (row or column), CSS Grid enables a structured, flexible design by defining both rows and columns simultaneously.

Application of CSS Grid

CSS Grid is particularly useful for complex layouts, such as multi-column designs, where elements need to be placed in specific grid areas. It provides a more intuitive way to create responsive designs without relying on floats or positioning hacks.

The following list outlines several advantages offered by CSS Grid:

- Provides full two-dimensional layout control over both rows and columns.
- Reduces reliance on floats and positioning, making layouts more manageable.
- Allows explicit and implicit grid definitions, adapting automatically to content.
- Supports alignment, spacing, and ordering of elements easily.
- Works well for complex layouts, such as dashboards, galleries, and responsive designs.

Note: **CSS Grid is particularly useful for creating complex web layouts, such as multi-column designs, where elements need to be placed in specific grid areas.**

Understanding the CSS Grid model

CSS Grid layout consists of a grid container and grid items. The grid container defines the overall structure, while grid items are the individual elements placed within that structure.

A CSS Grid layout consists of two key components:

- **Grid container**: The parent element that holds grid items. It is defined using `display: grid;`.
- **Grid items**: The child elements inside the grid container, which are placed in rows and columns.

Basic CSS Grid properties

CSS Grid provides several properties to control the layout and alignment of items within a grid container. The key properties include the following:

- **Grid container properties**: The following properties apply to the parent grid container:
  - **display: grid;**: Enables grid layout on the container.
  - **grid-template-columns**: Defines the number and size of columns.
  - **grid-template-rows**: Defines the number and size of rows.
  - **gap**: Specifies spacing between grid items.
  - **justify-items**: Aligns grid items along the horizontal axis.
  - **align-items**: Aligns grid items along the vertical axis.

    - **grid-auto-rows**: Automatically generates rows when needed.
    - **grid-auto-columns**: Automatically generates columns when needed.
- **Grid item properties**: The following properties apply to child elements (grid items):
    - **grid-column**: Specifies the column span of an item.
    - **grid-row**: Specifies the row span of an item.
    - **justify-self**: Aligns an individual item along the horizontal axis.
    - **align-self**: Aligns an individual item along the vertical axis.
    - **grid-area**: Defines an item's placement within the grid.

Creating a simple Grid layout

The following HTML and CSS code demonstrates a basic grid layout. The container **`<div>`** with the class **`grid-container`** is styled using CSS Grid, creating three equally sized columns with a 10px gap between items. Inside the container are three child **`<div>`** elements with the class **`grid-item`**, each styled with background color, padding, centered text, and a border to visually represent the grid structure. The details are as follows:

```
.grid-container {
display: grid;
grid-template-columns: auto auto auto; /* Three equal columns */
gap: 10px; /* Space between grid items */
}
.grid-item {
background-color: lightblue; padding: 20px;
text-align: center; border: 1px solid black;
}

<div class="grid container">
<div class="grid-item">1</div>
<div class="grid-item">2</div>
<div class="grid-item">3</div>
</div>
```

Creating a responsive Grid layout

CSS Grid makes it easy to create a responsive layout that automatically adjusts based on the screen size of the device. The following code demonstrates how to implement a flexible grid using the **`auto-fit`** and **`minmax()`** functions to ensure that grid items resize appropriately.

The following CSS code defines the grid structure. The **`.grid-container class uses display: grid`** and sets the columns to adjust responsively with **`grid-template-columns: repeat(auto-fit, minmax(200px, 1fr));`**, meaning the layout will fit as many 200px-wide columns as possible, stretching them if needed. A **`15px`** gap is added between the grid items. Each grid item, defined by the **`.grid-item`** class, has a light gray background, 20px padding, centered text, and a black border.

```
.grid-container {
display: grid;
grid-template-columns: repeat(auto-fit, minmax(200px, 1fr)); /* Responsive columns */
gap: 15px;
}
```

```
.grid-item {
background-color: lightgray; padding: 20px;
text-align: center; border: 1px solid black;
}
```

The following HTML code structures the content within the grid layout. The container **<div>** with the class **grid-container** wraps four child **<div>** elements, each having the class **grid-item** and labeled as Box 1 through Box 4. These items will automatically adjust their width and alignment based on the screen size, ensuring a responsive design.

```
<div class="grid-container">
<div class="grid-item">Box 1</div>
<div class="grid-item">Box 2</div>
<div class="grid-item">Box 3</div>
<div class="grid-item">Box 4</div>
</div>
```

In this example:

- **repeat(auto-fit, minmax(200px, 1fr))** dynamically adjusts the number of columns.
- **minmax(200px, 1fr)** ensures that each item is at least *200px* wide but can expand.
- The layout automatically adapts to screen size changes.

Grid layout for a web page

CSS Grid is a powerful layout system commonly used to design full-page web structures such as landing pages, admin dashboards, or content portals. It allows developers to define distinct areas of a page—such as headers, footers, sidebars, and main content sections, with precision and flexibility.

The following CSS code defines a page layout using named grid areas. The .grid-container uses **display: grid** along with the **grid-template-areas** property to structure the layout in three rows: a header at the top, a sidebar and content area side by side in the middle, and a footer at the bottom. The layout is controlled with **grid-template-rows** and **grid-template-columns** to set the height and width of the rows and columns, respectively, while the **gap** adds spacing between areas. Each section—header, sidebar, content, and footer—is assigned to its corresponding named grid area and styled with background color, padding, and alignment properties.

```
.grid-container {
display: grid;
grid-template-areas: "header header" "sidebar content" "footer footer";
grid-template-rows: 60px auto 50px; grid-template-columns: 200px auto; gap: 10px;
}

.header {
grid-area: header; background-color: lightblue; text-align: center;
padding: 15px;
}

.sidebar {
grid-area: sidebar; background-color: lightgray; padding: 15px;
}

.content {
grid-area: content; background-color: white; padding: 15px;
```

```
}

.footer {
grid-area: footer; background-color: lightblue; text-align: center;
padding: 10px;
}
```

The following HTML code structures the content using the defined grid areas. The outer **<div>** has the class **grid-container** and contains four child **<div>** elements, each assigned to a specific section of the layout: **header**, **sidebar**, **content**, and **footer**. These sections are placed on the page according to the grid layout defined in the CSS, creating a clean and organized web page structure.

```
<div class="grid-container">
<div class="header">Header</div>
<div class="sidebar">Sidebar</div>
<div class="content">Main Content</div>
<div class="footer">Footer</div>
</div>
```

In this layout, :**grid-template-areas** defines named regions for the layout structure. The header spans two columns, while the footer also spans two columns. The sidebar and content are arranged in two columns, making a structured page layout.

Best practices for using CSS Grid

Refer to the following list to optimize grid-based layouts:

- Use **grid-template-areas** for better readability and layout control.
- Combine grid and flexbox where necessary (e.g., flexbox inside grid items).
- Use **minmax()** with **auto-fit** or **auto-fill** for responsive grids.
- Avoid excessive manual column or row definitions; use **repeat()** instead.
- Set **gap** instead of **margin** for cleaner spacing between items.

Exercise: Create an HTML page that includes:

1. A well-structured CSS Grid layout with at least three rows and three columns.
2. A navigation menu styled using Flexbox.
3. A responsive grid-based section to display images or content boxes.

Note: CSS Grid is particularly useful for creating complex web layouts, such as multi-column designs, where elements need to be placed in specific grid areas. Ensure the layout is properly structured and responsive on different screen sizes.

The correct implementation should include:

- **A well-structured HTML document with an external CSS file.**
- **A navigation menu designed using Flexbox for proper alignment.**
- **A CSS Grid layout with auto-adjusting rows and columns for responsiveness.**
- **Proper CSS media queries to ensure the design adapts to different screen sizes.**

CSS colors and transparency

CSS allows defining colors for text, backgrounds, borders, and other elements using various color formats. Colors enhance readability, contrast, and the overall user experience. Furthermore, CSS3 introduced properties for controlling transparency and opacity, allowing for more dynamic visual effects.

Colors can be specified using keywords (e.g., **red**, **blue**), hexadecimal values (e.g., **#ff5733**), RGB (**rgb(255, 87, 51)**), RGBA (which includes an alpha transparency channel), HSL, and HSLA formats. The opacity property, ranging from 0 (completely transparent) to 1 (fully opaque), controls the transparency level of an entire element and its children.

For more precise transparency, the **rgba()** or **hsla()** functions allow setting opacity per color instead of affecting the entire element. This is especially useful for overlays, hover effects, and layered content designs.

Using appropriate color schemes and transparency can significantly impact a website's aesthetics, accessibility, and usability. Designers often use color contrast tools to ensure text remains legible across different background shades.

Foreground and background colors

CSS provides a way to set colors for text and backgrounds, enhancing the visual appeal of web pages. The **color** property sets the text color, while the **background-color** property sets the background color of elements.

The following properties are used to define colors in CSS:

- **color**: Defines the text (foreground) color.
- **background-color**: Defines the background color of elements.

The following example demonstrates how to set foreground and background colors for HTML elements:

```
/* Foreground and Background Colors */
h1 {
color: white;
background-color: black;
}

p {
color: blue;
background-color: lightgray;
}
```

CSS color formats

CSS supports various color formats to define colors, allowing flexibility in design. Each format has its own syntax and use cases, making it easier to choose the right one for specific needs.

CSS supports different ways to define colors:

- **Named colors**: (*red, blue, green*, etc.).
- **Hexadecimal colors**: (*#FF5733, #000000*).
- **RGB colors**: (*rgb(255, 0, 0)*).
- **RGBA colors**: (*rgba(255, 0, 0, 0.5)* - includes transparency).
- **HSL colors**: (*hsl(120, 100%, 50%)*).
- **HSLA colors**: (*hsla(240, 100%, 50%, 0.3)* - includes transparency).

The following example demonstrates the use of different color formats in CSS:

```
<!DOCTYPE html>
<html lang="en">
<head>
<meta charset="UTF-8">
<meta name="viewport" content="width=device-width, initial-scale=1.0">
<title>CSS Color Demonstration</title>
```

```
<style>
/* Named Color */
h1 {
color: red;
}

/* Hexadecimal Color */
h2 {
color: #FF5733;
}

/* RGB Color */
h3 {
color: rgb(0, 128, 0);
}

/* RGBA Color */

h4 {

}

color: rgba(0, 128, 0, 0.5);

/* HSL Color */
h5 {
color: hsl(240, 100%, 50%);
}

/* HSLA Color */
h6 {
color: hsla(240, 100%, 50%, 0.3);
}
</style>
</head>
<body>
<h1>Named Color: Red</h1>
<h2>Hexadecimal Color: #FF5733</h2>
<h3>RGB Color: rgb(0, 128, 0)</h3>
<h4>RGBA Color: rgba(0, 128, 0, 0.5)</h4>
<h5>HSL Color: hsl(240, 100%, 50%)</h5>
<h6>HSLA Color: hsla(240, 100%, 50%, 0.3)</h6>
</body>
</html>
```

This example demonstrates the use of different color formats in CSS. Each heading uses a different color format, showcasing how colors can be defined in various ways.

The rendered output of the preceding example will display headings with different colors based on the specified formats. Each heading will have a unique color, demonstrating the versatility of CSS color definitions as shown in the following figure:

Named Color: Red

Hexadecimal Color: #FF5733

RGB Color: rgb(0, 128, 0)

RGBA Color: rgba(0, 128, 0, 0.5)

HSL Color: hsl(240, 100%, 50%)

HSLA Color: hsla(240, 100%, 50%, 0.3)

Figure 2.2: *Output of CSS color formats example*

CSS3 opacity and transparency

CSS3 introduced new features for handling transparency and opacity, allowing developers to create visually appealing effects without relying on images or complex techniques. The **`opacity`** property and color functions like **`rgba()`** and **`hsla()`** enable fine control over element transparency, enhancing the overall design of web pages. The **`opacity`** property in CSS controls the transparency of an element, allowing for effects such as semi-transparent backgrounds or faded text. Additionally, the **`rgba()`** and **`hsla()`** color functions enable setting colors with transparency directly in the color definition.

The following properties are used to control opacity and transparency in CSS:

- **opacity**: Sets the transparency level of an element (0 to 1).
- **rgba()**: Defines a color with red, green, blue, and alpha (transparency) values.
- **hsla()**: Defines a color with hue, saturation, lightness, and alpha (transparency) values.

Opacity property

The **`opacity`** property controls the transparency of an element:

- **'opacity: 1'**: Fully visible.
- **'opacity: 0.5'**: Semi-transparent.
- **'opacity: 0'**: Fully hidden.

The following example demonstrates the use of the **`opacity`** property:

```
div {
background-color: blue; opacity: 0.5;
}
```

RGBA and HSLA colors

The **`rgba()`** and **`hsla()`** functions allow defining colors with transparency:

- **rgba (red, green, blue, alpha)**: Red, green, blue values with an alpha (transparency) value.
- **hsla (hue, saturation, lightness, alpha)**: Hue, saturation, lightness values with an alpha (transparency) value.
- Alpha value ranges from 0 (fully transparent) to 1 (fully opaque).

Note: The `rgba()` and `hsla()` formats allow setting both color and transparency in a single declaration. This is particularly useful for creating semi-transparent backgrounds or text colors.

The following example demonstrates the use of **`rgba()`** and **`hsla()`** functions in CSS:

```
/* RGBA Example */
p {
color: rgba(255, 0, 0, 0.5);
}

/* HSLA Example */
p {
color: hsla(240, 100%, 50%, 0.3);
}
```

Key points to remember are as follows:

- Use **`color`** to set text color and **`background-color`** for background.
- CSS supports multiple color formats, such as:
    - **Named colors** (e.g., red, blue, green)
    - **Hexadecimal** (HEX) color code (e.g., #ff5733)
    - **Red Green Blue** (RGB) (e.g., rgb(255, 87, 51))
    - **Red Green Blue Alpha** (RGBA) [includes transparency, e.g., rgba(255, 87, 51, 0.5)]
    - **Hue Saturation Lightness** (HSL) (e.g., hsl(9, 100%, 60%))
    - **Hue Saturation Lightness Alpha** (HSLA) [includes transparency, e.g., hsla(9, 100%, 60%, 0.5)]
- Opacity controls transparency of elements (**`opacity: 0.5`** makes it 50% transparent).
- Use **`rgba()`** or **`hsla()`** for transparent colors, which allow fine-tuned alpha (opacity) values.
- Higher contrast improves accessibility and ensures readability for all users.

CSS typography and text styling

A typeface is a design style that defines the shape of characters. A font is a specific variation of a typeface, such as bold or italic. Common typefaces include **`serif`**, **`sans-serif`**, **`monospace`**, and **`cursive`**.

CSS offers several properties to control typography and text appearance. The **`font-family`** property specifies the typeface, while **`font-size`** determines the size of the text. The **`font-weight`** property allows setting the thickness of characters (e.g., **`normal`**, **`bold`**), and **`font-style`** can be used for italic or oblique text.

Additional styling options include **`line-height`** for vertical spacing between lines, **`letter-spacing`** for adjusting space between characters, and word-spacing for controlling space between words. The **`text-align`** property aligns text left, right, center, or justify.

Typography plays a crucial role in user experience, readability, and accessibility. Selecting appropriate fonts and applying consistent text styles helps convey information clearly and maintain visual harmony throughout the webpage.

Techniques for choosing typefaces

Choosing the right typeface is crucial for effective communication and visual appeal. The following are some techniques to consider when selecting typefaces for web design:

- **Understand the purpose of the content**: Different typefaces convey different emotions and messages.

- **Consider readability**: Ensure that the typeface is legible at various sizes and on different devices.
- **Maintain consistency**: Use a limited number of typefaces to create a cohesive design.
- **Test across devices:** Check how the typeface appears on different screen sizes and resolutions.
- **Use web-safe fonts or web fonts**: Ensure compatibility across browsers and devices.

Key considerations are as follows:

- Serif fonts (e.g., Times New Roman) are often used for print and formal documents.
- Sans-serif fonts (e.g., Arial, Helvetica) are commonly used for web content due to their clean appearance.
- Monospace fonts (e.g., Courier New) are typically used for code snippets or technical content.
- Cursive fonts (e.g., Comic Sans) can add a playful touch but should be used sparingly.

Refer to the following list to understand the factors that are important to consider while choosing typefaces:

- **Readability**: Avoid overly decorative fonts.
- **Hierarchy**: Use different sizes and weights for emphasis.
- **Contrast**: Combine serif with sans-serif for better differentiation.

Specifying Typefaces in CSS

In CSS, typefaces are specified using the **`font-family`** property. You can list multiple fonts as fallbacks in case the preferred font is not available on the user's system. This ensures that the text remains readable even if the primary font fails to load. The **`font-family`** property allows you to specify the typeface for text elements. You can list multiple fonts as fallbacks, ensuring that if the first font is unavailable, the browser will use the next one in the list.

The following example demonstrates the way to specify typefaces in CSS:

```
/* Specify multiple fallback fonts */
body {
font-family: Arial, Helvetica, sans-serif;
}
```

Font size, type scales, and units

Font size is a crucial aspect of typography, affecting readability and user experience. CSS provides various units for specifying font sizes, allowing flexibility in design. Common units include pixels (*px*), ems (*em*), rems (*rem*), and percentages. Font size can be specified using different units, each with its own advantages and use cases. The most common units are as follows:

- **px**: Fixed size, commonly used for precise control.
- **em (relative to the parent element)**: Scales with the font size of the parent, useful for responsive designs.
- **relative to the root element (rem)**: Similar to **em**, but based on the root font size, providing consistency across the document.
- %: Relative to the parent element's font size, allowing for flexible scaling.
- **viewport width (vw) and viewport height (vh)**: Relative to the viewport size, useful for responsive typography.

The following example demonstrates how to set font sizes using different units in CSS:

```
p {
font-size: 16px;
}
```

```
h1 {
}
font-size: 2em;
h2 {
}
```

Using custom fonts with @font-face

In modern web design, custom fonts play a crucial role in enhancing the visual appeal and readability of a website. The `@font-face` rule in CSS allows developers to use custom fonts by specifying font files that are hosted on the server or externally. This feature eliminates the need for users to have the font installed on their local machines, ensuring consistent typography across different devices and browsers.

The key components of `@font-face` are as follows:

- **font-family**: Defines a name for the custom font, which is used later in the CSS.
- **src**: Specifies the path to the font file. Multiple formats (`woff2`, `woff`, `ttf`, etc.) are provided for broader compatibility.
- **format()**: Indicates the type of font file being used, ensuring that the browser selects the most efficient and compatible format.

Note: Steps to use custom fonts with `@font-face`:

1. **Obtain the font files (e.g., `woff2`, `woff`, `ttf`) from a reputable source or convert them using online tools.**
2. **Define the `@font-face` rule in the CSS file, specifying the font family name and the path to the font files.**
3. **Apply the custom font to the desired elements using the `font-family` property.**

The following example demonstrates how to define a custom font and apply it to the entire webpage:

```
@font-face {
font-family: 'CustomFont';
src: url('custom-font.woff2') format('woff2'), url('custom-font.woff') format('woff');
}

body {
font-family: 'CustomFont', sans-serif;
}
```

This example demonstrates how to define a custom font using the `@font-face` rule and apply it to the body of the webpage. The custom font is specified in both `woff2` and `woff` formats for compatibility across different browsers.

- The `@font-face` rule is used to define a new font named `'CustomFont'`.
- The `src` property specifies the location of the font files in `woff2` and `woff` formats, ensuring browser compatibility.
- The body selector applies the `CustomFont` as the primary typeface for the webpage, with `sans-serif` as a fallback option in case the custom font fails to load.
- Using `@font-face` effectively improves web typography and provides greater flexibility in designing visually appealing and accessible web pages.

Font weight, uppercase, lowercase, underline, and strike-through

CSS provides properties to modify font weight, text transformation, and text decoration. These properties enhance the visual hierarchy and emphasis of text elements, making them more engaging and readable.

The following properties are used to modify font weight and text decoration:

- **font-weight**: Sets the thickness of the font (e.g., `normal`, `bold`, `bolder`, `lighter`, or numeric values like `100`, `200`, etc.).
- **text-transform**: Controls the capitalization of text (e.g., `uppercase`, `lowercase`, `capitalize`).
- **text-decoration**: Adds decoration to text (e.g., `underline`, `line-through`, `overline`).
- **text-decoration-line**: Specifies the type of decoration (e.g., `underline`, `overline`, `line-through`).
- **text-decoration-color**: Sets the color of the text decoration.
- **text-decoration-style**: Defines the style of the text decoration (e.g., `solid`, `dashed`, `dotted`).
- **text-decoration-thickness**: Specifies the thickness of the text decoration line.
- **text-underline-offset**: Sets the space between the text and the underline.
- **text-decoration-skip-ink**: Controls whether the underline skips over descenders in text.
- **text-decoration-skip**: Specifies whether the text decoration should skip certain areas (e.g., descenders).
- **text-decoration-skip-ink**: Determines whether the underline skips descenders in text.

The following example demonstrates how to modify font weight, text transformation, and text decoration in CSS:

```
h1 {
font-weight: bold;
text-transform: uppercase;
}

p {
text-decoration: underline;
}

s {
text-decoration: line-through;
}
```

Line spacing, letter spacing, and word spacing

CSS allows control over line height, letter spacing, and word spacing to improve text readability and aesthetics. These properties help create visually appealing text layouts and enhance the overall user experience. The following properties are used to control line height, letter spacing, and word spacing:

- **line-height**: Sets the height of a line box, affecting the vertical spacing between lines of text.
- **letter-spacing**: Adjusts the space between individual characters in a text.
- **word-spacing**: Modifies the space between words in a text.
- **text-indent**: Indents the first line of a block of text.

The following example demonstrates how to adjust line height, letter spacing, and word spacing in CSS:

```
p {
line-height: 1.5; letter-spacing: 2px; word-spacing: 5px;
}
```

Text alignment, indenting, and shadow

CSS provides properties to align text, indent paragraphs, and add shadows to text. These properties enhance the visual presentation of text elements, making them more engaging and readable. The following properties are used to align text, indent paragraphs, and add shadows:

- **text-align**: Aligns text within an element (e.g., `left`, `right`, `center`, `justify`).
- **text-indent**: Indents the first line of a block of text.
- **text-shadow**: Adds shadow effects to text, enhancing its visibility and depth.
- **text-decoration**: Adds decoration to text (e.g., `underline`, `line-through`, `overline`).

The following example demonstrates how to align text, indent paragraphs, and add shadows in CSS:

```
h1 {
text-align: center;
text-shadow: 2px 2px 4px gray;
}

p {
text-indent: 20px;
}
```

Styling first letter or first line

CSS allows styling the first letter or first line of a paragraph to create visual emphasis. This technique is often used in articles and blogs to enhance the appearance of the text and draw attention to the beginning of a section The `::first-letter` and `::first-line` pseudo-elements are used to style the first letter or first line of a block-level element, such as a paragraph:

- **text-align**: Aligns text within an element (e.g., `left`, `right`, `center`, `justify`).
- **text-indent**: Indents the first line of a block of text.
- **text-shadow**: Adds shadow effects to text, enhancing its visibility and depth.
- **text-decoration**: Adds decoration to text (e.g., `underline`, `line-through`, `overline`).

The following example demonstrates how to style the first letter and first line of a paragraph in CSS:

```
p::first-letter {
font-size: 2em;
font-weight: bold;
}

p::first-line {
color: blue;
}
```

Styling links

CSS allows styling hyperlinks to improve their appearance and user experience. Links can be styled using various properties, including color, text decoration, and hover effects. Proper link styling enhances usability and accessibility, making it easier for users to identify clickable elements. The following properties are commonly used to style links:

- **color**: Sets the color of the link text.
- **text-decoration**: Specifies the decoration added to the text (e.g., `underline`, `none`).
- **font-weight**: Sets the weight (boldness) of the link text. Different link states can be styled using:
- **:hover**: When the mouse is over the link.
- **:active**: When the link is clicked.
- **:focus**: When the link is selected.

The following example demonstrates how to style links in CSS, including different states:

```
a {
color: blue;
text-decoration: none;
}

a:hover {
color: red;
}

a:active {
color: green;
}

a:focus {
outline: 2px solid orange;
}
```

CSS attribute selectors

CSS attribute selectors allow targeting elements based on their attributes and values. This feature enables more precise styling of elements without needing additional classes or IDs, enhancing the flexibility and maintainability of CSS code. Attribute selectors are defined using square brackets `[]`, allowing you to select elements with specific attributes or attribute values. The details are as follows:

- **[attribute]**: Selects elements with the specified attribute, regardless of its value.
- **[attribute="value"]**: Selects elements whose attribute exactly matches `"value"`.
- **[attribute~="value"]**: Selects elements whose attribute contains the word `"value"` (space- separated).
- **[attribute="value"]**: Selects elements whose attribute begins with `"value"` (a hyphen afterward).
- **[attribute^="value"]**: Selects elements whose attribute starts with `"value"`.
- **[attribute$="value"]**: Selects elements whose attribute ends with `"value"`.
- **[attribute*="value"]**: Selects elements whose attribute contains `"value"` as a substring.

The following example demonstrates how to use attribute selectors in CSS:

```
/* Select all inputs with type text */
input[type="text"] {
border: 1px solid black;
}
```

```
/* Select all links that open in a new tab */
a[target="_blank"] {
color: purple;
}
```

This example demonstrates the way to use attribute selectors to style input fields of type text and links that open in a new tab. The **input[type="text"]** selector applies styles to all text input fields, while the **a[target="_blank"]** selector targets links that have a **target** attribute set to **_blank**, indicating they open in a new tab.

The following are the key points to remember:

- CSS allows precise control over typography with font selection, size, weight, and spacing.
- Use **@font-face** to load custom fonts.
- Use **text-transform** to modify case and **text-decoration** for underline and strike-through.
- Styling links improves user experience, with states like **hover**, **active**, and **focus**.
- Attribute selectors enable targeting elements based on attributes (e.g., **[type="text"]**).

Styling lists, tables, and forms with CSS

CSS allows extensive styling of lists, tables, and forms to enhance their appearance, readability, and usability. Proper styling ensures that data is presented clearly, forms are user-friendly, and lists are visually distinct.

Styling lists in CSS

Lists in HTML (**<ul>**, **<ol>**, **<li>**) can be customized using CSS properties such as **list-style-type**, **list-style-image**, and **list-style-position**.

Different bullet point styles in CSS

The **list-style-type** property controls the appearance of list markers. It allows you to change the bullet points or numbering style of lists:

- **disc (default)**: Solid circle bullet.
- **circle**: Hollow circle bullet.
- **square**: Solid square bullet.
- **decimal**: Numbered list (1, 2, 3).
- **upper-roman**: Uppercase Roman numerals (I, II, III).
- **lower-alpha**: Lowercase letters (a, b, c).
- **none**: No bullet or numbering.

The following example demonstrates how to change the bullet points and numbering style of lists in CSS:

```
ul {

}

list-style-type: square;

ol {
```

```
list-style-type: upper-roman;
}
```

This will result in the following:

- Square bullet points for unordered lists.
- Upper Roman numerals (I, II, III) for ordered lists.

Adding images as bullet points in lists

The **`list-style-image`** property replaces default bullets with custom images. You can use any image URL as a bullet point:

- **list-style-image: url(image.png)**: Sets a custom image as the bullet point.
- If the image is not available, the default bullet style will be used.

The following example demonstrates how to use an image as a bullet point in CSS:

```
ul {
list-style-image: url('bullet.png');
}
```

Controlling the position of list markers

The **`list-style-position`** property determines whether bullets appear inside or outside the list item:

- **inside**: The bullet is placed inside the list item, aligning with the text.
- **outside (default)**: The bullet is placed outside the list item, creating a margin.
- **none**: No bullet or numbering.
- **list-style-position: inside;**: Bullets align with the text.
- **list-style-position: outside;**: Bullets remain outside the list item.
- **list-style-position: none;**:No bullets or numbering.

The following example demonstrates how to position the list marker in CSS:

```
ul {
list-style-position: inside;
}
```

If **`inside`** is used, the bullet aligns with the text. With **`outside`** (default), bullets remain outside the list item.

List styling shorthand

The **`list-style`** property is a shorthand for **`list-style-type`**, **`list-style-image`**, and **`list-style-position`**. It allows you to set all three properties in one declaration:

- **list-style - type image position;**: Combines all three properties.
- **Example** - **list-style**: Square **`url(bullet.png) inside;`** sets a square bullet with an image inside the list item.
- **list-style: none;**: Removes all bullets and numbering.

The following example demonstrates how to use the 'list-style' shorthand in CSS:

```
ul {
list-style: square inside;
}
```

Styling tables in CSS

Tables in HTML (**<table>**, **<tr>**, **<td>**, **<th>**) can be styled to improve readability and visual appeal. CSS provides properties to control borders, spacing, alignment, and more. The following properties are commonly used to style tables:

- **border**: Sets the border style, width, and color for table elements.
- **border-collapse**: Determines whether table borders are collapsed into a single border or separated.
- **border-spacing**: Sets the space between table cells when borders are not collapsed.
- **width and height**: Control the dimensions of the table.
- **text-align**: Aligns text within table cells (e.g., **left**, **center**, **right**).
- **vertical-align**: Aligns content vertically within table cells (e.g., **top**, **middle**, **bottom**).
- **padding**: Adds space inside table cells, improving readability.
- **background-color**: Sets the background color of table cells.
- **color**: Sets the text color within table cells.

Basic table styling

Basic table styling involves setting borders, width, and height to create a clean layout. The following example demonstrates basic table styling in CSS:

```
table {
border: 1px solid black; width: 80%;
height: auto;
}
```

Border on empty cells

The **empty-cells** property controls whether empty table cells have visible borders. It can be set to **show** (default) or **hide** to remove borders from empty cells.

The following example demonstrates how to hide borders on empty cells in CSS:

```
table {
empty-cells: hide;
}
```

Gaps between cells

The **border-spacing** property sets the space between table cells when borders are not collapsed. The **border-collapse** property determines whether table borders collapse into a single border or are separated. The **border-collapse** property can be set to:

- **collapse**: Collapses borders into a single border.
- **separate**: Keeps borders separate, allowing for spacing between cells.
- **hidden**: Hides borders entirely.
- **border-spacing**: Sets the space between cells when borders are not collapsed.
- **border-collapse**: Determines whether borders are collapsed or separated.

The following example demonstrates how to set gaps between cells and collapse borders in CSS:

```
table {
border-collapse: collapse; border-spacing: 10px;
}
```

This example sets the **border-collapse** property to **collapse**, which removes extra space between borders, and sets **border-spacing** to **10px**, creating a gap between cells when borders are not collapsed.

Note: The border-collapse property is crucial for controlling the appearance of table borders. Using border-collapse: collapse; removes extra space between borders, creating a cleaner look

Styling forms in CSS

Forms in HTML (**<form>**, **<input>**, **<textarea>**, **<button>**) can be styled to enhance usability and aesthetics. CSS provides properties to control the appearance of form elements, making them more user-friendly and visually appealing. The following properties are commonly used to style form elements:

- **'border'**: Sets the border style, width, and color for form elements.
- **'padding'**: Adds space inside form elements, improving usability.
- **'background-color'**: Sets the background color of form elements.
- **'color'**: Sets the text color within form elements.
- **'font-size'**: Controls the size of text in form elements.
- **'width' and 'height'**: Control the dimensions of form elements.
- **'margin'**: Adds space outside form elements, separating them from other content.
- **'display'**: Controls how form elements are displayed (e.g., **block**, **inline**, **flex**).
- **'cursor'**: Changes the mouse cursor when hovering over form elements (e.g., **pointer**, **text**).
- **Forms ('<form>', '<input>', '<textarea>', '<button>')**: It can be styled for better usability and design.

Styling text inputs

Basic text input fields can be styled using CSS properties like **border**, **padding**, and **background- color**. The following example demonstrates how to style text input fields in CSS:

```
input[type="text"] { border: 2px solid gray; padding: 5px;
}
```

Styling submit buttons

Submit buttons can be styled to improve their appearance and usability. Common styles include background color, text color, padding, and hover effects.

The following example demonstrates how to style submit buttons in CSS:

```
input[type="submit"] { background-color: blue; color: white;
padding: 10px;
}
```

Styling fieldsets and legends

Fieldsets and legends help group related form elements, improving accessibility and organization. The following example demonstrates how to style fieldsets and legends in CSS:

```
fieldset {
border: 2px dashed gray;
```

```
}

legend {
font-weight: bold;
}
```

Aligning form controls

Form controls may not align properly by default, leading to a disorganized appearance. This can be resolved using CSS techniques like Flexbox or Grid for better alignment and spacing.

Misaligned form controls

By default, form labels and inputs may not align properly. This can lead to a cluttered appearance and poor user experience.

To improve alignment, you can use the following CSS:

```
label {
display: block;
}
```

Using Flexbox for alignment

Using CSS Flexbox is an effective way to align form controls. It allows for flexible layouts and easy alignment of form elements.

The following example demonstrates how to use Flexbox to align form controls in CSS:

```
.form-container {
display: flex;
align-items: center;
}
```

Cursor styles in CSS

CSS allows you to change the appearance of the mouse cursor when hovering over elements. This enhances user experience by providing visual feedback on interactive elements. The **cursor** property in CSS is used to specify the type of cursor displayed when hovering over an element. Common cursor styles include the following:

- **'default'**: The default arrow cursor.
- **'pointer'**: A hand cursor, typically used for links.
- **'text'**: An I-beam cursor, indicating text selection.
- **'move'**: A four-direction arrow cursor, indicating draggable elements.
- **'not-allowed'**: A cursor indicating that an action is not allowed.
- **'wait'**: A spinning wheel or hourglass cursor, indicating a waiting state.
- **'crosshair'**: A crosshair cursor, often used for precision tasks.
- **'help'**: A question mark cursor, indicating help or information is available.
- **'progress'**: A cursor indicating that a task is in progress.
- **'zoom-in'**: A magnifying glass cursor, indicating zooming in is possible.
- **'zoom-out'**: A magnifying glass with a minus sign, indicating zooming out is possible.
- **'grab'**: A hand cursor indicating that an element can be grabbed or dragged.

- **'grabbing'**: A hand cursor indicating that an element is currently being dragged.
- **'alias'**: A cursor indicating that an element is an alias or shortcut.

The following example demonstrates how to change the cursor style in CSS:

```
button {
cursor: pointer;
}

.textbox {
cursor: text;
}
```

Hands-on project

In this project, you will create a personal portfolio webpage that showcases your skills, projects, and contact information. This project will help you apply the CSS concepts learned in this chapter and demonstrate your ability to create a well-styled, responsive webpage.

Project overview

You will build a personal portfolio webpage that includes sections for your introduction, skills, projects, and contact information. The webpage will be styled using an external CSS file, ensuring a clean separation of content and presentation. The design will be responsive, adapting to different screen sizes using CSS Flexbox or Grid. In this project, you will create a personal portfolio webpage that showcases your skills, projects, and contact information. This project will help you apply the CSS concepts learned in this chapter and demonstrate your ability to create a well-styled, responsive webpage.

Aim: Build a well-styled, responsive personal portfolio page using external CSS and best practices.

Project requirements

Your portfolio webpage should include the following:

- **External CSS file** linked to your HTML.
- **Responsive layout** using CSS Flexbox or Grid.
- Proper **Typography** (custom fonts via `@font-face`).
- Interactive navigation menu with hover and active states.
- Styled sections (About, Skills, Projects, Contact).
- At least one form with styled inputs and buttons.

Project steps

Follow these steps to complete the project:

1. Create a folder named `PortfolioProject` and inside it create `index.html` and `styles.css`.
2. Set up HTML structure including semantic tags (`<header>`, `<nav>`, `<section>`, `<footer>`).
3. Use CSS Grid or Flexbox to structure the main layout.
4. Implement external CSS styles for colors, fonts, and spacing.

5. Add responsive design using media queries.
6. Include hover and active effects for better interactivity.
7. Test across browsers and screen sizes.

Conclusion

In this chapter, we explored essential CSS concepts and techniques for styling web pages. We covered various CSS properties, selectors, and layout methods to create visually appealing and responsive designs. We learned about the importance of separating content from presentation, using external stylesheets for maintainability, and applying best practices for efficient CSS coding. By mastering these concepts, you can create well-structured, accessible, and user-friendly web pages that enhance the overall user experience. As you continue to learn web development, remember that CSS is a powerful tool that allows you to bring your creative vision to life. Practice applying these concepts in real-world projects, and explore advanced CSS techniques to further enhance your skills.

In the next chapter, you will learn about advanced CSS topics such as animations, transitions, media queries, and responsive design strategies to create dynamic and interactive web interfaces.

Exercises

1. Write the exact HTML line (one line) to link an external stylesheet named "site.css" from the <head> of a page.
2. Order these by cascade priority from highest to lowest: browser defaults, internal styles, inline styles, external stylesheets.
3. Two rules target the same <p>: (a) p { color: blue; } (b) #main .card > p.highlight::first-line { color: red; }. Which takes effect on the first line and why? State the winning selector and its specificity points.
4. Name two CSS properties that are inherited by default and two that are not. Give one short reason why inheritance helps maintainable CSS.
5. Fix the selector spelling and write a valid attribute selector that styles all inputs whose type is "text" with a 1px solid black border.
6. Given content width 300px, padding 10px on all sides, border 2px on all sides, and no margin: compute the total rendered width for (a) box-sizing: content-box; and (b) box-sizing: border-box;. Show both numbers.
7. Write CSS to center a child <div> horizontally and vertically inside a 300px-tall container using Flexbox (do not use absolute positioning).
8. Create a responsive Grid container with columns that auto-fit to at least 200px and stretch to fill the row, with a 15px gap between items. Write only the CSS for the grid container.
9. Choose one color and write it in three formats: HEX, rgb(), and hsl(). Use the same color value across all formats.
10. Write a minimal @font-face rule that loads "CustomFont" from custom-font.woff2 and custom-font.woff, then apply it to the whole page with a sans-serif fallback.
11. Write CSS that makes the first letter of paragraphs large and bold, and makes the first line blue. Use proper pseudo-elements.
12. Style links so that default links are blue with no underline, :hover links turn red, :active links turn green, and :focus shows a 2px solid orange outline. Write the CSS.
13. Write CSS to style a table with collapsed borders, 8px cell padding, striped rows (alternate light gray), and hidden borders on empty cells.

14. Write a compact form layout that aligns labels and inputs on a single row using Flexbox. Include styles for a primary submit button with a hover effect. Provide only the CSS and the minimal HTML wrapper.
15. Build a small responsive layout: a top navigation bar laid out with Flexbox (space-between) and a main content area below laid out with CSS Grid (two columns on wide screens, one column on small screens). Provide only the CSS and minimal HTML structure.

Chapter 3
Advanced CSS Concepts

Introduction

As web interfaces grow more complex, **Cascading Style Sheets** (**CSS**) must evolve beyond basic styling into powerful layout, positioning, and interactive capabilities. In this chapter, we will understand advanced CSS techniques that professional developers use to build responsive, maintainable, and performant designs. You will learn how to leverage browser DevTools for real-time debugging of forms and styles, master positioning schemes (static, relative, absolute, fixed, floats, and clears), and understand the nuances of screen sizes, resolutions, and grid systems like the 960px 12-column pattern. We will explore modern CSS frameworks, Bootstrap, Tailwind, and Foundation, and see how they accelerate development. You will also discover how media queries, relative units (*rem/em*), Flexbox, and CSS Grid combine to create fluid, adaptive layouts. Finally, we will cover animations, transitions, trans- forms, CSS variables, and advanced selectors to craft interactive, accessible user experiences. By the end of this chapter, you will have a toolbox of advanced CSS strategies to tackle real-world design challenges.

Structure

This chapter covers the following topics:

- Web developer toolbar
- CSS frameworks for layouts
- Tailwind CSS for layouts
- Choosing a CSS framework
- Grid and flexbox layouts
- CSS variables and selectors
- Responsive webpage design with CSS
- Screen sizes, resolutions, and page sizes
- Bootstrap grid layouts
- Foundation grids
- Media queries
- Advanced CSS techniques
- Pseudo-classes and pseudo-elements

Objectives

By the end of this chapter, the readers will be able to use browser DevTools to inspect and debug form styles and layouts in real-time, and apply static, relative, absolute, fixed, and float positioning effectively. They will learn to design fluid and liquid layouts that adapt to various screen sizes and resolutions, implement a 960px, 12-column grid system, and customize it for responsive designs. The chapter will guide them in leveraging CSS frameworks such as Bootstrap, Tailwind, and Foundation to accelerate development and in writing media queries to create a mobile-first, responsive experience. They will also understand how to choose and apply relative units such as rem and em for scalable typography, and combine Flexbox with CSS Grid to build complex, adaptive layouts. Additionally, the readers will develop the ability to create smooth animations, transitions, and transforms to enhance interactivity, as well as define and use CSS variables and advanced selectors for writing clean, maintainable code.

Web developer toolbar

The web developer toolbar, also known as **DevTools**, comes built into modern browsers and empowers developers to inspect, debug, and modify web pages in real time. By revealing the underlying HTML structure, CSS rules, and

JavaScript behavior, it helps identify layout issues, catch scripting errors, and optimize page performance without leaving the browser.

To examine any element on a page, right-click it and choose *Inspect*, or press F12 (or Ctrl+Shift+I). DevTools opens and highlights that element in the *Elements* panel, where you can see its tag hierarchy, attributes, and applied styles. Tweak CSS properties or HTML attributes here and watch changes appear instantly in the page.

When you work with forms, DevTools offers the following specialized panels and workflows:

- **Elements**: Verify that each `<input>`, `<select>`, and `<textarea>` uses the correct `name`, `id`, and `type` attributes.
- **Console**: Look for JavaScript errors thrown during validation or submission, and use `console.log()` to trace event handlers.
- **Network**: Watch form submission requests, inspect headers and payloads, and confirm server responses.
- **Sources**: It sets up breakpoints in your validation or submit-handler scripts to step through code and examine variable values.
- **Computed styles**: Review the final, cascade-resolved CSS on your form elements, including inherited and overridden rules.
- **Accessibility**: Identify missing labels, ARIA roles, or tabindex issues that could hinder users relying on assistive technologies.
- **Performance**: Profile form interactions to spot rendering jank or slow scripts that delay feedback.
- **Application**: Inspect cookies, local storage, and session storage entries related to form data.

Inspecting and debugging a simple form

The following depicts a basic HTML form and its styling. Use DevTools to step through each element, validate the structure, and experiment with CSS rules on the fly:

```
<!DOCTYPE html>
<html lang="en"><head>
<meta charset="UTF-8">
<meta name="viewport" content="width=device-width, initial-scale=1.0">
<title>Demo</title>
<style>
ul{list-style:square inside}
table{border:1px solid #000;width:80%;border-collapse:collapse} td,th{border:1px solid
#000;padding:6px} input[type=text]{border:1px solid #888;padding:4px} input[type=submit]
{background:blue;color:#fff;padding:6px} fieldset{border:1px dashed #888;padding:5px}
legend{font-weight:bold}
</style>
</head><body>
<h2>List</h2>
<ul><li>Item 1</li><li>Item 2</li></ul>
<h3>Table</h3>
<table>
<tr><th>H1</th><th>H2</th></tr>
<tr><td>Data 1</td><td>Data 2</td></tr>
</table>
<h3>Form</h3>
<form><fieldset><legend>Info</legend>
```

```
<label>Name:<input type="text" name="name"></label>
<input type="submit" value="Go">
</fieldset></form>
</body></html>
```

The following are the key takeaways:

- Use **list-style-type**, **list-style-image**, and **list-style-position** to customize lists.
- Tables can be styled using **border-collapse**, **border-spacing**, and **empty-cells**.
- Form elements should be styled for better usability.
- Use *cursor* styles to change pointer behavior on different elements.
- Browser DevTools help debug and inspect CSS styles.

CSS Layout and positioning techniques

CSS controls the placement and stacking of elements using five positioning schemes, which are **static**, **relative**, **absolute**, **fixed**, and **sticky**. A **static** element follows the normal document flow. A **relative** element shifts from its original spot without affecting siblings. An **absolute** element exists in the flow and positions itself relative to the nearest ancestor that has a non–static position. A **fixed** element locks itself to the viewport and stays visible during scrolling. A **sticky** element behaves like **relative** until it crosses a specified scroll threshold, then behaves like **fixed**. Mastering these modes enables precise control over layout, layering, and overlap.

Containing elements

Setting **position: relative** on a container creates a new positioning context. Absolutely positioned children then calculate their offsets (*top, right, bottom, left*) against that container's edges instead of the viewport. This method keeps related elements together, avoids unexpected shifts when content or screen size changes, and simplifies responsive layouts. The following is a simple example that positions a **New** badge in the top-right corner of a card:

```
<style>
.card {
position: relative; width: 200px; height: 120px;
border: 1px solid #ccc;
padding: 10px;
}
.badge {
position: absolute; top: 8px;
right: 8px; background: red; color: white; padding: 2px 6px; border-radius: 4px; font-size: 0.8em;
}
</style>

<div class="card">
<div class="badge">New</div>
<p>Product details go here.</p>
</div>
```

Normal flow

By default, every element uses **position: static.** In this mode, elements follow the normal document flow, stacking vertically (or horizontally for inline elements) and ignoring **top**, **left**, **right**, and **bottom** offsets. Margins collapse naturally between adjacent block elements.

The following is an example of two static paragraphs with margin and background styling:

```
<!DOCTYPE html>
<html lang="en">
<head>
<meta charset="UTF-8">
<meta name="viewport" content="width=device-width, initial-scale=1.0">
<style>
.stat {
position: static;        /* default */
margin: 20px 0;  /* vertical margins collapse */
padding: 10px;
background-color: #eef;
}
</style>
</head>
<body>
<p class="stat">First paragraph in normal flow.</p>
<p class="stat">Second paragraph in normal flow.</p>
</body>
</html>
```

Relative positioning

The following is an example of relative positioning. The element stays in its normal spot within the document flow, but its rendered box shifts by the specified offsets without affecting surrounding elements.

```
div {
position: relative;      /* remain in flow */
top: 10px;         /* move down 10px */
left: 20px;        /* move right 20px */
margin: 0.5em;     /* maintain spacing */
padding: 0.5em;  /* inner padding */
background-color: #fde8e8;  /* visual highlight */
}
```

Absolute positioning

The following is an example of absolute positioning. An absolutely positioned element is removed from the normal flow and aligned relative to its nearest ancestor that has a **non-static** position (or the viewport if none exists).

```
div {
position: absolute;      /* removed from flow */
top: 50px;         /* 50px down from container's top */
right: 20px;       /* 20px in from container's right */
width: 150px;      /* fixed width for clarity */
padding: 0.5em;  /* inner spacing */
background-color: #e8f0fd;  /* visual highlight */
}
```

Fixed positioning

The following is an example of fixed positioning. A fixed element stays anchored to the viewport, remaining visible as the user scrolls. It exists outside the normal flow and may overlap with other content.

```
header {
position: fixed; /* lock to viewport */
top: 0; /* align at top */
left: 0;/* align at left */
width: 100%;     /* span full width */ background-color: #000; /* dark background */ color: #fff;
/* light text */
padding: 0.5em; /* inner spacing */
z-index: 1000;  /* sit above other elements */
}
```

Overlapping elements

The **z-index** property determines the stacking order of positioned elements. Only elements with **position set to relative, absolute, fixed, or sticky** will respect **z-index**. Elements with higher

z-index values render above those with lower values. If two elements share the same stacking context, the one declared later in the HTML appears on top.

The following is an example that draws two overlapping boxes, where the green box sits above the red box:

```
<style>
.box {
position: absolute; width: 100px; height: 100px;
}
.box1 {
background: lightcoral; top: 20px;
left: 20px;
z-index: 1;  /* renders below .box2 */
}
.box2 {
background: lightseagreen; top: 40px;
left: 40px;
z-index: 2;  /* renders above .box1 */
}
</style>

<div class="box box1"></div>
<div class="box box2"></div>
```

Floating elements

The **float** property takes an element out of the normal block flow and shifts it to the left or right, allowing inline content to wrap around it. Floats commonly wrap text around images or create simple multi-column layouts. To prevent parent containers from collapsing around floats, use a clearing strategy (for example, apply **overflow: auto** to the container or insert a cleared element after the floats).

The following is an example of floating an image to the left with a margin for spacing:

```
img {
float: left;      /* align image at left edge */
margin: 0 10px 10px 0;  /* add space to the right and below */
}
```

Elements side-by-side

You can align multiple content blocks horizontally by floating each block and assigning a width. After floating, apply a clearfix to the parent so it expands to contain its children.

The following is an example of two side-by-side columns with a clearfix:

```
<style>
.container::after { content: ""; display: table; clear: both;
}
.column { float: left; width: 50%;
box-sizing: border-box; padding: 0.5em; background: #f4f4f4; border: 1px solid #ddd;
}
</style>

<div class="container">
<div class="column">Column 1 content</div>
<div class="column">Column 2 content</div>
</div>
```

Clearing floats

The **clear** property stops elements from flowing alongside floated siblings. By applying **clear: both**, an element begins below any previous floats on either side. A common pattern uses a clearfix pseudo-element on the container to ensure it expands around its floated children.

The following is an example of a clearfix that clears both left and right floats:

```
.clearfix::after { content: ""; display: table; clear: both;
}
```

Parents of floated elements

When all child elements are floated, they exit the normal flow, and the parent's height collapses to zero. This collapse can break backgrounds, borders, or any layout that depends on the parent's dimensions.

The following is an example of using the **overflow** trick to force the parent to contain its floated children:

```
.parent {
overflow: hidden; /* makes parent expand around floats */
}
```

Multi-column layouts with floats

Floats can arrange content into columns by assigning each block a proportional width and floating them side by side. Applying a clearfix on the parent container ensures it expands to contain all floated children. This technique builds responsive, multi-column layouts without using Flexbox or Grid.

The following is an example of a simple three-column layout using floats:

```
<style>
.container::after { content: ""; display: table; clear: both;
}
.column {
float: left; width: 33.33%;
box-sizing: border-box; padding: 0.5em;
background-color: #f9f9f9;
border: 1px solid #ddd;
```

```
}
</style>

<div class="container">
<div class="column">Column 1 content</div>
<div class="column">Column 2 content</div>
<div class="column">Column 3 content</div>
</div>
```

Screen sizes, resolutions, and page sizes

Modern devices span a wide range of pixel dimensions, aspect ratios, and display densities. Designing for this variety requires understanding three core concepts—the browser's layout viewport (measured in CSS pixels), the device's physical pixel dimensions, and the **device pixel ratio** (**DPR**). By combining fluid units and media queries, a page can adapt seamlessly from small phones to large desktops, and even to printed page sizes when needed.

Device pixels vs. CSS pixels

Browsers map CSS pixels to physical device pixels. On a standard screen, one CSS pixel equals one device pixel. High-density screens (for example, Retina or AMOLED displays) may pack two, three, or more device pixels into a single CSS pixel. The JavaScript property **`window.devicePixelRatio`** reveals this ratio. To deliver crisp images, provide multiple resolutions, and use the **`srcset`** attribute:

```
<img src="logo.png"
srcset="logo@2x.png 2x, logo@3x.png 3x" alt="Company Logo">
```

Responsive units

Relative units adapt to viewport size or root font size. Common choices include the following:

- vw, vh: **`1vw`** equals 1% of viewport width; **`1vh`** equals 1% of viewport height
- rem: Based on the root **`font-size`**.
- em: Based on the current element's **`font-size`**.

For example, a layout container can span almost the full width while capping at a readable maximum:

```
.container {
width: 90vw;
max-width: 1200px;
margin: 0 auto;
}
```

Media queries and breakpoints

Media queries apply different styles based on viewport characteristics like width, height, and resolution. They enable responsive design by allowing you to define breakpoints where the layout changes to suit different screen sizes. A common mobile-first approach starts with base styles for small screens, then adds media queries for larger devices.

The following is an example of a simple responsive layout using media queries:

```
/* Base (mobile) */
.header { padding: 1em; font-size: 1.1rem; }

/* Tablet and up */
@media (min-width: 600px) {
```

```
.header { padding: 1.5em; }
.nav    { display: block; }
}

/* Desktop and up */
@media (min-width: 1024px) {
.sidebar { float: right; width: 300px; }
.content { margin-right: 320px; }
}
```

By combining fluid units with strategically placed breakpoints, pages remain legible, usable, and visually balanced across screens, and print layouts can be handled via a dedicated `@media print` stylesheet.

Layout grids

Grid systems divide a page into columns and gutters, creating a predictable framework that improves alignment, readability, and responsiveness. The classic 960 px, 12-column grid splits a 960 px-wide container into twelve 80 px-wide columns separated by 20 px gutters. You can adapt this pattern to other widths or column counts as needed.

Grid system

In web design, a grid system provides a structured layout that helps maintain visual consistency and organization. It allows designers to create balanced, harmonious designs by aligning elements along a predefined set of columns and gutters. This approach simplifies the design process, enhances readability, and ensures that content is presented in a clear, logical manner.

A grid system streamlines design and development by the following:

- Ensuring consistent alignment across sections.
- Organizing content into readable, balanced blocks.
- **Simplifying maintenance**: Updating column widths automatically adjusts all related elements.
- **Supporting responsiveness**: The columns collapse or reflow gracefully on smaller screens
- **Scaling layouts**: You can easily mix and match column spans (for example, 4-column vs. 8-column blocks).

Popular column grid

In web design, a grid system provides a structured layout that helps maintain visual consistency and organization. It allows designers to create balanced, harmonious designs by aligning elements along a predefined set of columns and gutters. This approach simplifies the design process, enhances readability, and ensures that content is presented in a clear, logical manner.

The 960 px, 12-column grid divides the page into twelve equal-width columns, with gutters between them. This grid is commonly used for fixed-width layouts, providing a clean and organized structure for content. The grid consists of the following:

- **Columns**: Vertical divisions that hold content.
- **Guflers**: Horizontal spaces between columns to separate content visually.
- **Margins**: Outer spaces around the grid to center it within the viewport.
- **Container**: The overall width of the grid, typically set to 960 px.
- **Row**: A horizontal grouping of columns, which can contain multiple columns.
- **Column span**: The number of columns a block occupies, allowing for flexible layouts.

- **Breakpoints**: Media queries that adjust column widths and layout for different screen sizes.
- **Responsive design**: Adapting the grid to various devices, ensuring usability and readability.
- **Fluid layouts**: Using percentage-based widths to allow the grid to scale with the viewport.
- **Fixed layouts**: Maintaining a consistent width (960 px) across devices, often used for desktop-focused designs.
- **Nested grids**: Creating sub-grids within columns for more complex layouts.
- **Alignment**: Ensuring elements within columns align properly, using CSS properties like text-align, flexbox, or grid.
- **Accessibility**: Ensuring the grid structure supports screen readers and other assistive technologies.
- **Visual hierarchy**: Using the grid to establish a clear visual flow, guiding users through the content.
- **Typography**: Ensuring text within the grid is legible and well-spaced, using appropriate font sizes and line heights.
- **Images and media**: Ensuring images and other media fit within the grid, maintaining aspect ratios and responsiveness.
- **Testing and validation**: Regularly testing the grid layout across different devices and browsers to ensure consistent appearance and functionality.
- **Performance optimization**: Minimizing CSS and JavaScript to ensure fast loading times, especially for complex grid layouts.
- **Cross-browser compatibility**: Ensuring the grid works consistently across all major browsers, using vendor prefixes if necessary.
- **Custom breakpoints**: Defining specific breakpoints for different devices, allowing for tailored layouts that enhance user experience.
- **Grid systems in CSS frameworks**: Many CSS frameworks (like Bootstrap, Foundation, Tailwind) provide built-in grid systems that simplify implementation and ensure responsiveness.

In the 960 px grid, each column is 80 px wide, and the gutters between columns are 20 px wide.

The total width of the grid is calculated as follows:

- Each column measures 80 px.
- Each gutter (space between columns) measures 20 px.
- Total width = (12 × 80 px) + (11 × 20 px) = 960 px.

You can implement this with modern CSS using Flexbox or grid layout instead of manual floats.

Implementing a basic grid

Use a flex container and percentage-based column widths to recreate the 12-column grid. The following is a minimal CSS setup for a 12-column grid:

```
.grid-container { width: 960px; margin: 0 auto; display: flex; flex-wrap: wrap;
}
.column {
width: 8.33%;    /* 100% ÷ 12 */ padding: 10px;    /* gutter space */ box-sizing: border-box;
background: #f0f0f0;
border: 1px solid #ccc;
}
```

And here is the corresponding HTML:

```
<div class="grid-container">
<div class="column">1</div>
…
<div class="column">12</div>
</div>
```

Responsive grid adjustments

To adapt the grid for tablets and phones, redefine column widths at breakpoints: The following media queries collapse columns on narrower screens:

```
@media (max-width: 768px) {
.column { width: 50%; } /* two columns per row */
}
@media (max-width: 480px) {
.column { width: 100%; } /* full-width blocks */
}
```

Common layout patterns

By combining column spans, you can create the following versatile layouts:

- **Full-width banner**: One block spans all 12 columns (width: 100%).
- **Two-column section**: Each block spans 6 columns (width: 50%).
- **Three-column row**: Each block spans 4 columns (width: 33.33%).
- **Four-column row**: Each block spans 3 columns (width: 25%).

Best practices

Follow these guidelines and the best practices for a robust grid:

- Use relative (%) widths instead of fixed pixels for better flexibility.
- Apply `box-sizing: border-box` so padding does not inflate column widths.
- Avoid manual floats; prefer Flexbox or CSS Grid for easier alignment and ordering.
- Maintain a consistent gutter size for visual harmony.
- Leverage media queries to adjust layouts at logical breakpoints.

CSS frameworks for layouts

CSS frameworks deliver ready-made grid systems, components, and responsive utilities that accelerate development and enforce design consistency. By adopting a framework, the need to write boilerplate CSS for common layout patterns vanishes, allowing focus on unique design requirements and application logic.

Using a CSS framework effectively

Choosing a CSS framework is essential when a project demands the following:

- **Rapid prototyping**: Built-in grids and components let you assemble interfaces in minutes.
- **Responsive behavior**: Predefined breakpoints and fluid layouts adapt automatically to mobile, tablet, and desktop.

- **Design uniformity**: A shared set of styles and utilities ensures visual harmony across pages and components.
- **Cross-browser support**: Framework authors handle quirks in legacy and modern browsers, reducing your QA burden.
- **Custom theming**: Most frameworks expose Sass or configuration files so you can tweak colors, spacing, and typography to match your brand.

Popular frameworks

Several mature frameworks dominate the landscape. Each takes a different approach. The details are as follows:

- **Bootstrap**: A mobile-first, component-rich framework built on a 12-column grid. It offers cards, navbars, modals, and extensive JavaScript plugins.
- **Tailwind CSS**: A utility-first toolkit that encourages composing small, single-purpose classes directly in your HTML. It ships with a customizable design system and **just-in-time** (JIT) mode for a minimal bundle size.
- **Foundation**: Similar in scope to Bootstrap, Foundation emphasizes semantic markup and accessibility. It provides flexible XY grids and off-canvas menus.
- **Bulma**: A modern, Flexbox-based framework with a clean API and no JavaScript dependencies. It excels at simple column layouts and typography.

Quick start with Bootstrap

The following is a minimal HTML snippet that loads Bootstrap via **Content Delivery Network** (CDN) and creates a two-column layout. Swap in any grid or utility classes from your chosen framework in a similar fashion.

```
<!DOCTYPE html>
<html lang="en">
<head>
<meta charset="UTF-8">
<meta name="viewport" content="width=device-width, initial-scale=1.0">
<title>Framework Grid Demo</title>
<link
href="https://cdn.jsdelivr.net/npm/bootstrap@5.3.0/dist/css/bootstrap.min.css" rel="stylesheet">
</head>
<body>
<div class="container my-4">
<div class="row">
<div class="col-md-6 bg-light p-3"> Left panel
</div>
<div class="col-md-6 bg-secondary text-white p-3"> Right panel
</div>
</div>
</div>
</body>
</html>
```

Bootstrap grid layouts

Bootstrap provides a responsive, mobile-first grid built on Flexbox. It divides the page into twelve columns inside a container and uses rows to wrap columns. You can easily apply the right classes, and Bootstrap will handle sizing, spacing, and wrapping.

Core grid components

Bootstrap's grid relies on the following three building blocks:

- **.container / .container-fluid:** `.container` centers and caps the width; .container-fluid spans the full viewport.
- **.row:** Wraps columns and applies negative margins to align gutters.
- **.col-*-*:** Defines column span and breakpoint, for example `.col-md-6 spans` 6 of 12 columns on `screens≥768 px`.

Two-column layout

In Bootstrap, you can create a two-column layout by using the `.row` and `.col-` classes. Each column can be sized using the grid system, which allows for responsive design.

The following is an example of a simple two-column layout using Bootstrap's grid:

```
<!DOCTYPE html>
<html lang="en">
<head>
<meta charset="UTF-8">
<meta name="viewport"
content="width=device-width, initial-scale=1.0">
<link
href="https://cdn.jsdelivr.net/npm/bootstrap@5.3.0/dist/css/bootstrap.min.css" rel="stylesheet">
</head>
<body>
<div class="container my-4">
<div class="row">
<div class="col-md-6 bg-light p-3">Column 1</div>
<div class="col-md-6 bg-secondary text-white p-3"> Column 2
</div>
</div>
</div>
</body>
</html>
```

Responsive breakpoints

Bootstrap's grid system is responsive by default. It uses media queries to adjust column widths based on the viewport size. You can specify different column spans for various breakpoints, allowing for flexible layouts that adapt to different devices.

Bootstrap adjusts columns at the following five breakpoints:

- **.col-:** Extra-small (<576 px)
- **.col-sm-:** Small (≥576 px)
- **.col-md-:** Medium (≥768 px)
- **.col-lg-:** Large (≥992 px)
- **.col-xl-:** Extra-large (≥1200 px)

Combine the following classes to change the layout across devices. The following is an example where columns stack on phones and sit side-by-side on tablets and larger screens:

```
<div class="container">
<div class="row">
<div class="col-12 col-md-6"> Full width on xs, half on md+
</div>
<div class="col-12 col-md-6"> Full width on xs, half on md+
</div>
</div>
</div>
```

Tailwind CSS for layouts

Tailwind CSS adopts a utility-first approach, offering single-purpose classes that you compose directly in your HTML. This method avoids custom CSS files, keeps your styles consistent, and speeds up development by reusing a well-defined design system.

Utility-first philosophy

Tailwind's utility classes cover spacing, sizing, typography, colors, and more. By combining these classes, you can build custom components without writing new CSS. The following are the key benefits:

- **Consistency**: A shared scale for margins, padding, and fonts prevents drift across components.
- **Reusability**: Single-purpose classes reduce duplication and make refactoring easier.
- **Predictability**: Class names map directly to CSS properties, so you always know what each utility does.

The following is an example that uses utilities to style a card container and a button:

```
<div class="max-w-sm mx-auto p-6 bg-white rounded-lg shadow-lg">
<h2 class="text-xl font-semibold mb-4">Card Title</h2>
<p class="text-gray-700 mb-6">
This card uses padding, rounded corners, and a drop shadow.
</p>
<button class="px-4 py-2 bg-blue-500 hover:bg-blue-600 text-white font-medium rounded">
Action
</button>
</div>
```

Responsive grid utilities

Tailwind's grid utilities enable you to define column counts and gaps at each breakpoint without writing custom media queries. Use **`grid-cols-n`** for column count and **`gap-n`** for spacing.

The following is an example that shows one column on small screens and two columns on medium and larger screens:

```
<div class="grid grid-cols-1 md:grid-cols-2 gap-6 p-4">
<div class="bg-gray-200 p-4">Column 1</div>
<div class="bg-gray-700 text-white p-4">Column 2</div>
</div>
```

Flexbox utilities

Tailwind provides concise classes for Flexbox layouts. Control direction, wrapping, and alignment with **flex-**, **justify-**, and **items-** utilities.

The following example creates a responsive row of cards that wrap on narrow screens:

```
<div class="flex flex-col sm:flex-row sm:space-x-4 space-y-4 sm:space-y-0 p-4">
<div class="flex-1 bg-blue-100 p-4">Card A</div>
<div class="flex-1 bg-blue-300 p-4">Card B</div>
<div class="flex-1 bg-blue-500 text-white p-4">Card C</div>
</div>
```

Configuration and customization

Tailwind's configuration file (**tailwind.config.js**) enables you to extend defaults or add new utilities. You can define custom colors, spacings, and even new grid variants.

The following snippet adds a 16-column grid and a custom gap size:

```
/* tailwind.config.js */
module.exports = {
theme: { extend: {
gridTemplateColumns: {
'16': 'repeat(16, minmax(0, 1fr))',
},
gap: {
'7': '1.75rem',
},
},
},
};
```

Bootstrap vs. Tailwind

Although both frameworks enable rapid, responsive layouts, they differ fundamentally. Tailwind first explains each utility's effect and then applies it directly in markup, while Bootstrap offers pre-styled components. Tailwind's JIT compiler generates only the CSS you use, resulting in minimal bundle sizes, whereas Bootstrap ships its full stylesheet by default. Finally, Tailwind grants pixel-level control at the cost of longer class lists, while Bootstrap simplifies markup with higher-level abstractions.

Foundation grids

Foundation provides a mobile-first, flexbox-based grid. Wrap content in a **.grid-container** (fixed width) or **.grid-container fluid** (full width). Inside, define rows with **.grid-x** and gutters with **.grid-padding-x**, then assign each column a **.cell** class plus size modifiers (e.g., **small-6**, **medium-4**) to span a fraction of the 12-unit grid.

Grid setup

Rows use **.grid-x** and **.grid-padding-x** to establish a horizontal layout. Each **.cell** class represents one or more of the twelve default columns. Foundation calculates gutter widths automatically, so you only need to specify column spans.

The following is an example of two equal columns on all screen sizes:

```
<div class="grid-container">
<div class="grid-x grid-padding-x">
<div class="cell small-6"> Column 1
</div>
<div class="cell small-6"> Column 2
</div>
</div>
</div>
```

Responsive cells

Foundation supports three breakpoints, which are **small**, **medium**, and **large**. You can combine size classes to adjust each cell's width at different viewport widths.

The following example makes each cell full-width on small screens, half-width on medium, and one-third width on large devices:

```
<div class="grid-container">
<div class="grid-x grid-padding-x">
<div class="cell small-12 medium-6 large-4">Box 1</div>
<div class="cell small-12 medium-6 large-4">Box 2</div>
<div class="cell small-12 medium-6 large-4">Box 3</div>
</div>
</div>
```

Offsets and order

Use **small-offset-#** to shift cells right by a given number of columns and **small-order-#** to change their source order on small screens. This helps center content or rearrange blocks for better flow. The following example centers a 6-column cell and reorders two others:

```
<div class="grid-container">
<div class="grid-x grid-padding-x">
<div class="cell small-6 small-offset-3"> Centered block
</div>
<div class="cell small-6 small-order-2"> Second on small
</div>
<div class="cell small-6 small-order-1"> First on small
</div>
</div>
</div>
```

Nested grids

You can nest rows inside any cell to create more complex layouts. Each nested **.grid-x** starts a fresh 12-column context within its parent.

The following example nests two 6-column blocks inside an 8-column parent, alongside a 4-column sidebar:

```
<div class="grid-container">
<div class="grid-x grid-padding-x">
<div class="cell small-8">
<div class="grid-x grid-padding-x">
<div class="cell small-6">Nested A</div>
<div class="cell small-6">Nested B</div>
```

```
</div>
</div>
<div class="cell small-4"> Sidebar
</div>
</div>
</div>
```

Choosing a CSS framework

Choosing the right CSS framework can significantly impact your project's development speed, maintainability, and user experience. This section compares popular frameworks like Bootstrap, Tailwind CSS, and Foundation across key criteria to help you make an informed decision. Following is a table summarizing the main features of each framework:

Feature	Bootstrap	Tailwind CSS	Foundation
Ease of use	High	Medium	Medium
Customization	Low to medium	High	Medium
Performance	Medium	High (JIT)	Medium
Style	Pre-styled components	Utility-first	Semantic markup
Ecosystem	Large (components, plugins)	Growing (plugins)	Mature (components, plugins)

Table 3.1: *Comparison of CSS frameworks*

Table 3.1 summarizes the main features of each framework, helping the reader to quickly compare their strengths and weaknesses. The following is a brief overview of each framework's strengths and weaknesses:

- **Bootstrap**: Best for rapid prototyping and teams needing a low barrier to entry. It provides a comprehensive set of pre-styled components, but it can feel opinionated in design.
- **Tailwind CSS**: It is ideal for developers who want granular control over styles without writing custom CSS. Its first approach utility allows for high customization but may lead to verbose class names.
- **Foundation**: It offers a balance between Bootstrap and Tailwind, with a focus on semantic markup and accessibility. It provides flexible grids and components, but has a steeper learning curve than Bootstrap.
- **Bulma**: A modern, Flexbox-based framework that is easy to use and has a clean API. It excels at simple column layouts and typography, but lacks JavaScript components.
- **Semantic UI**: It focuses on human-friendly HTML and a rich set of components. It provides a unique approach to styling, but can be heavy and complex for simple projects.

Framework criteria

Selecting a CSS framework requires balancing setup effort, flexibility, performance, visual style, and ecosystem support. Consider the following factors:

- **Ease of use**: *How quickly can developers scaffold layouts and components?*
- **Customization**: *Can you override defaults or extend the design system to match your brand?*
- **Performance**: *Does the framework include a purge mechanism to remove unused CSS?*
- **Style**: *Does the framework impose a distinctive look, or allow granular control over every property?*
- **Ecosystem**: *Are components, plugins, and community support readily available?*

Ease of use

Bootstrap shines when teams need a low barrier to entry. Its semantic grid classes and pre-styled components allow developers to assemble responsive pages with minimal configuration.

The following is a basic Bootstrap layout with two columns:

```
<link href="https://cdn.jsdelivr.net/npm/bootstrap@5.3.0/dist/css/bootstrap.min.css"        \
\ rel="stylesheet">

<div class="container my-4">
<div class="row">
<div class="col-md-6 p-3 bg-light">Left panel</div>
<div class="col-md-6 p-3 bg-secondary text-white">Right panel</div>
</div>
</div>
```

Customization

Tailwind CSS uses a configuration file to expose every design token, colors, spacing, and font sizes for easy theming. You can add or override scales and generate only the utilities you need.

The following is a **`tailwind.config.js`** snippet that extends the default color palette and grid columns:

```
/* tailwind.config.js */
module.exports = { theme: {
extend: { colors: {
primary: '#1e40af', accent: '#fbbf24',
},
gridTemplateColumns: {
'16': 'repeat(16, minmax(0, 1fr))',
},
},
},
};
```

Performance

Frameworks can ship large CSS files. Tailwind's JIT compiler and PurgeCSS remove unused classes, yielding minimal bundles. Bootstrap also offers a Sass build to include only the required components.

The following is a PostCSS config that purges Tailwind CSS in production:

```
/* postcss.config.js */
module.exports = { plugins: {
tailwindcss: {}, autoprefixer: {},
...(process.env.NODE_ENV === 'production' && { '@fullhuman/postcss-purgecss': {
content: ['./src/**/*.html'],
defaultExtractor: content => content.match(/[\w-/:]+(?<!:)/g) || []
}
})
}
};
```

Style

Bootstrap enforces a cohesive look out of the box, ideal for consistency across teams. Tailwind and Foundation, by contrast, give full control over spacing, colors, and typography, at the cost of writing more classes.

The following is a simple comparison of card styling in each framework:

```
<!-- Bootstrap card -->
<div class="card" style="width: 18rem;">
<div class="card-body">
<h5 class="card-title">Bootstrap</h5>
<p class="card-text">Pre-styled component</p>
</div>
</div>

<!-- Tailwind card -->
<div class="max-w-sm p-6 bg-white rounded-lg shadow-lg">
<h5 class="text-xl font-semibold mb-2">Tailwind</h5>
<p class="text-gray-700">Utility-first styling</p>
</div>

<!-- Foundation card -->
<div class="card">
<div class="card-divider">Foundation</div>
<div class="card-section">Flexible grid and components</div>
</div>
```

Comparison example

This fragment shows three frameworks side by side in a minimal layout. Swap classes as needed to explore differences:

```
<!DOCTYPE html>
<html lang="en">
<head>
<!-- Bootstrap -->
<link href="https://cdn.jsdelivr.net/npm/bootstrap@5.3.0/dist/css/bootstrap.min.css"        \
\ rel="stylesheet">
<!-- Tailwind -->
<script src="https://cdn.tailwindcss.com"></script>
<!-- Foundation -->
<link rel="stylesheet" href="https://cdnjs.cloudflare.com/ajax/libs/foundation/6.7.4/cs    \
\ s/foundation.min.css">
</head>
<body class="p-4">

<!-- Bootstrap -->
<div class="container mb-4">
<div class="row">
<div class="col-6 bg-light p-3">Bootstrap</div>
<div class="col-6 bg-secondary text-white p-3">Demo</div>
</div>
```

```
</div>

<!-- Tailwind -->
<div class="grid grid-cols-2 gap-4 mb-4">
<div class="bg-blue-100 p-3">Tailwind</div>
<div class="bg-blue-700 text-white p-3">Demo</div>
</div>

<!-- Foundation -->
<div class="grid-container">
<div class="grid-x grid-padding-x">
<div class="cell small-6 bg-gray p-3">Foundation</div>
<div class="cell small-6 bg-black text-white p-3">Demo</div>
</div>
</div>

</body>
</html>
```

Media queries

Responsive design adapts page layouts to varying screen characteristics by applying CSS rules conditionally. Media queries detect features like viewport width, pixel density, and orientation, then apply targeted styles. This technique ensures readable text, usable navigation, and optimized resource loading on phones, tablets, desktops, and high-density displays.

Approach

Developers follow two main strategies. The mobile-first approach writes base styles for small viewports, then uses **`min-width`** queries to enhance designs on larger screens. This yields lean core CSS and prioritizes essential content. The desktop-first approach starts with wide-screen styles, then uses **`max-width`** queries to adjust for smaller devices. Mobile-first generally leads to simpler, more performant code.

The following is an example that applies a light gray background on viewports at least 768 px wide:

```
@media (min-width: 768px) {
body {
background-color: lightgray;
}
}
```

Standard breakpoints

Designers often target three ranges—phones (up to 600 px), tablets (601–1024 px), and desktops (1025 px and up). These breakpoints match common device widths and keep layouts coherent across screens.

Sample queries are as follows:

```
/* Phones */
@media (max-width: 600px) {
.menu { font-size: 14px; }
}

/* Tablets */
```

```
@media (min-width: 601px) and (max-width: 1024px) {
.menu { font-size: 16px; }
}

/* Desktops */
@media (min-width: 1025px) {
.menu { font-size: 18px; }
}
```

Orientation

Orientation queries apply styles when a device is in landscape or portrait mode. Use them to adjust layouts and images for the current orientation.

The following is an example that changes the page background in landscape:

```
@media (orientation: landscape) {
body {
background-color: lightblue;
}
}
```

High-density

High-density displays pack more device pixels into each CSS pixel. Use **`min-resolution or device-pixel-ratio`** queries to serve higher-resolution assets or adjust UI scaling.

The following is an example that halves the image width on Retina screens:

```
@media (min-resolution: 2dppx) {
img.responsive {
width: 50%;
}
}
```

Combined conditions

Combine multiple features in one query with `and` or comma separators to fine-tune styles for complex scenarios.

An example that targets tablets in landscape orientation is as follows:

```
@media (min-width: 601px) and (max-width: 1024px) and (orientation: landscape) {
.sidebar {
display: block;
}
}
```

Scalable units

Relative units like **`rem`** and **`em`** scale dimensions based on font size, improving accessibility and consistency. They adapt naturally when users adjust base font settings or when you change a single root value.

Root em

The **`rem`** unit derives from the root **`html`** font size. Setting a base of 16 px makes **`1rem`** equal to 16 px everywhere. Changing the root size scales all `rem`-based values proportionally.

The following is an example of using **rem** for typography:

```
html {
font-size: 16px;  /* 1rem = 16px */
}
h1 {
font-size: 2rem;  /* 32px */
margin-bottom: 1.5rem;  /* 24px */
}
p {
line-height: 1.6rem;  /* 25.6px */
}
```

Element em

The **em** unit calculates relative to the current element's font size. It is ideal for components that scale internally when you adjust their font size.

The following is an example that sizes a button and its icon using **em**:

```
.button {
font-size: 1rem; /* inherits root size (16px) */
padding: 0.75em 1.25em; /* 12px vertical, 20px horizontal */
}
.button .icon {
font-size: 1.25em;        /* 20px (1.25 × 16px) */
margin-right: 0.5em;      /* 8px */
}
```

Grid and flexbox layouts

Responsive designs adapt to varying screen sizes without excessive media queries. CSS Grid manages two-dimensional layouts with rows and columns, while Flexbox distributes items along a single axis. Combining both delivers powerful, adaptable interfaces.

Grid layout

CSS Grid defines a grid container with **grid-template-rows** and **grid-template-columns**, uses `gap` for spacing, and supports named areas for semantic placement. It excels at complex layouts that require precise control over both axes.

The following is an example of a three-column grid that collapses to two and then one column via media queries:

```
.container {
display: grid;
grid-template-columns: repeat(3, 1fr);
gap: 16px;
}
@media (max-width: 768px) {
.container { grid-template-columns: repeat(2, 1fr); }
}
@media (max-width: 480px) {
.container { grid-template-columns: 1fr; }
}
```

Flexbox layout

Flexbox uses **display: flex** and **flex-direction** to arrange items in a row or column. Properties like **justify-content** and **align-items** control alignment, and **flex-grow**, **flex-shrink**, and **flex- basis** manage sizing. Flexbox suits toolbars, menus, and simple one-axis layouts.

The following is an example of a horizontal navigation that stacks vertically on narrow screens:

```
.nav {
display: flex;
justify-content: space-between;
}
@media (max-width: 600px) {
.nav {
flex-direction: column; align-items: center;
}
}
```

Combined layout

Use Grid for the overall page structure and Flexbox within grid items for alignment and spacing. Grid defines regions; Flexbox centers or distributes content inside them.

The following is an example of a two-column layout where the content area uses Flexbox to center its inner elements:

```
.page {
display: grid;
grid-template-columns: 1fr 3fr;
gap: 24px;
}
.sidebar {
background: #f4f4f4;
}
.content {
display: flex;
flex-direction: column; justify-content: center; align-items: center;
}
```

Responsive visibility

Control which elements appear on different devices by changing their **display** in media queries. Hiding nonessential content on small screens improves focus and performance.

The following example hides a sidebar on small viewports:

```
@media (max-width: 600px) {
.sidebar {
display: none;
}
}
```

Auto grid

The **auto-fit** and **auto-fill** keywords with **minmax()** create fluid grids that adapt without explicit breakpoints. Columns wrap automatically based on available space.

The following is an example of a responsive gallery that fits as many 200px columns as the viewport allows:

```
.gallery {
display: grid;
grid-template-columns: repeat(auto-fit, minmax(200px, 1fr));
gap: 16px;
}
```

The summary is as follows:

- CSS Grid handles two-dimensional layouts with precise control over rows and columns.
- Flexbox excels at one-dimensional alignment and distribution.
- Combining Grid for structure and Flexbox for inner alignment delivers maximum flexibility.
- Use media queries to adjust both grid and flex layouts for different screen sizes.
- Leverage **`auto-fit`** and **`auto-fill`** to reduce manual breakpoints.
- Toggle element visibility with `display` rules to optimize small-screen experiences.

Advanced CSS techniques

Modern web interfaces benefit from interactive effects that guide user attention and provide visual feedback. CSS offers built-in mechanisms, transitions, transformations, and animations that run entirely in the browser's rendering engine. These tools enable smooth state changes, element movements, and complex keyframe-driven sequences without JavaScript.

Transitions

Transitions animate changes to CSS properties when their values update (for example, on hover or focus). You specify which property to animate, how long the change takes, the easing curve, and an optional delay. Transitions suit simple hover effects, link underlines, and form feedback.

The following is an example that darkens a button and lifts it upward on hover:

```
.button {
background: #3490dc;
color: #fff;
padding: 0.75rem 1.5rem;
border: none;
transition: background 0.3s ease, transform 0.3s ease;
}
.button:hover {
background: #2779bd;
transform: translateY(-4px);
}
```

Transformations

Transformations reposition or reshape elements in 2D or 3D space. Common functions include **`translate()`**, **`scale()`**, **`rotate()`**, and **`skew()`**. The **`transform-origin`** property sets the pivot point for rotations and scales. Transforms never affect document flow, avoiding layout recalculations. Following is an example that slightly enlarges and tilts an image on hover:

```
.card img {
display: block; width: 100%;
transition: transform 0.4s;
```

```
transform-origin: center center;
}
.card:hover img {
transform: scale(1.05) rotate(2deg);
}
```

Animations

Animations define keyframes that describe intermediate states of CSS properties. You assign the animation name, duration, timing function, delay, iteration count, and direction. Animations handle loading indicators, attention-grabbers, and looping effects.

The following is an example of a continuous spinner using a simple rotation animation:

```
@keyframes spin {
to { transform: rotate(360deg); }
}
.spinner { width: 40px; height: 40px;
border: 4px solid #ccc; border-top-color: #3490dc; border-radius: 50%;
animation: spin 1s linear infinite;
}
```

Performance tips

For smooth animations, animate only properties that trigger compositor layers, such as **`transform`** and **`opacity`**. Avoid animating layout-affecting properties like **`width`**, **`height`**, or **`box-shadow`**, which force reflows. Use the **`will-change`** hint sparingly to let the browser prepare for upcoming changes. The following is an example that signals the browser to optimize for upcoming transforms:

```
.card {
will-change: transform, opacity;
}
```

CSS variables and selectors

CSS custom properties, or variables, enable you to store reusable values, such as colors, spacing, and font sizes, in your style sheet. They follow the cascade and inherit through the DOM, making theme updates and component-level overrides straightforward. Advanced selectors allow precise targeting of elements based on attributes, position, and state, reducing the need for extra classes or JavaScript.

Defining variables

You declare variables using custom property syntax within any rule set. Variables defined on the **`:root`** selector act globally, while those inside a specific selector apply only within that scope. Use the **`var()`** function to retrieve a variable's value, optionally providing a fallback.

The following is an example of defining global and local variables and using them:

```
:root {
--primary-color: #1e90ff;
--base-padding: 16px;
}
.card {
--card-bg: #f4f4f4;
background-color: var(--card-bg);
```

```
padding: var(--base-padding);
}
h1 {
color: var(--primary-color);
margin-bottom: var(--base-padding);
}
```

Variable scope

Variables inherit like normal properties. A variable defined on a parent is available to its descendants unless it is overridden by a more specific declaration. The local variables inside a component or utility class can shadow global definitions, enabling per-component theming.

The following is an example of scope and inheritance:

```
:root {
--font-size: 18px;
}
.container {
font-size: var(--font-size);
}
.container .highlight {
--font-size: 24px;       /* overrides only within .highlight */
font-size: var(--font-size);
}
```

Dynamic updates

You can change variables in response to user interaction or state changes using pseudo-classes or JavaScript. Transitions on custom properties allow smooth interpolation when values change.

The following is an example that updates a color variable on hover:

```
.button {
--btn-color: #3490dc;
background-color: var(--btn-color);
transition: background-color 0.3s ease;
}
.button:hover {
--btn-color: #2779bd;
}
```

Variables in media queries

Redefine variables inside media queries to adapt values globally for different viewports. This technique centralizes responsive adjustments and minimizes repetition.

The following is an example that adjusts the base font size based on screen width:

```
:root {
--base-font: 16px;
}
@media (max-width: 600px) {
:root {
--base-font: 14px;
```

```
}
}
body {
font-size: var(--base-font);
}
```

Advanced selectors

Advanced selectors allow you to target elements by attributing values, structural position, state, and more often, without adding extra class details as follows:

- `[attr=value]` selects elements with a specific attribute value.
- `E > F` selects direct children.
- `E + F` selects the next sibling.
- `E ~ F` selects all the following siblings.
- `:nth-child(n)` targets elements by index.
- `:not(selector)` excludes matches.
- `::before and ::`after inserting generated content.

The following is an example combining several selectors:

```
<style>
/* attribute selector */
input[type="email"] { padding: 8px; }

/* child combinator and pseudo-class */
nav > ul > li:nth-child(1) a::after {
content: " (Home)";
}

/* adjacent sibling */
h2 + p { margin-top: 0.5em; }

/* negation */
button:not(.disabled):hover {
opacity: 0.8;
}
</style>
```

Pseudo-classes and pseudo-elements

Pseudo-classes and pseudo-elements allow you to target elements and their parts without extra HTML. Pseudo-classes match elements based on state or position, while pseudo-elements style or insert parts of an element, such as its first letter or generated content.

Pseudo-classes

Pseudo-classes apply styles when elements enter certain states or occupy specific positions. Structural pseudo-classes like `:nth-child()` and`:first-of-type` match elements by their order within a parent. State pseudo-classes, such as: `hover` and: `focus`, respond to user interactions. This approach adapts styles dynamically without JavaScript or extra classes.

The following is an example that highlights every second item and bolds the first paragraph:

```
li:nth-child(2n) {
background-color: lightgray;
}
p:first-of-type {
font-weight: bold;
}
```

Pseudo-elements

Pseudo-elements treat portions of an element as separate objects. You can insert content before or after an element (**::before**, **::after**) or style its first letter or line (**::first-letter**, **::first-line**). They enable decorative effects without additional markup.

The following is an example that adds star icons around headings:

```
h1::before { content: "? "; color: gold;
}
h1::after { content: " ?"; color: gold;
}
```

Combinators

Combinators describe relationships between selectors, refining your target elements. The descendant combinator (a space) selects any nested element. The child combinator (>) matches direct children only. The adjacent sibling combinator (+) targets the immediate next sibling. The general sibling combinator (~) applies to all following siblings.

The following is an example showing each combinator:

```
/* Descendant */
div p {
color: blue;
}
/* Child */
div > p {
font-weight: bold;
}
/* Adjacent sibling */
div + p {
color: red;
}
/* General sibling */
div ~ p {
text-decoration: underline;
}
```

Negation

The **:not()** pseudo-class excludes elements that match a given selector. It simplifies exclusion logic and reduces the need for extra utility classes. You can combine it with other selectors to refine your rules.

The following is an example that styles every button except those marked danger:

```
button:not(.danger) { background-color: blue; color: white;
padding: 0.5em 1em; border: none; border-radius: 4px;
}
```

Variables

Custom properties (variables) integrate with selectors and pseudo-classes to enable dynamic theming. Variables are inherited through the cascade and updated across all affected elements when redefined. You can adjust variables in media queries or on hover to create responsive or interactive effects.

The following is an example that uses a variable for border color and applies it on hover:

```
:root {
--border-color: blue;
}
.card {
border: 2px solid var(--border-color);
padding: 1em;
transition: border-color 0.3s;
}
.card:hover {
--border-color: red;
}
```

The following list outlines the summary:

- Pseudo-classes adapt styles based on element state or document structure.
- Pseudo-elements insert or style parts of an element without extra HTML.
- Combinators refine selection by describing element relationships.
- The `:not()` selector excludes specific elements from a rule.
- Custom properties work with selectors and pseudo-classes for dynamic, maintainable themes.

Responsive webpage design with CSS

Exercise: In this hands-on project, you will design a responsive webpage using CSS. The webpage will include a navigation bar, a content section with a grid layout, and a styled form. You will implement CSS Flexbox and Grid for layout, media queries for responsiveness, and CSS variables for maintainability.

Project requirements

The following list outlines the project requirements:

- A navigation bar using Flexbox with links styled in different states.
- A grid-based content section displaying three content cards with images and text.
- A contact form with styled input fields and a submit button.
- Use of CSS variables for colors and font sizes.
- Media queries to ensure a mobile-friendly design.

Step 1: HTML structure

Create an HTML file (**index.html**) with the following structure:

```
<!DOCTYPE html>
<html lang="en">
<head>
<meta charset="UTF-8">
```

```
<meta name="viewport" content="width=device-width, initial-scale=1.0">
<title>Responsive CSS Project</title>
<link rel="stylesheet" href="styles.css">
</head>
<body>

<nav class="navbar">
<a href="#">Home</a>
<a href="#">About</a>
<a href="#">Services</a>
<a href="#">Contact</a>
</nav>

<section class="content">
<div class="card">
<img src="image1.jpg" alt="Image 1">
<p>Content description here.</p>
</div>
<div class="card">
<img src="image2.jpg" alt="Image 2">
<p>Content description here.</p>
</div>
<div class="card">
<img src="image3.jpg" alt="Image 3">
<p>Content description here.</p>
</div>
</section>

<section class="contact">
<h2>Contact Us</h2>
<form>
<input type="text" placeholder="Your Name">
<input type="email" placeholder="Your Email">
<textarea placeholder="Your Message"></textarea>
<button type="submit">Send Message</button>
</form>
</section>

</body>
</html>
```

Step 2: Styling with CSS

Create a CSS file (**`styles.css`**) with the following styles:

```
/* Define CSS Variables */
:root {
--primary-color: #3498db;
--secondary-color: #2ecc71;
--font-size: 16px;
```

```
}

/* Reset and basic styles */
body {
font-family: Arial, sans-serif; margin: 0;
padding: 0;
}
/* Navigation Bar */
.navbar {
display: flex;
justify-content: space-around; background-color: var(--primary-color); padding: 10px;
}

.navbar a {
color: white;
text-decoration: none;
font-size: var(--font-size);
}

.navbar a:hover {
color: var(--secondary-color);
}

/* Grid Content */
.content {
display: grid;
grid-template-columns: repeat(auto-fit, minmax(250px, 1fr));
gap: 20px;
padding: 20px;
}

.card {
background: lightgray; padding: 15px;
text-align: center; border-radius: 8px;
}

/* Contact Form */
.contact {
text-align: center;
padding: 20px;
}

form {
display: flex;
flex-direction: column; gap: 10px;
max-width: 400px;
margin: auto;
}
```

```
input, textarea {
padding: 10px;
border: 1px solid #ccc;
}

button {
background-color: var(--primary-color);
color: white; border: none; padding: 10px; cursor: pointer;
}

/* Responsive Design */
@media (max-width: 600px) {
.navbar {
flex-direction: column; align-items: center;
}

.content {
grid-template-columns: 1fr;
}
}
```

Project output

Once the project is complete, the webpage should:

- Have a fully functional navigation bar that changes color on hover.
- Display content in a responsive grid layout, adjusting for small screens.
- Include a styled contact form with input fields and a submit button.
- Adapt to different screen sizes using CSS media queries.

You can test the project by opening the **index.html** file in a web browser. Resize the browser window to see how the layout adjusts for different screen sizes.

The following figure depicts the expected output for the responsive CSS project:

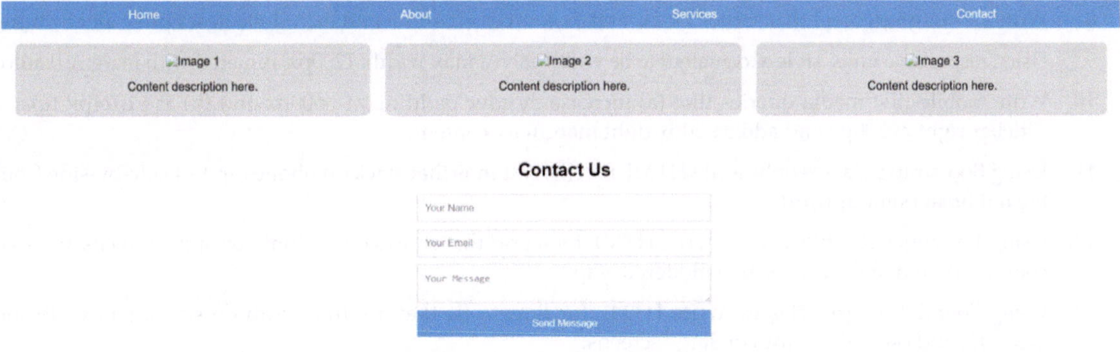

Figure 3.1: Responsive CSS project output

Conclusion

In this chapter, we have explored a wide range of advanced CSS concepts essential for modern web development: from using the web developer toolbar to debug and fine-tune form elements, through mastering layout and positioning techniques, static, relative, absolute, fixed, float, and clear, to designing responsive, grid-based systems such as the 960px 12-column layout. We examined how leading CSS frameworks (Bootstrap, Tailwind, Foundation) simplify and standardize responsive design, while media queries and relative units (rem, em) ensure fluidity across screen sizes. We combined CSS Grid and Flexbox to create adaptive layouts and an enriched user experience with animations, transitions, and transforms. Finally, we introduced CSS variables and advanced selectors to write DRY, maintainable stylesheets.

In *Chapter 4, JavaScript Fundamentals*, we will shift focus from static styling to dynamic behavior. You will learn what JavaScript is and how it integrates with the browser's DOM, trace its evolution from ES5 to the latest ES features, and set up your development environment with VS Code and Node.js. We will cover the basics, variables, data types, statements, expressions, and operators, then dive into control structures, functions, objects, and arrays. Finally, we will introduce asynchronous programming with callbacks, promises, and async/await, laying the foundation for building interactive, data-driven web applications.

Exercises

1. State two ways to open browser DevTools and name three panels useful for form debugging with one-line purposes for each (e.g., Elements, Console, Network).
2. Given <div class="card"><div class="badge">New</div>...</div>, write minimal CSS that positions .badge at the card's top-right using a proper positioning context.
3. Explain, in one sentence each, how static, relative, absolute, fixed, and sticky positioning behave in layout.
4. Two absolutely positioned boxes overlap: .box1 { z-index: 1; } and .box2 { z-index: 2; } inside the same stacking context. Which renders on top and why?
5. Floated children cause a parent's height to collapse. Propose two different fixes and write the minimal CSS for each fix.
6. Create two 50% columns using floats and apply a clearfix so the parent expands. Write the minimal HTML and CSS.
7. Write CSS for a responsive gallery that uses Grid with repeat(auto-fit, minmax(200px, 1fr)) and a 16px gap.
8. Write an <img> element that serves 1x, 2x, and 3x sources via srcset and includes a descriptive alt attribute.
9. Using responsive units, style a .container to be width: 90vw, max-width: 1200px, centered with margin: 0 auto.
10. Write mobile-first media queries that (a) increase .header padding at ≥600px and (b) at ≥1024px float a .sidebar right at 300px and add a 320px right margin to .content.
11. Using Bootstrap 5 classes only, write HTML for two columns that stack on phones and sit side-by-side from the md breakpoint upward.
12. Using Tailwind CSS utilities only, write HTML for a grid that shows one column on small screens and two columns on md and above with a moderate gap.
13. Using Foundation grid classes, write HTML for three cells that are full-width on small, half-width on medium, and one-third width on large screens.
14. Create a button whose background color is controlled by a CSS variable; on :hover, change the variable so the background transitions smoothly.
15. Write CSS that animates a card on hover using only transform and opacity with a 0.3s transition and includes a will-change hint.

CHAPTER 4

JavaScript Fundamentals

Introduction

JavaScript is the backbone of dynamic, interactive web applications. In this chapter, we will understand the fundamentals of JavaScript: its definition, history, and role in the browser; core syntax elements such as statements, expressions, and comments; variable declarations (var, let, const) and data types (primitive and non-primitive); and essential programming constructs including type conversion/coercion, operators, control structures (conditionals and loops), and functions (declarations, expressions, arrow functions, default parameters, callbacks, and higher-order functions). We also explore object-oriented features—object literals, constructors, prototypes, and ES6 classes, alongside array manipulation methods (map, filter, reduce), the spread/rest operators, and destructuring. Asynchronous programming is introduced through callbacks, Promises, async/await, and the event loop, culminating in a hands-on To-Do List project that reinforces these concepts. By mastering these fundamentals, you will be prepared to write robust, maintainable JavaScript that drives modern web experiences.

Structure

This chapter covers the following topics:

- JavaScript overview
- JavaScript history
- JavaScript vs. other languages
- Statements and expressions
- Comments in JavaScript
- Data types in JavaScript
- JavaScript operators
- Loops in JavaScript
- Functions
- Object prototypes classes
- Spread and rest operators with destructuring
- Polyfills and transpilation
- JavaScript and the browser
- Development environment
- Statements
- Variables
- Type conversion and coercion
- Conditional statements
- Loop control
- Error handling
- Arrays and array methods
- Asynchronous JavaScript

Objectives

In this chapter, we will begin by defining JavaScript and tracing its evolution from ES5 through ES6 and beyond, then examine how JavaScript executes in the browser via the Document Object Model. The readers will learn to declare variables using var, let, and const, understand their scoping rules, and distinguish between primitive and non-primitive data types. They will perform explicit type conversions and identify common pitfalls of implicit coercion. They will apply arithmetic, comparison, logical, and bitwise operators, and construct conditional statements and loops to control program flow. You will define and invoke functions, including arrow functions, callbacks, and higher-order functions, for modular, reusable code. The readers will also create and manipulate objects using literals, constructor functions with prototypes, and ES6 classes, and will manage arrays with built-in methods as well as spread/rest syntax and destructuring for concise expressions. The readers will further implement asynchronous logic using callbacks, Promises, and async/await, gaining insight into the event loop. Finally, they will reinforce these skills by building an interactive To-Do List application.

JavaScript overview

JavaScript stands as a high-level interpreted language that brings web pages to life. Browsers embed a JavaScript engine to manipulate HTML and CSS, respond to user actions, and fetch data without reloading. On the server side, Node.js executes JavaScript to handle **input/output (I/O)** and serve content, enabling developers to use a single language across the entire stack.

Language characteristics

JavaScript uses dynamic typing and a prototype-based object model. Variables can hold any value, and functions are first-class citizens; they can be assigned to variables, passed as arguments, or returned from other functions. Its event-driven architecture, combined with asynchronous callbacks and promises, excels at handling user interactions and I/O-bound tasks without blocking the main thread.

The following is an example of a function used as a callback:

```
function
  greet(name)
  { console.
  log(`Hello,
  ${name}!`);
}
const sayHello = greet;
sayHello('Alice'); // prints "Hello, Alice!"
```

Basic syntax

JavaScript syntax covers variables, control flow, and data structures. Use **`let`** and **`const`** to declare block-scoped variables, or **`var`** for legacy function scope. Objects group named **`values;`** **`arrays`** hold ordered lists. Arrow functions provide a concise way to define callbacks.

The following example shows variable declarations, an object, and arrow function:

```
const user = { name: 'Bob', age: 30 };
let count = 0;
const increment = () => { count += 1;
    console.log(count);
  };

for (let i = 0;
  i < 3; i++) {
  increment();
}
// prints 1, 2,3
```

Browser API

Browsers expose a rich **application programming interface (API)** to JavaScript for interacting with the **Document Object Model (DOM)**, handling events, and making network requests. You can query and update page elements, attach event listeners, and use the fetch API to retrieve JSON or other resources asynchronously.

The following example attaches a click listener and loads data from an API:

```
document.getElementById('loadBtn').
  addEventListener('click', () => { fetch('/api/data')
    .then(res => res.json())
    .then(data => {
      document.getElementById('output').textContent = data.message;
    })
    .catch(err => console.error(err));
});
```

Server environment

Node.js runs JavaScript outside the browser, offering built-in modules for file I/O, networking, and process management. Its non-blocking I/O model, powered by the event loop, makes it suitable for scalable network applications.

The following example creates a simple HTTP server with Node.js:

```
const http = require('http');

const server = http.createServer((req,
  res) => { res.writeHead(200, {
  'Content-Type': 'text/plain' });
  res.end('Hello from Node.js\n');
});

server.listen(3000, () => {
  console.log('Server running at http://localhost:3000');
});
```

Ecosystem and tooling

The JavaScript ecosystem features npm for package management, plus build tools like **Webpack** and **Rollup**. **Transpilers** (e.g., Babel) enable you to use modern syntax while targeting older environments. Frameworks such as **React**, **Angular**, and **Vue** provide structure for large applications.

The following example shows an **ECMAScript** (**ES**) module import and using a third-party library:

```
// Install with: npm install lodash
import _ from 'lodash';

const nums =
[1, 2, 3, 4];
console.log(_.
shuffle(nums));
// prints nums in random order
```

Polyfills and transpilation

Modern JavaScript features (*ES6+*) may not run in older browsers or runtimes. Transpilation uses tools like **Babel** to convert new syntax into backwards-compatible code, while polyfills (e.g. `core- js`) supply missing APIs at runtime. Together, they ensure broad compatibility without sacrificing modern syntax or features.

The following presents a basic Babel setup with core-js polyfills:

```
// Install Babel and core-js
npm install --save-dev @babel/core @babel/cli @babel/preset-env core-js
```

The following shows a sample **.babelrc** configuring preset-env and automatic polyfilling based on target environments:

```
"presets": [ ["@babel/reset-env", {
    "useBuiltIns": "usage",
    "corejs": 3,
    "targets": {
      "browsers": [">0.25%", "not dead"]
          }
          }]
]
}
```

The following code demonstrates how modern code is transpiled and polyfilled:

```
// Original ES2021 code
const squares = [1,2,3].map(n => n**2); console.
log(squares.includes(4));

// Transpiled + polyfilled ES5 output (simplified)
"use strict";

require("core-js/modules/es.array.
includes"); require("core-
js/modules/es.array.map");
require("core-js/modules/
es.number.constructor");

var squares = [1, 2, 3].map(function (n) {
  return Math.pow(n, 2);
});
console.log(squares.includes(4));
```

JavaScript history

JavaScript began as a simple scripting language for adding interactivity to web pages. Since its introduction in 1995, it has evolved through formal standardization (ECMA-262) and annual editions, transforming into a versatile language for both client-side and server-side development.

Origins

Brendan Eich wrote the first JS interpreter (then called **Mocha**) in 10 days for Netscape Navigator 2.0. Renamed to **LiveScript** and finally JavaScript, the language was standardized as ECMA-262 Edition 1 in 1997. Early JS featured function declarations, a global object, and a prototype-based inheritance model—no modules, strict mode, or modern APIs existed yet.

The following is a snippet in the style of early JS:

```
var greet = function(name) {
  return 'Hello, ' + name + '!';
};
console.log(greet('World')); // Hello, World!
```

ES5 standard

ECMAScript 5 (*2009*) introduced major improvements for robustness and JSON support. **`use strict`** enforced safer coding by disallowing silent errors and prohibiting certain bad practices. Native methods like **`Array.prototype.forEach`**, **`map`**, **`filter`**, and **`reduce`** made array processing declarative. **`JSON.parse`** and **`JSON.stringify`** simplified data interchange. Getters, setters, and **`Object.create`** enabled more powerful object definitions.

The following example shows strict mode and JSON parsing:

```
'use strict';
var data = '{"user":"Alice","age":30}';
var obj = JSON.
parse(data);
obj.age = obj.
age + 1;
console.log(JSON.stringify(obj)); // {"user":"Alice","age":31}
```

Strict mode

Strict mode enforces a stricter variant of JavaScript, catching common errors and disallowing problematic syntax. It prevents accidental globals, forbids assigning to non-writable properties, disallows duplicate parameter names, and makes **`this`** undefined in functions that are not methods. Enabling strict mode improves code safety and allows engines to optimize more aggressively.

The following list presents key strict mode behaviors:

- Implicit **`globals`** throw **`ReferenceError`** instead of silently creating a global.
- Assigning non-writable or non-existent properties throws an error.
- Duplicate parameter names in functions generate a **`SyntaxError`**.
- The **`with`** statement is disallowed.
- In strict mode, when a function is called on its own (not as a method of an object), the value of `this` is undefined instead of defaulting to the global object.

The following demonstrates enabling strict mode and its effects:

```
"use strict";

// Implicit global is now an error
function setValue() {
  undeclared = 5; // ReferenceError: undeclared is not defined
}

// Duplicate parameters are not allowed
function sum(a, a) {
  return a + a; // SyntaxError: Duplicate parameter name not allowed in this context
}

// 'this' is undefined in a normal function
function showThis() { console.log(this); // undefined
}

setValue();
```

ES6 standard

ECMAScript 2015 (ES6) represented a significant milestone in the evolution of JavaScript. Block-scoped let and const replaced var. Arrow functions (=>) provide concise syntax and lexically bind this. Template literals (backticks) enabled interpolation. Destructuring unpacked arrays and objects. Default parameters, rest/spread operators, classes, modules (**import/export**), and Promises for asynchronous workflows rounded out a modern toolkit.

The following example combines several ES6 features:

```
const users = ['Alice','Bob','Carol'];
const greetAll = names => {
  names.forEach(name => {
    console.log(`Hello, ${name}!`);
  });
};
greetAll(users);
// Hello, Alice!
// Hello, Bob!
// Hello, Carol!
```

Modules

JavaScript modules enable you to split code into reusable files, manage **dependencies**, and **optimize loading**. Two main module systems exist: **ES Modules** (**ESM**) with static **import/export**, and **CommonJS** (**CJS**) with **require** and **module. exports**. Modern bundlers like **Webpack**, **Rollup**, and **Vite** resolve and bundle modules for browsers, support code-splitting via dynamic **import()**, and enable tree-shaking to remove unused code.

The following presents key aspects of each system:

- **ESM**:
  - Use **export** to expose bindings and **import** to consume them.
  - Static analysis enables tree-shaking and better optimization.
  - Supported natively in modern browsers and Node.js (when using **.mjs** or setting **"type":"module"**).
- CJS:
  - Use **module.exports** to expose and **require()** to import.
  - Synchronous loading suited to server environments.
  - Ubiquitous in older Node.js codebases.
- **Dynamic import**:
  - import(**'path/to/module'**) returns a Promise, enabling code-splitting and on-demand loading.
- **Bundlers**:
  - Webpack, Rollup, and Vite transform and bundle modules for browsers.
  - Support plugins for loading assets, transpiling, and **hot-module replacement** (**HMR**).

The following demonstrates ES Module syntax:

```
// math.js
export function add(a, b) {
  return a + b;
}
export const PI = 3.14;
```

```
// app.js
import { add, PI } from './math.
js'; console.log(add(2, 3), PI);
// 5 3.14
```

The following demonstrates dynamic import for code-splitting:

```
button.addEventListener('click',
  async () => { const { Chart } =
  await import('./chart.js'); new
  Chart(/* ... */);
});
```

The following demonstrates CommonJS syntax in Node.js:

```
// util.js
function greet(name) {
  return `Hello, ${name}!`;
}
module.exports = { greet };

// server.js
const { greet } = require('./util'); console.
log(greet('Alice')); // Hello, Alice!
```

The following table presents a minimal Webpack configuration for bundling ES Modules:

entry	`{ './src/app.js' }`
output	`{ path: path.resolve( dirname, 'dist'),` `filename: 'bundle.js' }`
module.rules	Use babel-loaderto transpile modern syntax for older browsers

Table 4.1: *Minimal Webpack configuration*

Modern updates

Since ES6, yearly editions have added async/await (ES2017) for linear async code, object and array spread (ES2018), optional chaining and nullish coalescing (ES2020), BigInt for large integers, dynamic **`import()`** for code splitting, and logical assignment operators (ES2021). The pipeline operator, decorators, and record and tuple syntax are in proposal stages, promising further expressiveness.

The following example uses **`async`**/**`await`** and optional chaining:

```
async function loadUser(id) {
  const res = await fetch(`/
  api/users/${id}`); const data
  = await res.json(); console.
  log(data?.profile?.name ??
  'Unknown');
}
loadUser(42);
```

Modern ES features

Recent ECMAScript editions (ES2020 and later) added handy operators and module enhancements that simplify code and improve safety. These include optional chaining, nullish coalescing, logical assignment operators, dynamic **`import()`**, and even top-level **`await`** in modules.

The following list presents the key modern features:

- Optional chaining ('a?.b?.c') lets you safely access deeply nested properties without throwing if an intermediate is null or undefined.
- Nullish coalescing ('x ?? y') returns the right-hand side only when the left is null or undefined, not for other falsy values.
- Logical assignment ('x &&= y', 'x | | = y', 'x ??= y') combines logical operators with assignment for more concise defaults and guards.
- Dynamic import ('import('...')') returns a Promise, enabling on-demand module loading and code-splitting.
- Top-level await allows using await outside functions in ES modules, simplifying startup code.

The following demonstrates optional chaining:

```
const user = { profile: { name: 'Alice' } };
console.log(user.profile?.name);
// 'Alice' console.log(user.address?.street);
// undefined, no error
```

The following demonstrates nullish coalescing:

```
let count = 0;
console.log(count ?? 10);          // 0 (only null/undefined fall back)
let name = null;
console.log(name ?? 'Guest'); // 'Guest'
```

The following demonstrates logical assignment:

```
let a;
a ||= 5;          // a = a || 5 → 5

let b = true;
b &&= false; // b = b && false → false

let c = null;
c ??= 'fallback'; // c = c ?? 'fallback' → 'fallback'
```

The following demonstrates dynamic import and top-level await (in an ES module, e.g. **`main.mjs`**):

```
// dynamic import
button.addEventListener('click', async () => {
  const { init } = await import('./module.js');
  init();
});

// top-level await
const data = await fetch('/data.json').then(r =>
r.json()); console.log(data);
```

JavaScript and the browser

JavaScript runs inside the browser by interacting with the DOM. It can read and modify HTML and CSS, respond to user events, fetch data from servers, and store information locally.

DOM

The DOM exposes page content as a tree of nodes and provides methods to query, create, update, or remove elements. Scripts can change text, attributes, styles, or structure at any time, enabling dynamic updates without reloading the page.

The following is an example that changes a heading's text and appends a new list item:

```
// Change an existing element
document.getElementById('title').textContent = 'Updated Heading';

// Create and append a new list item const li = document.createElement('li'); li.textContent =
'New item';
document.querySelector('ul').appendChild(li);
```

Events

Events fire when users interact with the page: clicks, form submissions, key presses, mouse moves, and more. You register callbacks with **`addEventListener`** to respond and optionally stop propagation or prevent default behavior.

The following is an example that toggles a menu's visibility on button click:

```
const btn = document.getElementById('menuBtn');
const menu = document.getElementById('menu');

btn.addEventListener('click', () => { menu.classList.toggle('visible');
});
```

Fetch API

The Fetch API replaces the older XMLHttpRequest for network requests. It returns Promises that resolve to **`Response`** objects, from which you can parse JSON, text, or blobs.

The following is an example that loads JSON data and inserts it into the page:

```
fetch('/api/users')
  .then(res => res.json())
  .then(users => {
    const list = document.
    getElementById('userList'); users.
    forEach(u => {
      const li = document.
      createElement('li'); li.textContent
      = `${u.name} (${u.email})`; list.
      appendChild(li);
    });
  })
  .catch(err => console.error(err));
```

Timers

Timers schedule code execution. **setTimeout** runs a function once after a delay; **setInterval** repeats it at fixed intervals. You cancel them with **clearTimeout** or **clearInterval**.

The following is an example of a simple countdown:

```
let count = 5;
const intervalId = setInterval(() => { console.log(count);
  if (--count < 0) { clearInterval(intervalId);
    console.log('Liftoff!');
  }
}, 1000);
```

Storage

Browsers offer key–value storage via **localStorage** and **sessionStorage**. **localStorage** persists across sessions; **sessionStorage** clears when the tab closes. Both stores only store the strings.

The following is an example that saves and retrieves user preferences:

```
// Save preference
localStorage.setItem('theme', 'dark');

// Load preference
const theme = localStorage.getItem('theme') || 'light'; document.documentElement.
setAttribute('data-theme', theme);
```

DevTools

Browser DevTools integrate a JavaScript debugger, console, network inspector, and performance profiler. Use **console.log**, breakpoints, and live editing to diagnose issues and test changes instantly.

The following is an example of logging object details for debugging:

```
const user = { name: 'Alice', age: 28 }; console.log('User data:', user);
console.table([{ name: 'Alice' }, { name: 'Bob' }]);
```

Performance

Efficient rendering and responsive interfaces require careful control of animation and event handling. The browser's **requestAnimationFrame** API schedules updates at the optimal time, while debouncing and throttling prevent excessive function calls in response to rapid events.

The following presents key techniques for smooth, performant code:

- **requestAnimationFrame** for synchronized, high-performance animations.
- Debouncing to group rapid events into a single call after a delay.
- Throttling to limit a handler to at most one call per time interval.

The following code demonstrates **requestAnimationFrame** for a simple draw loop:

```
const canvas = document.querySelector('canvas');
const ctx = canvas.getContext('2d');
let x = 0;
function draw() {
  ctx.clearRect(0, 0, canvas.width, canvas.height); ctx.fillRect(x, 50, 50, 50);
```

```
  x = (x + 2) % canvas.width; requestAnimationFrame(draw);
}

requestAnimationFrame(draw);
```

The following code demonstrates a debounce helper that delays execution until events stop:

```
function debounce(fn, delay) {
  let timer;
  return (...args) => { clearTimeout(timer);
    timer = setTimeout(() => fn(...args), delay);
  };
}

const onResize = debounce(() => { console.log('Resized to', window.innerWidth);
}, 200);

window.addEventListener('resize', onResize);
```

The following demonstrates a throttle helper that ensures regular but limited calls:

```
function throttle(fn, interval) {
  let last = 0;
  return (...args) => {
    const now = Date.now();
    if (now - last >= interval) { last = now;
      fn(...args);
}
       };
}

const onScroll = throttle(() => { console.log('Scrolled to', window.scrollY);
}, 100);

window.addEventListener('scroll', onScroll);
```

JavaScript vs. other languages

JavaScript, Python, and Java each occupy distinct niches yet overlap in server- and client-side development. JavaScript pairs event-driven, asynchronous code with prototype-based objects. Python prioritizes clear syntax, rich standard libraries, and dynamic typing. Java offers static typing, strong performance via the JVM, and mature tooling for large systems.

Feature comparison

JavaScript runs in browsers and Node.js with an event loop for non-blocking I/O. Python excels in scripting, AI, and data analysis with asyncio for concurrency. Java compiles to bytecode on the JVM, leveraging threads and a robust standard API.

The following table presents a detailed comparison of various popular programming languages with respect to their usage:

Feature	JavaScript	Python	Java
Typing	Dynamic, duck typing	Dynamic, strong emphasis on readability	Static I compile-time checked
Paradigm	Functional and prototype OOP	Multi-paradigm, OOP focus	Class-based OOP
Execution model	Interpreted and JIT in engines	Interpreted (CPython)	Compiled to bytecode on JVM
Concurrency	Event loop (async/await)	Threads and asyncio	Threads and concurrency APIs
Primary use	Web I front/end I full- stack via Node.js	Scripting, data science, web back-end	Enterprise, I Android, large systems

***Table 4.2:** Features comparison of popular programming languages*

Typing model

JavaScript and Python use dynamic typing, letting variables hold any value and perform type coercion at runtime. This speeds prototyping but can introduce type errors. Java's static types catch mismatches at compile time, improving reliability in large codebases.

The following examples illustrate how different programming languages handle typing and type conversion:

- **JavaScript example**:

```
let x = '42';
x = x * 1;          // coerces to number 42
```

- **Python example**:

```
x = '42'
x = int(x)        # explicit conversion to integer
```

- **Java example**:

```
int x = Integer.parseInt("42");
// x is statically typed as int
```

Concurrency

JavaScript's single-threaded event loop handles I/O via callbacks, Promises, or async/await, avoiding thread overhead. Python supports threads and the asyncio library for cooperative multitasking. Java leverages true multithreading with synchronized blocks and high-level concurrency utilities.

The following examples demonstrate how JavaScript, Python, and Java implement concurrency and asynchronous operations using their respective mechanisms:

- **JavaScript async/await**:

```
async function fetchData() {
  const res = await fetch('/data'); const json = await res.json(); console.log(json);
}
fetchData();
```

- **Python asyncio**:

```
import asyncio, aiohttp

async def fetch():
async with aiohttp.ClientSession() as s:
async with s.get('https://api.example.com') as r: print(await r.json())
```

```
asyncio.run(fetch())
```

- **Java threads**:

```
new Thread(() -> {
  // blocking I/O here
  System.out.println("Done");
}).start();
```

Ecosystem

NPM hosts millions of JavaScript packages, focused on front-end tooling and full-stack frameworks. **Python Package Index** (**PyPI**) caters to scientific computing, web frameworks, and scripting utilities. Maven Central manages Java libraries for enterprise, mobile, and big data.

The following example demonstrates the installation process in various programming languages:

```
// JavaScript
npm install express

# Python
pip install requests

# Java (Maven)
<dependency>
  <groupId>org.springframework</groupId>
  <artifactId>spring-web</artifactId>
  <version>5.3.0</version>
</dependency>
```

Performance

JavaScript engines (V8, SpiderMonkey) use JIT compilation and hidden classes to optimize hot code paths. CPython remains interpreter-bound, though PyPy offers JIT. The JVM employs tiered compilation and garbage collection tuned for throughput or latency.

The following example demonstrates a benchmark pattern:

```
// measure loop duration console.time('loop'); for(let i=0;i<1e7;i++); console.timeEnd('loop');
```

Security fundamentals

Web applications face risks such as **cross-site scripting** (**XSS**) and unauthorized cross-origin access. Mitigating these threats requires sanitizing any user-supplied content before injecting it into the DOM, configuring CORS headers to restrict external requests, and enforcing a **Content Security Policy** (**CSP**) to limit where scripts and other resources can load from.

The following list outlines key security practices:

- Sanitize or escape user input before inserting it into the DOM to prevent XSS attacks.
- Set appropriate CORS headers (`Access-Control-Allow-Origin, Access-Control-Allow-Methods`) to control which origins may access your API.
- Use a strict CSP header to restrict script sources, disallow inline scripts, and block unauthorized resource loading.

The following demonstrates sanitizing input in the browser:

```
function sanitize(input) {
  const div = document.createElement('div'); div.appendChild(document.createTextNode(input));
  return div.innerHTML;
}
const userInput = '<img src=x onerror=alert(1)//>'; const safeHtml = sanitize(userInput);
document.getElementById('output').innerHTML = safeHtml;
```

The following code demonstrates setting CORS headers in a Node.js server:

```
res.setHeader('Access-Control-Allow-Origin', 'https://example.com'); res.setHeader('Access-Control-Allow-Methods', 'GET,POST,OPTIONS');
```

The following shows a sample CSP header:

```
Content-Security-Policy: \ default-src 'self'; \
script-src 'self' https://cdn.example.com; \ object-src 'none'
```

CSRF mitigation

Cross-Site Request Forgery (**CSRF**) tricks a user's browser into making unwanted requests. To prevent it, servers issue per-session tokens and enforce same-site cookie policies.

The following presents common CSRF defenses:

- Synchronizer token paflern includes a secret token in every state-changing form or AJAX request, and validates its server-side.
- SameSite cookies Set *SameSite=Lax* or *Strict* so cookies are not sent on cross-site navigations.
- Custom request headers: Require a custom header (e.g. *X-CSRF-Token*) which browsers would not attach on cross-site *<form>* submissions.

The following code demonstrates embedding and validating a CSRF token in a fetch request:

```
// On page render, server injects a token into a meta tag
// <meta name="csrf-token" content="abc123">

const token = document.querySelector('meta[name="csrf-token"]').content; fetch('/api/update', {
  method: 'POST', headers: {
    'Content-Type': 'application/json', 'X-CSRF-Token': token
  },
  body: JSON.stringify({ data: '...' })
});
// Server checks that `X-CSRF-Token` matches the user's session token
```

Content Security Policy reporting hooks

Besides blocking unauthorized loads, CSP can report violations back to your server. Reporting hooks enable you to monitor and fine-tune your policy in production.

The following presents a CSP header with a reporting endpoint:

```
// In your HTTP response:
Content-Security-Policy: \ default-src 'self'; \
  script-src 'self' https://cdn.example.com; \ report-to csp-endpoint

Report-To: {
  "group":"csp-endpoint", "max_age":10886400,
  "endpoints":[{"url":"https://report.example.com/csp"}]
}
```

The following code demonstrates handling a report on the server (Node.js/Express):

```
app.post('/csp', express.json(), (req, res) => { console.log('CSP violation:', req.body);
  // Log or alert based on req.body.csp-report details
  res.status(204).end();
});
```

Web Workers

Web Workers enable running computation in background threads, keeping the main **user interface (UI)** thread responsive. Workers run in their own context, cannot access the DOM directly, and communicate with the main thread via **postMessage** and **onmessage**.

The following code demonstrates a simple Web Worker implementation:

```
// worker.js
self.onmessage = function(e) {
  const n = e.data;
  let sum = 0;
  for (let i = 1; i <= n; i++) { sum += i;
  }
  postMessage(sum);
};
```

The following shows how to instantiate and use this worker from the main script:

```
// main.js
const worker = new Worker('worker.js');

worker.onmessage = function(e) { console.log('Computed sum:', e.data);
};

worker.onerror = function(err) {
  console.error('Worker error:', err.message);
};

// Offload heavy computation to the worker
worker.postMessage(1000000000);
```

Memory and closures

Closures capture variables from their outer scope, which can unintentionally keep those variables (and any referenced DOM elements or data) in memory, causing leaks. Understanding how and when to release references helps maintain a healthy memory footprint.

The following presents common leak patterns and prevention techniques:

- Timers and callbacks retaining closures beyond their useful life: always call **clearTimeout** or **clearInterval**.
- Event listeners holding onto DOM nodes after removal: remove listeners before discarding elements.
- Caches or long-lived data structures capturing large objects: use size limits or **WeakMap** to allow garbage collection.

The following code demonstrates a simple closure leak and its fix:

```
// Leak: interval callback retains the count variable forever
function startCounting() {
```

```
  let count = 0;
  const id = setInterval(() => { console.log(count++);
  }, 1000);
  // Without clearInterval(id), 'count' and the callback persist
  return id;
}

const timerId = startCounting();

// ...later, to prevent the leak:
clearInterval(timerId); // releases the closure and allows 'count' to be garbage-collected
```

Choosing the right tool

Selecting the right language hinges on project requirements and team skills. Consider the following factors:

- **Runtime environment**: Browser, server, data pipeline, or embedded system.
- **Concurrency model**: Event loop versus threads or processes.
- **Ecosystem**: Available libraries, frameworks, and community support.
- **Performance**: Throughput, latency, and resource footprint.
- **Maintainability**: Type safety, tooling, and code readability.

JavaScript excels at interactive user interfaces and real-time services. Its single-threaded event loop and async/await syntax handle I/O without blocking. The same code runs in the browser and on servers via Node.js, enabling full-stack development.

The following example demonstrates a JavaScript environment:

```
// Simple real-time server with WebSocket
import { WebSocketServer } from 'ws';
const wss = new WebSocketServer({ port: 8080 }); wss.on('connection', ws => {
  ws.on('message', msg => ws.send(`Echo: ${msg}`));
});
```

Python shines in data analysis, machine learning, and scripting. Its clear syntax and powerful libraries (like pandas and TensorFlow) speed up prototyping. The asyncio framework and multiprocessing module offer concurrency options for I/O-bound and CPU-bound tasks.

The following example demonstrates a Python environment:

```
import pandas as pd

df = pd.read_csv('data.csv')
summary = df.groupby('category').value.mean() print(summary)
```

Java provides static typing, the JVM's JIT optimizations, and mature frameworks (such as Spring Boot). It suits large-scale, high-performance back ends and Android applications. Java's thread model and concurrency utilities handle heavy workloads with predictable behavior.

The following example demonstrates a Java Spring Boot environment:

```
import org.springframework.boot.*;
import org.springframework.boot.autoconfigure.*; import org.springframework.web.bind.annotation.*;

@SpringBootApplication @RestController
public class App {
```

```
  public static void main(String[] args) { SpringApplication.run(App.class, args);
  }
  @GetMapping("/hello")
  public String hello() {
    return "Hello from Java";
  }
}
```

By evaluating environment, concurrency needs, ecosystem maturity, and performance targets, teams can choose the language that aligns best with their project goals.

Development environment

A solid development environment boosts productivity and code quality. This section covers setting up **Visual Studio Code (VS Code)**, installing Node.js for server-side scripting, and using the browser console for quick tests.

VS Code setup

VS Code is a lightweight yet powerful editor with built-in support for JavaScript.

Extensions add linting, formatting, debugging, and live reloading. Customize your workspace by tweaking settings and installing recommended plugins.

Install VS Code from the official site and then add these popular extensions:

- **ESLint**: It highlights syntax and style errors.
- **Prettier**: It enforces consistent code formatting on save.
- **Debugger for chrome/edge**: Step through code running in the browser.
- **Live Server**: It launches a local HTTP server with live reload.

Use the following code to streamline formatting and linting in your `settings.json`:

```
{
  "editor.formatOnSave": true, "editor.codeActionsOnSave": {
    "source.fixAll.eslint": true
  },
  "eslint.validate": ["javascript", "javascriptreact"],
  "files.eol": "\n"
}
```

Node.js setup

Node.js provides a runtime for executing JavaScript on the server or locally. Its package manager (**npm**) handles libraries and scripts. Install the LTS version for stability, then verify installation.

After downloading from nodejs.org and running the installer, check the following versions:

```
node -v # e.g. v18.15.0
npm -v  # e.g. 9.5.0
```

- **Initialize a new project and install dependencies**:

  ```
  mkdir my-app && cd my-app npm init -y
  npm install express      # example dependency
  ```

- **Create an entry script** index.js **and run it**:

```
// index.js
const express = require('express');
const app = express();
app.get('/', (req, res) => res.send('Hello from Node')); app.listen(3000, () => console.
log('Listening on port 3000'));
node index.js
```

Use **npx nodemon index.js** for automatic restarts on file changes.

Browser console

Every modern browser includes a JavaScript console for testing snippets, inspecting variables, and debugging. You can run code instantly or embed scripts in HTML files served by Live Server or a local HTTP server.

Open Developer Tools (*F12* or *Ctrl+Shift+I*) and switch to the **Console** tab. Enter any statement, for example:

```
console.log('Hello, JavaScript!');
// Define a function and invoke it function multiply(a, b) { return a * b; } console.
log(multiply(6, 7)); // 42
```

To test modules in the browser, serve an HTML file with **type="module"**:

```
<!DOCTYPE html>
<html lang="en">
<head>
  <meta charset="UTF-8">
  <title>Module Test</title>
</head>
<body>
  <script type="module">
    import { greet } from './
    greet.js'; greet('World');
  </script>
</body>
</html>
```

Use the Live Server extension or **npx http-server** to avoid CORS issues when importing modules.

Debugging

Browser DevTools provide a full-featured debugger that lets you pause execution, step through code, inspect variables, and profile performance. You can also insert the **debugger** statement directly into your code to trigger a breakpoint.

The following code demonstrates the **debugger** statement:

```
function calculate(a, b) {
  debugger; // execution will pause here when DevTools is open
  return a + b;
}

calculate(2, 3);
```

The following list presents key DevTools debugging tools:

- **Breakpoints**: Set in the Sources panel or via the debugger statement.
- **Step controls**: Step over, step into, and step out of functions.

- **Watch expressions**: Monitor specific variables or expressions as you debug.
- **Call stack**: View the chain of function calls that led to the current line.
- **Scope panel**: Inspect local, closure, and global variables at a breakpoint.
- **Performance profiler**: Record JavaScript and rendering performance to identify bottlenecks.
- **Network inspector**: See exactly which resources load when, their timing, and payload sizes.

Testing basics

Automated testing helps catch regressions early and ensures code works as intended. For quick sanity checks, use **`console.assert`** in development. For more comprehensive coverage, popular frameworks like **Jest** and **Mocha** enable unit and integration tests with rich reporting.

The following demonstrates using **`console.assert`** for lightweight checks:

```
// This assertion passes silently
console.assert(2 + 2 === 4, 'Math is broken');

// This assertion fails and logs the message
console.assert(2 + 2 === 5, 'Expected 2 + 2 to equal 5');
```

The following lists some common JavaScript testing frameworks:

- **Jest**: Batteries-included, snapshot testing, and built-in coverage.
- **Mocha**: Flexible test runner often paired with Chai for assertions.
- **Jasmine**: Standalone framework with spies and mocks.
- **AVA**: Minimalistic, concurrent test runner.

Package management and scripts

The **`package.json`** file defines project metadata, dependencies, and custom scripts. Using the **`scripts`** section, you can centralize commands, for example, building, linting, testing, and running a development server, and invoke them with **`npm run <name>.`**

The following presents a sample **`package.json`** configuration:

```
{
  "name": "my-app",
  "version": "1.0.0",
  "scripts": {
    "dev": "vite",
    "start": "node dist/server.js", "build": "webpack --mode production", "lint": "eslint
    'src/**/*.{js,jsx}'", "test": "jest"
  },
  "dependencies": {
    "react": "^18.0.0"
  },
  "devDependencies": {
    "vite": "^4.0.0",
    "webpack": "^5.0.0",
    "eslint": "^8.0.0",
    "jest": "^29.0.0"
  }
}
```

The following list demonstrates how to run these scripts from the command line:

- **npm run dev**: Start the development server with hot reload.
- **npm run build**: Produce production-ready bundles.
- **npm run lint**: Check code style and catch errors early.
- **npm run test**: Execute the test suite with Jest.

Key points to remember

This section distills the most important concepts and techniques you have seen so far. It reinforces how JavaScript enables dynamic interfaces, modern syntax features, DOM manipulation, language trade-offs, and the tools that streamline your workflow.

Dynamic web applications

JavaScript powers interactive interfaces by responding to user actions and updating page content without full reloads. Event listeners capture clicks, form submissions, and other events to modify the DOM or fetch new data.

The following demonstrates a button click that reveals hidden content:

```
<button id="showBtn">Show Details</button>
<div id="details" style="display:none;">Here are the details...</div>
<script> document.getElementById('showBtn')
    .addEventListener('click', () => {
      const d = document.getElementById('details');
      d.style.display = d.style.display === 'none' ? 'block' : 'none';
    });
</script>
```

Modern features

ES6 and later editions introduced syntax and APIs that streamline code, reduce errors, and support asynchronous workflows. Block-scoped declarations, concise arrow functions, template literals, and async/await improve readability and maintainability.

The following demonstrates let, const, arrow functions, template literals, and **`async`/`await`**:

```
const fetchUser = async id => {
  let response = await fetch(`/api/users/${id}`); let user = await response.json(); console.
  log(`User ${user.name}, age ${user.age}`);
};

let userId = 5; fetchUser(userId);
```

DOM interactions

The DOM API exposes page elements as a tree of nodes. Scripts can query, create, update, or remove elements dynamically. Efficient updates and batching (via document fragments) prevent layout thrashing.

The following demonstrates creating, updating, and removing list items:

```
// Create new list item
const ul = document.querySelector('ul'); const newLi = document.createElement('li'); newLi.
textContent = 'Dynamic item'; ul.appendChild(newLi);
```

```
// Update the first item
ul.firstElementChild.textContent = 'First item (edited)';

// Remove the last item
ul.removeChild(ul.lastElementChild);
```

Tooling

Modern JavaScript development relies on editors, linters, formatters, and runtime environments. VS Code, Node.js, and browser DevTools form a powerful toolchain for writing, testing, and debugging code.

The following points highlight essential tools and extensions:

- VS Code with ESLint, Prettier, and Live Server.
- Node.js (LTS) and npm or yarn for package management.
- Browser DevTools (Elements, Console, Network, Performance).
- Bundlers and task runners like Webpack, Rollup, or Vite.
- Transpilers like Babel for backward compatibility.

Statements and expressions

JavaScript programs consist of statements that direct the engine to perform actions and expressions that evaluate values. Understanding their distinction helps write clear, predictable code and leverage the language's flexibility, such as embedding expressions in conditional tests or function arguments.

Note: A statement instructs JavaScript to execute an action, such as declaring variables or control-ling flow. An expression computes a value and can be embedded inside statements.

Statements

Statements form the building blocks of control flow and declarations. They include variable declarations (**`let`**, **`const`**, **`var`**), control flow statements (**`if`**, **`else`**, **`switch`**, **`for`**, **`while`**), declaration statements (**`function`**, **`class`**), block statements (**`{...}`**), and expression statements (standalone expressions like function calls). Statements do not themselves produce values to their surrounding code, and they cannot be used in places where an expression is expected.

The following demonstrates various statement types:

```
// Variable declaration
let count = 0;

// Conditional statement
if (count < 5) { count++;
} else { count = 0;
}

// Function declaration
function greet(name) { console.log('Hello, ' + name);
}

// Loop statement
for (let i = 0; i < 3; i++) { greet('User' + i);
}
```

Expressions

Expressions produce values and can appear wherever JavaScript expects one. They range from simple literals and arithmetic operations to function calls, arrow functions, and object or array literals. Since expressions return values, they can be used in assignments, as arguments, or inside other expressions, enabling concise and flexible code.

The following demonstrates a variety of expressions:

```
// Literal expressions
42
"hello"

// Arithmetic expression
let sum = 5 + 7;
// Function call expression
console.log(sum);

// Arrow function expression
const square = x => x * x;

// Object and array expressions
let user = { name: "Alice", age: 30 };
let numbers = [1, 2, 3].map(n => n * 2);

// Ternary expression
let status = count > 0 ? 'active' : 'inactive';
```

Comparison

Statements and expressions serve different roles but often intermingle and intermix. Recognizing which constructs return values and which direct control flow is key to writing valid and idiomatic JavaScript.

The following table presents a comparison of statements and expressions:

Attribute	Statements	Expressions
Definition	Instruct the engine to perform actions	Compute and return a value
Return value	No	Yes
Examples	**`if`**, **`for`**, **`let`**, **`function`**	**`42`**, **`a + b`**, **`func()`**, **`x => x*2`**
Usage	Standalone lines in code	Within assignments, arguments, or other expressions

Table 4.3: *Comparison of statements and expressions in JavaScript*

Comments in JavaScript

Comments improve code readability, document intent, and assist team collaboration. JavaScript supports several comment styles to annotate logic, disable code for testing, and generate external documentation.

Note: JavaScript provides single-line comments, multi-line comments, and JSDoc comments for structured documentation.

Purpose

Comments explain non-obvious code, mark future tasks, and supply metadata for documentation tools. They help new maintainers understand intent, facilitate debugging by disabling code sections, and enable automatic API reference generation.

The following presents common uses for comments:

- Clarify complex algorithms or business-logic.
- Indicate TODO and FIXME items.
- Temporarily disable code during debugging.
- Provide structured data for documentation generators (JSDoc).

Types

JavaScript supports three comment styles, which include brief notes, detailed explanations, and API documentation, and each is suited to different needs.

The following presents a comparison of comment styles:

Style	Syntax	Use case
Single-line comment	`// comment`	Brief notes, disabling code lines
Multi-line comment	`/* ... */`	Detailed explanations
JSDoc comment	`/** ... */`	API docs, parameter/type annotations

Table 4.4: *Comparison of comment styles in JavaScript*

Single-line

Single-line comments begin with `//` and extend to the end of the line. They are ideal for inline notes and quickly disabling a statement.

The following demonstrates single-line comments:

```
// Initialize counter
let count = 0;

// Increment when button clicked
button.addEventListener('click', () => count++);
```

Multi-line

Multi-line comments start with `/*` and end with `*/`. They accommodate longer descriptions spanning several lines.

The following demonstrates multi-line comments:

```
/*
  Function: calculateTotal Parameters:
    - prices: array of numbers
    - taxRate: decimal
  Returns the sum of prices plus tax.
*/
function calculateTotal(prices, taxRate) {
  // ...
}
```

Documentation

JSDoc comments (`/** ... */`) annotate function signatures, parameters, return types, and other metadata. Tools like JSDoc or TypeScript can generate HTML documentation from these comments.

The following demonstrates a JSDoc comment:

```
/**
  * Calculates the area of a rectangle.
  * @param {number} width  - The rectangle's width.
  * @param {number} height - The rectangle's height.
  * @returns {number} The computed area.
  */
function getArea(width, height) {
  return width * height;
}
```

Best practices

Effective comments are concise, up-to-date, and avoid restating obvious code. Focus on *why* rather than *what*, and remove or update comments when the code changes. Use JSDoc for public APIs and line/block comments for implementation details.

The following presents best practices for commenting:

- Explain rationale, not code mechanics.
- Keep comments synchronized with code changes.
- Use TODOs sparingly and track them in issue trackers.
- Leverage JSDoc for generating external documentation.

Variables

Variables store and track data in JavaScript. They enable programs to remember values, perform computations, and manage state across functions and blocks. ECMAScript defines three declaration keywords, like **`var`**, **`let`**, and **`const`**, each with its own scoping, hoisting, and mutability rules.

Note: JavaScript provides three keywords for declaring variables: Following are their key behaviors:

- **var: Function-scoped, hoisted, allows redeclaration and reassignment.**
- **let: Block-scoped, hoisted into a temporal dead zone, disallows redeclaration in the same scope, allows reassignment.**
- **const: Block-scoped, hoisted into a temporal dead zone, disallows redeclaration, requires initialization, prohibits reassignment.**

Declaration

Variable declarations define identifiers and optionally assign initial values. Choosing the correct keyword prevents unintended scope leaks or accidental constant mutation. Use **`const`** by default for values that should not change, **`let`** for reassignable variables, and reserve **`var`** for legacy patterns.

The following demonstrates basic declarations:

```
var a = 10;           // function-scoped, can be redeclared
let b = 20;           // block-scoped, cannot redeclare in same block
const c = 30; // block-scoped, must initialize, cannot reassign
```

Scope

Scope determines where a variable is accessible. **var** creates a variable in the enclosing function or global scope, while **let** and **const** restrict visibility to the enclosing block (between {} braces). Proper scoping avoids name collisions and ensures predictable lifetimes.

The following demonstrates scope differences:

```
function demo() {
  var x = 1; let y = 2; if (true) {
    var x = 3;  // same x as above
    let y = 4;          // new y in this block
    console.log(x, y); // 3, 4
  }
  console.log(x, y);   // 3, 2
}
```

Hoisting

Hoisting moves declarations to the top of their scope at runtime. **var** declarations hoist the name but leave the initialization in place, resulting in **undefined** if accessed early. **let** and **const** also hoist names, but remain inaccessible until the declaration is evaluated, creating a *temporal dead zone* that throws a **ReferenceError** if accessed beforehand.

The following demonstrates hoisting behavior:

```
console.log(a); // undefined
var a = 5;

console.log(b); // ReferenceError
let b = 6;
```

Comparison

You can compare the three declaration keywords across scope, redeclaration, and reassignment rules. Understanding these distinctions prevents subtle bugs and aids maintainable code design. The following table presents a comparison of **var**, **let**, and **const**:

Keyword	Scope	Redeclaration	Reassignment
var	Function	Yes	Yes
let	Block	No	Yes
const	Block	No	No

Table 4.5: *Comparison of variable declaration keywords*

Data types in JavaScript

JavaScript values fall into two categories—primitive types, which represent single immutable values, and reference types, which handle collections and complex structures. Knowing how each type behaves, especially with respect to equality, copying, and memory, helps write reliable code.

Primitive types

Primitive values are immutable and compared by value. They include basic data units and unique identifiers. ES2020 added **`BigInt`** to handle integers beyond the safe **`Number`** range.

The following lists JavaScript's primitive types:

- **String**: Text data, e.g., **`"hello"`**.
- **Number**: Floating-point values, e.g., **`42, 3.14`**.
- **BigInt**: Arbitrary-precision integers, e.g., **`9007199254740991n`**.
- **Boolean**: Logical values **`true`** or **`false`**.
- **Undefined**: Variables declared but not assigned.
- **Null**: Intentional absence of any object value.
- **Symbol**: Unique, immutable identifiers.

The following demonstrates primitive declarations:

```
let name = "Alice";          // String
let age = 25;
// Number let big =
9007199254740991n;   //
BigInt let isValid =
true;        // Boolean
let notSet;                          // Undefined
let empty = null;                    // Null
let key = Symbol("key");   // Symbol
```

Reference types

Reference types are objects that store collections or complex data. Variables hold references to these objects, not the object itself. Modifying a referenced object affects all its references.

The following lists common reference types:

- **Object**: Unordered key–value pairs.
- **Array**: Ordered lists of values.
- **Function**: Callable blocks of code (first-class objects).
- **Date**: Date and time objects.
- **Map and set**: Collections of keyed or unique values.

The following demonstrates reference type usage:

```
let person = { name: "Alice", age: 25 };              // Object let numbers = [1, 2, 3, 4];
// Array function greet() { return "Hello!"; }        // Function let now = new Date(); // Date
let idMap = new Map([["a", 1], ["b", 2]]);            // Map
let uniqueSet = new Set([1,2,3]);                     // Set
```

Date and time

JavaScript's built-in **`Date`** object represents a moment in time as milliseconds since the Unix epoch. It supports multiple constructors and methods for parsing, manipulating, and formatting dates, but developers must beware of timezone quirks and inconsistent parsing. The modern **`Intl.DateTimeFormat`** API offers robust, locale-aware formatting.

The following presents the various date constructor forms:

Syntax	Description
`new Date()`	Current date and time
`new Date(ms)`	UTC date at **ms** milliseconds since epoch
`new Date(dateString)`	Parses an ISO-formatted string
`new Date(yyyy, m-1, d, h, m, s, ms)`	Local date from components

Table 4.6: Date constructor variants

The following demonstrates common **Date** usage and **Intl** formatting:

```
// Constructing dates
const now          = new Date();
const epoch        = new Date(0);
const isoDate      = new Date('2021-05-01T12:00:00Z');
const localDate = new Date(2021, 4, 1, 12, 0, 0);

// Parsing and conversion
console.log(now.toISOString());                // e.g. "2025-06-16T14:23:30.123Z"
console.log(now.toString());                   // Locale string with timezone

// Beware: Date.parse is implementation-dependent
console.log(Date.parse('2021/05/01'));          // May differ across engines

// Intl.DateTimeFormat for locale-aware output
const formatter = new Intl.DateTimeFormat('en-GB', { dateStyle: 'full',
  timeStyle: 'long', timeZone: 'Europe/London'
});
console.log(formatter.format(now));            // e.g. "Monday, 16 June 2025 at 15:23:30 GMT+1"
```

Type checking

JavaScript's **typeof** operator and structural checks help distinguish types. Be aware that **typeof null** returns **"object"**, a legacy quirk, and that arrays require **Array.isArray**.

The following table presents type inspection methods:

Expression	Result	Notes
typeof "text"	**"string"**	—
typeof 123	**"number"**	—
typeof 1n	**"bigint"**	ES2020
typeof true	**"boolean"**	—
typeof undefined	**"undefined"**	—
typeof null	**"object"**	Legacy quirk
Array.isArray([])	**true**	Detects arrays
myMap instanceof Map	**true**	Detects Map instances

Table 4.7: Common type checking expressions

Regular expressions

Regular expressions (**regex**) are patterns used to match character combinations in strings. JavaScript's regex literals start and end with slashes, with optional flags to modify behavior. Common methods like **`test()`**, **`exec()`**, **`String.prototype.match()`**, **`replace()`**, and **`split()`** let you validate, parse, search, and transform text efficiently.

The following table presents the most-used regex flags:

Flag	Description
`g`	Global match (find all)
`i`	Case-insensitive match
`m`	Multiline anchors (^ and $)
`u`	Unicode; full code point support
`y`	Sticky; matches at lastIndex only
`s`	Dotall; . matches newline

Table 4.8: *Common regex flags*

The following demonstrates regex creation and the core methods:

```
// literal with flags
const re = /ab\d+/gi;

// test() returns true/false
console.log(re.test('AB123')); // true

// exec() returns match details re.lastIndex = 0; console.log(re.exec('xxAb123yy'));
// ["Ab123"], index: 2, input: "xxAb123yy"

// match() on string
const hits = ‚ab1 AB2 ab3'.match(/ab\d/gi); console.log(hits); // [„ab1","AB2","ab3"]

// replace() to transform
const clean = '2021-04-30'.replace(/-(\d{2})-/g, '/$1/'); console.log(clean); // "2021/04/30"

// split() on pattern
const parts = 'one,two;three|four'.split(/[,;|]/); console.log(parts); //
["one","two","three","four"]
```

Type conversion and coercion

JavaScript often needs to reconcile values of different types during operations. When you explicitly convert a value, you control the process; when the engine coerces a value, it does so according to built-in rules. Mastering both helps avoid bugs and write clear, predictable code.

Note: Type Conversion (casting) happens when you explicitly invoke built-in functions such as `Number()`, `String()`, or `Boolean()`. Type Coercion occurs when JavaScript quietly converts values during operations, for example, turning "5" into 5 when you subtract.

Explicit conversion

When you need a guaranteed type, use explicit conversion. This ensures your values are exactly what you expect before performing calculations, concatenations, or logical checks. Common functions include **`String()`**, **`Number()`**, **`parseInt()`**, **`parseFloat()`**, and **`Boolean()`**.

The following presents common explicit conversion methods:

- **Convert to string: `String(value)` or `value.toString()`**
- **Convert to number: `Number(value)`, `parseInt(value, 10)`, `parseFloat(value)`**
- **Convert to boolean: `Boolean(value)`**

The following demonstrates explicit conversions and a parseInt radix example:

```
// String to number
let s = "42";
let n = Number(s);                    // n === 42 (number)
console.log(typeof n, n);


// Number to string
let a = 100;
let str = String(a);                  // str === "100"
console.log(typeof str, str);


// To integer with radix
let oct = parseInt("08", 10); // always decimal: 8
console.log(oct);


// To boolean
let flag = Boolean(0);                // 0 is falsy, so flag === false
console.log(flag);
```

Implicit coercion

JavaScript applies coercion when values of different types mix in expressions. Understanding these rules prevents surprising results and helps you write more resilient code. Coercion occurs in arithmetic, concatenation, comparisons, and logical contexts.

The following presents common implicit coercion scenarios:

- **String concatenation**: "5" + 3 □ "53"
- **Numeric operations**: "5" - 3 □ 2
- **Boolean contexts**: values convert based on truthiness in if or logical operators
- **Arithmetic with non-numeric strings**: produces NaN

The following demonstrates implicit coercion and **`NaN`**:

```
// Concatenation coerces to string
let r1 = "5" + 3;           // "53"

// Subtraction coerces to number
let r2 = "5" - 3;           // 2
```

```
// Non-numeric arithmetic yields NaN
let r3 = "foo" * 2; // NaN

// Truthy and falsy checks
if ("hello") console.log("truthy");                // runs
if (0) console.log("won't run"); else console.log("falsy"); // "falsy"
```

Falsy values

Certain values coerce to **false** in boolean contexts. Knowing them helps avoid logic errors in conditionals and loops.

The following presents common falsy values:

Value	Description
false	Boolean false
0	Numeric zero
""	Empty string
null	Null value
undefined	Undefined variable
NaN	Not a Number

Table 4.9: JavaScript falsy values

JavaScript treats all other values as truthy, including non-empty strings, non-zero numbers, objects, and symbols.

Understanding explicit conversion and implicit coercion together allows you to write code that behaves consistently, avoiding pitfalls like unintended string concatenation or unexpected **NaN** results.

JavaScript operators

Operators perform actions on one or more operands and return a result. JavaScript categorizes operators into arithmetic, comparison, logical, assignment, and bitwise groups. Mastering these operators—and understanding their precedence and type coercion rules—enables concise, expressive, and bug-free code.

Arithmetic operators

Arithmetic operators execute mathematical calculations on numeric values. Beyond the basic addition, subtraction, multiplication, division, and modulus, JavaScript supports exponentiation, unary operations, and increment/decrement operators. Be mindful that non-numeric operands will be coerced to numbers when possible, which can sometimes yield **NaN**.

The following demonstrates common arithmetic operators:

```
// Basic operations
```

let sum	= 10 + 5;	// 15
let diff	= 10 - 5;	// 5
let prod	= 10 * 5;	// 50
let quot	= 10 / 5;	// 2
let rem	= 10 % 3;	// 1

```
// Advanced operations
```

`let pow`	`= 2 ** 3;`	`// 8 (exponentiation)`
`let neg`	`= -sum;`	`// -15 (unary negation)`
`let incPrefix`	`= ++sum;`	`// sum becomes 16, returns 16`
`let decPostfix`	`= sum--;`	`// returns 16, then sum becomes 15`

Comparison operators

Comparison operators evaluate relationships between two values and return a Boolean. Loose equality (`==`, `!=`) coerces types before comparison, while strict equality (`===`, `!==`) requires identical type and value. Relational operators (`>`, `<`, `>=`, `<=`) compare numeric or string values based on lexicographic or numeric ordering.

The following demonstrates comparison operators:

`let looseEq`	`= (10 == "10");`	`// true (coerced comparison)`
`let strictEq`	`= (10 === "10");`	`// false (different types)`
`let notEqual`	`= (10 != "10");`	`// false`
`let strictNe`	`= (10 !== "10");`	`// true`
`let greater`	`= (10 > 5);`	`// true`
`let lessOrEq`	`= (5 <= 5);`	`// true`

Logical operators

Logical operators combine Boolean values or expressions. The AND operator (**&&**) returns the first falsy operand or the last truthy one, while the OR operator (`||`) returns the first truthy operand or the last falsy one. The NOT operator (`!`) inverts a Boolean value. Logical operators use short-circuit evaluation, which can skip evaluating parts of the expression.

The following demonstrates logical operators and short-circuit behavior:

```
let andRes = true && false;             // false let orRes = true || false;         // true let
notRes = !true;                         // false

// Short-circuit examples
function foo() { console.log('foo'); return true; }
let v1 = false && foo();                // foo() not called, v1 is false
let v2 = true || foo();                 // foo() not called, v2 is true
```

Assignment operators

Assignment operators set or update variable values. The simple assignment (`=`) assigns the right-hand value to the left-hand variable. Compound assignment operators combine an operation with assignment (`+=`, `-=`, `*=`, `/=`, `%=`, `**=`) for concise updates.

The following demonstrates assignment operators:

`let x = 10;`	`// basic assignment`	
`x += 5;`	`// equivalent to x = x + 5`	→ 15
`x **= 2;`	`// x = x ** 2`	→ 225
`x -= 10;`	`// x = x - 10`	→ 215
`x %= 7;`	`// x = x % 7`	→ 5

Bitwise operators

Bitwise operators treat their operands as 32-bit integers and perform bit-level operations. AND (**&**), OR (**|**), XOR (**^**), and NOT (**~**) operate on each bit. Shift operators (**<<**, **>>**, **>>>**) move bits left or right, with signed or zero-fill modes.

The following demonstrates bitwise operations:

let a	= 5;	// binary: 000...0101
let b	= 1;	// binary: 000...0001

let and	= a & b;	// 1	(0001)
let or	= a | b;	// 5	(0101)
let xor	= a ^ b;	// 4	(0100)
let notA	= ~a;	// -6	(two's complement)

```
let shl  = a << 1; // 10  (1010)
let shr  = a >> 1; // 2          (0010, sign-propagating)
let ushr = a >>> 1;// 2          (0010, zero-fill)
```

Conditional statements

Conditional statements control which code runs based on evaluated expressions. They form the basis of branching logic, allowing programs to respond differently to varying inputs or states. JavaScript offers several constructs—**if**, **else**, **else if**, and **switch**—to cover simple tests and complex multi-way decisions.

Note: JavaScript provides the following conditional constructs:
- **if executes a block when its condition is truthy.**
- **else supplies an alternative when the if condition is falsy.**
- **else if tests additional conditions in sequence.**
- **switch evaluates one expression against multiple case values.**

If statement

The simplest branching structure, the **if** statement, evaluates a Boolean expression. If the expression yields true, the subsequent code block executes. Conditions coerce non-Boolean values—only **false**, **0**, **""**, **null**, **undefined**, and **NaN** count as falsy; everything else is truthy. Always use braces to avoid unintended behavior when adding lines later.

The following demonstrates an **if** statement checking voting eligibility:

```
let age = 18;
if (age >= 18) {
  console.log("You are eligible to vote.");
}
```

If else statement

The **if else** construct introduces a fallback path. When the **if** condition is false, the code inside the **else** block runs. This pattern ensures one of two exclusive branches executes. Use **else** sparingly; if you find many **else if** clauses, consider **switch** or lookup tables for clarity.

The following demonstrates an **if else** statement for voting age:

```
let age = 16;
if (age >= 18) { console.log("You can vote.");
} else {
  console.log("You are too young to vote.");
}
```

If else if statement

When you need to test several conditions in order, use an **if**, followed by one or more **else if** clauses, and an optional **else** at the end. JavaScript evaluates each condition in sequence and runs only the first matching block. Use **else if** for mutually exclusive ranges or categories.

The following demonstrates grading logic with **if else if**:

```
let score = 85;
if (score >= 90) { console.log("Grade A");
} else if (score >= 75) { console.log("Grade B");
} else if (score >= 60) {
  console.log("Grade C");
} else { console.log("Grade D");
}
```

Switch statement

The **switch** statement selects one of many branches based on a single expression's value. It compares using strict equality (===) and executes the matching `case` block. Without a **break**, execution *falls through* to subsequent cases. Always include a **default** case to handle unexpected values. The following demonstrates a **switch** statement for weekdays:

```
let day = "Monday";
switch (day) {
  case "Monday":
    console.log("Start of the work week.");
    break;
  case "Friday": console.log("Weekend is near!"); break;
  case "Saturday":
  case "Sunday":
    console.log("Enjoy the weekend!");
    break; default:
    console.log("Regular day.");
}
```

Loops in JavaScript

Loops execute a block of code repeatedly, enabling you to process collections, perform calculations, and manage asynchronous tasks in a controlled manner. JavaScript provides several loop constructs: **for**, **while**, and do … while—each suited to different scenarios. Understanding their syntax, behavior, and control mechanisms helps write efficient, maintainable code.

Note: JavaScript's main loop types are:
for – repeat a known number of times.
while – repeat while a condition remains true.
do … while – execute once, then repeat while a condition remains true.

For loop

The **for** loop initializes a counter, checks the condition before each iteration, and updates the counter after each pass. Use it when you know exactly how many times to run the loop, such as iterating through arrays or generating sequences. You can control flow inside the loop with **break** (exit early) and **continue** (skip to next iteration), and even nest loops for multi-dimensional data.

The following demonstrates a basic for loop iterating five times:

```
for (let i = 1; i <= 5; i++) { console.log("Iteration:", i);
}
```

The following demonstrates using break and continue inside a for loop:

```
for (let i = 1; i <= 5; i++) {
  if (i === 3) continue; // skip when i is 3 if (i === 5) break;  // exit when i is 5 console.
  log("Value:", i);
}
// Output: 1, 2, 4
```

The following demonstrates a nested for loop for matrix-like iteration:

```
for (let row = 1; row <= 3; row++) {
  for (let col = 1; col <= 3; col++) { console.log(`Cell [${row},${col}]`);
  }
}
// Outputs coordinates of a 3×3 grid
```

While loop

The **while** loop evaluates its condition before each iteration, running as long as the condition remains truthy. It is ideal when the number of iterations is unknown in advance, such as reading from a data stream or awaiting user input. Always ensure the loop's condition will eventually become false to avoid infinite loops.

The following demonstrates a basic **while** loop:

```
let count = 1;
while (count <= 5) { console.log("Count:", count); count++;
}
```

The following demonstrates a sentinel-controlled **while** loop and how to avoid infinite repetition:

```
let input;
const valid = ["yes","no"];
while (!valid.includes(input)) {
  input = prompt("Enter yes or no").toLowerCase();
}
// Loop ends once user enters a valid response
```

Do while loop

The **do … while** loop guarantees that its body executes at least once before checking the condition. Use it when an initial action must occur (for example, prompting a user) before deciding whether to repeat.

The following demonstrates a basic **do … while** loop:

```
let num = 1;
do {
  console.log("Number:", num); num++;
} while (num <= 5);
```

The following compares **`while`** and **`do ... while`**, highlighting that **`do ... while`** always runs once:

```
// Condition false initially
let x = 10;
while (x < 5) { console.log("Won't run");
}
do {
  console.log("Runs once");
} while (x < 5);
// Outputs: "Runs once"
```

Iteration protocols

Iteration protocols let you loop over any object that implements the iterator interface. Built-in constructs like arrays and strings expose a default iterator via **`[Symbol.iterator]`**, which powers **`for…of`** loops. By contrast, **`for…in`** walks object keys, and array-specific methods such as **`forEach()`** provide a functional style. You can even create your own iterable by defining a **`[Symbol.iterator]`** method.

The following lists the main iteration techniques:

- **for…in**: It iterates over the enumerable property names of an object.
- **for…of**: It iterates over the values produced by an iterable (arrays, strings, Maps, Sets, etc.).
- **Array.prototype.forEach**: It calls a callback for each array element.
- **Iterator interface**: Any object with a **`[Symbol.iterator]()`** method returning an object with a **`next()`** method.

The following demonstrates **`for…in vs for…of vs forEach()`**:

```
// for…in over keys
const obj = { a: 1, b: 2 };
for (let key in obj) { console.log(key); // 'a', 'b'
}

// for…of over values
const arr = [10, 20];
for (let value of arr) { console.log(value); // 10, 20
}

// forEach over elements
arr.forEach((v, i) => console.log(i, v));
// 0 10
// 1 20
```

The following shows how to build a custom iterable using the iterator protocol:

```
// Define an iterable that yields 1, 2, 3 then stops
const counter = { [Symbol.iterator]() {
    let i = 1;
```

```
        return { next() {
            if (i <= 3) {
              return { value: i++, done: false };
            } else {
              return { done: true };
            }
          }
        };
    }
};

    for (let n of counter) { console.log(n); // 1, 2, 3
    }
```

Loop control

Loop control statements let you alter the normal iteration flow. The **break** statement exits a loop immediately, while **continue** skips the rest of the current iteration and proceeds to the next one.

Both can be used with labels to affect outer loops. Proper use of these statements can simplify complex loops, but overuse may reduce readability.

break statement

The **break** statement stops loop execution and transfers control to the first statement following the loop. In nested loops, prefixing `break` with a label allows you to exit an outer loop from within an inner loop. Use labeled breaks sparingly, only when they genuinely simplify the logic. The following demonstrates a simple **break** exiting a **for** loop:

```
for (let i = 1; i <= 10; i++) {
  if (i === 5) {
    break; // Exits loop when i equals 5
  }
  console.log(i);
}
// Output: 1 2 3 4
```

The following demonstrates a labeled **break** exiting an outer loop:

```
// Label the outer loop
outer:
for (let i = 1; i <= 3; i++) {
  for (let j = 1; j <= 3; j++) {
    if (i * j > 4) {
      break outer; // Exit both loops
    }
    console.log(i, j);
  }
}
// Output: 1 1, 1 2, 1 3, 2 1
```

continue statement

The **continue** statement skips the remaining code in the current iteration and jumps directly to the loop's next cycle. When used with a label, **continue** can skip iterations of an outer loop. This helps avoid deeply nested **if** statements and clarifies intent by isolating the cases you want to process.

The following demonstrates **continue skipping** a specific iteration:

```
for (let i = 1; i <= 5; i++) {
  if (i === 3) {
    continue; // Skip logging when i equals 3
  }
  console.log(i);
}
// Output: 1 2 4 5
```

The following demonstrates a labeled **continue** in nested loops:

```
outer:
for (let i = 1; i <= 3; i++) {
  for (let j = 1; j <= 3; j++) {
    if ((i + j) % 2 === 0) {
      continue outer; // Skip to next i when sum is even
    }
    console.log(i, j);
  }
}
// Output: 1 2, 2 1, 2 3, 3 2
```

Functions

Functions in JavaScript are first-class values that encapsulate reusable logic. They can be declared, assigned, passed around, and invoked dynamically. Understanding their forms, scope, and behavior, especially with respect to this, hoisting, and closures, is essential for building modular, maintainable code.

Definition and invocation

A function groups statements and returns a value when invoked. Parameters receive input, and the return value passes output back to the caller. Every invocation creates a new execution context with its own **arguments** object and local variables.

The following demonstrates a named function declaration and invocation:

```
// Function declaration
function greet(name) {
  return `Hello, ${name}!`;
}

// Invocation
console.log(greet("Alice")); // Hello, Alice!
```

Declaration and expression

JavaScript supports two primary forms for defining functions. Declarations are hoisted, allowing calls before their definition. Expressions assign functions to variables and are not hoisted, requiring definition before use.

The following presents distinguishing features:

- **Function declaration**:
  - Named function available throughout its scope.
  - Hoisted and can be called before the definition.
- **Function expression**:
  - Can be anonymous or named.
  - Not hoisted and must be defined before invocation.
  - Useful for callbacks and IIFEs.

The following demonstrates both forms:

```
// Declaration
function add(a, b) {
  return a + b;
}
console.log(add(2, 3)); // 5


// Expression
const multiply = function(a, b) {
  return a * b;
};
console.log(multiply(4, 5)); // 20
```

Arrow functions

Arrow functions provide concise syntax and lexical `this`. They implicitly return expressions in their single-expression form and cannot be used as constructors.

The following demonstrates arrow syntax variants:

```
// Single-expression
const square = x => x * x;

// Multiple parameters
const sum = (a, b) => a + b;

// Block body with explicit return
const diff = (a, b) => { const result = a - b; return result;
};

console.log(square(5), sum(2,3), diff(5,2)); // 25 5 3
```

Parameters

Functions accept parameters for input. JavaScript supports default, rest, and the legacy **`arguments`** object. Defaults provide fallbacks; rest gathers extra arguments into an array.

The following presents parameter types:

- Default parameters assign a value when an argument is **undefined**.

- Rest parameters **(...args)** collect remaining arguments into an array.
- **arguments** object provides all arguments in non-arrow functions.

The following demonstrates parameter usage:

```
// Defaults
function greet(name = "Guest") { console.log(`Hello, ${name}!`);
}
greet(); // Hello, Guest!

// Rest
function join(separator, ...items) {
  return items.join(separator);
}
console.log(join(", ", "a","b","c")); // "a, b, c"

// arguments object
function legacy() { console.log(arguments[0], arguments[1]);
}
legacy("x", "y"); // "x" "y"
```

Closures

Closures give inner functions access to variables in their defining scope, even after the outer function has returned. They enable data privacy and factory patterns.

The following demonstrates a closure for a private counter:

```
function makeCounter() {
  let count = 0;
  return function() { count += 1; return count;
  };
}

const counter = makeCounter();
console.log(counter(), counter(), counter()); // 1 2 3
```

Recursion

A function can call itself to solve problems by breaking them into smaller subproblems. Ensure a base case to terminate recursion.

The following demonstrates recursive solutions:

```
// Factorial
function factorial(n) {
  return (n <= 1) ? 1 : n * factorial(n - 1);
}
console.log(factorial(5)); // 120

// Fibonacci
function fib(n) {
  return (n < 2) ? n : fib(n - 1) + fib(n - 2);
}
console.log(fib(6)); // 8
```

Methods and bind

When functions are methods of objects, **this** refers to the calling object. **bind**, **call**, and **apply** control **this** and argument passing.

The following presents method invocation and binding:

```
const obj = { x: 10 };
function show() { console.log(this.x);
}

// As method obj.show = show; obj.show(); // 10

// As standalone const f = obj.show; f(); // undefined// bind
const bound = show.bind(obj); bound(); // 10
```

The following table presents call vs apply vs. bind:

Method	Description
`fn.call(thisArg, a, b, …)`	Invokes `fn` with `thisArg` and arguments list.
`fn.apply(thisArg, [args])`	Invokes `fn` with `thisArg` and arguments array.
`fn.bind(thisArg, a, b, …)`	Returns a new function with `thisArg` and preset arguments.

Table 4.10: *Call, apply, and bind* usage

IIFE

Immediately Invoked Function Expressions (**IIFE**) run once to create an isolated scope, avoiding global pollution.

The following demonstrates an IIFE:

```
(function() {
  const secret = 42; console.log("IIFE ran");
})();
// secret is not accessible here
```

Generators

Generator functions yield multiple values over time and maintain state between yields. They return iterator objects.

The following demonstrates a simple generator:

```
function* idGenerator() {
  let id = 1;
  while (true) {
    yield id++;
  }
}
const gen = idGenerator(); console.log(gen.next().value, gen.next().value); // 1 2
```

Hoisting

Function declarations are hoisted to the top of their scope, allowing calls before definition. Function expressions and arrow functions are not hoisted.

The following demonstrates hoisting behavior:

```
console.log(foo()); // "bar"
function foo() { return "bar"; }

try { console.log(baz());
} catch (e) {
  console.log(e.message); // baz is not a function
}
const baz = function() { return "baz"; };
```

Error handling

Robust applications must anticipate and handle failures. JavaScript provides the **`throw`** statement to signal errors and **`try / catch / finally`** blocks to intercept them. You can define custom error types by extending **`Error`**. Proper propagation and logging ensure that errors surface at the right level and carry useful context.

throw and try catch finally

Use **`throw`** to signal an error and wrap risky code in **`try`**. The **`catch`** block receives the thrown value (usually an **`Error object`**), and **`finally`** runs cleanup code regardless of success or failure.

The following presents the basic syntax:

```
function parseJSON(text) {
  try {
    return JSON.parse(text);
  } catch (err) {
    console.error("Invalid JSON:", err.message);
    return null;
  } finally {
    console.log("Parsing attempt finished");
  }
}

const data = parseJSON('{"a":1}');
const bad  = parseJSON('not json');
```

Custom error types

Creating specialized error classes helps distinguish error sources and attach extra data. Extend the built-in **`Error`** class, set the **`name`**, and capture the stack trace.

The following presents a custom error subclass:

```
class ValidationError extends Error {
  constructor(field, message) {
    super(message);
    this.name = "ValidationError";
    this.field = field;
  }
}

function validateAge(age) {
  if (age < 0 || age > 150) {
```

```
    throw new ValidationError("age", "Age must be between 0 and 150");
  }
}


try {
  validateAge(-5);
} catch (err) {
  if (err instanceof ValidationError) { console.warn(`${err.field} error: ${err.message}`);
  } else {
    throw err; // re-throw unexpected errors
  }
}
```

Propagation and logging

Errors should bubble up to the level that can handle or report them. Avoid suppressing errors silently; log them with context and, if necessary, re-throw to be caught by higher-level handlers (such as global exception listeners in browsers or middleware in Node.js).

The following presents best practices for propagating and logging:

- Catch only when you can handle or transform the error.
- Add contextual information (operation, identifiers) before re-throwing.
- Use a centralized logger (e.g., **`console.error`**, external services) to record stack traces and metadata.

The following demonstrates enriching and re-throwing an error:

```
function loadConfig(path) {
  try {
    // assume readFileSync may throw
    const json = fs.readFileSync(path, "utf8");
    return JSON.parse(json);
  } catch (err) {
    err.message = `Failed to load config from ${path}: ${err.message}`; throw err;
  }
}


try { loadConfig("/invalid/path.json");
} catch (err) {
  console.error(err); // includes updated message and stack
}
```

Objects prototypes classes

Objects form the foundation of JavaScript's data model. Every object is a collection of properties, each a key-value pair, and a link to a prototype object. Prototypes implement inheritance—when you request a property on an object, JavaScript first looks for that property on the object itself, then follows the prototype chain until it either finds it or reaches the end.

Object basics

Every JavaScript object stores zero or more own properties and may reference another object as its prototype. You can create objects in several ways: literals, constructors, **Object.create**, and manipulate their properties at runtime, adding, updating, or deleting keys as needed.

The following list demonstrates common object operations:

- Creating an object literal with properties.
- Accessing properties via dot or bracket notation.
- Adding or updating properties dynamically.
- Deleting properties with the **delete** operator.
- Checking for own properties via **hasOwnProperty**.

The following demonstrates these operations:

```
const book = { title: '1984', author: 'Orwell' };

// access
console.log(book.title);                // "1984"
console.log(book['author']);            // "Orwell"

// add/update
book.year = 1949;
book.title = 'Nineteen Eighty-Four';

// delete
delete book.author;

// check
console.log(book.hasOwnProperty('author')); // false
console.log('year' in book);                         // true
```

Prototype chain

Every object in JavaScript has an internal link ([[Prototype]]) to another object. This *prototype chain* is used for property lookups. If a property is not found on the object itself, the engine checks its prototype, then that object's prototype, and so on, until it either finds the property or reaches null.

The following table presents a comparison of own versus inherited properties:

	Own property	Inherited property
Storage location	Stored directly on the object	Stored on the prototype object
Enumeration	Shown by **Object.keys()**	Not shown by **keys()**, but appears in **for...in**
Deletion	Can be deleted	Cannot delete via own object; delete affects prototype

***Table 4.11**: Own properties versus inherited properties*

The following demonstrates inspecting the prototype chain:

```
const parent = { greet() { return 'hi'; } }; const child = Object.create(parent); child.name =
'Alice';
```

console.log(child.name);	// "Alice"	(own)
console.log(child.greet());	// "hi"	(inherited)

```
console.log(child.hasOwnProperty('greet'));        // false console.log(child._proto_ === parent);
// true console.log(Object.getPrototypeOf(child));        // parent object
```

Constructor functions

Before ES6 classes, constructor functions were the main way to create many objects sharing the same prototype. By convention, these functions are named with an uppercase first letter and invoked with the **new** keyword. Inside the constructor, **this** refers to the newly created object.

The following demonstrates defining and using a constructor function:

```
// Define constructor
function Person(name, age) {
  this.name = name;
  this.age  = age;
}

// Share methods via prototype
Person.prototype.describe = function() {
  return `${this.name}, ${this.age} years old`;
};

// Create instances
const alice = new Person('Alice', 25);
const bob         = new Person('Bob',      30);

console.log(alice.describe()); // "Alice, 25 years old"
console.log(bob.describe());            // "Bob, 30 years old"
```

Classes

ES6 introduced the `class` syntax as a clearer, more concise way to define constructor functions and their prototypes. Under the hood, classes still use prototypes, but they bundle constructor and method definitions in a familiar object-oriented style. In addition, `extends` and `super` handles inheritance cleanly.

The following demonstrates defining and extending classes:

```
class Animal {
     constructor(name) {
        this.name = name;
  }
  speak() {
    console.log(`${this.name} makes a sound`);
  }
}

class Dog extends Animal {
  constructor(name, breed) {
    super(name);              // call parent constructor
    this.breed = breed;
```

```
  }
  speak() {
    console.log(`${this.name} barks`);
  }
}

const dog = new Dog('Rex', 'Labrador'); dog.speak();      // "Rex barks" console.log(dog instanceof
Animal); // true
```

Arrays and array methods

Arrays are ordered collections of values accessible by numeric indices. They can hold elements of any type, primitives, objects, even other arrays, and resize dynamically as you add or remove items. Arrays provide a rich set of methods for traversal, transformation, search, and manipulation, making them indispensable in JavaScript development.

Array basics

An array groups related values under a single variable. Each value is stored at a zero-based index, and the `length` property reflects the count of elements. Arrays are objects under the hood, so you can augment them at runtime, though modifying built-in behavior is generally discouraged.

The following demonstrates array creation and basic operations:

- Literal syntax with square brackets
- Accessing elements by index
- Checking length
- Modifying elements in place

The following demonstrates these basics:

```
const fruits = ['Apple', 'Banana', 'Cherry'];

// access
console.log(fruits[0]);                // "Apple"

// length
console.log(fruits.length); // 3

// modify
fruits[1] = 'Blueberry';
console.log(fruits);                   // ['Apple','Blueberry','Cherry']
```

Adding and removing elements

JavaScript arrays provide methods to push or pop elements at the end, unshift or shift elements at the front, and splice elements anywhere in the middle. These operations adjust the `length` automatically.

The following is an overview of insertion and removal methods:

Method	Effect	Returns
`push(...)`	Add one or more elements to the end.	New length
`pop()`	Remove the last element.	Removed element
`unshift(...)`	Add one or more elements to the front.	New length
`shift()`	Remove the first element.	Removed element
`splice(start, deleteCount, ...)`	Remove or replace or insert at the start.	Array of removed elements

Table 4.12: Common methods for adding and removing array elements

The following demonstrates these methods in practice:

```
let items = [1, 2, 3];

// end operations
items.push(4);          // [1,2,3,4]
items.pop();            // [1,2,3]

// front operations
items.unshift(0); // [0,1,2,3]
items.shift();          // [1,2,3]

// splice: remove and insert
items.splice(1, 1, 'a','b');
// removes 1 element at index 1, inserts 'a','b'
// result: [1,'a','b',3]
```

Iteration techniques

Traversing an array to read or process each element can be done with classic loops or declarative methods. In addition to **`for`** and **`while`**, ES6 introduced **`for…of`**, and all arrays support **`forEach`** for callback-driven iteration.

The following demonstrates various iteration patterns:

- Traditional **`for`** loop for index control.
- **`for…of`** for direct value access.
- **`forEach`** for callback-based processing.

The following shows these in action:

```
const nums = [10, 20, 30];

// for loop
for (let i = 0; i < nums.length; i++) { console.log(nums[i]);
}

// for…of
for (const n of nums) { console.log(n);
}

// forEach
nums.forEach((n, idx) => { console.log(idx, n);
});
```

Transform filter reduce

Arrays can be transformed into new arrays or aggregated values via **map**, **filter**, and**. map** projects each element, **filter** selects elements matching a predicate, and **reduce** combines all elements into a single result.

The following demonstrates transformation and aggregation:

- **map** applies a function to each element.
- **filter** returns elements that satisfy a condition.
- **reduce** accumulates a single value.

The following shows examples:

```
const values = [1, 2, 3, 4, 5];

// map to squares
const squares = values.map(x => x * x);
// [1,4,9,16,25]

// filter evens
const evens = values.filter(x => x % 2 === 0);
// [2,4]

// sum via reduce
const sum = values.reduce((acc, x) => acc + x, 0);
// 15
```

Finding and sorting

To locate elements, arrays provide **find**, **findIndex**, **includes**, and **indexOf**. For ordering, **sort** (with optional comparator) arranges elements in place, and **reverse** flips the sequence.

The following demonstrates search and sort methods:

- **find** returns the first matching element
- **findIndex** returns its index or **-1**
- **includes** tests for presence
- **indexOf** finds the first occurrence
- **sort** orders elements; beware of string coercion
- **reverse** inverts the array

The following shows these in practice:

```
const arr = [3, 1, 4, 1, 5, 9];

// find and index
console.log(arr.find(x => x > 4));              // 5
console.log(arr.findIndex(x => x > 4));// 4

// includes and indexOf
console.log(arr.includes(1));                   // true
console.log(arr.indexOf(1));                    // 1
```

```
// sort ascending
arr.sort((a, b) => a - b);
// [1,1,3,4,5,9]

// reverse
arr.reverse();
// [9,5,4,3,1,1]
```

Destructuring

Array destructuring unpacks elements into distinct variables using a concise syntax. You can skip elements, assign defaults, and collect the rest into an array with the rest pattern.

The following demonstrates destructuring patterns:

- Basic unpacking of fixed positions.
- Skipping elements with commas.
- Default values for missing entries.
- Rest element to gather leftovers.

The following shows destructuring in action:

```
const coords = [10, 20, 30, 40];

// basic
const [x, y] = coords;
// x===10, y===20

// skip third
const [, , z] = coords;
// z===30

// defaults
const [a=1, b=2, c=3, d=4, e=5] = [10];
// a===10, b===2, c===3, d===4, e===5

// rest
const [first, ...rest] = coords;
// first===10, rest===[20,30,40]
```

Multidimensional arrays

Arrays can nest arbitrarily to represent matrices or grids. ES2019 introduced **`flat`** and **`flatMap`** to collapse nested arrays by a specified depth.

The following demonstrates nested arrays and flattening:

```
const matrix = [ [1, 2],
  [3, 4],
  [5, [6, 7]]
];

// one-level flatten
```

```
console.log(matrix.flat());
// [1,2,3,4,5,[6,7]]

// full flatten
console.log(matrix.flat(2));
// [1,2,3,4,5,6,7]

// flatMap example
const words = ['hello world', 'foo bar']; console.log(words.flatMap(s => s.split(' ')));
// ['hello','world','foo','bar']
```

Object methods

Objects are not just bags of data, but you can also transform and inspect them with built-in utilities. Methods on the **Object** constructor help you enumerate keys, merge defaults, and enforce immutability at a fine-grained level.

The following demonstrates common object utilities:

- **Object.keys(obj)** returns an array of own property names.
- **Object.values(obj)** returns an array of own property values.
- **Object.entries(obj)** returns an array of [key, value] pairs.
- **Object.assign(target, …)** merges source objects into the target.
- **Object.fromEntries(entries)** builds an object from **[key, value]** pairs.

The following demonstrates these in action:

```
const defaults = { theme: 'light', lang: 'en' };
const userOpts = { lang: 'fr' };

// merge with defaults
const config = Object.assign({}, defaults, userOpts);
// inspect
console.log(Object.keys(config));              // ['theme','lang'] console.log(Object.
values(config)); // ['light','fr'] console.log(Object.entries(config));
// [['theme','light'],['lang','fr']]

// rebuild from entries
const obj2 = Object.fromEntries([['x',1],['y',2]]); console.log(obj2); // { x:1, y:2 }
```

Array methods beyond map, filter, and reduce

In addition to **map**, **filter**, and **reduce**, JavaScript arrays offer a rich set of helpers for searching, slicing, and flattening.

The following demonstrates advanced array methods:

- **find(fn)** returns the first element matching the predicate.
- **some(fn) / every(fn)** test whether any or all elements pass a check.
- **flat(depth)** flattens nested arrays up to the given depth.
- **flatMap(fn)** combines a map and a single-level flatten.
- **sort(fn)** orders an array in place based on a comparator.
- **splice(start, deleteCount, ...items)** adds/removes elements in place.

The following demonstrates these methods:

```
const nums = [1,2,3,4,5,6];

// find
console.log(nums.find(n => n % 2 === 0)); // 2

// some / every
console.log(nums.some(n => n > 5)); // true
console.log(nums.every(n => n < 10)); // true

// flatten
const nested = [1, [2,3], [[4]]];
console.log(nested.flat(2)); // [1,2,3,4]

// flatMap
const pairs = ['a','b'].flatMap(c => [c, c.toUpperCase()]);
console.log(pairs); // ['a','A','b','B']

// sort
const unsorted = [3,1,4,1,5]; unsorted.sort((a,b)=>a-b); console.log(unsorted); // [1,1,3,4,5]

// splice
const arr = [ 'x','y','z' ];
arr.splice(1, 1, 'Y1','Y2'); console.log(arr); // ['x','Y1','Y2','z']
```

Destructuring in practice

Destructuring lets you pull values out of objects and arrays in a concise, declarative way, especially useful after applying those preceding methods.

The following demonstrates real-world use cases:

- Pull only the fields you need from an API response.
- Swap variables without a temporary.
- Extract function arguments with defaults.
- Collect *the rest* of an array or object into a new variable.

The following shows these patterns:

```
// object destructuring with defaults & rest
const user = { id:123, name:'Alice', role:'admin' };
const { id, name, ...meta } = user; console.log(id, name, meta);
// 123 'Alice' { role:'admin' }

// array destructuring & swap
let a=1,b=2;
[ a, b ] = [ b, a ]; console.log(a,b); // 2 1

// function params
function signup({ email, password, newsletter=false }) {
  // ...
```

```
}
signup({ email:'x@x.com', password:'p' });


// nested destructuring
const data = { items:[{id:1},{id:2}] }; const [{id:firstId}] = data.items; console.log(firstId); // 
1
// default values on missing const [x=10, y=20] = [5]; console.log(x,y); // 5 20
```

Spread and rest operators with destructuring

Modern JavaScript introduces the spread and rest operators, both using the same **`syntax (...)`**, to simplify working with arrays, objects, and function parameters. These operators enable concise cloning and merging of data structures, collection of function arguments, and unpacking of values. Destructuring complements them by providing a readable syntax to extract values from arrays or object properties into standalone variables.

Spread and rest

The spread operator expands an iterable (like an array or string) or object properties into individual elements. In contrast, the rest operator collects multiple elements or properties into a single array or object. Their dual nature depends on context: when used in an assignment or function call, they spread; when used in a parameter list or destructuring pattern, they rest.

The following list presents common use cases for spread and rest:

- Clone or merge arrays and objects without mutating originals.
- Pass an array of values as individual function arguments.
- Capture remaining function arguments into an array.
- Separate parts of an array or object from the rest.

The following demonstrates spread in array and object contexts:

```
// Array cloning and merging
const arr1 = [1, 2];
const arr2 = [...arr1, 3, 4]; // [1,2,3,4]
const clone = [...arr2];              // shallow copy of arr2

// Object cloning and merging
const obj1 = { a: 1, b: 2 };
const obj2 = { ...obj1, c: 3 }; // { a:1, b:2, c:3 }
const cloneObj = { ...obj2 };

// Function call with spread
function sum(x, y, z) { return x + y + z; }
const nums = [5, 10, 15]; console.log( sum(...nums) );    // 30
```

The following demonstrates rest in function parameters and destructuring:

```
// Rest in function parameters
function join(separator, ...items) {
  return items.join(separator);
}
console.log( join(', ', 'a','b','c') ); // "a, b, c"
```

```
// Rest in array destructuring
const [first, second, ...others] = [10, 20, 30, 40];
console.log(first, second, others);              // 10 20 [30,40]

// Rest in object destructuring
const { a, b, ...restProps } = { a:1, b:2,
c:3, d:4 }; console.log(a, b, restProps);
// 1 2 { c:3, d:4 }
```

Destructuring

Destructuring enables unpacking values from arrays or properties from objects into distinct variables in a single, expressive statement. It supports defaults for missing values, skipping of elements, nested patterns, and renaming of object properties.

The following presents key destructuring features:

- Extract array elements by position.
- Skip unwanted elements with commas.
- Provide default values when data is absent.
- Pull object properties by name, with optional renaming.
- Handle nested structures in one pattern.

The following demonstrates array destructuring patterns:

```
const data = [100, 200, 300, 400];

// Basic unpacking
const [x, y] = data;                    // x=100, y=200

// Skip elements
const [, second,, fourth] = data;
 // second=200, fourth=400

// Defaults
const [m = 1, n = 2, o = 3] = [10];
 // m=10, n=2, o=3

// Nested destructuring
const nested = [1, [2, 3], 4];
const [p, [q, r], s] = nested;
 // p=1, q=2, r=3, s=4
```

The following demonstrates object destructuring patterns:

```
const person = { name: 'Alice', age: 30,
  address: { city: 'Wonderland', zip: '12345' }
};

// Basic extraction
const { name, age } = person;
```

```
// Renaming and defaults
const { name: firstName, height = 170 } = person;
// firstName='Alice', height=170
// Nested destructuring
const {
                                    address: { city, zip },
} = person;
// city='Wonderland', zip='12345'

// Combine with rest
const { name: nme, ...otherProps } = person;
// nme='Alice', otherProps={ age:30, address:{...} }
```

Asynchronous JavaScript

Asynchronous programming lets JavaScript run long-running tasks, network requests, timers, and file **input/output (I/O)**, without blocking the main thread. Behind the scenes, the event loop, task queues, and microtask queues coordinate callbacks, **`Promises`**, and **`async/await`** so your UI stays responsive even while work continues in the background.

Event loop and task queues

The event loop continuously pulls tasks from two queues:

- **Macrotasks (or task queue)**: Callbacks from setTimeout, setInterval, I/O events, and rendering.
- **Microtasks (or microtask queue):** Promise callbacks (.then/.catch/.finally) and queueMicrotask.

When the call stack is empty, the event loop first drains all microtasks, then runs the next macrotask, giving Promise handlers priority over timers and I/O.

The following demonstrates the ordering of a macrotask vs. a microtask:

```
// Schedule a macrotask
setTimeout(() => console.log('timeout'), 0);

// Schedule a microtask
Promise.resolve().then(() => console.log('promise'));
console.log('sync');
// Expected output:
//        sync
//        promise
//        timeout
```

Callback patterns

Callbacks were the original async building block in JavaScript, and you pass a function to be invoked later. While straightforward, deeply nested callbacks lead to *callback hell*, which makes code hard to read and maintain.

The following shows a nested-callback pattern:

```
function step1(cb) {
  setTimeout(() => { console.log('step1'); cb(); }, 500);
}
function step2(cb) {
```

```
  setTimeout(() => { console.log('step2'); cb(); }, 500);
}
function step3() {
  setTimeout(() => console.log('step3'), 500);
}

// callback hell
step1(() => {
                                                   step2(() => {
                                                     step3();
  });
});
```

Promises and chaining

Promises encapsulate an eventual value or error and let you chain operations rather than nest them. Each **`.then`** returns a **`new Promise`**, so you can linearize your logic.

The following demonstrates **`Promise`** chaining:

```
function task(duration) {
  return new Promise(resolve =>
    setTimeout(() => resolve(duration), duration)
  );
}

task(300)
  .then(d => { console.log('first', d); return task(200);
  })
  .then(d => { console.log('second', d); return task(100);
  })
  .then(d => console.log('third', d))
  .catch(err => console.error('error', err))
  .finally(() => console.log('all done'));
```

Async await

`async/await` builds on Promises to let you write asynchronous code in a synchronous style. An **`async`** function always returns a Promise; **`await`** pauses execution until the Promise settles, then returns its value or throws its error.

The following demonstrates **`async`**/**`await`** with error handling:

```
async function fetchUser(id) {
  try {
    let res = await fetch(`/api/users/${id}`);
    if (!res.ok) throw new Error(res.statusText); let user = await res.json(); console.
    log('user', user);
  } catch (err) {
    console.error('fetch failed', err);
  } finally {
    console.log('fetch attempt complete');
  }
}
fetchUser(42);
```

Microtasks vs. macrotasks

Because microtasks run before the next macrotask, they can starve timers if you queue too many. Use microtasks for quick, light-weight jobs (Promise reactions) and macrotasks for work that can safely wait.

The following presents the interplay in a compact form:

```
console.log('start');

Promise.resolve()
  .then(() => console.log('microtask 1'))
  .then(() => console.log('microtask 2'));

setTimeout(() => console.log('macrotask 1'), 0);
setTimeout(() => console.log('macrotask 2'), 0);

console.log('end');
// Output order:
//        start
//        end
//        microtask 1
//        microtask 2
//        macrotask 1
//        macrotask 2
```

Conclusion

In this chapter, we introduced JavaScript's core building blocks that enable interactive web experiences. We began by defining the language and tracing its evolution, then explored how it integrates with the browser's DOM. Fundamental syntax elements, statements, expressions, comments, variables, and data types, were covered before moving on to control structures, loops, and operators that direct program flow. Functions were examined in depth, including modern arrow functions and callback patterns, followed by object-oriented techniques with constructors, prototypes, and ES6 classes. We then manipulated collections using arrays and methods like map, filter, and reduce, leveraging spread/rest operators and destructuring for cleaner code. Finally, we tackled asynchronous programming, using callbacks, Promises, and async/await, and demystified the event loop. A hands-on To-Do List project consolidated these principles in a real-world context.

Next, in *Chapter 5, JavaScript and DOM Manipulation*, we will focus on interacting with HTML pages. You will learn to select, traverse, and modify DOM elements; handle user events via listeners and delegation; validate forms and persist data with Web Storage; and harness Web APIs such as Fetch, WebSockets, Geolocation, Canvas, and Notifications. We will also cover performance optimizations like throttling and debouncing, enabling you to build highly responsive, production-ready web applications.

Exercises

1. Define a statement and an expression in JavaScript, and give one short example of each.
2. Write one sentence each to describe the scope and reassignment rules for var, let, and const. Include one line of code per keyword to illustrate.
3. Predict the console output and justify each line:
    a. console.log(a);
    b. var a = 5;

   c. console.log(b);

   d. let b = 6;

4. List all JavaScript primitive types and give one literal example for each. Then state why typeof null returns "object".

5. Given const person = { firstName: 'Ada', lastName: 'Lovelace', city: 'London' }; and const nums = [10, 20, 30], write destructuring assignments to: (a) extract firstName as name, (b) get the first two numbers into a and b, and the rest into rest.

6. Using spread and rest, write code that (a) clones and extends an array const a = [1,2,3] to [1,2,3,4], and (b) defines function sum(...vals) that returns the total.

7. Using array methods only, transform [1,2,3,4,5,6] to the sum of squares of even numbers (i.e., 2^2 + 4^2 + 6^2). Write the one-liner using map/filter/reduce.

8. Show three comparisons that highlight the difference between == and ===. For each, write the expression and the Boolean result.

9. Write (a) a function declaration add(a,b) that returns a+b, (b) a function expression multiply(a,b), and (c) an arrow function diff(a,b). Call all three with sample inputs.

10. Write makeCounter() that uses a closure to return a function which increments and returns a private count each time it is called. Show three successive calls and outputs.

11. Convert this Promise chain to async/await with try/catch: fetch('/api/user/7').then(r => r.json()).then(u => console.log(u.name)).catch(err => console.error(err));

12. Order the logs produced by the event loop and explain briefly:

   a. console.log('A');

   b. setTimeout(() => console.log('B'));

   c. Promise.resolve().then(() => console.log('C'));

   d. console.log('D');

13. Write minimal DOM code that adds a click listener to a button with id="loadBtn", fetches JSON from "/api/data", and inserts data.message into an element with id="output" using textContent.

14. Save the string 'dark' to localStorage under the key 'theme' and read it back on page load; if no value exists, default to 'light' and set a data-theme attribute on <html>. Write the code.

15. Create a simple Web Worker example that sums numbers from 1..n in worker.js and returns the result to the main thread; write both the worker code and the main thread code that receives and logs the result.

Join our Discord space

Join our Discord workspace for latest updates, offers, tech happenings around the world, new releases, and sessions with the authors:

https://discord.bpbonline.com

CHAPTER 5
JavaScript and DOM Manipulation

Introduction

In modern web development, mastering advanced JavaScript concepts and the **Document Object Model** (**DOM**) is essential for creating truly interactive applications. In this chapter, we explore how to select, traverse, and modify DOM elements dynamically, respond to user events with listeners and delegation, and optimize event handling through throttling and debouncing. We will validate form inputs, persist data in the browser using localStorage and sessionStorage, and handle errors gracefully with try–catch and Chrome DevTools. You will also organize code with ES6+ features—modules, template literals, destructuring, optional chaining, and nullish coalescing, and leverage a variety of web **application programming interfaces** (**APIs**), like Fetch, XHR, WebSockets, Geolocation, Canvas, Drag-and-Drop, and Notifications. Hands-on projects, including an interactive To-Do List and a Calculator, will reinforce these techniques in real-world scenarios.

Structure

This chapter will cover the following topics:

- DOM overview
- Selecting elements
- Modifying HTML and CSS dynamically
- Event listeners and event delegation
- Handling form input and validation
- Web storage
- DOM traversal and update
- Interactive todo app
- User interactions
- Error handling and debugging
- JavaScript modules
- Template literals
- Destructuring objects
- Destructuring arrays
- Symbols and BigInts
- Optional chaining
- Nullish coalescing
- Event-driven programming
- Event bubbling and capturing
- Event delegation
- Custom events
- Throttling and debouncing
- JavaScript and the Web API
- WebSockets
- Geolocation API
- Canvas API
- Drag and drop API
- Notification API
- Permission
- Hands-on project interactive calculator

Objectives

By the end of this chapter, the readers will learn how to select and manipulate DOM elements using methods such as **getElementById**, **querySelector**, and by traversing parent, child, and sibling nodes to update page content dynamically. They will implement event-driven programming by attaching listeners for clicks, keypresses, and scroll events, and apply delegation, throttling, and debouncing techniques to optimize performance. They will validate form inputs to ensure data accuracy and leverage **localStorage** and **sessionStorage** for persistent and session-based client-side data management. They will write robust, maintainable code by organizing logic into ES6 modules, using template literals, destructuring assignments, optional chaining, and nullish coalescing. They will also debug JavaScript effectively with **try-catch** blocks, breakpoints, and console methods in Chrome DevTools. Finally, the readers will integrate a variety of Web APIs, Fetch, XHR, WebSockets, Geolocation, Canvas, Drag-and-Drop, and Notifications, to build interactive, real-time web applications reinforced by hands-on projects.

DOM overview

The DOM is a platform and language-neutral interface that represents HTML (and XML) documents as a hierarchical tree of nodes. Each node corresponds to parts of the document, which are elements, text, comments, attributes, and more, and provides properties and methods for inspection and modification. Through the DOM API, JavaScript can traverse this tree, read or change element content and attributes, adjust styles, and respond to user events, enabling fully dynamic and interactive web pages.

The following table presents key node types in the DOM:

Node type	Description	Example
Document	The root of the node tree	**document**
Element	Represents an HTML or XML element	**<div>**
Text	The text content inside an element	Text between tags
Comment	A comment in the source	**<!-- ... -->**
Attribute	A name–value pair associated with an element	**id="main"**

Table 5.1: *Common DOM node types*

The following demonstrates selecting and modifying elements:

```
// Select the first <h1> and change its text const heading = document.querySelector('h1'); heading.
textContent = 'Updated Heading';

// Add a class to an element
const box = document.getElementById('box'); box.classList.add('highlight');

// Create and insert a new list item
const list = document.querySelector('ul'); const item = document.createElement('li'); item.
textContent = 'New Item'; list.appendChild(item);
```

The preceding example shows how to locate elements using CSS selectors and ID lookup, update their content and classes, and dynamically create and append new nodes to the document tree.

Selecting elements

Selecting elements is the first step to interact with the page structure. JavaScript offers multiple methods, each with its own performance characteristics and use cases. Understanding return types (single element vs. collections) and whether collections are live or static helps you write efficient, bug-free code. When working with the DOM,

JavaScript provides several built-in methods to select elements. Each method differs in speed, return type, and how it responds to DOM updates.

The following approaches illustrate the most commonly used techniques:

- **By ID**: Selecting by ID returns a single element or **null** if no match is found. This method is very fast because IDs are unique in the DOM. Use it when you know the exact element you need to manipulate.

  The following demonstrates selecting an element by its ID:

```
// Returns the element with id="header" or null const header = document.
getElementById("header"); if (header) {
  header.textContent = "Welcome!";
}
```

- **By class**: Selecting by class name returns an **HTMLCollection** of all matching elements. This collection is live, meaning it updates automatically when the DOM changes. To work with array methods, convert it to an array first.

  The following demonstrates selecting by class and converting to an array:

```
// Live HTMLCollection of elements with class="item"
const itemsCollection = document.getElementsByClassName("item");
// Convert to an array for array methods const items = Array.from(itemsCollection); items.
forEach(el => el.style.color = "blue");
```

- **By tag**: Selecting by tag name returns a live **HTMLCollection** of all elements with the given tag. Use this when you need to process all headings, paragraphs, or other tag-specific elements.

  The following demonstrates selecting by tag name:

```
// Live collection of all <p> elements
const paragraphs = document.getElementsByTagName("p");
for (let p of paragraphs) { p.classList.add("text-paragraph");
}
```

Query selector

querySelector accepts any valid CSS selector and returns the first matching element or **null**. This method is flexible but slightly slower than ID or class selectors.

The following demonstrates using **querySelector**:

```
// First <a> inside .nav-menu
const firstLink = document.querySelector(".nav-menu a"); firstLink.setAttribute("target", "_blank");
```

All selectors

querySelectorAll returns a static **NodeList** of all matching elements. This list does not update when the DOM changes, but it supports **forEach** directly and can be spread into an array.

The following demonstrates **querySelectorAll** and list conversion:

```
// Static NodeList of all links
const allLinks = document.querySelectorAll("a.external");
// Direct forEach iteration
allLinks.forEach(link => link.rel = "noopener");
// Convert to array for advanced methods
const linkArray = [...allLinks];
```

Method comparison

Choosing the right method depends on whether you need a single element or multiple, and whether you require live updates. The following table summarizes key differences between the selection methods:

Method	Returns	Count	Live	Selector type
`getElementById`	`Element/null`	Single	n/a	ID only
`getElementsByClassName`	`HTMLCollection`	Multiple	Live	Class only
`getElementsByTagName`	`HTMLCollection`	Multiple	Live	Tag only
`querySelector`	`Element/null`	Single	Static snapshot	CSS
`querySelectorAll`	`NodeList`	Multiple	Static snapshot	CSS

Table 5.2: Comparison of DOM selection methods

Modifying HTML and CSS dynamically

Dynamic modification of HTML and CSS lies at the heart of interactive web pages. JavaScript can update text, change attributes, adjust inline styles, manage CSS classes, and even create or remove elements on the fly. These capabilities enable you to respond to user actions, fetch data, and animate **user interface** (**UI**) changes without reloading the page.

Content updates

Updating the content of an element lets you display new information or feedback to the user. You can replace plain text safely via **`textContent`** or **`innerText`**, or inject **Hypertext Markup Language** (**HTML**) fragments with **`innerHTML`**, noting that **`innerHTML`** may introduce security risks if used with untrusted input.

The following demonstrates updating text and HTML content:

```
// Replace plain text safely
const title = document.getElementById("header"); title.textContent = "Welcome Back!";
// Inject HTML (use with trusted data only)
const container = document.querySelector(".message"); container.innerHTML = "<strong>Success:</
strong> Data loaded.";
```

Attribute updates

Many behaviors and resources depend on element attributes. You can read or modify any attribute with **`getAttribute`** and **`setAttribute`**, or use direct properties (e.g., **`src`**, **`href`**, **`value`**) for common attributes. Data attributes (**`data-*`**) map to the **`dataset`** object.

The following demonstrates attribute manipulation:

```
// Change image source
const img = document.querySelector("img"); img.setAttribute("src", "newimage.png");

// Update link target via property
const link = document.querySelector("a.read-more"); link.href = "https://example.com";
link.target = "_blank";

// Work with data-attributes
const item = document.querySelector(".product"); item.dataset.id = "12345";  // sets data-
id="12345"
```

Style updates

Inline styles allow per-element customization without altering external stylesheets. The style object exposes CSS properties in camelCase. For bulk style changes or transitions, consider toggling CSS classes instead of many inline assignments.

The following demonstrates inline style updates:

```
// Highlight the introduction section
const intro = document.querySelector(".intro"); intro.style.backgroundColor = "lightgreen"; intro.
style.padding = "1em";
intro.style.borderRadius = "4px";

// Animate opacity
const box = document.getElementById("box"); box.style.transition = "opacity 0.5s"; box.style.
opacity = 0.5;
```

Class manipulation

Managing CSS classes via the classList API provides a clean way to apply pre-defined styles. It supports adding, removing, toggling, and checking for classes without string concatenation errors.

The following demonstrates common classList methods:

```
// Add and remove classes
const card = document.querySelector(".card"); card.classList.add("highlighted"); card.classList.
remove("collapsed");

// Toggle a class on click
const btn = document.getElementById("toggleBtn"); btn.addEventListener("click", () => {
  card.classList.toggle("expanded");
});

// Check for a class
if (card.classList.contains("highlighted")) { console.log("Card is highlighted");
}
```

The following presents a summary of **classList** methods:

Method	Description
`add(class)`	Adds the specified class if not already present.
`remove(class)`	Removes the specified class if present.
`toggle(class)`	Adds class if missing, removes if present.
`contains(class)`	Returns **true** if the class is present.
`replace(a,b)`	Replaces class **a** with class **b**.

Table 5.3: Common classList methods

Element creation

Beyond modifying existing elements, you can generate new nodes at runtime. Use **createElement**, set its properties or children, and insert it into the DOM with methods like **appendChild**, **insertBefore**, or **insertAdjacentHTML**.

The following demonstrates creating and inserting elements:

```
// Create a new list item
const ul = document.getElementById("taskList"); const newLi = document.createElement("li"); newLi.
textContent = "New Task"; newLi.classList.add("task-item");

// Append to the end of the list
ul.appendChild(newLi);

// Insert HTML snippet before the list
ul.insertAdjacentHTML("beforebegin",
  '<p class="notice">You have new tasks!</p>'
);
```

Element removal

Removing elements helps keep the page clean and free of obsolete nodes. Use **removeChild** on the parent node or call **remove()** directly on the element in modern browsers. Ensure any associated event listeners are also cleaned up to prevent memory leaks.

The following demonstrates element removal:

```
// Remove via parent
const toRemove = document.querySelector(".obsolete"); toRemove.parentNode.removeChild(toRemove);

// Or use remove() directly
const oldBanner = document.getElementById("oldBanner"); oldBanner.remove();
```

Event listeners and event delegation

Event handling is at the core of interactive web pages. By listening for user actions, clicks, keystrokes, and form submissions, you can update the UI, validate input, or trigger network requests. JavaScript's **addEventListener** API provides a flexible, standards-compliant way to register handlers on any DOM node. Event delegation builds on this by leveraging event propagation to manage large or dynamic sets of elements efficiently.

Adding event listeners

Listening to events involves specifying the event type, a callback function, and optional behavior flags. The callback receives an **Event** object that carries details such as the event target, type, and phase. You can prevent default browser behavior or stop propagation to parent listeners. Modern browsers support options like **capture**, **once**, and **passive** to fine-tune how listeners behave.

The following demonstrates a common listener options list:

- **capture**: When true, the listener runs during the capture phase before the target phase.
- **once**: When true, the listener is removed automatically after its first invocation.
- **passive**: When true, indicates the listener will not call **preventDefault()**, allowing optimized scrolling and touch handling.

The following demonstrates basic and advanced event listener usage:

```
// Basic click listener
const btn = document.getElementById("btn-submit"); btn.addEventListener("click", function(event) {
  alert("Submit clicked");
});
```

```
// Named handler and removal
function onKeyPress(e) { console.log("Key pressed:", e.key);
}
document.addEventListener("keypress", onKeyPress);
// Later, to remove:
document.removeEventListener("keypress", onKeyPress);

// Listener with options
window.addEventListener("scroll", function() { console.log("Scrolled");
}, { passive: true, once: false });
```

Event delegation

Attaching separate listeners to each child element can be inefficient, especially when elements are created or removed dynamically. Event delegation solves this by placing one listener on a common ancestor. Since most events bubble up from the target to the document root, the ancestor can intercept them and determine the original source via **event.target** or **event.currentTarget**. This pattern reduces memory use and ensures new elements automatically inherit the behavior.

The following demonstrates simple list delegation:

```
// Delegate clicks on list items
const taskList = document.getElementById("task-list"); taskList.addEventListener("click",
function(event) {
  if (event.target.tagName === "LI") {
    console.log("Task clicked:", event.target.textContent);
                                        }
                                     });
```

Often, you need to handle clicks on elements matching a selector within the parent. Using **closest()** lets you find the nearest ancestor of the clicked node that satisfies the selector. The following demonstrates delegation with selector matching:

```
// Delegate on dynamically added buttons
document.body.addEventListener("click", function(event) {
  const btn = event.target.closest(".remove-btn");
  if (!btn) return;
  const item = btn.closest(".item"); item.remove();
});
```

Handling form input and validation

Form validation ensures that user-submitted data meets expected formats and constraints before processing. Browser-native constraint validation provides basic checks (e.g., required fields, email formats), while JavaScript enables custom rules, real-time feedback, and integration with Constraint API methods such as **setCustomValidity()** and **reportValidity()**. Combining HTML attributes with JS handlers delivers a robust, user-friendly experience.

Validation overview

Validation can be declarative, using HTML attributes like **required** or **pattern**, or programmatic via JavaScript. The constraint validation API exposes properties (**validity**, **validationMessage**) and methods (**checkValidity**, **reportValidity**) to inspect and control validation state. Use declarative checks for common rules and script-driven checks for bespoke logic.

The following table presents common HTML validation attributes:

Aflribute	Description
required	Field must be non-empty.
type="email"	Value must match email format.
minlength="n"	Minimum number of characters.
maxlength="n"	Maximum number of characters.
pattern="regex"	Custom regular expression.

Table 5.4: *Common HTML validation attributes*

Basic validation

Basic validation intercepts the form's **submit** event, inspects input values, and prevents submission on failure. Use **event.preventDefault()** to halt sending data until corrections are made.

The following demonstrates basic form validation using the submit event:

```
// Basic form validation
document.getElementById("user-form").addEventListener("submit", function(event) {
    const username = document.getElementById("username").value.trim();
    if (username === "") {
        alert("Username cannot be empty."); event.preventDefault();
    }
});
```

Custom validation

For rules beyond HTML attributes, the Constraint API allows setting custom error messages and validity states. After evaluating a field, call **setCustomValidity(message)** to attach a message, then **reportValidity()** to display feedback.

The following demonstrates custom validation with Constraint API:

```
// Custom password match validation
const form = document.getElementById("signup-form");
const pwd1 = form.querySelector("#password");
const pwd2 = form.querySelector("#confirm-password");

form.addEventListener("submit", function(event) {
    if (pwd1.value !== pwd2.value) { pwd2.setCustomValidity("Passwords do not match"); pwd2.
        reportValidity();
        event.preventDefault();
    } else {
        pwd2.setCustomValidity("");
    }
});
```

Live feedback

Real-time validation enhances usability by checking input as the user types. Attach handlers to **input** or **change** events and toggle visual cues (e.g., CSS classes) to indicate validity state.

The following demonstrates real-time validation on the input event:

```
// Real-time email format check
```

```
const emailField = document.getElementById("email");
const feedback = document.getElementById("email-feedback");

emailField.addEventListener("input", function() {
    if (emailField.validity.typeMismatch) {
        feedback.textContent = "Please enter a valid email address."; emailField.classList.
        add("invalid");
    } else {
        feedback.textContent = ""; emailField.classList.remove("invalid");
    }
});
```

Web storage

Web storage provides a simple key–value store in the browser, separate from cookies and without network overhead. It enables persisting user preferences or session data, improving performance and user experience. Two storage areas exist, where one lasts beyond browser restarts, and one is tied to a single session.

Local storage

Local storage retains data even after the browser or tab is closed, until explicitly cleared. It is ideal for long-term settings such as themes, language preferences, or cached application state. Stored values are strings; complex data must be serialized (e.g., with JSON).

The following demonstrates **localStorage** usage:

```
// Persist a theme setting
localStorage.setItem("theme", "dark");
// Retrieve and apply the theme
const theme = localStorage.getItem("theme");
if (theme) {
  document.documentElement.setAttribute("data-theme", theme);
}
```

Session storage

Session storage keeps data only for the duration of the page session. Once the tab or window is closed, stored values are discarded. This makes it suitable for transient data like form drafts or navigation state that should not persist indefinitely.

The following demonstrates **sessionStorage** usage:

```
// Store a draft input between reloads
sessionStorage.setItem("draftComment", "This is a draft");
// Load the draft when reloading the page
const draft = sessionStorage.getItem("draftComment");
if (draft) { document.getElementById("commentBox").value = draft;
}
```

DOM traversal and update

DOM manipulation often requires first locating elements in relation to one another, then changing their content, attributes, or structure. Traversal methods navigate the node tree, while update methods insert, remove, or modify elements dynamically.

DOM traversal

Traversing the DOM uses relationships between nodes—parents, children, and siblings. Familiar methods include **parentNode**, **children**, **firstElementChild**, **nextElementSibling**, and the iterator returned by **querySelectorAll**. Custom loops or methods like **for...of** can iterate over element collections.

The following demonstrates common traversal patterns:

```
// Start from a known element
const item = document.getElementById("current-item");

// Navigate to its parent and siblings
const parent = item.parentNode;
const firstChild = parent.firstElementChild;
const nextSibling = item.nextElementSibling;

// Iterate over all list items
const list = document.querySelectorAll("#menu li");
for (const li of list) { console.
  log(li.textContent);
}
```

DOM update

After locating nodes, you can change their content, attributes, classes, or even the document structure. Methods such as **textContent**, **setAttribute**, **classList**, **appendChild**, **removeChild**, and **insertBefore** enable fine-grained updates.

The following demonstrates dynamic DOM updates:

```
// Modify an element's text and attribute const header = document.querySelector("h1"); header.
textContent = "Welcome Back";
header.setAttribute("title", "Updated Page Title");

// Create and insert a new element
const newItem = document.createElement("li"); newItem.textContent = "New Menu Item"; document.
querySelector("#menu").appendChild(newItem);

// Remove an element
const obsolete = document.getElementById("old-section"); obsolete.parentNode.
removeChild(obsolete);
```

Interactive todo app

An interactive todo list combines form input, event handling, dynamic DOM updates, and data persistence. Users add, complete, and remove tasks, with state saved across sessions via web storage.

HTML structure

The HTML provides a text input, a button for adding tasks, and a list container. Minimal CSS classes distinguish completed tasks, enabling visual feedback.

The following demonstrates the HTML skeleton:

```
<!DOCTYPE html>
<html lang="en">
```

```
<head>
  <meta charset="UTF-8">
  <title>Todo List</title>
  <style>
    .done { text-decoration: line-through; color: gray; }
  </style>
</head>
<body>
  <h2>Todo List</h2>
  <input id="taskInput" placeholder="Enter new task">
  <button id="addBtn">Add</button>
  <ul id="tasks"></ul>
  <script src="app.js"></script>
</body>
</html>
```

Script logic

The script listens for clicks on the **Add** button, creates and inserts list items, and toggles their completion state on click. It also handles removal when tasks are clicked twice.

The following demonstrates task creation and interaction:

```
// app.js

const input = document.getElementById("taskInput"); const list = document.getElementById("tasks");
const btn        = document.getElementById("addBtn");

// Add task on button click
btn.addEventListener("click", () => {
  const text = input.value.trim();
  if (!text) { alert("Enter a task"); return;
  }
  const li = document.createElement("li"); li.textContent = text;
  // Toggle done on single click
  li.addEventListener("click", () => { li.classList.toggle("done");
    saveTasks();
  });
  // Remove on double click
  li.addEventListener("dblclick", () => { list.removeChild(li);
    saveTasks();
  });
  list.appendChild(li); input.value = ""; saveTasks();
});
```

Data persistence

Tasks and their completion states are stored in **`localStorage`** as JSON. On page load, stored tasks are restored; on any change, the list is re-serialized.

The following demonstrates saving and loading tasks:

```
// Load tasks on startup
window.addEventListener("DOMContentLoaded", () => {
  const saved = JSON.parse(localStorage.getItem("tasks")) || [];
  for (const t of saved) {
    const li = document.createElement("li"); li.textContent = t.text;
    if (t.done) li.classList.add("done");
    // reuse click handlers from above
    li.addEventListener("click", () => { li.classList.toggle("done"); saveTasks();
    });
    li.addEventListener("dblclick", () => { list.removeChild(li);
      saveTasks();
    });
    list.appendChild(li);
  }
});

// Serialize tasks to storage
function saveTasks() {
  const tasks = [];
  for (const li of document.querySelectorAll("#tasks li")) {
    tasks.push({ text: li.textContent, done: li.classList.contains("done") });
  }
  localStorage.setItem("tasks", JSON.stringify(tasks));
}
```

User interactions

User interactions drive dynamic behavior in web applications. By handling events such as clicks, key presses, and scrolling, developers can create responsive interfaces that adapt to user actions. Effective event handling enhances usability, accessibility, and overall engagement.

Click events

Click events fire when users press and release a pointing device button on an element. These are fundamental for buttons, links, and interactive controls.

User agents dispatch a `click` event after processing pointer-down and pointer-up. The event object provides details such as `target`, `currentTarget`, and modifier keys. Handlers can call **`event.preventDefault()`** to stop default behaviors (e.g., form submission) or **`event.stopPropagation()`** to limit bubbling.

The following demonstrates adding a click listener:

```
// Single-click handler
document.getElementById("btnAction")
  .addEventListener("click", function(event) { console.
    log("Clicked:", event.currentTarget.id);
    // Prevent a link from navigating
    event.preventDefault();
  });
```

The following demonstrates toggling a navigation menu:

```
<button id="menuToggle">Menu</button>
<nav id="navMenu" style="display:none">
  <ul><li>Home</li><li>About</li><li>Contact</li></ul>
</nav>
<script>
  const btn = document.
  getElementById("menuToggle"); const menu =
  document.getElementById("navMenu"); btn.
  addEventListener("click", () => {
    menu.style.display = menu.style.display === "none" ? "block" : "none";
  });
</script>
```

Keypress events

Keyboard events capture users' keystrokes, enabling shortcuts, form handling, and accessibility features. Modern browsers fire **keydown**, **keypress**, and **keyup** events; **keydown** is recommended for reliably detecting all keys. The event object's **key**, **code**, and modifier properties (**ctrlKey**, **altKey**, etc.) allow fine-grained control. Use **event.preventDefault()** to suppress default actions like scrolling or form submission.

The following demonstrates logging key presses:

```
document.addEventListener("keydown", function(event) { console.log(`Key down: ${event.key}
  (${event.code})`);
});
```

The following demonstrates a *Ctrl+S* shortcut:

```
document.addEventListener("keydown", function(event) {
  if (event.ctrlKey && event.
    key === "s") { event.
    preventDefault();
    alert("Save triggered");
          }
        });
```

Scroll events

Scroll events fire whenever the document or an element is scrolled. They enable features such as lazy loading, infinite scroll, or UI updates based on scroll position. Since these fires frequently occur while scrolling, handlers should be throttled or debounced to avoid performance issues.

The **window.scrollY** (or **scrollTop** on elements) gives the current scroll offset. Developers can use **requestAnimationFrame** or utility functions to limit handler invocation. The following demonstrates a basic scroll listener:

```
window.addEventListener("scroll", () => { console.log("Scroll position:", window.scrollY);
});
```

The following demonstrates a scroll-to-top button:

```
<button id="toTop" style="display:none;position:fixed;bottom:20px;right:20px">
                      ↑ Top
                    </button>
<script>
  const btn = document.getElementById("toTop"); window.addEventListener("scroll", () => {
    btn.style.display = window.scrollY > 200 ? "block" : "none";
  });
```

```
btn.addEventListener("click", () => { window.scrollTo({ top: 0, behavior: "smooth" });
});
                                    </script>
```

Error handling and debugging

Error handling and debugging are essential for building reliable JavaScript applications. By anticipating and managing runtime failures, you prevent crashes and provide meaningful feedback. Debugging tools then help you trace, inspect, and resolve issues efficiently.

Common errors

JavaScript errors fall into distinct categories. Understanding these helps you diagnose issues quickly and apply the appropriate fix.

The following tables present common error types:

Error type	Cause	Example
`SyntaxError`	Invalid JavaScript syntax	Missing bracket
`ReferenceError`	Undefined variable or property	Accessing an undeclared var
`TypeError`	Invalid operation on a value type	Calling non-function
`RangeError`	Value outside allowable range	Creating an array with a negative length

Table 5.5: Common JavaScript error types

The following demonstrates these errors:

```
// SyntaxError
// console.log("Hello";

// ReferenceError
// console.log(noSuchVar);

// TypeError
let num = 5;
// num.toUpperCase();

// RangeError
// let arr = new Array(-1);
```

Try catch finally

The **`try`** / **`catch`** / **`finally`** construct lets you handle exceptions gracefully. Code in **`try`** runs normally; if an error occurs, control flows to **`catch`**. The **`finally`** block always executes, useful for cleanup.

The following demonstrates basic try–catch:

```
try {
  let result = JSON.parse("invalid"); console.log(result);
} catch (err) {
  console.error("Parse failed:", err.message);
}
```

The following demonstrates finally usage:

```
try { console.log("Start"); throw new Error("Oops");
} catch (err) {
  console.warn("Caught:", err.message);
} finally { console.log("Cleaning up");
}
```

Custom errors

Creating custom error subclasses helps differentiate failure modes and attach context. Extend **Error**, set **name**, and add properties as needed. The following demonstrates a custom error:

```
class ValidationError extends Error {
  constructor(field, message) {
    super(message);
    this.name = "ValidationError";
    this.field = field;
  }
}

function validateAge(age) {
  if (age < 0 || age > 150) {
    throw new ValidationError("age", "Age out of range");
  }
}

try {
  validateAge(-5);
} catch (err) {
  if (err instanceof ValidationError) { console.error(`${err.field} error: ${err.message}`);
  } else {
    throw err;
  }
}
```

DevTools

Chrome DevTools offers powerful features for inspecting and debugging JavaScript in the browser. You can set breakpoints, step through code, watch variables, and profile performance.

The following demonstrates opening DevTools:

- Press *F12* or *Ctrl+Shift+I* (Windows/Linux)
- Press *Cmd+Option+I* (Mac)

The following demonstrates setting breakpoints:

- In the Sources panel, click the line number to add a breakpoint.
- Reload the page to pause at that point.

The following demonstrates the **debugger** statement:

```
function compute(x) {
  debugger; return x * 2;
}
compute(5);
```

Console methods

The console API provides multiple methods to log, group, and inspect data, aiding quick debugging and visualization.

The following list presents common console methods:

- **console.log() – standard logging**
- **console.warn() – warning messages**
- **console.error() – error messages**
- **console.table() – tabular data display**
- **console.group() / console.groupEnd() – grouped logs**

Logging basics

The following demonstrates log, warn, and error:

```
console.log("Info message"); console.warn("Warning message"); console.error("Error message");
```

Table output

The following demonstrates a console table:

```
const users = [
  { name: "Alice", age: 25 },
  { name: "Bob",          age: 30 }
];
console.table(users);
```

Grouped logs

The following demonstrates grouping:

```
console.group("User Details"); console.log("Name: Alice"); console.log("Age: 25"); console.
groupEnd();
```

JavaScript modules

Modular code organization improves maintainability, testability, and reuse by splitting functionality into self-contained files. JavaScript ES6 introduced native modules with **import** and **export**, enabling static analysis, tree-shaking, and asynchronous loading.

Module basics

Modules encapsulate code and explicitly expose interfaces. Each file can export values, functions, objects, primitives, and import what it needs from other modules. Static imports allow bundlers and engines to optimize dependency graphs.

The following demonstrates basic export and import usage:

```
// File: math.js
export function add(a, b) {
  return a + b;
}
```

```
// File: main.js
import { add } from './math.js'; console.log(add(5, 3)); // Output: 8
```

Named exports

Named exports let you expose multiple bindings from a module. Consumers import only the pieces they require, reducing bundle size and avoiding namespace collisions.

The following presents named export and import:

```
// File: mathUtils.js
export function add(a, b) {
  return a + b;
}
export const PI = 3.14159;

// File: app.js
import { add, PI } from './mathUtils.js'; console.log(add(2, 2));          // Output: 4 console.
log(`PI is ${PI}`);                              // Output: PI is 3.14159
```

Default export

A module may designate one default export, representing its primary functionality. Importing a default export does not require curly braces and can be renamed freely.

The following demonstrates a default export:

```
// File: greet.js
export default function greet(name) {
  return `Hello, ${name}!`;
}

// File: app.js
import greet from './greet.js'; console.log(greet('Alice'));      // Output: Hello, Alice!
```

Combined exports

Modules often include both a default export and additional named exports. This pattern provides a primary API alongside utility functions or constants.

The following demonstrates combining both export types:

```
// File: utilities.js
export default function formatDate(date) {
  return date.toISOString().slice(0,10);
}
export function parseDate(str) {
  return new Date(str);
}

// File: app.js
import formatDate, { parseDate } from './utilities.js'; const d = parseDate('2025-01-01');
console.log(formatDate(d));             // Output: 2025-01-01
```

Practical example

In a real-world app, separate concerns into modules for API interaction, data formatting, and UI updates. This structure promotes clarity and ease of testing.

The following list presents a simple module layout:

- **api.js**: Handles network requests
- **utils.js**: Data formatting and helpers
- **app.js**: Application logic and DOM updates

The following demonstrates each module's code and integration:

- **api.js**:

```
export async function fetchUser(id) {
  const res = await fetch(`https://jsonplaceholder.typicode.com/users/${id}`);
  if (!res.ok) throw new Error('Network error');
  return await res.json();
}
```

- **utils.js**:

```
export default function formatUser(user) {
  return `${user.name} <${user.email}>`;
}
export function capitalize(text) {
  return text.charAt(0).toUpperCase() + text.slice(1);
}
```

- **app.js**:

```
import formatUser, { capitalize } from './utils.js';
import { fetchUser } from './api.js';

async function showUser(id) {
  try {
    const user = await fetchUser(id);
    const display = capitalize(formatUser(user)); document.getElementById('user').
    textContent = display;
  } catch (err) {
    console.error('Error loading user:', err);
  }
}

showUser(1);
```

Template literals

Template literals provide a more powerful and readable way to work with strings by allowing embedded expressions, multi-line text, and custom interpolation. They use backticks (``) instead of quotes and can contain placeholders delimited by `${}`. This feature simplifies concatenation and improves maintainability when constructing complex strings.

> **Note: Template literals are string literals enclosed by backticks that support embedded expressions, multi-line content, and tagged templates for custom processing.**

The following demonstrates embedding expressions and multi-line text:

```
let user = { name: "Alice", age: 30 }; let greeting = `Hello, ${user.name}! You are ${user.age}
years old.`; console.log(greeting);
/* Output:
Hello, Alice!
You are 30 years old.
*/
```

Destructuring objects

Destructuring objects allows unpacking properties into distinct variables in a concise syntax. This feature reduces boilerplate when extracting multiple fields and supports default values, renaming, and nested patterns.

The following demonstrates basic object destructuring and default values:

```
const settings = { theme: "dark", fontSize: 14 }; const { theme, fontSize, language = "en" } =
settings; console.log(theme, fontSize, language); // dark 14 en
```

Destructuring supports renaming and nested objects:

```
const config = {
  server: { host: "localhost", port: 8080 }, debug: true
};
const {
  server: { host: hostname, port }, debug
} = config;
console.log(hostname, port, debug); // localhost 8080 true
```

Destructuring arrays

Array destructuring provides a clear syntax to unpack elements into variables, skip items, and gather the remainder into a rest array. It is especially useful when working with tuples or fixed-structure lists.

The following demonstrates basic array destructuring:

```
const rgb = [255, 100, 50];
const [red, green, blue] = rgb; console.log(red, green, blue); // 255 100 50
```

The rest pattern collects remaining elements:

```
const numbers = [1, 2, 3, 4, 5];
const [first, second, ...rest] = numbers; console.log(first, second, rest); // 1 2 [3,4,5]
```

Symbols and BigInt

Symbols and BigInt are two modern primitive types introduced to address unique identifier needs and large integer arithmetic beyond the 53-bit limit of Number.

Symbols

Symbols create truly unique identifiers, preventing property name collisions in object-oriented designs and libraries.

Note: A Symbol is a primitive type whose instances are guaranteed to be unique, making them ideal for object property keys when name clashes must be avoided.

The following demonstrates creating and using symbols as object keys:

```
const ID = Symbol("id");
const obj = {}; obj[ID] = 123;
```

```
console.log(obj[ID]);                 // 123
console.log(Object.keys(obj)); // [] (symbol-keyed properties are non-enumerable)
```

BigInt

BigInt allows representing and operating on integers larger than **Number.MAX_SAFE_INTEGER** (2^{53}**-1**) without loss of precision.

Note: A BigInt is a numeric primitive that can handle arbitrarily large integer values, denoted by appending n to the literal or using the BigInt() constructor.

The following demonstrates BigInt arithmetic and comparisons:

```
const big1 = 9007199254740991n;             // MAX_SAFE_INTEGER
const big2 = big1 + 2n;
console.log(big2);                          // 9007199254740993n
console.log(typeof big2);                   // bigint

// Mixed operations with Number throw TypeError
// big2 + 1 // TypeError: Cannot mix BigInt and other types
```

Optional chaining

Optional chaining provides a concise, safe way to access nested object properties. If any reference in the chain is **null** or **undefined**, the entire expression gracefully yields **undefined** rather than throwing.

Note: Optional chaining (?.) is an operator that short-circuits property access or method calls when an intervening value is null or undefined.

The following demonstrates optional chaining for property and method access:

```
const user = { profile: { name: "Bob" } }; console.log(user.profile?.name); // Bob console.log(user.
address?.street);                                  // undefined

// Safe method call
const fn = null;
console.log(fn?.());                               // undefined, no error
```

Nullish coalescing

Nullish coalescing distinguishes between **null/undefined** and other falsy values, providing defaults only when a value is truly absent.

Note: The nullish coalescing operator (??) returns the right-hand operand when the left-hand operand is null or undefined, otherwise returns the left-hand operand.

The following demonstrates nullish coalescing versus logical OR:

```
let count = 0;
console.log(count || 10);          // 10  (0 is falsy)
console.log(count ?? 10);          // 0   (0 is not nullish)

let name = null;
console.log(name ?? "Guest"); // Guest
```

Event-driven programming

Event-driven programming enables JavaScript to react to user and system actions by registering callbacks for named events. Instead of running code in a fixed sequence, applications listen for events, such as clicks, keystrokes, or network responses—and invoke handlers when those events occur, creating highly interactive and responsive interfaces.

Note: Event-driven programming is a paradigm where registered callbacks execute in response to dispatched events, decoupling event sources from event handlers.

The following demonstrates registering a simple click listener:

```
// Attach a click listener to a button
const button = document.getElementById('myButton'); button.addEventListener('click', () => {
  console.log('Button was clicked');
});
```

Event bubbling and capturing

Events propagate through the DOM in two main phases: capturing (from the root down to the target) and bubbling (from the target back up to the root). Understanding both phases is essential for precise event handling and delegation.

Bubbling

Event bubbling starts at the event's target element and then travels upward through its ancestors. By default, most listeners react during the bubbling phase, allowing parent elements to handle child events without attaching listeners to every descendant.

The following demonstrates bubbling and stopping its propagation:

```
// Child listener fires first
document.getElementById('child').addEventListener('click', (e) => { console.log('Child
  clicked');
  // e.stopPropagation(); // prevents parent handler
});

// Parent listener fires after child
document.getElementById('parent').addEventListener('click', () => { console.log('Parent
  clicked');
});
```

Capturing

Event capturing (also called *trickling*) invokes listeners on ancestors before the event reaches its target. To use capturing, pass a third argument of `true` to `addEventListener`.

The following demonstrates capturing in action:

```
// Parent listener in capture phase
document.getElementById('parent').addEventListener('click', () => { console.log('Parent
  clicked (capturing)');
}, true);

// Child listener in bubble phase
document.getElementById('child').addEventListener('click', () => { console.log('Child
  clicked');
});
```

Event delegation

Event delegation leverages bubbling to manage events for many child elements via a single listener on a common ancestor. This technique reduces memory usage and simplifies dynamic content handling.

The following presents a delegation for a list of items:

```
const list = document.getElementById('itemList'); list.addEventListener('click', (e) => {
      // Only handle clicks on list items
      if (e.target && e.target.tagName === 'LI') { console.log('Item clicked:', e.target.
        textContent);
      }
    });
```

Custom events

Custom events allow developers to define and dispatch application-specific events, facilitating communication between decoupled components.

The following demonstrates creating and dispatching both a basic **Event** and a **CustomEvent** with data:

```
// Basic custom event
const basicEvent = new Event('basic'); document.addEventListener('basic', () => {
  console.log('Basic event triggered');
});
document.dispatchEvent(basicEvent);

// CustomEvent with detail payload
const detailEvent = new CustomEvent('dataReady', { detail: { items: [1,2,3], timestamp: Date.now()
  }
});
document.addEventListener('dataReady', (e) => { console.log('Data received', e.detail);
});
document.dispatchEvent(detailEvent);
```

Throttling and debouncing

In many web applications, rapid event firing—such as scrolling, resizing, or typing- can overwhelm handlers and degrade performance. Throttling and debouncing are two common patterns that control the rate at which functions execute in response to frequent events, ensuring responsive interfaces and efficient resource usage.

Throttling

Throttling limits a function so it runs at most once during a specified interval, regardless of how many times the event fires. This pattern is ideal when you need regular updates but want to cap the execution rate, common in handling window resize, scroll, or mousemove events. Throttling maintains performance by discarding intermediate calls until the cooldown period elapses.

The following demonstrates a basic throttle implementation and its use with the resize event:

```
function throttle(func, limit) {
  let inThrottle = false; return function(...args) {
    if (!inThrottle) { func.apply(this, args); inThrottle = true;
      setTimeout(() => inThrottle = false, limit);
       }
```

```
        };
    }
window.addEventListener('resize', throttle(() => {
      console.log('Resized at most once per second');
  }, 1000)
);
```

The following presents common throttling use cases:

- Updating layout on **resize** without flooding the handler.
- Tracking scroll position for infinite scrolling or lazy loading.
- Handling rapid **mousemove** events in interactive graphics.

Debouncing

Debouncing postpones a function's execution until a specified time has passed with no additional calls. This pattern is ideal when an action should fire only after a burst of events completes—common in input validation, search-as-you-type, or resizing interfaces. Debouncing ensures the handler runs only once, after the user input *settles*.

The following demonstrates a basic debounce implementation and its use with the scroll event:

```
function debounce(func, delay) {
  let timerId;
  return function(...args) { clearTimeout(timerId);
    timerId = setTimeout(() => func.apply(this, args), delay);
  };
}

window.addEventListener('scroll', debounce(() => {
    console.log('Scrolled and idle for 500ms');
  }, 500)
);
```

The following presents optional debounce configuration options:

Option	Behavior
leading	Invoke callback immediately on the first call within the delay period.
trailing	Invoke the callback after the delay period ends if calls occurred.

***Table 5.6:** Debounce execution options*

Many utility libraries (e.g., Lodash's **_.throttle** and **_.debounce**) provide these patterns with additional configuration for leading/trailing execution, making integration concise and robust.

JavaScript and the Web API

Web APIs are interfaces provided by browsers that extend JavaScript beyond core language features, granting access to networking, graphics, audio/video, device hardware, geolocation, storage, and more. By leveraging these APIs, developers build rich, interactive applications that communicate with servers, manipulate media, and store data on the client.

Fetch API

The Fetch API is a modern, Promise-based interface for making HTTP requests. It replaces the older XMLHttpRequest, providing a cleaner syntax, better support for streaming, and straightforward handling of various response types

(JSON, text, blobs, etc.). Fetch requests return a **`Response`** object, whose methods **`(.json(), .text(), .blob())`** parse the response body. Errors such as network failures or non-OK HTTP statuses must be handled explicitly.

The following demonstrates common response parsing methods:

- **response.json()**: Parses JSON payload
- **response.text()**: Returns raw text
- **response.blob()**: Returns binary blob
- **response.ok**: Boolean for status in 200–299

The following demonstrates a basic fetch with error handling:

```
fetch('https://api.example.com/data')
  .then(response => {
    if (!response.ok) {
      throw new Error(`HTTP error ${response.status}`);
    }
    return response.json();
  })
  .then(data => console.log('Received', data))
  .catch(err => console.error('Fetch failed', err));
```

The following demonstrates an **`async`**/**`await`** variant with a timeout via **`AbortController`**:

```
const controller = new AbortController();

setTimeout(() => controller.abort(), 5000);

async function loadData() {
  try {
    const response = await fetch('/api/items', { signal: controller.signal });
    if (!response.ok) throw new Error(response.
    statusText); const items = await response.json();
    console.log(items);
  } catch (err) {
    console.error('Request error', err);
  }
}

loadData();
```

XHR basics

The **XMLHttpRequest** (**XHR**) API is the classic way to send HTTP requests in JavaScript. It supports callbacks for state changes, progress events, and detailed control over headers and response types. While largely supplanted by Fetch, XHR remains important for legacy code and fine-grained event hooks.

The following presents the **`readyState`** values:

State	Description
0	**UNSENT**: `open()` not called
1	**OPENED**: `send()` not called

2	**HEADERS_RECEIVED**: headers received
3	**LOADING**: response body loading
4	**DONE**: operation complete

Table 5.7: *XMLHttpRequest readyState values*

The following demonstrates a basic **GET** request:

```
const xhr = new XMLHttpRequest(); xhr.open('GET', '/api/data', true); xhr.onreadystatechange =
() => {
  if (xhr.readyState === 4) {
    if (xhr.status === 200) {
      const data = JSON.parse(xhr.responseText); console.log('Data', data);
    } else {
      console.error('Error', xhr.status);
    }
  }
};
xhr.send();
```

The following demonstrates sending JSON via POST:

```
const form = document.getElementById('user-form'); form.addEventListener('submit', event => {
  event.preventDefault();
  const xhr = new XMLHttpRequest(); xhr.open('POST', '/api/users', true);
  xhr.setRequestHeader('Content-Type', 'application/json'); xhr.onload = () => {
    if (xhr.status === 201) {
      console.log('User created', JSON.parse(xhr.responseText));
      } else {
      console.error('Create failed', xhr.status);
       }
      };
  const user = { name: form.name.value }; xhr.send(JSON.stringify(user));
});
```

Handling JSON data

JavaScript Object Notation (JSON) is the de facto format for client-server data exchange. JavaScript provides **`JSON.parse()`** to convert JSON strings into objects, and **`JSON.stringify()`** to serialize objects into JSON. Both methods accept optional functions—*reviver* for parsing and *replacer* for stringifying, to transform values during conversion.

The following demonstrates parsing and stringifying:

```
const jsonString = '{"user":"Alice","age":25}'; const obj = JSON.parse(jsonString); console.
log(obj.user, obj.age); // Alice 25

const newJson = JSON.stringify(obj); console.log(newJson); // {"user":"Alice","age":25}
```

The following demonstrates using a reviver to convert dates:

```
const data = '{"date":"2025-06-20T12:00:00Z"}';
const parsed = JSON.parse(data, (key, value) => key === 'date' ? new Date(value) : value
);
console.log(parsed.date instanceof Date); // true
```

The following demonstrates storing and retrieving JSON in local storage:

```
const prefs = { theme: 'dark', notifications: true }; localStorage.setItem('prefs', JSON.
stringify(prefs));

const stored = JSON.parse(localStorage.getItem('prefs')); console.log(stored.theme, stored.
notifications); // dark true
```

WebSockets

WebSockets provide a full-duplex communication channel over a single TCP connection, enabling real-time data exchange between client and server without the overhead of repeated HTTP requests. Once established, the connection remains open, allowing both parties to push messages at any time, which is ideal for chat apps, live notifications, and collaborative tools.

States

WebSocket connections transition through well-defined states accessible via the **readyState** property. Understanding these states helps manage connection logic and handle reconnection strategies.

The following presents the WebSocket state values:

State	Description
0 (CONNECTING)	Connection is being established
1 (OPEN)	Connection is open and ready to communicate
2 (CLOSING)	Connection is in the process of closing
3 (CLOSED)	Connection is closed or could not be opened

Table 5.8: *WebSocket connection states*

Usage

The WebSocket API exposes event handlers (**onopen**, **onmessage**, **onerror**, **onclose**) and a **send()** method to transmit data. Proper error handling and reconnection logic ensure resilience in real-world applications.

The following demonstrates a basic **WebSocket** setup:

```
const socket = new WebSocket('wss://example.com/socket');

// Send a greeting once open
socket.onopen = () => { socket.send('Hello, server!');
};

// Log incoming messages
socket.onmessage = event => { console.log('Received:', event.data);
};
// Handle errors
socket.onerror = err => { console.error('WebSocket error:', err);
};

// Clean up on close
socket.onclose = () => { console.log('Connection closed');
};
```

The following demonstrates a simple real-time chat example:

```
<input id="chatInput" placeholder="Type a message">
<button id="sendBtn">Send</button>
<div id="chatMessages"></div>

<script>
  const socket = new WebSocket('wss://chat.example.com');

  socket.onmessage = event => {
    const msgDiv = document.createElement('div'); msgDiv.textContent = event.data; document.
    getElementById('chatMessages').appendChild(msgDiv);
  };

  document.getElementById('sendBtn').onclick = () => { const input = document.
    getElementById('chatInput'); socket.send(input.value);
    input.value = '';
  };
</script>
```

Geolocation API

The Geolocation API enables web applications to query the user's physical location, leveraging GPS, Wi-Fi, or IP-based positioning. Access requires explicit user permission, and the API offers both one-time lookups and continuous tracking.

Methods

The API provides two primary methods—**`getCurrentPosition()`** for a one-time read and **`watchPosition()`** for ongoing updates—each accepting a success callback, an optional error callback, and an options object to tune accuracy, timeout, and caching.

The following presents the method signatures:

- **`getCurrentPosition(success, error, options)`**
- **`watchPosition(success, error, options)`**
- **`clearWatch(watchId)`**

Errors

If the location cannot be obtained, the error callback receives a **`PositionError`** object with a **`code`** and **`message`**. Handling these codes improves user experience when permissions are denied or timeouts occur.

The following presents common error codes:

Code	Condition
1 (PERMISSION_DENIED)	User denied permission
2 (POSITION_UNAVAILABLE)	Location unavailable
3 (TIMEOUT)	Request timed out

***Table 5.9:** Geolocation error codes*

Examples

Applications commonly fetch a single position or track movement, then use the coordinates in mapping or location-based services.

The following demonstrates a basic position lookup:

```
navigator.geolocation.
  getCurrentPosition( pos => {
    console.log('Latitude:', pos.coords.latitude);
    console.log('Longitude:', pos.coords.longitude);
  },
  err => console.error('Location error:', err)
);
```

The following demonstrates finding nearby points of interest:

```
function findNearby() { navigator.geolocation.getCurrentPosition(pos => {
    const { latitude, longitude } = pos.coords; fetch(`/api/
    nearby?lat=${latitude}&lon=${longitude}`)
      .then(r => r.json())
      .then(data => console.log('Nearby places:', data))
      .catch(err => console.error(err));
  }, () => alert('Cannot access location'));
}
```

Canvas API

The Canvas API exposes a 2D rendering context on an HTML **<canvas>** element, enabling dynamic drawing of shapes, text, images, and animations entirely in JavaScript. It forms the basis for games, data visualizations, and drawing applications.

Drawing

The 2D context offers methods to draw filled and stroked shapes, paths, text, and images. Managing state via **save()** and **restore()** allows complex compositions.

The following presents key drawing methods:

- **fillRect(x,y,w,h) and strokeRect(x,y,w,h)**
- **clearRect(x,y,w,h)**
- **beginPath(), moveTo(), lineTo(), arc()**
- **fill(), stroke()**
- **fillText(text,x,y) and drawImage(img,x,y)**

The following demonstrates drawing a blue square:

```
<canvas id="c" width="200" height="200"></canvas>
<script>
  const ctx = document.getElementById('c').
  getContext('2d'); ctx.fillStyle = 'blue';
  ctx.fillRect(50, 50, 100, 100);
</script>
```

Animation

Animations use **requestAnimationFrame()** to synchronize updates to the browser's refresh rate, ensuring smooth motion and efficient CPU usage.

The following demonstrates a moving rectangle animation:

```
const canvas = document.getElementById('c');
const ctx = canvas.getContext('2d');
let x = 0;
function animate() { ctx.clearRect(0,0,canvas.width,canvas.height); ctx.fillRect(x,50,50,50);
  x = (x + 2) % canvas.width; requestAnimationFrame(animate);
}
requestAnimationFrame(animate);
```

The following demonstrates a simple drawing tool:

```
<canvas id="draw" width="400" height="300" style="border:1px solid #000"></canvas>
<script>
  const cv = document.getElementById('draw');
  const c = cv.getContext('2d');
  let drawing = false;
  cv.addEventListener('mousedown', ()=> drawing = true); cv.addEventListener('mouseup', ()=>
  drawing = false);
  cv.addEventListener('mousemove', e => {
    if (drawing) {
      c.fillRect(e.offsetX, e.offsetY, 4, 4);
      }
    });
</script>
```

Drag and Drop API

The Drag and Drop API enables intuitive drag-and-drop interactions by firing a sequence of events (**dragstart**, **dragover**, **drop**) and using the **DataTransfer** object to carry data between source and target.

Events

Key events in the drag-and-drop lifecycle allow customizing visuals and data transfer. The following presents the main events:

- **dragstart**: When dragging begins
- **dragover**: When a dragged item moves over a drop zone
- **dragleave**: When it leaves a drop zone
- **drop**: When the item is released
- **dragend**: When dragging ends

Data transfer

The **DataTransfer** object holds the data payload and drag effects. Use **setData()** on drag start and **getData()** on drop, and configure permitted operations (copy, move, link). The following presents common **DataTransfer** methods:

- setData(format, data): Store data
- getData(format): Retrieve data
- effectAllowed: Allowed operations (e.g. *copyMove*)
- dropEffect: Visual feedback (e.g. *move*)

Example

A simple example where a draggable element can be dropped into a target zone demonstrates the full flow from **dragstart** to **drop**.

The following demonstrates a basic drag-and-drop implementation:

```
<div id="item" draggable="true">Drag me</div>
<div id="zone" style="width:200px;height:150px;border:1px solid #000"></div>

<script>
  const item = document.getElementById('item');
  const zone = document.getElementById('zone');

  item.addEventListener('dragstart', e => { e.dataTransfer.setData('text/plain', e.target.id);
    e.dataTransfer.effectAllowed = 'move';
  });

  zone.addEventListener('dragover', e => { e.preventDefault(); // allow drop e.dataTransfer.
    dropEffect = 'move';
  });

  zone.addEventListener('drop', e => { e.preventDefault();
    const id = e.dataTransfer.getData('text/plain'); zone.appendChild(document.
    getElementById(id));
  });
</script>
```

Notification API

The Notification API enables web applications to display system-level notifications to users, even when the page is not in focus. Notifications enhance engagement by alerting users to important events, messages, or updates. To avoid misuse, browsers require explicit permission from the user before notifications can be shown.

Permissions

Before creating notifications, an application must check and request permission. There are three permission states, namely **default** (user has not chosen), **granted** (user approved), and **denied** (user refused). Handling these states ensures respectful use of notifications.

The following presents the permission workflow:

- Check **Notification.permission** to see the current state.
- If the state is **default**, call **Notification.requestPermission()**.
- Handle the returned promise to detect **granted** or **denied**.

The following demonstrates requesting permission:

```
if (Notification.permission === 'default') { Notification.requestPermission().then(permission => {
    console.log('Permission status:', permission);
  });
}
```

Creating notifications

Once permission is granted, notifications can be created via the **`Notification`** constructor. Each notification displays a title and optional settings to customize its appearance and behavior.

The following demonstrates basic notification creation:

```
if (Notification.permission === 'granted') {
  new Notification('Hello!', {
    body: 'This is a system notification.', icon: '/assets/notification-icon.png'
  });
}
```

Notification options

Notifications accept an options object to control their content and behavior. Common options include the message body, icon, action buttons, and data payload for later use.

The following presents common notification options:

Property	Type	Description
`body`	String	Main text of the notification
`icon`	String (URL)	URL to an icon image
`badge`	String (URL)	Small monochrome icon for status bars
`tag`	String	Identifier to replace existing notifications
`actions`	Array	Buttons with `action` and `title`
`data`	Any	Arbitrary data accessible in event handlers
`requireInteraction`	Boolean	Keeps notification open until user interacts
`timestamp`	Number	Custom timestamp for display

***Table 5.10:** Notification option properties*

The following demonstrates a notification with actions:

```
new Notification('New Message', {
  body: 'You have received a new message.', icon: '/assets/msg-icon.png',
  actions: [
    { action: 'open', title: 'Open App' },
    { action: 'dismiss', title: 'Dismiss' }
  ],
  data: { messageId: 12345 },
  tag: 'msg-12345'
});
```

Notification events

Notifications emit events to handle user interactions and lifecycle changes. Listening to these events allows the application to respond to clicks, errors, and closures.

The following presents key notification events:

- **Onclick**: Fired when the notification is clicked.

- **Onclose**: Fired when the notification is closed.
- **Onerror**: Fired if an error occurs displaying the notification.
- **Onshow**: Fired when the notification is displayed.

The following demonstrates attaching event handlers:

```
const note = new Notification('Reminder', { body: 'Meeting starts in 10 minutes.', tag: 'meeting-
  reminder'
});

note.onclick = () => { window.focus();
  console.log('Notification clicked');
};

note.onclose = () => console.log('Notification closed'); note.onerror = () => console.
error('Notification error'); note.onshow = () => console.log('Notification shown');
```

Best practices

Effective use of notifications respects user preferences and context. Request permission at a logical point in the user flow, avoid spamming, group related updates with tags, and use actions to provide quick responses. For push notifications beyond page lifetime, integrate with Service Workers and the Push API.

The following lists highlights best practices:

- Request permission only when needed, not on page load.
- Use descriptive titles and concise bodies.
- Group similar notifications using tag.
- Provide action buttons for meaningful interactions.
- Handle denied permissions gracefully, with in-app fallbacks.
- Employ Service Workers for background and push notifications.

Hands-on project interactive calculator

An interactive calculator is an ideal way to apply core JavaScript concepts, variables, data types, operators, DOM manipulation, event handling, and error management, in a cohesive example. This project guides you through building a web-based calculator that performs basic arithmetic and handles user input errors gracefully.

Design and implement a web-based calculator that demonstrates core JavaScript concepts by accepting input from buttons and the keyboard, building and validating an expression string, evaluating it safely, and updating the display with clear error feedback.

Implementation

The build proceeds in three stages. Define the HTML structure, style it with a responsive grid, and add JavaScript behavior. Use clear IDs and classes so DOM selection stays simple and reliable during event handling. Implement guarded evaluation, keyboard support, and recovery from invalid input to keep the interface responsive and fault-tolerant. The following subsections present each part with concise explanations and complete code.

HTML structure

HTML defines an input display and a grid of buttons for digits, operators, equals, and clear. Proper IDs and classes enable easy selection in JavaScript.

The following demonstrates the calculator HTML:

```
<!DOCTYPE html>
<html lang="en">
<head>
    <meta charset="UTF-8">
    <title>Interactive Calculator</title>
    <link rel="stylesheet" href="style.css">
</head>
<body>
    <div id="calculator">
        <input type="text" id="display" disabled>
        <div id="buttons">
            <!-- row 1 -->
            <button class="btn clear"       data-value="C"    data-area="clear">C</button>
            <button class="btn operator"    data-value="%"    data-area="percent">%</button>
            <button class="btn operator"    data-value="+-" data-area="plusminus">±</button>
            <button class="btn operator"    data-value="/"    data-area="divide">/</button>

            <!-- row 2 -->
            <button class="btn"             data-value="7"    data-area="seven">7</button>
            <button class="btn"             data-value="8"    data-area="eight">8</button>
            <button class="btn"             data-value="9"    data-area="nine">9</button>
            <button class="btn operator"    data-value="*"    data-area="multiply">*</button>
            <!-- row 3 -->
            <button class="btn"             data-value="4"    data-area="four">4</button>
            <button class="btn"             data-value="5"    data-area="five">5</button>
            <button class="btn"             data-value="6"    data-area="six">6</button>
            <button class="btn operator"    data-value="-"    data-area="subtract">-</button>
            <!-- row 4 -->
            <button class="btn"             data-value="1"    data-area="one">1</button>
            <button class="btn"             data-value="2"    data-area="two">2</button>
            <button class="btn"             data-value="3"    data-area="three">3</button>
            <button class="btn operator"    data-value="+"    data-area="add">+</button>
            <!-- row 5 -->
            <button class="btn"             data-value="."    data-area="dot">.</button>
            <button class="btn"             data-value="0"    data-area="zero">0</button>
```

```
            <button class="btn backspace" data-value="back"data-area="back">&larr;</
            button><button class="btn equals"      data-value="="     data-area="equals">=</
            button>
        </div>
        </div>
    <script src="script.js"></script>
    </body>
</html>
```

CSS styling

CSS creates a responsive grid layout, styles buttons by purpose, and ensures the display is legible. Flexbox or simple percentage widths can be used.

The following demonstrates the CSS styling (**style.css**):

```
    /* container                                                                      */
        #calculator{
        width: 360px; margin: 40px auto; padding: 20px; background:#f7f7f7; border-radius:18px;
    box-shadow:0 4px 20px rgba(0,0,0,.12);
}

    /* display                                                                        */
        #display{
        width:100%;
        height:56px;
        text-align:right; font-size:2.1em;
    border:1px solid #ddd; border-radius:8px; padding:6px 14px; margin-bottom:18px; box-
    sizing:border-box; background:#ffffff; color:#555;
}


    /* grid                                                                           */
        #buttons{
        display:grid;
        grid-template-columns:repeat(4,1fr); grid-template-rows:repeat(5,64px); grid-gap:12px;
        grid-template-areas:
            "clear     percent   plusminus    divide"
            "seven     eight     nine         multiply"
            "four      five      six          subtract"
            "one       two       three        add"
            "dot       zero      back         equals";
 }
    /* generic button style                                                           */
    .btn{
        font-size:1.6em; font-weight:500;
        border:1px solid #cfcfcf; border-radius:10px; background:#ffffff; cursor:pointer;
        transition:background .15s;
    }
```

```
.btn:active{background:#eaeaea;}
```

The following demonstrates the CSS styling (**style.css**):

```
/* functional colours                */
.operator{background:#ff9900;color:#fff;border-color:#ff9900;}
.equals {background:#4caf50;color:#fff;border-color:#3d8b40;}
.clear    {background:#f44336;color:#fff;border-color:#c62828;}
.backspace{background:#9e9e9e;color:#fff;border-color:#757575;}

/* assign grid areas                 */
button[data-area="clear"]         {grid-area:clear;} button[data-
area="percent"]{grid-area:percent;}
button[data-area="plusminus"] grid-area:plusminus;}
button[data-area="divide"] grid-area:divide;}
button[data-area="seven"] {grid-area:seven;}
button[data-area="eight"]         grid-area:eight;}
button[data-area="nine"]          grid-area:nine;}
button[data-area="multiply"]{grid-area:multiply;}
button[data-area="four"]          {grid-area:four;}
button[data-area="five"]          {grid-area:five;}
button[data-area="six"]           {grid-area:six;}
button[data-area="subtract"]{grid-area:subtract;
button[data-area="one"]           {grid-area:one;}
button[data-area="two"]           grid-area:two;}
button[data-area="three"]         {grid-area:three;
button[data-area="add"]           {grid-area:add;}
button[data-area="dot"]           {grid-area:dot;}
button[data-area="zero"]          grid-area:zero;}
button[data-area="back"]          {grid-area:back;}
button[data-area="equals"]        {grid-area:equals;}
```

Calculator logic

The JavaScript selects all buttons, listens for clicks, builds an expression string, evaluates it with **eval()**, and handles errors. The display is updated after each input or operation.

The following demonstrates the JavaScript logic (script.js):

```
const display     = document.getElementById("display");
const buttons     = document.querySelectorAll(".btn");
let    expression = "";

/* helper          */
const update = () => (display.value = expression || "0");

/* click handling */
buttons.forEach(btn => btn.addEventListener("click", ()=>{
     const val = btn.dataset.value;
     if(val === "C"){                          // clear
          expression = "";
     }else if(val === "back"){                 // backspace
          expression = expression.slice(0,-1);
```

```
        }else if(val === "%"){                          // percent
            try{ expression = (eval(expression)/100).toString(); }
            catch{ expression = ""; display.value = "Error"; return; }
        }else if(val === "+-"){                         // plus/minus
            try{ expression = ( -eval(expression) ).toString(); }
            catch{ expression = ""; display.value = "Error"; return; }
        }else if(val === "="){                          // equals
            try{ expression = eval(expression).toString(); }
            catch{ expression = ""; display.value = "Error"; return; }
        }else{
            expression += val;
          }
          update();
        }));
```

Error handling

To avoid unhandled exceptions when the user enters an invalid expression, the evaluation is wrapped in **`try...catch`**. On error, the display shows *Error,* and the expression resets.

Keyboard support

Enhance usability by allowing keyboard entry. A **keydown listener** appends digits/operators or triggers evaluation on *Enter* and clear on Escape.

The following demonstrates keyboard handling (**`script.js`**):

```
/* keyboard support                                                          */
document.addEventListener("keydown", e=>{
    const k = e.key;
    if(/[0-9\.+\-*/]/.test(k)){ expression += k; }
    else if(k === "Enter"){ e.preventDefault(); buttons.namedItem("=")?.click(); }
    else if(k === "Backspace"){ buttons.forEach(b=>b.dataset.value==="back"&&b.click()); }
    else if(k === "%"){ buttons.forEach(b=>b.dataset.value==="%"&&b.click()); }
    else if(k === "Escape"){ buttons.forEach(b=>b.dataset.value==="C"&&b.click()); }
    update();
});
```

Project output

The completed calculator provides a clean, responsive UI that supports both mouse and keyboard input. It displays the current expression or result in a read-only field at the top. Invalid expressions produce an *Error* message, and pressing the **clear button** (**C**) or the Escape key resets the calculator to its initial state.

The following figure shows the styled calculator interface with all controls in place:

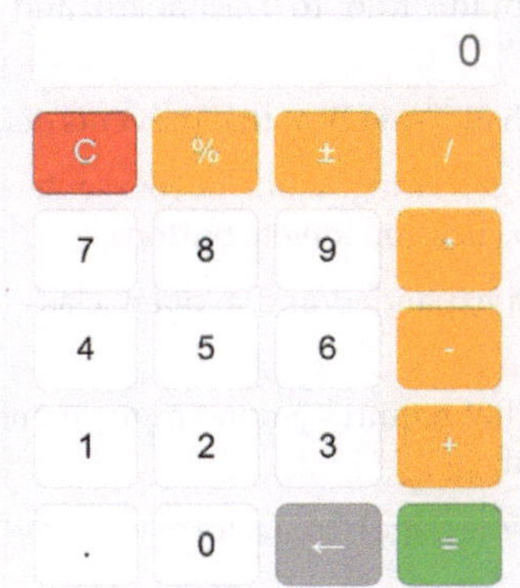

***Figure 5.1:** Final interactive calculator output*

Key aspects of this output include:

- A prominent display area showing *0* when empty, updating live as users enter numbers or operators.
- Digit buttons (0–9) and a decimal point for numerical input.
- Operator buttons for division (/), multiplication (*), subtraction (–), and addition (+) styled in orange for quick identification.
- A percentage (%) and plus/minus (±) button for common calculator functions.
- An equals button (=) in green to evaluate the expression, also triggered by the Enter key.
- A clear button (C) in red and a backspace button (⌫) in gray for error correction, both keyboard-accessible (Escape for clear, Backspace for delete).
- Graceful error handling: malformed expressions result in *Error* rather than a broken UI.

Conclusion

In this chapter, we mastered advanced JavaScript and DOM techniques to transform static pages into dynamic, responsive web applications. We began by selecting, traversing, and modifying DOM elements, then handled user interactions with event listeners, delegation, throttling, and debouncing. Form validation, localStorage, and sessionStorage demonstrated client-side state management. We improved code reliability with error handling and Chrome DevTools debugging. ES6+ features - modules, template literals, destructuring, optional chaining, and nullish coalescing, helped us write cleaner, modular code. Finally, we consumed key Web APIs, Fetch, XHR, WebSockets, Geolocation, Canvas, Drag-and-Drop, and Notifications, and cemented our learning with hands-on To-Do List and Calculator projects.

Next, in *Chapter 6, Web Technology Fundamentals*, we will step back to understand the web's underpinnings. You will learn how HTTP and HTTPS enable secure client-server communication, dissect the request-response cycle, and work with headers, cookies, and sessions. We will explore the client-server model, introduce CORS for cross-origin security, and design RESTful APIs. A hands-on Node.js and Express project will demonstrate building a basic web server. These fundamentals are crucial for developing scalable, secure, and performant web applications.

Exercises

1. Select the first <ul> on the page and append a new <li> with the text 'New item' using DOM methods only (no innerHTML).

2. Change the text of an element with id="title" to 'Dashboard' and add a class 'highlight' without removing existing classes.
3. Add a click listener to a button with id="saveBtn" that prevents default form submission and logs 'Saving…'.
4. Explain event bubbling and event capturing in one or two sentences, then attach a delegated click handler on a parent .list that reacts only to clicks on .delete buttons.
5. Write minimal code to toggle aria-expanded and a 'open' class on a dropdown trigger and its menu for accessibility.
6. Create a form validation snippet that requires a non-empty 'name' and a valid email; show an inline error message next to each invalid input.
7. Serialize form fields (name, email, message) from a form with id="contactForm" into a JSON object without using external libraries.
8. Use fetch to POST JSON { name, email } to /api/subscribe, handle non-2xx responses by throwing an Error, and show a success or error message in #status.
9. Debounce a search input (#q) so that handleSearch runs 300ms after the user stops typing; write a reusable debounce utility and apply it.
10. Throttle a scroll handler to run at most once every 100ms and update a progress bar width based on page scroll position.
11. Store a 'theme' preference ('light' or 'dark') in localStorage when a toggle is clicked, and apply it on page load via a data-theme attribute on <html>.
12. Write code that safely inserts user-provided text into #output without risk of XSS; then contrast it with an unsafe approach in one sentence.
13. Create and use a <template> element to add a new card with title and description to a .cards container on button click.
14. Build a minimal custom event named 'cart:add' that carries a productId detail; dispatch it from an Add to Cart button and listen for it on document.
15. Write worker.js that sums 1..n and postMessage(s) the result, and main-thread code that sends n and logs the returned sum; include basic error handling.

Join our Discord space

Join our Discord workspace for latest updates, offers, tech happenings around the world, new releases, and sessions with the authors:

https://discord.bpbonline.com

CHAPTER 6
Web Technology Fundamentals

Introduction

The **World Wide Web** (**WWW**) underpins nearly every aspect of modern digital life, enabling the exchange of information and the delivery of dynamic, interactive experiences. At its core lies a suite of protocols and standards—chief among them the **HyperText Transfer Protocol** (**HTTP**), that govern how clients (browsers) and servers communicate over the internet. This chapter delves into the fundamentals of web technology: we begin by exploring the stateless, text-based nature of HTTP and its various request methods (GET, POST, PUT, DELETE, etc.), then follow the life of a request through the **Domain Name System** (**DNS**) lookup, server processing, response delivery, and browser rendering. We examine **secure HTTP** (**HTTPS**), the mechanics of cookies and sessions for maintaining state, and the role of HTTP headers in conveying metadata. Finally, we survey higher-level concepts such as the client-server architecture, **Cross-Origin Resource Sharing** (**CORS**), and RESTful **application programming interface** (**API**) design, and apply this knowledge in hands-on projects and a real-world case study. By understanding these building blocks, you will be prepared to design and debug robust, secure web applications.

Structure

This chapter covers the following topics:

- Understanding HTTP
- Request-response cycle
- Secure HTTP
- Cookies and sessions
- HTTP headers and cookies
- Common HTTP request and response headers
- Custom headers
- Understanding cookies
- Cookie management with JavaScript
- Cookie security
- Client-server model
- CORS mechanism
- REST APIs
- Building a simple web server with Node.js

Objectives

After completing this chapter, the readers will be able to articulate how HTTP underlies every web interaction by defining its stateless, text-based nature and distinguishing among its core methods (GET, POST, PUT, DELETE, and more). They will trace the full request–response cycle, from DNS resolution through server processing to browser rendering, and contrast HTTP with its secure counterpart, HTTPS, explaining the benefits of **Transport Layer Security/Secure Sockets Layer** (**TLS/SSL**) encryption, data integrity, and authentication. Readers will demonstrate how cookies and sessions maintain user state across otherwise stateless requests, compare client-side versus server-side storage mechanisms, and identify the roles of common request and response headers (including custom headers) in conveying metadata and enforcing security. They will describe the client-server architecture's advantages and limitations, configure CORS headers to enable safe cross-origin resource sharing, and apply REST principles to design and consume stateless APIs with proper HTTP verbs and **JavaScript Object Notation** (**JSON**) payloads. Finally, they will build and test a simple Node.js/Express web server and analyze real-world network traffic in your browser's developer tools, reinforcing their understanding with practical, hands-on experience. The WWW is an essential platform for sharing information and building web applications. The foundation of web technologies includes protocols, markup languages, scripting, and databases that work together to deliver interactive and dynamic experiences. This chapter covers fundamental concepts such as HTTP, the request-response cycle, and how the web operates.

Understanding HTTP

HTTP is the fundamental protocol that governs how web clients and servers exchange information. It operates on top of **Transmission Control Protocol/Internet Protocol** (**TCP/IP**) and defines a simple request–response pattern, because HTTP is stateless, each interaction is self-contained, and servers do not inherently remember previous requests unless stateful mechanisms (such as cookies or sessions) are layered on top. HTTP messages are encoded in plain text, making them both human-readable and easy to debug.

Key HTTP features

HTTP provides a number of design principles that make it both powerful and flexible. Its stateless nature simplifies server implementation and scaling. The textual format of messages allows developers to inspect and diagnose issues easily. Built-in extensibility via headers supports authentication, caching, compression, and other cross-cutting concerns. Finally, HTTP's support for arbitrary media types makes it suitable for everything from plain HTML to JSON APIs and multimedia streaming.

The following demonstrates the core features of HTTP:

- **Statelessness**: Each request is independent, with no built-in memory of prior transactions. To maintain continuity, the application layer uses cookies, sessions, or tokens.
- **Textual format**: Requests and responses are plain text, with a start line, headers, a blank line, and an optional body. This human-readability eases manual testing and debugging.
- **Media flexibility**: Through the `Content-Type` header, HTTP can transport **HyperText Markup Language** (**HTML**), JSON, **eXtensible Markup Language** (**XML**), images, audio, video, and more.
- **Extensibility** Custom and standard headers allow conveying metadata such as authentication credentials (`Authorization`), caching directives (`Cache-Control`), and content negotiation (`Accept`).

Request methods

HTTP defines a small set of methods to indicate the desired action on a resource. Each method carries semantic meaning regarding safety, idempotence, and expected effects. Web applications rely on these verbs to structure RESTful APIs, perform **Create, Read, Update, and Delete** (**CRUD**) operations, and negotiate capabilities between client and server.

The following table presents the most common HTTP request methods:

Method	Purpose	Idempotent
`GET`	Retrieve a representation of a resource.	Yes
`POST`	Create or process a subordinate resource.	No
`PUT`	Replace or create a resource at the target URI.	Yes
`DELETE`	Remove the resource at the target URI.	Yes
`HEAD`	Same as GET, but returns only headers.	Yes
`OPTIONS`	Discover supported methods and features.	Yes

Table 6.1: Common HTTP request methods

The following figure depicts the architecture of the HTTP request and response exchange:

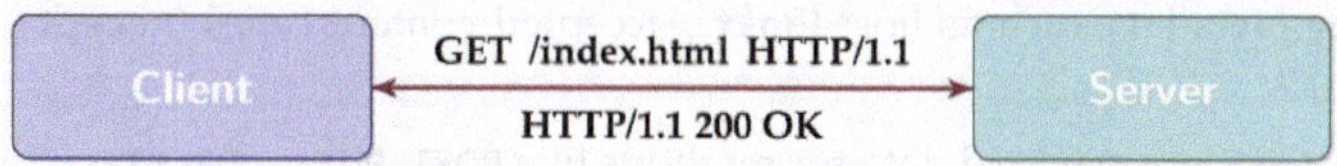

Figure 6.1: HTTP request-response exchange

Request-response cycle

The HTTP request-response cycle underpins all web interactions. A client issues a request to a server, which then processes that request and returns an appropriate response. This exchange is stateless by design, meaning the server does not retain memory of previous requests unless additional mechanisms (such as cookies or sessions) are employed.

Process steps

Each HTTP interaction follows a clear sequence of steps, from user initiation to browser rendering. Understanding these phases helps diagnose latency, failures, and performance bottlenecks.

The following presents the core stages of the cycle:

1. **Client sends request**: The user action—typing a **Uniform Resource Locator** (**URL**), clicking a link, or submitting a form, triggers the browser to construct and dispatch an HTTP request.
2. **DNS lookup**: The domain name is resolved to an IP address via the DNS, directing the request to the correct server.
3. **Server processing**: The server receives the request, routes it through application logic or static file handlers, and generates a response payload.
4. **Response delivery**: The server returns an HTTP response containing a status line, headers, and optionally a body with HTML, JSON, or other data.
5. **Browser rendering**: The client parses the response, applies styles, executes scripts, and displays the final page to the user.

The following figure shows the complete cycle of HTTP request-response:

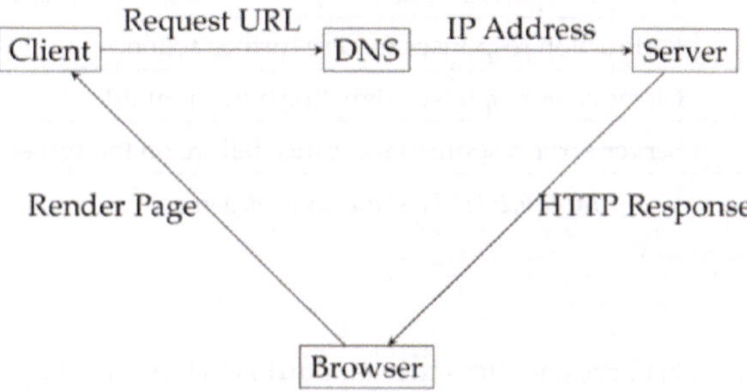

Figure 6.2: HTTP request-response cycle

Request structure

An HTTP request is composed of three main parts, which are the start line, headers, and an optional body. Together, they instruct the server on which resource to fetch, how to interpret data, and what client capabilities are.

The following demonstrates a typical request format:

- **Start line**: Specifies the method (e.g., `GET`), the path (e.g.,`/index.html`), and the HTTP version.
- **Headers**: Convey metadata such as host (`Host`), accepted content types (`Accept`), and user agent (`User-Agent`).
- **Body (optional)**: Contains payload data for methods like `POST`, `PUT`, or `DELETE`.

The following is an example of a simple `GET` request:

```
GET /index.html HTTP/1.1 Host: www.example.com User-Agent: Mozilla/5.0 Accept: text/html
```

Response structure

A server response mirrors the request format, which consists of a status line, headers, and a body. The status line indicates success or failure, headers provide context, and the body carries the requested content. The following demonstrates a standard response format:

- **Status line**: Contains the HTTP version, status code (e.g., `200`), and reason phrase (e.g., `OK`).
- **Headers**: Describe response metadata such as `Content-Type`, `Content-Length`, and caching policies.
- **Body**: The actual resource data includes HTML, JSON, image bytes, or other media.

The following is an example of a minimal HTTP response:

```
HTTP/1.1 200 OK
Content-Type: text/html Content-Length: 1024

<html>...</html>
```

Status code classes

HTTP status codes are grouped by their leading digit to indicate the general outcome of a request. Familiarity with these classes aids debugging and API design.

The following table shows the five status code categories:

Class	Meaning
1xx	Informational responses indicating request receipt.
2xx	Success responses confirming the request was processed.
3xx	Redirection responses require further action.
4xx	Client error responses signaling a bad request.
5xx	Server error responses indicate a failure on the server side.

***Table 6.2:** HTTP status code categories*

Secure HTTP

Secure HTTP, commonly known as HTTPS, enhances the standard HTTP protocol by encrypting all traffic between client and server using TLS. This encryption prevents eavesdropping, tampering, and impersonation, ensuring that data remains confidential and unaltered in transit.

Benefits

HTTPS delivers multiple security and functional advantages that are essential for modern web applications.

The following list outlines key benefits of HTTPS:

- **Encryption**: All data exchanged is encrypted, preventing third parties from reading sensitive information.
- **Integrity**: TLS ensures that messages cannot be modified in transit without detection.
- **Authentication**: Digital certificates verify that users are communicating with the legitimate server.
- **SEO boost**: Search engines favor HTTPS sites, improving visibility and rankings.

TLS handshake

Before secure data transfer begins, the client and server perform a handshake to agree on encryption parameters and authenticate the server.

The following figure presents the TLS handshake sequence:

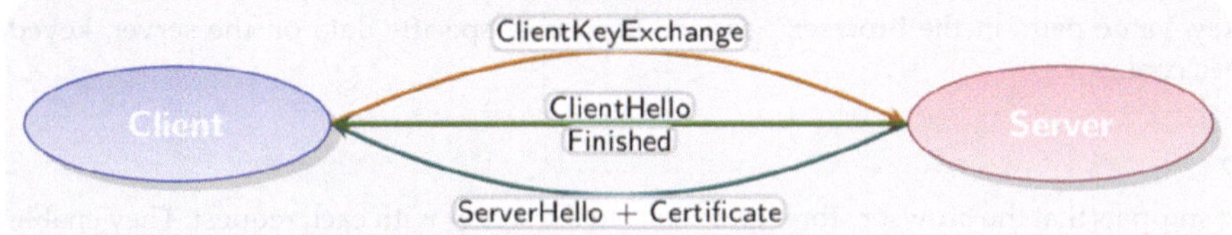

Figure 6.3: *TLS handshake process*

Certificate chain

Web browsers trust servers based on a chain of certificates rooted in well-known **certificate authorities** (**CAs**). Each certificate in the chain vouches for the next until the root CA is reached.

The following statement presents TLS version support and deprecation status:

Version	Status
TLS 1.0	Deprecated
TLS 1.1	Deprecated
TLS 1.2	Widely supported
TLS 1.3	Recommended

Table 6.3: *TLS version support status*

Redirect example

To ensure all visitors use HTTPS, servers often redirect HTTP requests to the secure scheme automatically.

The following statement demonstrates an Apache redirect to HTTPS:

```
RewriteEngine On RewriteCond %{HTTPS} off
RewriteRule ^(.*)$ https://%{HTTP_HOST}%{REQUEST_URI} [L,R=301]
```

Server setup

Enabling TLS on a Node.js server requires supplying the private key and certificate to the HTTPS module.

The following statement presents a minimal Node.js HTTPS server setup:

```
const https = require('https');
const fs = require('fs');

const options = {
```

```
  key: fs.readFileSync('key.pem'), cert: fs.readFileSync('cert.pem')
};

https.createServer(options, (req, res) => { res.writeHead(200, {'Content-Type': 'text/plain'});
  res.end('Hello Secure World');
}).listen(443, () => {
  console.log('HTTPS server running on port 443');
});
```

Cookies and sessions

Cookies and sessions are mechanisms to preserve state across multiple HTTP requests. Cookies reside on the client, storing small key–value pairs in the browser. Sessions keep user-specific data on the server, keyed by a session identifier sent via cookie.

Cookies

Cookies are text snippets that the browser stores and sends to the server with each request. They enable features such as remembering user preferences, maintaining authentication, and tracking behavior across pages.

The following presents common cookie uses:

- Storing user preferences such as theme or language.
- Maintaining login state across visits.
- Tracking user behavior for analytics and personalization.

The following demonstrates setting and reading a cookie:

```
// Set a cookie that expires in 7 days
document.cookie = "theme=dark; max-age=" + 7*24*60*60 + "; path=/";

// Read all cookies
console.log(document.cookie); // "theme=dark; other=..."
```

Sessions

Sessions store user data on the server side, offering stronger security for sensitive information. A unique session ID is stored in a cookie or URL parameter, allowing the server to retrieve the corresponding session data.

The following presents the session benefits:

- Secure storage of sensitive data on the server.
- Automatic expiry when the browser closes or after a timeout.
- Prevention of client-side tampering.

The following demonstrates a simple Express.js session setup:

```
const express = require('express');
const session = require('express-session');

const app = express(); app.use(session({
  secret: 'keyboard cat', resave: false, saveUninitialized: true
}));

app.get('/', (req, res) => {
```

```
  req.session.views = (req.session.views || 0) + 1;
  res.send(`Views: ${req.session.views}`);
});

app.listen(3000);
```

The following table presents a comparison of cookies and sessions:

Feature	Cookies (Client)	Sessions (Server)
Storage location	Browser	Server memory or storage.
Data size	Up to 4 kilobytes (KB) per cookie	Limited only by server capacity.
Security	Visible to client, editable	Hidden from the client.
Expiration	Configurable **time to live (TTL)**	On browser close or timeout.
Usage	Preferences, tracking	Authentication, cart contents.

Table 6.4: Comparison of cookies and sessions

Cycle steps

The HTTP request-response cycle describes how a browser and server exchange data.

The following list presents the cycle steps:

1. **Client request**: Browser sends an HTTP request with cookies.
2. **Server processing**: Server reads cookies or session ID, processes logic.
3. **Server response**: Server sends back headers, body, and may set cookies.
4. **Browser update**: Browser stores cookies and renders the response.

HTTP example

The following statement demonstrates an HTTP GET request:

```
GET /dashboard
HTTP/1.1 Host:
example.com
Cookie: theme=dark; connect.sid=abc123
```

The following statement demonstrates HTTP response:

```
HTTP/1.1 200 OK
Set-Cookie: theme=light; Max-Age=86400;
HttpOnly Content-Type: text/html

<html>…</html>
```

HTTP headers and cookies

HTTP headers and cookies work together to convey metadata and state between client and server. Headers are key–value pairs included in both requests and responses, while cookies are special headers that store small pieces of data on the client.

Header overview

Headers augment HTTP messages with information about content, caching, authentication, and more. They fall into several logical groups, each serving a different purpose in request/response processing.

The following presents header categories:

- **Request headers**: Convey client details (e.g., `User-Agent`, `Accept`, `Authorization`).
- **Response headers**: Convey server metadata (e.g., `Content-Type`, `Set-Cookie`, `Cache-Control`).
- **Entity headers**: Describe the message body (e.g., `Content-Length`, `Content-Encoding`).
- **Security headers**: Enforce policies (e.g., `Strict-Transport-Security`, `Content-Security- Policy`).

The following presents common headers in each category:

Category	Header	Purpose
Request	`Accept`	Media types the client can handle
	`User-Agent`	Client application identification
	`Authorization`	Credentials for authentication
Response	`Content-Type`	Media type of the response body
	`Set-Cookie`	Instructs the browser to store a cookie
	`Cache-Control`	Caching directives for clients/proxies
Entity	`Content-Length`	Size of the message body in bytes
	`Content-Encoding`	Compression applied to the body
Security	`Strict-Transport-Security`	Enforce HTTPS use
	`Content-Security-Policy`	Whitelist for resource loading

Table 6.5: Common HTTP headers

Header examples

These are some sample HTTP messages illustrating request and response headers in action. The following demonstrates a GET request with headers:

```
GET /dashboard HTTP/1.1 Host: example.com
User-Agent: Mozilla/5.0 (Windows NT 10.0;
Win64; x64) Accept:
text/html,application/xhtml+xml Authorization:
Bearer abcdef123456
```

The following demonstrates a response with headers:

```
HTTP/1.1 200 OK
Content-Type: text/html; charset=UTF-8
Content-Length: 1024
Cache-Control: max-age=3600
Set-Cookie: sessionId=xyz789; HttpOnly; Secure; SameSite=Lax
```

Cookie mechanics

Cookies are conveyed via the `Set-Cookie` response header and sent back by the client in the `Cookie` request header. They enable stateful interactions such as session management and user preferences.

The following list presents common cookie attributes:

- `HttpOnly` prevents JavaScript access, mitigating **cross-site scripting** (XSS) risks.
- `Secure` ensures cookies are sent only over HTTPS.

- `SameSite` controls cross-site sending (`Lax`, `Strict`, `None`).
- `Max-Age` or `Expires` sets the cookie's lifetime.
- `Path` and `Domain` restrict where the cookie is sent.

The following demonstrates setting and reading cookies in JavaScript:

```
// Set a cookie valid for 1 day
document.cookie = "theme=light; Max-Age=" + 24*60*60 + "; Path=/; Secure; SameSite=Lax";

// Read cookies
const cookies = document.cookie.split('; ').map(c =>c.split('='));
console.log(cookies); // [ ['theme','light'], ... ]
```

Common HTTP request and response headers

HTTP headers accompany every request and response, conveying metadata such as content negotiation, authentication credentials, caching directives, and cross-origin policies. Clients include request headers to inform servers of their capabilities and context, while servers return response headers to direct client behavior and convey resource properties. Understanding these headers is essential for debugging, security, and performance optimization.

Request headers

Request headers provide information about the client's environment, preferences, and authorization. They enable servers to tailor responses based on supported formats, security tokens, and the origin of the request. Proper use of request headers ensures efficient content negotiation and secure access control.

The following demonstrates a sample HTTP request with headers:

```
GET /index.html HTTP/1.1
Host: www.example.com
User-Agent: Mozilla/5.0 (Windows NT 10.0; Win64; x64)
Accept: text/html,application/xhtml+xml
Authorization: Bearer abc123token
Referer: https://www.example.com/home
```

The following presents key request headers:

- `Host` specifies the domain and port of the server.
- `User-Agent` identifies the client application and version.
- `Accept` lists of media types the client can process.
- `Authorization` carries credentials for protected resources.
- `Referer` indicates the URL of the referring resource.

Response headers

Response headers inform the client about the returned content, caching rules, security policies, and any cookies to store. They guide browsers and intermediaries in handling the response data correctly and securely.

The following demonstrates a sample HTTP response with headers:

```
HTTP/1.1 200 OK
Content-Type: text/html; charset=UTF-8
Content-Length: 1234
Cache-Control: max-age=3600, public
Set-Cookie: sessionId=xyz789; HttpOnly; Secure; SameSite=Lax
```

```
Access-Control-Allow-Origin: https://app.example.com
Access-Control-Allow-Credentials: true
```

The following presents key response headers:

- **Content-Type** specifies the media type and character encoding of the body.
- **Content-Length** indicates the size of the response body in bytes.
- **Cache-Control** controls caching mechanisms and lifetimes.
- **Set-Cookie** instructs the client to store cookies with attributes.
- **Access-Control-Allow-Origin** defines permitted cross-origin requests

Custom headers

Custom headers enable applications to transmit metadata or control information beyond the standard HTTP header set. Historically, non-standard headers were prefixed with **X-** (for example, **X-Requested-With**) to avoid collisions. Although RFC 6648 discourages the **X-** convention in favor of unprefixed header names, many APIs and legacy systems still use custom headers. When designing custom headers, choose clear, descriptive names and document their purpose. Be aware that using non-simple headers in cross-origin requests often triggers CORS preflight checks.

The following demonstrates an HTTP request with a custom header:

```
GET /api/resource
HTTP/1.1 Host:
api.example.com
Authorization: Bearer
abc123token X-Custom-Header:
MyCustomValue
```

Custom headers may carry application tokens, versioning information, feature flags, or debugging hints. Always ensure they do not expose sensitive data inadvertently.

The following demonstrates setting a custom header in JavaScript:

```
// Using Fetch API with a custom header
fetch('https://api.example.com/resource', { method: 'GET',
  headers: {
    'Authorization': 'Bearer abc123token', 'X-Custom-Header': 'MyCustomValue'
  }
})
  .then(response => response.json())
  .then(data => console.log(data))
  .catch(err => console.error('Fetch error:', err));
```

Understanding cookies

Cookies are small pieces of data that browsers store on the client's device to maintain stateful sessions and carry information across HTTP requests. Each cookie consists of a name-value pair and optional attributes, such as expiration, path, domain, and security flags, that control its scope and lifetime. Cookies enable features like login persistence, user preferences, and tracking, but they also introduce privacy considerations and size limitations (typically around 4 KB per cookie and a maximum of 20–50 cookies per domain).

Cookie types

There are several kinds of cookies, each serving distinct purposes and lifecycles. The following statements categorize cookies by their behavior and scope:

- **Session cookies**: Exist only for the browser session and are deleted when the user closes the browser.
- **Persistent cookies**: Remain on the client until a specified expiration date or until manually deleted.
- **Secure cookies**: Sent to the server only over encrypted HTTPS connections, protecting them from eavesdropping.
- **HttpOnly cookies**: Inaccessible to JavaScript's `document.cookie` API, mitigating cross-site scripting risks.
- **SameSite cookies**: Restrict cross-site sending: `Strict`, `Lax`, or `None` control whether cookies accompany cross-origin requests.

Cookie attributes

Every cookie can include attributes that define its scope and security. The following table outlines common cookie attributes and their purposes:

Attribute	Description
`Expires`	**Absolute expiration date (UTC)** after which the cookie is discarded.
`Max-Age`	Lifetime in seconds; takes precedence over `Expires`.
`Domain`	Hosts for which the cookie is sent; defaults to the host that set it.
`Path`	URL path that must exist in the request URL for the cookie to be sent.
`Secure`	If present, the cookie is sent only over HTTPS.
`HttpOnly`	If present, the cookie is inaccessible to JavaScript.
`SameSite`	Controls cross-site sending: `Strict`, `Lax`, or `None`.

Table 6.6: Common cookie attributes and descriptions

Setting cookies

Cookies can be created or updated by sending a `Set-Cookie` header from the server or via JavaScript's `document.cookie` API. When setting cookies in a script, you must format the string correctly and include any desired attributes.

The following is a code snippet that illustrates how to set a cookie with attributes in JavaScript:

```
// Set a persistent, secure cookie
document.cookie = [ "sessionId=abc123",
  "Max-Age=3600",              // 1 hour
  "Path=/",
  "Secure",                    // send only over HTTPS
  "SameSite=Lax"
].join("; ");
```

Accessing and deleting cookies

Reading and removing cookies require parsing the `document.cookie` string and issuing a new cookie with a past expiration date to delete it. The following examples demonstrate utilities for reading and deleting cookies:

```
// Read a cookie by name
function getCookie(name) {
  const pattern = new RegExp('(?:^|; )' + name + '=([^;]*)');
  const match = document.cookie.match(pattern);
  return match ? decodeURIComponent(match[1]) : null;
}
```

```
// Delete a cookie by name
function deleteCookie(name, path = '/') {
  document.cookie = `${name}=; Max-Age=0; Path=${path};`;
}

// Usage
console.log(getCookie('sessionId')); // e.g. "abc123"
deleteCookie('sessionId');
```

Cookie management with JavaScript

Cookies are small text entries that browsers store and send with HTTP requests to maintain state across page loads. JavaScript can manage cookies via the **document.cookie** API, enabling creation, retrieval, update, and deletion of cookies. Proper handling requires encoding values, specifying attributes such as expiration and path, and understanding security implications.

Set cookie

Creating a cookie involves writing a string to **document.cookie** that combines a name-value pair with optional attributes. Attributes control the cookie's lifetime, scope, and security flags. Without an explicit expiration, cookies default to session cookies that expire when the browser closes.

The following code shows how to set a cookie with attributes:

```
document.cookie = "username=Alice; \ expires=Fri, 31 Dec 2023 23:59:59 UTC; \ path=/;
SameSite=Lax";
```

Read cookie

Reading cookies returns a single string containing all name-value pairs separated by semicolons. To access individual cookies, you must split and parse this string, decoding each value as needed. The following demonstrates parsing **document.cookie** into an object:

```
// Retrieve raw cookie string
const raw = document.cookie; // e.g. "username=Alice; theme=dark"
// Parse into an object
const cookies = raw.split("; ").reduce((acc, pair) => {
  const [name, value] = pair.split("="); acc[name] = decodeURIComponent(value); return acc;
}, {});
console.log(cookies.username); // "Alice"
```

Delete cookie

To remove a cookie, overwrite it with the same name and set its expiration date to a past time. Ensure you match the original path and domain, so the browser removes the correct cookie.

The following code shows how to delete a cookie by expiring it:

```
document.cookie = "username=; \ expires=Thu, 01 Jan 1970 00:00:00 UTC; \ path=/; SameSite=Lax";
```

Cookie security

Modern browsers support cookie attributes that enhance security by limiting when and how cookies are sent. These flags help prevent common vulnerabilities like cross-site request forgery and script-based cookie theft.

The following list highlights the main security flags for cookies:

- **Secure**: Sent only over HTTPS, protecting against eavesdropping.
- **HflpOnly**: Inaccessible to JavaScript, mitigating XSS-based theft.
- **SameSite**: Controls cross-site sending: `Strict`, `Lax`, or `None`.
- **Domain and path**: Restrict which hosts and URL paths receive the cookie.

The following is an HTTP header example, which shows a secure, `HttpOnly` cookie with `SameSite` protection:

```
Set-Cookie: sessionId=abc123; Secure; HttpOnly; SameSite=Strict;
 Path=/; Max-Age=3600
```

Client-server model

The client-server architecture divides responsibilities between clients and servers in networked applications. Clients, such as web browsers or mobile apps, initiate requests for resources or services. Servers host applications, manage business-logic and data storage, and return appropriate responses. This separation promotes scalability, centralized management, and consistent security controls.

The following figure depicts client and server roles:

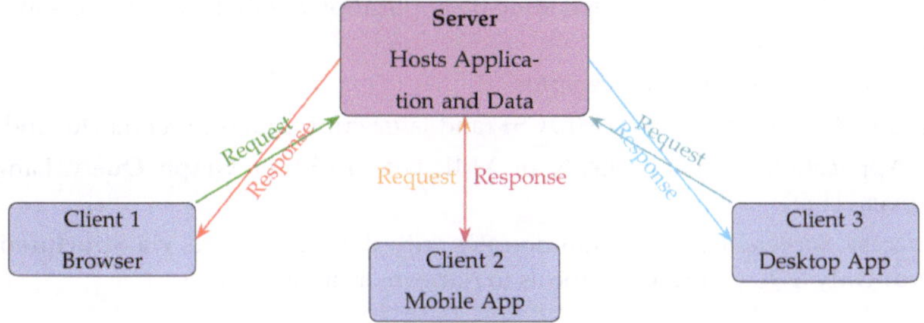

Figure 6.4: Interaction between clients and server

Client and server roles

In this model, each side has distinct duties. Clients present user interfaces and send requests for resources or actions. Servers listen for these requests, execute application logic, query or update databases, and formulate responses. This clear delineation enables efficient distribution of workloads and centralized enforcement of business rules and security.

Core roles in the client-server model are as follows:

- **Clients**: User agents (browsers, mobile or desktop apps) that issue HTTP requests to consume services.
- **Servers**: Backend systems that process incoming requests, perform computations or data access, and return HTTP responses.

Request example

An HTTP request comprises a request line, headers, and an optional body. The request line specifies the method, resource path, and protocol version. Headers convey metadata such as accepted formats and authentication tokens.

The following code demonstrates a typical HTTP GET request structure:

```
GET /home HTTP/1.1
Host: www.example.com
User-Agent: Mozilla/5.0 (Windows NT; Win64; x64)
Accept: text/html,application/xhtml+xml
```

Response example

An HTTP response begins with a status line indicating the protocol version, status code, and message. Response headers follow, providing metadata about the payload. The optional body contains the resource content, such as HTML or JSON.

The following code presents a standard HTTP response:

```
HTTP/1.1 200 OK
Content-Type: text/html; charset=UTF-8
Content-Length: 92

<html>
  <head><title>Example</title></head>
  <body><h1>Welcome to Example</h1></body>
</html>
```

Communication examples

Client-server interactions take various forms depending on application requirements. Understanding these patterns helps design robust, efficient systems.

The following are some common interaction scenarios:

- **Web browsing**: Browsers request HTML, CSS, and JavaScript from web servers to render pages.
- **API calls**: Applications exchange JSON or XML with REST or **Graph Query Language** (**GraphQL**) endpoints over HTTP.
- **Database access**: Server-side code communicates with database servers via **Structured Query Language** (**SQL**) or **Not Only SQL** (**NoSQL**) protocols to retrieve or update data.

Advantages and limitations

The client-server model offers clear benefits but also presents challenges. Centralizing logic and data on servers simplifies maintenance and enhances security. However, it introduces potential single points of failure and latency concerns.

The following table summarizes the pros and cons of the client-server model:

Aspect	Advantages	Limitations
Management	Centralized updates and consistent policies.	Single point of failure on the server side.
Scalability	Servers handle many concurrent clients.	Performance bottlenecks under heavy load.
Security	Central enforcement of access controls.	The entire system is compromised if the server is breached.
Maintenance	Simplified backups, monitoring, and disaster recovery.	Requires robust infrastructure and high availability.

***Table 6.7**: Advantages and limitations of the client-server model*

CORS mechanism

CORS is a browser security feature that controls how web pages from one origin can interact with resources from another. By default, browsers enforce the **Same-Origin Policy** (**SOP**), which restricts scripts on one domain from accessing data on a different domain. CORS relaxes SOP by using HTTP headers that explicitly grant or deny cross-origin access. When a browser issues a cross-origin request, it may send a *preflight* OPTIONS request to check what is permitted. The server's response headers then determine whether the browser proceeds with the actual request.

The following figure demonstrates the basic CORS request flow:

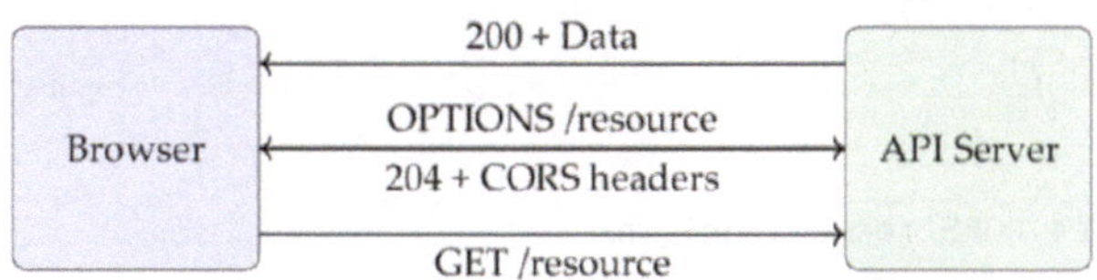

***Figure 6.5:** Simple CORS preflight and actual request flow*

Need for CORS

By default, scripts loaded from one origin cannot interact with resources on another, preventing many legitimate use cases such as calling third-party APIs or serving assets from a **Content Delivery Network** (CDN). Modern applications often rely on microservices, cloud APIs, or external storage, all of which typically reside on different domains. CORS provides a controlled way to grant access only to trusted origins, ensuring both flexibility and security.

The following code demonstrates a CORS-blocked request:

```
Access to fetch at 'https://api.example.com/data' from origin 'https://mywebsite.com' has been blocked
by CORS policy: No 'Access-Control-Allow-Origin' header is present.
```

This error shows that the API server did not include the `Access-Control-Allow-Origin` header in its response, so the browser refused to share the response with the calling script.

CORS error handling

When a CORS error occurs, developers can choose among several strategies to resolve it while preserving security:

The following list presents common handling approaches:

- **Server-side CORS headers**: Servers send headers like `Access-Control-Allow-Origin` or `Access-Control-Allow-Methods` to explicitly permit cross-origin requests.
- **Proxy servers**: A same-origin proxy forwards client requests to the external API, avoiding direct cross-origin calls by the browser.
- **JSONP (Deprecated)**: JSONP uses `<script>` tags for cross-domain data loading but is limited to GET requests and poses security risks.

The following table presents common CORS headers:

Header	Description
Access-Control-Allow-Origin	Specifies allowed origin(s)
Access-Control-Allow-Methods	Specifies allowed HTTP methods
Access-Control-Allow-Headers	Specifies allowed request headers
Access-Control-Allow-Credentials	Indicates whether credentials are allowed

***Table 6.8:** Common CORS headers*

Server CORS setup

Most web frameworks offer simple middleware or configuration for setting the necessary CORS headers automatically. By tailoring these settings, servers can either allow all origins or restrict access to a specific list of trusted domains.

Refer to the following code, which demonstrates enabling CORS for all origins in Express.js:

```
const express = require("express");
const cors = require("cors");

const app = express();
app.use(cors()); // Enables CORS for all origins

app.get("/data", (req, res) =>
  { res.json({ message: "CORS
  enabled" });
});

app.listen(3000, () => console.log("Server running on port 3000"));
```

With this setup, any website can request **/data**. To tighten security, you can specify exactly which origins are permitted:

The following demonstrates restricting CORS to one origin:

```
const express = require("express");
const cors = require("cors");
const app = express();

const corsOptions = {
  origin: 'https://mywebsite.com', optionsSuccessStatus: 200
};

app.use(cors(corsOptions));

app.get("/data", (req, res) => {
  res.json({ message: "CORS enabled for mywebsite.com" });
});

app.listen(3000, () => console.log("Server running on port 3000"));
```

This configuration ensures that only scripts served from **https://mywebsite.com** can access your API, preventing other domains from successfully making requests.

REST APIs

RESTful APIs follow an architectural style defined by Roy Fielding that enables scalable, maintainable, and stateless web services. Clients interact with named resources on servers using standard HTTP methods. Each resource is identified by a URI, and representations (typically JSON or XML) are exchanged over the network, because REST enforces statelessness, each request contains all information needed for processing. This simplifies server design and allows horizontal scaling, as servers need not store session data.

Server and client roles

In the REST model, servers and clients have distinct responsibilities. Servers host resources, handle business-logic, enforce validation, and return responses. Clients initiate requests, parse responses, render data, and manage user interactions. By cleanly separating concerns, RESTful design promotes modularity and reuse.

The following list outlines the responsibilities of servers and clients:

- **Servers**: Receive HTTP requests, perform authentication and validation, access databases or other services, and send back status codes with resource representations.
- **Clients**: Construct and send HTTP requests, handle response codes, parse JSON or XML payloads, update the UI or data store, and manage retries or error handling.

REST principles

REST rests on a set of architectural constraints that ensure consistency, performance, and simplicity. By adhering to these principles, API designers create services that are intuitive and easy to evolve.

Core REST guidelines are as follows:

- **Statelessness**: Every request includes all information needed; servers do not retain client context between requests.
- **Resource URIs**: Resources are addressed via unique, hierarchical URIs (e.g., `/users/42/orders`).
- **HTTP Verbs**: Use standard methods like `GET` (read), `POST` (create), `PUT/PATwCH` (update), `DELETE` (remove).
- **Representations**: Transfer resource state in formats like JSON or XML, with appropriate `Content-Type` headers.
- **Uniform interface**: A consistent set of conventions for URIs, verbs, headers, and status codes makes APIs predictable.

REST API example

A typical REST API returns structured data in response to client requests. Clients can easily parse and use this data for rendering or further processing.

A typical REST response is as follows:

```
{
  "users": [
    { "id": 1, "name": "Alice" },
    { "id": 2, "name": "Bob" }
  ]
}
```

HTTP methods

HTTP methods in REST carry specific semantics that guide resource operations. Correct usage ensures APIs behave consistently and predictably.

The following demonstrates HTTP method usage:

```
GET /users HTTP/1.1 Host: api.example.com

POST /users HTTP/1.1 Host: api.example.com
Content-Type: application/json

{ "name": "Charlie" }

PUT /users/2 HTTP/1.1 Host: api.example.com
Content-Type: application/json

{ "name": "Robert" }

DELETE /users/2 HTTP/1.1 Host: api.example.com
```

Building a simple web server with Node.js

In this hands-on project, the objective is that we will be building a basic web server using Node.js and Express. The server will handle HTTP requests and serve a simple web page.

Project setup

To complete this project, ensure that Node.js is installed on your system. Refer to the following steps:

1. Install Node.js from **https://nodejs.org/**.
2. Open a terminal and create a project folder:
   ```
   mkdir web-server cd web-server
   ```
3. Initialize a Node.js project:
   ```
   npm init -y
   ```
4. Install Express:
   ```
   npm install express
   ```

Implementation of the web server

Create a file named **`server.js`** and add the following code:

server.js

```
const express = require("express");
const app = express();
const port = 3000;

// Define a route for handling HTTP GET requests
app.get("/", (req, res) => {
    res.send("<h1>Welcome to My Web Server</h1>");
});

// Start the server
app.listen(port, () => {
    console.log(`Server running at http://localhost:${port}`);
});
```

Running the server

To run the web server, execute the following command in the terminal:

```
node server.js
```

Testing the web server

Refer to the following steps to test a web server:

1. Open a web browser and visit: **http://localhost:3000**
2. The message **`Welcome to My Web Server`** should be displayed as shown in the following figure:

Figure 6.6: Output of the web server with Node.js

Extending the project

To extend this project, add support for handling additional routes:

`Enhanced Code: server.js`

```
// Additional route
app.get("/about", (req, res) => {
    res.send("<h1>About Page</h1><p>This is a basic web server.</p>");
});
```

Restart the server and visit **http://localhost:3000/about** to see the new page.

Project summary: In this project, we implemented a simple web server using Node.js and Express, demonstrated how to handle HTTP requests, and extended the functionality with additional routes.

Conclusion

In this chapter, we have established the foundational principles of web communication. You have learned how HTTP functions as a stateless protocol carrying requests and responses over TCP/IP, and seen how secure HTTPS exchanges guarantee confidentiality and integrity. We dissected the request–response cycle, detailed the structures of HTTP messages, and surveyed crucial status codes. By exploring cookies and sessions, you now understand how state is managed across stateless exchanges. HTTP headers empower metadata exchange and security controls, while the client-server model underlies every web interaction. We tackled CORS to enable safe cross-origin access, and embraced RESTful API design for scalable, stateless services. Hands-on projects solidified your ability to implement a simple Express server and inspect real-world traffic, and the e-commerce case study illustrated these mechanisms in practice.

In the next chapter, we will shift our focus to *Modern Frontend Frameworks*, starting with React. You will discover how component-based architectures, virtual **Document Object Model** (**DOM**) diffing, and unidirectional data flow transform JavaScript from a scripting language into a powerful tool for building highly interactive, maintainable single-page applications. Prepare to explore **JavaScript XML** (**JSX**) syntax, state and props, hooks, and the vast React ecosystem as we bridge from low-level protocols to high-level user interfaces.

Exercises

1. Define HTTP in one sentence and explain why it is called a stateless protocol.
2. Write the general structure of a raw HTTP request (start line, two example headers, blank line, optional body). Use a GET /index.html example with a Host header.
3. Classify these status codes by class and meaning in one short line each: 200, 301, 403, 404, 500.
4. List five common HTTP methods (GET, POST, PUT, DELETE, HEAD) and state for each whether it is safe and/or idempotent.

5. Name four important request headers and four important response headers and state the purpose of each in 4–8 words.
6. Explain the complete HTTP request–response cycle in 5 bullet sentences including DNS lookup and browser rendering steps.
7. Describe the core differences between HTTP and HTTPS and list three benefits of TLS (encryption, integrity, authentication).
8. Write a minimal Node.js + Express server that responds 'Hello' to GET / and listens on port 3000 (about 8–10 lines).
9. Extend the server: add POST /data that accepts JSON and echoes it back; include express.json() and a simple console log of method and URL.
10. Show a Node.js HTTPS server setup snippet that reads key.pem and cert.pem and serves plain text 'Secure OK' on port 443 (about 10–12 lines).
11. Set a cookie named sessionId with value abc123 that lasts 1 hour, has Path=/, Secure, HttpOnly, and SameSite=Lax using (a) a Set-Cookie header line and (b) document.cookie JavaScript.
12. State two differences between cookies and sessions, and give one use case where sessions are safer than cookies.
13. Write short Express code to enable sessions using express-session that counts and returns the number of views at GET / (about 8–10 lines).
14. Explain what a CORS preflight request is, when it triggers, and why browsers enforce it.
15. Write Express CORS configuration that (a) allows only https://app.example.com, (b) allows credentials, and (c) exposes the X-Total-Count header.

Chapter 7
React

Introduction

Modern web applications demand robust, maintainable, and dynamic user interfaces. React, a JavaScript library developed by Facebook, addresses these needs with its component-based architecture, declarative **JavaScript XML** (**JSX**) syntax, and virtual **Document Object Model** (**DOM**) for efficient rendering. In this chapter, you will set up your React environment, scaffold a new project, and organize its folder structure. We will explore how Babel transforms JSX into JavaScript and examine both functional and class components—leveraging props, children, and defaultProps. You will learn state management with the useState and useReducer hooks, side-effect control via useEffect, and event handling with React's synthetic event system. We will configure client-side routing with React Router, introduce global state via the Context API, and build custom hooks for reusable logic. You will apply performance optimizations using memoization techniques (useMemo, useCallback, React.memo), handle controlled and uncontrolled forms with validation, test components using Jest and React Testing Library (including snapshots), and style your **user interface** (**UI**) with CSS Modules, Tailwind CSS, styled-components, or CSS-in-JS. Finally, we will survey advanced patterns, best practices, and the wider React ecosystem to equip you for real-world development.

Structure

This chapter covers the following topics:

- Getting started
- JavaScript XML basics
- Components
- State management
- Effect hook
- Event handling
- Routing
- Context API
- Custom hooks
- Performance
- Forms
- Testing
- Styling
- State libraries
- Build and deploy
- Ecosystem
- Advanced patterns
- Best practices
- Hands-on project

Objectives

By the end of this chapter, the readers will have configured a React development environment and organized its folder structure. They will write and transform JSX, grasp Babel's role, and build both function and class components leveraging props, children, and defaultProps. They will manage component state using useState and useReducer, lift state upward, and orchestrate side effects with useEffect, including dependency arrays and cleanup. Readers will also handle synthetic events and context binding, and configure client-side routing with dynamic parameters and nested routes using React Router. They will create, provide, and consume global state via the Context **application programming interface** (**API**), and author reusable custom hooks. They will optimize performance with memoization, useMemo, useCallback, and React.memo. They will build controlled and uncontrolled forms, validate inputs, test components with Jest and React Testing Library (including snapshot tests), and apply styling using CSS Modules, Tailwind CSS, styled-components, and CSS-in-JS. Finally, they will apply advanced patterns and best practices for code organization and performance.

Getting started

This section guides you through the initial steps required to start a React project. It covers installing essential tools, creating a new application from a template, and understanding the default project layout. Following these steps ensures a smooth development experience and provides a solid foundation for building React applications.

Environment setup

Developing with React requires a recent version of Node.js and a JavaScript package manager. Node.js provides the runtime for development tools and build processes, while npm (or Yarn) handles package installation. A code editor with syntax highlighting and linting, such as **Visual Studio Code** (**VS Code**), enhances productivity. Optionally, installing the **TypeScript** compiler globally allows adding static types later.

The following list presents the required tools:

- **Node.js (v14 or above)**: JavaScript runtime for development scripts and bundling.
- **npm or Yarn**: Package manager for installing libraries and running scripts.
- **Code Editor**: VS Code recommended, with ESLint and Prettier extensions.
- **TypeScript (optional)**: For adding types: `npm install -g typescript`.

The following demonstrates installation commands:

```
# Install Node.js (Ubuntu)
curl -fsSL https://deb.nodesource.com/setup_20.x | sudo -E bash -
sudo apt-get install -y nodejs

# Verify versions
node --version     # e.g. v16.13.0
npm --version      # e.g. 8.1.0

# (Optional) Install Yarn globally
npm install -g yarn

# (Optional) Install TypeScript
npm install -g typescript
```

Project creation

Creating a React project typically starts with a tool that sets up the development server, build pipeline, and a clean folder layout. **Create React App** (**CRA**) suits learning and small demos, while Vite is a modern option that starts fast and keeps hot reload responsive. For production applications that need routing, server-side rendering, and structured data loading patterns out of the box, React frameworks such as Next.js and Remix are also widely used.

The following demonstrates using CRA:

```
# Using npm
npx create-react-app my-app

# Or using Yarn
yarn create react-app my-app
```

```
# Navigate into project
cd my-app

# Start development server
npm start
```

The following demonstrates using Vite:

```
# Scaffold with Vite (React + JavaScript)
npm create vite@latest my-app -- --template react

# Install dependencies
cd my-app
npm install

# Start dev server
npm run dev

# (Optional) Next.js (React framework)
npx create-next-app@latest my-next-app
cd my-next-app
npm run dev

# (Optional) Remix (React framework)
npx create-remix@latest my-remix-app
cd my-remix-app
npm install
npm run dev
```

Folder structure

After scaffolding, the project folder contains configuration files, source code, and assets. Understanding this layout helps locate code, assets, and build output efficiently. Customizing or extending the structure should follow these conventions to maintain consistency.

The following table demonstrates the default folder layout:

Path	Purpose
node_modules/	Installed dependencies for the project.
public/	Static assets and HTML template (**index.html**).
src/	Application source code (components, styles, tests).
src/index.js	Entry point that renders the root component.
src/App.js	Main application component.
package.json	Project metadata and scripts (start, build, test).
package-lock.json	Exact dependency tree (npm) **vite.config.js**.
node_modules/	Installed dependencies for the project.

Table 7.1: *Default project folder structure*

JavaScript XML basics

JSX is a syntax extension that allows writing HTML-like code within JavaScript. It provides a declarative, familiar way to define UI components by combining markup and logic. Under the hood, JSX is transformed into standard JavaScript function calls (e.g., **React.createElement**). This transformation enables efficient updates via the Virtual

DOM and keeps component definitions concise and readable. By blending structure and behavior, JSX streamlines component development and aligns with React's component-centric paradigm.

JSX syntax

JSX syntax closely resembles HTML but follows JavaScript rules. Elements must be properly closed, attribute names use camelCase (e.g., `className`), and JSX tags can be nested. Components are referenced using capitalized names. Every JSX expression must return a single root element; if multiple siblings are needed, they can be wrapped in a fragment (`<> </>`).

The following presents common syntax rules:

- **Elements must close**: <img />, <div></div>
- **Attributes use camelCase:** className, htmlFor
- **JavaScript expressions in braces:** {user.name}
- **Fragment wrapper:** <></>

The following demonstrates JSX element examples:

```
function Profile() {
  return (
    <>
      <h1 className="title">Welcome</h1>
      <img src="/avatar.png" alt="User avatar" />
      <label htmlFor="nameInput">Name</label>
      <input id="nameInput" placeholder="Enter name" />
    </>
  );
}
```

Expressions in JSX

JSX allows embedding any JavaScript expression inside curly braces. This includes variables, function calls, ternaries, and array methods. Expressions must resolve to a renderable value (string, number, element, array of elements). Complex logic should reside outside the return statement to maintain readability. Conditional rendering and list rendering are common patterns.

The following list presents expression usage:

- Variable interpolation: `{count}`
- Conditional rendering: `{isLoggedIn ? <Home /> : <Login />}`
- List rendering: `{items.map(item => <li key={item.id}>{item.name}</li>)}`

The following demonstrates JSX expressions:

```
function ItemsList({ items, isLoading
                                       }) {
if (isLoading) return <p>Loading...</
                                       p>;

  return (
    <ul>
      {items.length === 0
        ? <li>No items found</li>
```

```
            : items.map(item => (
                <li key={item.id}>{item.name}</li>
            ))
        }
    </ul>
  );
}
```

JSX and Babel

Browsers do not understand JSX natively. Babel, a JavaScript compiler, transforms JSX into **React.createElement** calls. A Babel configuration with the **@babel/preset-react** preset enables this transformation. During build time, Babel processes files, applies plugins, and outputs browser-compatible JavaScript. Integrating Babel with bundlers like Webpack or Vite automates JSX compilation.

Most modern React setups hide this complexity. Tools such as Create React App and Vite already include the required JSX transform in their build pipeline, so JSX works out of the box. In typical projects, there is no need to edit Babel configuration files manually. Manual Babel configuration is mainly relevant when building a custom Webpack setup, adding uncommon language features, or maintaining older toolchains.

The following script demonstrates a minimal Babel configuration:

```
{
  "presets": [ "@babel/preset-env", "@babel/preset-react"
  ],
  "plugins": [
    "@babel/plugin-transform-runtime"
  ]
}
```

The following table presents a transformation example:

JSX input	Transformed output

`<h1>Hello {name}</h1>`	`React.createElement(`
	`'h1',`
	`null, 'Hello ', name`
	`);`

Table 7.2: JSX to JavaScript via Babel

Components

React components are the building blocks of a React application. Each component encapsulates its own structure, behavior, and styling, enabling modular and reusable UI elements. Components can be simple functions or classes and can manage internal state, accept external data via props, and respond to user interactions. By composing components together, complex interfaces can be built from small, testable pieces.

Function components

Function components are JavaScript functions that return React elements. They are concise and, since React 16.8, can manage state and side effects using hooks. Function components are preferred for their simplicity and performance benefits, as they avoid the overhead of class instantiation and lifecycle methods when not needed.

The following presents key traits of function components:

- Defined as plain functions
- Use hooks (**useState**, **useEffect**) for state and effects
- Do not have `this` context
- Easier to test and reason about

The following demonstrates a function component example:

```
// src/Timer.jsx
import React, { useEffect, useState } from "react";

function Timer() {
    const [seconds, setSeconds] = useState(0);
    useEffect(() => {
        const id = setInterval(() => {
            setSeconds((s) => s + 1);
        }, 1000);

        // cleanup on unmount
        return () => clearInterval(id);
    }, []);

    return (
        <div style={{ fontFamily: "Arial, sans-serif", padding: 16 }}>
            <h2 style={{ marginTop: 0 }}>Timer (useState + useEffect)</h2>
            <p style={{ fontSize: 18 }}>Elapsed: {seconds}s</p>
        </div>
    );
}

export default Timer;

// src/App.js
import Timer from "./Timer";

export default function App() {
  return (
      <div style={{ maxWidth: 640, margin: "40px auto", padding: "0 16px" }}>
        <Timer />
      </div>
  );
}
```

The following browser output figure confirms that a function component can manage time-based behavior using hooks. The **useState** hook stores the **seconds** value, and the component re-renders whenever this state changes. The **useEffect** hook starts a **setInterval** timer once after the first render because the dependency array is empty (**[]**). Every 1000 ms, the interval updates state using the functional form setSeconds**(s => s + 1)**, which always uses the latest state value. The effect also returns a cleanup function that clears the interval, which prevents extra timers and avoids memory leaks when the component unmounts.

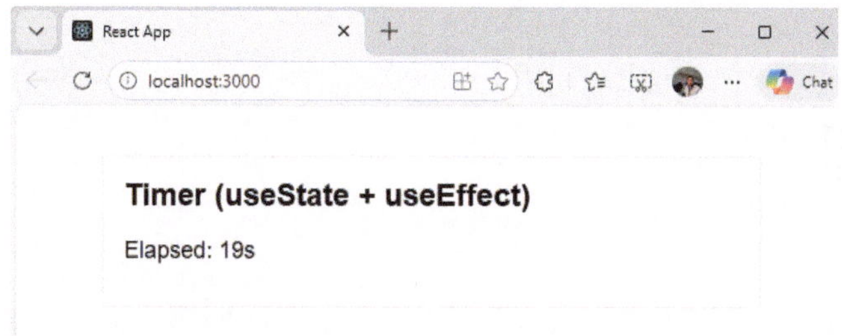

Figure 7.1: Browser output of the Timer function component

The component updates the elapsed seconds once per second using **useState**, and schedules/cleans the interval using **useEffect**.

Class components

Class components extend **React.Component** and use lifecycle methods plus internal state. Modern React development primarily uses function components with hooks, so class components are best treated as legacy knowledge for maintaining older codebases. Class components still appear in many real projects, and understanding **render()** and key lifecycle methods helps when reading or migrating existing code.

Note: Default approach in new projects: write function components and use hooks (useState, useEffect, useReducer). Use class components only when working with an existing codebase that already follows the class style.

The following presents a lifecycle method overview:

Method	Purpose
constructor	Initialize state and bind event handlers.
render	Return JSX that describes the UI.
componentDidMount	Run side effects after first render (fetch data, subscriptions, timers).
componentDidUpdate	Respond to prop/state changes (re-run effects with conditions).
componentWillUnmount	Cleanup before removal (clear timers, remove listeners).

Table 7.3: Class component lifecycle methods

The following example shows the pattern commonly found in older React codebases:

```
import React from 'react';

class Clock extends React.Component {
  constructor(props) {
    super(props);
    this.state = { time: new Date() };
  }

  componentDidMount() {
    this.timerID = setInterval(() => {
      this.setState({ time: new Date() });
```

```
    }, 1000);
  }

  componentWillUnmount()
    { clearInterval(this.
    timerID);
  }

  render() {
    return <h2>Time: {this.state.time.toLocaleTimeString()}</h2>;
  }
}

export default Clock;
```

Component properties

Properties (**Props**) are read-only inputs passed from a parent component to a child. They allow components to be reusable and configurable. Props can include data of any type—strings, numbers, objects, or even functions.

The following presents prop usage patterns:

- **Passed as attributes in JSX**: `<Greeting name="Alice" />`.
- Accessed via **props** argument in function components.
- Accessed via **this.props** in class components.
- Immutable within the child component.

The following demonstrates a props example:

```
function Greeting(props) {
  return <p>Hello, {props.name}!</p>;
}

// Usage: <Greeting name="Alice" />
```

Children prop

The **children** prop is a special prop that represents nested content inside a component. It enables wrapping arbitrary JSX or other components, making container components flexible.

The following presents children's prop usage:

- Automatically populated with inner JSX.
- Useful for layout or wrapper components.
- Can be any renderable React node.

The following demonstrates a children's prop example:

```
function Card(props) {
  return (
    <div className="card">
      {props.children}
    </div>
  );
```

```
}

// Usage:
// <Card>
//   <h3>Title</h3>
//   <p>Content goes here.</p>
// </Card>
```

Default props

Default props provide fallback values when a parent does not supply a prop. Defining default props ensures components behave predictably even if certain props are omitted.

The following presents the default props setup:

- Defined as **`Component.defaultProps`**.
- Works for both function and class components.
- Applied before prop type validation.

The following demonstrates a default props example:

```
function Button(props) {
  return <button>{props.label}</button>;
}

Button.defaultProps = { label: 'Click me'
};

// Usage without label prop:
// <Button /> renders "Click me"
```

State management

State in React represents dynamic data that determines how components render and behave. Managing state efficiently ensures UI consistency, predictable updates, and easier debugging. React provides hooks and patterns to handle state within components, share state between components, and coordinate complex state logic. This section covers local state with **`useState`**, more advanced local state with **`useReducer`**, and sharing state via lifting.

useState hook

The **`useState`** hook allows function components to hold and update local state. It returns a state value and a setter function. Calling the setter schedules a re-render with the new state. The initial state can be a value or a function for lazy initialization. **`useState`** is ideal for simple states like form fields, toggles, or counters.

The following presents **`useState`** signature:

```
const [state, setState] = useState(initialValue);
```

- **`initialValue`** can be a primitive, an object, an array, or a function returning the initial state.
- Calling **`setState(newValue)`** enqueues an update and re-renders the component.
- **Setter accepts a function form**: **`setState(prev => computeNext(prev))`**.

The following demonstrates a counter example:

```
import React, { useState } from 'react';
```

```
function Counter() {
  const [count, setCount] = useState(0);

  return (
    <div>
      <p>Count is {count}</p>
      <button onClick={() => setCount(c => c + 1)}>
        Increment
      </button>
    </div>
  );
}

export default Counter;
```

useReducer hook

The `useReducer` hook manages complex state logic by using a reducer function that takes the current state and an action, then returns the next state. It mirrors Redux's reducer pattern but operates locally. `useReducer` is suitable when state transitions involve multiple sub-values or when the next state depends on the previous state in non-trivial ways.

The following presents `useReducer` signature:

- `const [state, dispatch] = useReducer(reducer, initialState);`
- `reducer` is `(state, action) => newState`.
- `dispatch(action)` triggers the reducer to compute and set a new state.
- Optional `init` function can lazily initialize state.

The following table presents a comparison of hooks:

Criterion	useState	useReducer
Complexity	Simple state	Complex state logic
Update logic	Inline setter calls	Centralized I reducer function
Related updates	Multiple setters	Single dispatch for all updates
Performance	Fine for a few state vars	Better for many updates
Readability	Local logic	Encapsulated I in I reducer

Table 7.4: useState versus useReducer

The following demonstrates a reducer example:

```
import React, { useReducer } from 'react';

const initialState = {
  values: { name: '', email: '', password: '' },
  errors: {},
  isSubmitting: false
};

function validate(values) {
  const errors = {};
```

```
  if (!values.name.trim()) errors.name = 'Name is required.';
  if (!/^\S+@\S+\.\S+$/.test(values.email)) errors.email = 'Enter a valid email.';
  if (values.password.length < 6) errors.password = 'Password must be at least 6 characters.';

  return errors;
}

function reducer(state, action) {
  switch (action.type) {
    case 'updateField': {
      const values = { ...state.values, [action.field]: action.value };
      return { ...state, values };
    }

    case 'submitStart':
      return { ...state, isSubmitting: true };

    case 'submitValidate': {
      const errors = validate(state.values);
      const hasErrors = Object.keys(errors).length > 0;
      return { ...state, errors, isSubmitting: !hasErrors };
    }

    case 'submitSuccess':
      return { ...initialState };

    case 'reset':
      return { ...initialState };

    default:
      throw new Error('Unknown action type');
  }
}
```

The following is the continuation of the reducer example:

```
function SignupFormReducer() {
  const [state, dispatch] = useReducer(reducer, initialState);
  const { values, errors, isSubmitting } = state;

  function handleChange(e) {
    dispatch({
      type: 'updateField',
      field: e.target.name,
      value: e.target.value
    });
  }

  function handleSubmit(e) {
    e.preventDefault();
    dispatch({ type: 'submitStart' });
    dispatch({ type: 'submitValidate' });

    // If validation passed, "submit" the form (demo purpose)
    const nextErrors = validate(values);
    if (Object.keys(nextErrors).length === 0) {
```

```
      console.log('Submitted:', values);
      dispatch({ type: 'submitSuccess' });
    }
  }

  return (
      <form onSubmit={handleSubmit}>
        <label>Name</label>
        <input name="name" value={values.name} onChange={handleChange} />
        {errors.name && <p className="error">{errors.name}</p>}

        <label>Email</label>
        <input name="email" value={values.email} onChange={handleChange} />
        {errors.email && <p className="error">{errors.email}</p>}

        <label>Password</label>
        <input
            name="password"
            type="password"
            value={values.password}
            onChange={handleChange}
        />
        {errors.password && <p className="error">{errors.password}</p>}

        <button type="submit" disabled={isSubmitting}>
          Sign up
        </button>

        <button type="button" onClick={() => dispatch({ type: 'reset' })}>
          Reset
        </button>
      </form>
  );
}

export default SignupFormReducer;
```

This example shows why **useReducer** helps in real apps. One reducer centralizes updates for related fields, validation errors, and the submit flow. The component stays readable because it dispatches actions instead of managing many **useState** calls that can become scattered.

Lifting state

Lifting state involves moving shared state up to the closest common ancestor of the components that need it. This pattern avoids duplication and ensures a single source of truth. Child components receive the state and updater via props. Lifting is critical for coordinating sibling component interactions and consolidating state logic.

The following presents lifting steps:

1. Identify the minimal common parent of components sharing a state.
2. Move the state and updater function into that parent.
3. Pass state and updater down via props to child components.
4. Children call updater to modify parent state, triggering a re-render.

The following demonstrates a lifting state example:

```
import React, { useState } from 'react';

function TemperatureInput({ scale, temp, onTempChange }) {
  return (
    <fieldset>
      <legend>Enter temperature in {scale}:</legend>
      <input
        value={temp}
        onChange={e => onTempChange(e.target.value)}
      />
    </fieldset>
  );
}

function Calculator() {
  const [celsius, setCelsius] = useState('');
  const [fahrenheit, setFahrenheit] = useState(,‘);

  function handleCelsiusChange(value) { setCelsius(value);
    setFahrenheit((value * 9/5 + 32).toFixed(1));
  }

  function handleFahrenheitChange(value) {
    setFahrenheit(value);
    setCelsius(((value - 32) * 5/9).toFixed(1));
  }

  return (
    <div>
      <TemperatureInput scale="Celsius" temp={celsius}
        onTempChange={handleCelsiusChange}
      />
      <TemperatureInput scale="Fahrenheit" temp={fahrenheit}
        onTempChange={handleFahrenheitChange}
       />
     </div>
   );
}

export default Calculator;
```

Effect hook

The Effect hook (**useEffect**) lets function components perform side effects, operations that interact with outside systems or mutate state outside the render. Effects run after render, ensuring the UI is updated before the operation. Common uses include data fetching, subscriptions, manually updating the DOM, and timers. By declaring effects, React can coordinate when and how they run, improving consistency and avoiding race conditions.

useEffect usage

The **useEffect** hook takes a function that React runs after rendering. This function can optionally return a cleanup function. Effects run on initial mount and, by default, after every update. Using **useEffect** moves side-effect logic out of the render phase, keeping render pure and predictable.

The following presents basic **useEffect** usage:

```
import React, { useEffect, useState } from "react";

function DataFetcher({ url }) {
    const [data, setData] = useState(null);
    const [error, setError] = useState("");

    useEffect(() => {
        const controller = new AbortController();

        async function load() {
            try {
                setError("");
                const res = await fetch(url, { signal: controller.signal });
                if (!res.ok) throw new Error("Request failed");
                const json = await res.json();
                setData(json);
            } catch (e) {
                if (e.name !== "AbortError") setError("Failed to load data.");
            }
        }

        load();
        return () => controller.abort();
    }, [url]);

    if (error) return <p role="alert">{error}</p>;
    if (!data) return <p>Loading…</p>;
    return <pre>{JSON.stringify(data, null, 2)}</pre>;
}
```

Dependency array

The dependency array (second argument to **useEffect**) tells React when to re-run the effect. An empty array (**[]**) runs the effect only once after mount. Including variables causes the effect to run whenever any dependency changes. Omitting the array runs the effect after every render, which may hurt performance.

The following table presents dependency behaviors:

Dependencies	Run timing
None (omit)	After every render
[]	Once on the mount
[x]	On mount and when x changes
Multiple	On mount and when any listed changes

Table 7.5: Dependency array behaviors

The following demonstrates a conditional effect:

```
function WindowWidth() {
  const [width, setWidth] = useState(window.innerWidth);

  useEffect(() => {
    const onResize = () => setWidth(window.innerWidth); window.
    addEventListener('resize', onResize);
    return () => window.removeEventListener('resize', onResize);
  }, []); // empty array: setup once

  return <p>Width: {width}px</p>;
}
```

Cleanup functions

Effects can return a cleanup function that React calls before the component unmounts or before the next effect run. Cleanups prevent memory leaks and stale subscriptions. Use them to remove event listeners, cancel timers, or abort fetch requests.

The following presents cleanup patterns:

- Remove event listeners
- Clear intervals or timeouts
- Cancel network requests

The following demonstrates the cleanup in effect:

```
function Clock() {
  const [time, setTime] = useState(new Date());

  useEffect(() => {
    const id = setInterval(()
      => { setTime(new
      Date());
    }, 1000);
    return () => clearInterval(id); // cleanup on unmount
  }, []);

  return <h2>{time.toLocaleTimeString()}</h2>;
}
```

Event handling

Event handling in React connects user interactions, clicks, form entries, and keyboard input to component logic. React uses handler props (e.g., **`onClick`**) to attach callback functions. Handlers receive a React **`SyntheticEvent`** object that normalizes browser differences. By keeping event handling declarative, React ensures predictable updates and integrates seamlessly with the Virtual DOM.

Handling events

Handlers in React are passed as props using camelCase names. Instead of **Hypertext Markup Language** (**HTML**) strings, you provide functions. Handlers can call state setters, perform side effects, or prevent default browser behavior. Inline arrow functions or pre-bound methods can be used.

The following demonstrates attaching handlers:

```
function Clicker() {
  function handleClick() { alert('Button clicked');
  }

  return (
    <button onClick={handleClick}> Click me
    </button>
  );
}
```

The following presents a form handling example:

```
function NameForm() {
  const [name, setName] = useState('');

  function handleSubmit(e) { e.preventDefault(); console.log('Submitted name:', name);
  }

  return (
    <form onSubmit={handleSubmit}>
      <input
        value={name}
        onChange={e => setName(e.target.value)}
      />
      <button type="submit">Submit</button>
    </form>
  );
```

Synthetic events

React wraps native events in **`SyntheticEvent`** for cross-browser consistency. The wrapper provides the same interface across browsers and batches updates for performance. In React 17+, event pooling is removed, so accessing event properties asynchronously is safe without calling **`e.persist()`**.

The following presents common event properties:

Property	Description
`type`	Event type (e.g., **`click`**, **`submit`**)
`target`	Element that triggered the event `currentTarget`
`currentTarget`	element where the handler is attached
`preventDefault()`	stops the default browser action
`stopPropagation()`	stops bubbling

***Table 7.6**: SyntheticEvent properties*

The following demonstrates accessing the event object:

```
function LinkPreventer() {
  function handleClick(e) { e.preventDefault(); console.log('Default prevented');
  }
```

```
  return (
    <a href="https://example.com" onClick={handleClick}> Go to example.com
    </a>
  );
}
```

Binding context

In class components, handler methods lose their **`this`** context unless explicitly bound. You can bind in the constructor, use public class fields with arrow functions, or bind inline in JSX. Binding ensures **`this.props`** and **`this.state`** are accessible within handlers.

The following presents binding strategies:

- **Constructor binding**: **`this.handleClick = this.handleClick.bind(this)`**
- **Public class field**: **`handleClick = () => { … }`**
- **Inline bind**: **`onClick={e => this.handleClick(e)}`**

The following demonstrates constructor binding:

```
class ButtonClass extends React.Component {
  constructor(props) {
    super(props);
    this.handleClick = this.handleClick.bind(this);
  }

  handleClick() { console.
    log('Clicked in
    class');
  }

  render() {
    return <button onClick={this.handleClick}>Click</button>;
  }
}
```

The following demonstrates public field syntax:

```
class ButtonField extends React.
  Component { handleClick = () => {
    console.log('Clicked via field');
  };

  render() {
    return <button onClick={this.handleClick}>Click</button>;
  }
}
```

Routing

Routing enables React applications to display different UI based on the **Uniform Resource Locator** (**URL**). By defining route paths and associated components, routers manage navigation without full page reloads. React Router provides a declarative API to map URLs to components, handle dynamic segments, and nest routes for complex layouts. Proper routing enhances user experience by maintaining browser history, supporting deep linking, and enabling efficient code splitting.

Router setup

Before defining routes, install and configure the router in the application entry. Wrap the root component with a router provider (e.g., **BrowserRouter**). Inside, use **Routes** and **Route** to declare path-component mappings. This setup ensures that URL changes render the correct components and update the browser history.

The following presents the installation step:

```
npm install react-router-dom
```

The following demonstrates a basic setup:

```
import React from 'react';
import { BrowserRouter, Routes, Route, Link } from 'react-router-dom';
import Home from './Home';
import About from './About';

function App() {
 return (
    <BrowserRouter>
     <nav>
        <Link to="/">Home</Link> | <Link to="/about">About</Link>
     </nav>
      <Routes>
        <Route path="/" element={<Home />} />
        <Route path="/about" element={<About />} />
      </Routes>
    </BrowserRouter>
  );
}

export default App;
```

Route parameters

Route parameters allow routes to capture dynamic values from the URL, such as user IDs. Define parameters in the path using a colon prefix (e.g., **:id**). In the component, use the **useParams** hook to access parameter values and fetch or display corresponding data.

The following presents parameterized route syntax:

```
<Routes>
  <Route path="/users/:id" element={<UserProfile />} />
</Routes>
```

The following demonstrates accessing parameters:

```
import { useParams } from 'react-router-dom';

function UserProfile() {
  const { id } = useParams();
  // Fetch user data with id
  return <h2>User ID is {id}</h2>;
}
```

Nested routes

Nested routes let you define child routes within a parent route, enabling shared layouts and UI nesting. Use the **Outlet** component in the parent to render matched child routes. This pattern supports modular page structures and reduces duplication by collocating layout and route definitions.

The following presents a nested route configuration:

```
<BrowserRouter>
  <Routes>
    <Route path="/dashboard" element={<DashboardLayout />}>
      <Route index element={<DashboardHome />} />
      <Route path="stats" element={<Stats />} />
      <Route path="settings" element={<Settings />} />
    </Route>
  </Routes>
</BrowserRouter>
```

The following demonstrates a parent layout with **Outlet**:

```
import { Outlet, Link } from 'react-router-dom';

function DashboardLayout() {
  return (
    <div>
      <nav>
        <Link to="">Home</Link> |
        <Link to="stats">Stats</Link> |
        <Link to="settings">Settings</Link>
      </nav>
      <section>
        <Outlet />
      </section>
    </div>
  );
}
```

The following figure illustrates the route hierarchy:

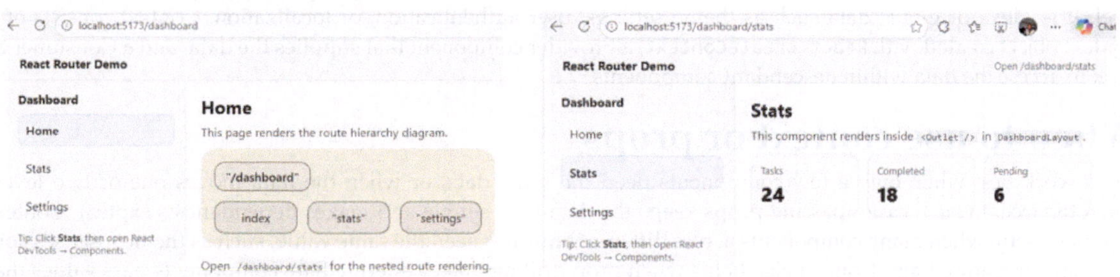

Figure 7.2: Route hierarchy

The following figure illustrates the React demo:

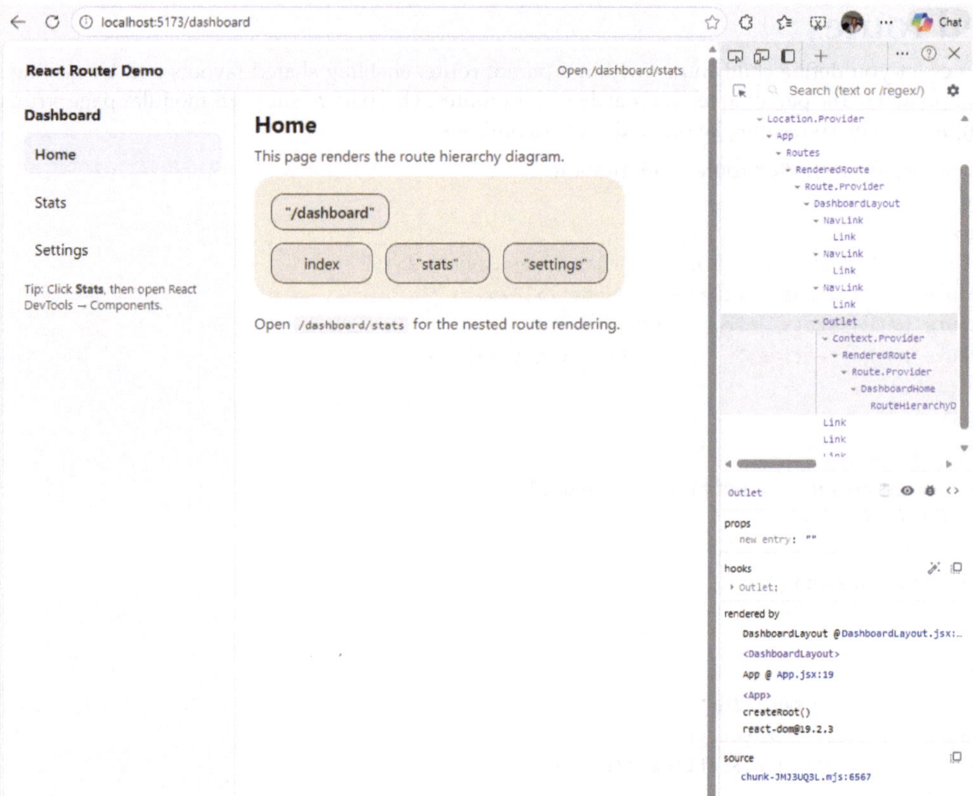

Figure 7.3: Nested routing under/dashboard *in React Router*

The **DashboardLayout** keeps the sidebar layout fixed, while child routes (**index**, **stats**, **settings**) render inside **<Outlet/>**. The browser views show **/dashboard** and **/dashboard/stats**, and React DevTools confirms the active route by highlighting the mounted child component in the component tree.

Context API

The Context API provides a way to share data across the component tree without passing props manually at every level. It is ideal for global data such as theme settings, user authentication, or localization. Context consists of a Context object created with **React.createContext**, a Provider component that supplies the data, and a Consumer or hook to access the data within descendant components.

When to use context or props

Props work best when only a few components need the same data, or when the data moves one or two levels down the tree. In such cases, passing props keeps the data flow simple and makes dependencies explicit. Context becomes useful when many components across different branches need the same value, such as theme, user session, language, or feature flags. Context also helps when prop drilling makes intermediate components pass values that they do not use.

A simple rule can guide the decision. Use props when the value is local to a feature and only a small subtree needs it. Use context when the same value is needed in many places, and updates should automatically reach all consumers.

Avoid Context for rapidly changing values (for example, mouse position) because it can trigger wide re-renders unless optimized.

Creating context

Creating a context involves calling **React.createContext** and exporting the resulting Context object. You can specify a default value, which is used if a matching Provider is not found higher in the tree. The Context object contains two components: **Provider** and **Consumer**.

The following demonstrates context creation:

```
import React from 'react';

// Create context with default value
export const ThemeContext = React.createContext('light');
```

Providing context

To make context available to components, wrap part of your tree with the Context **Provider**, supplying a **value** prop. All descendants will receive updates when the **value** changes. Avoid recreating the value object on every render to prevent unnecessary re-renders.

The following demonstrates provider usage:

```
import React, { useState } from 'react';
import { ThemeContext } from './ThemeContext';

function App() {
  const [theme, setTheme] = useState('light');

  return (
    <ThemeContext.Provider value={{ theme, setTheme }}>
      <Toolbar />
    </ThemeContext.Provider>
  );
}
```

The following table presents a comparison of patterns:

Prop drilling	Context API
Pass props through every	Provide value once at the top level
Coupling between intermediate	Decoupled consumer logic ate components
Boilerplate and verbose code	Cleaner component APIs
Hard to refactor deeply	Easy to add new consumers to nested trees

Table 7.7: *Prop drilling versus context*

Consuming context

Descendant components can access context via the **useContext** hook or the Context's **Consumer** component. The hook is the simplest approach in functional components, returning the current context value. Using **Consumer** involves a render prop pattern, suitable in class components or when needing more control.

The following demonstrates **useContext** hook:

```
import React, { useContext } from 'react';
import { ThemeContext } from './ThemeContext';

function ThemedButton() {
  const { theme, setTheme } = useContext(ThemeContext);
  return (
    <button className={theme}
    onClick={() => setTheme(theme === 'light' ? 'dark' : 'light')}> Current theme: {theme}
    </button>
  );
}
```

The following demonstrates **Context.Consumer**:

```
import React from 'react';
import { ThemeContext } from './ThemeContext';

function Label() {
  return (
    <ThemeContext.Consumer>
      {({ theme }) => (
        <span className={`label ${theme}`}>Theme is {theme}</span>
      )}
    </ThemeContext.Consumer>
  );
}
```

The following figure illustrates context flow:

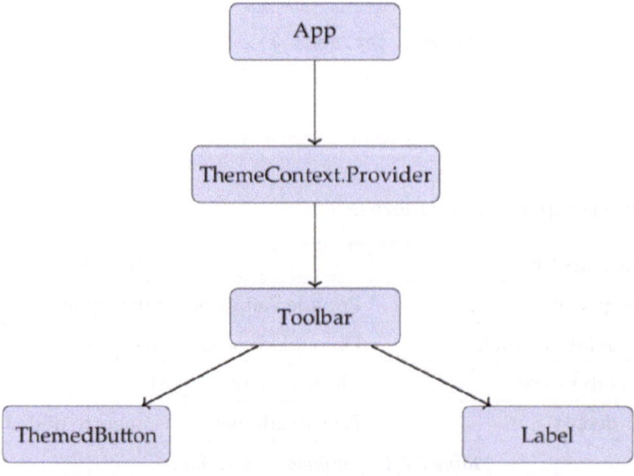

***Figure 7.4**: Context propagation from provider to consumers*

In practice, context becomes easiest to understand through common app-wide needs. The next two examples show typical scenarios where Context reduces prop drilling and keeps shared data consistent across many components. The first example uses a **ThemeContext** to switch light and dark styles from any component. The second example uses an **AuthContext** to store the logged-in user and protect pages so only authenticated users can access them. Each example follows the same pattern: create a context, wrap the app with a provider, and consume the value using **useContext** (or **Context.Consumer** when needed).

Example 1: Common UI setting theme

Theme is a good Context use case because many components (buttons, cards, pages) may need it, and prop drilling would quickly become repetitive.

The following example demonstrates the theme context for UI setting:

```
// ThemeContext.js
import React, { useState, useMemo } from "react";

export const ThemeContext = React.createContext(null);

export function ThemeProvider({ children }) {
    const [theme, setTheme] = useState("light");

    const value = useMemo(() => ({ theme, setTheme }), [theme]);

    return (
        <ThemeContext.Provider value={value}>
            {children}
        </ThemeContext.Provider>
    );
}

// App.jsx
import React from "react";
import { ThemeProvider } from "./ThemeContext";
import Toolbar from "./Toolbar";

export default function App() {
    return (
        <ThemeProvider>
            <Toolbar />
        </ThemeProvider>
    );
}

// ThemedButton.jsx
import React, { useContext } from "react";
import { ThemeContext } from "./ThemeContext";

export default function ThemedButton() {
    const { theme, setTheme } = useContext(ThemeContext);

    return (
        <button
            className={theme}
            onClick={() => setTheme(theme === "light" ? "dark" : "light")}
        >
            Current theme: {theme}
        </button>
    );
}
```

Example 2: Authentication, user session across the app

Authentication state is another strong Context use case because many screens need to know whether a user is logged in and who the user is.

The following implementation presents authentication of the user session across the application:

```
// AuthContext.js
import React, { useState, useMemo } from "react";

export const AuthContext = React.createContext(null);

export function AuthProvider({ children }) {
    const [user, setUser] = useState(null);

    function login(email) {
        setUser({ email }); // replace with real API call in production
    }

    function logout() {
        setUser(null);
    }

    const value = useMemo(() => ({ user, login, logout }), [user]);

    return <AuthContext.Provider value={value}>{children}</AuthContext.Provider>;
}

// ProtectedRoute.jsx (simple pattern)
import React, { useContext } from "react";
import { AuthContext } from "./AuthContext";

export default function ProtectedRoute({ children }) {
    const { user } = useContext(AuthContext);
    if (!user) return <p>Please login to continue.</p>;
    return children;
}

// Usage example
import React from "react";
import { AuthProvider } from "./AuthContext";
import ProtectedRoute from "./ProtectedRoute";
import Dashboard from "./Dashboard";

export default function App() {
    return (
        <AuthProvider>
            <ProtectedRoute>
                <Dashboard />
            </ProtectedRoute>
        </AuthProvider>
    );
}
```

Note: Context is not a full replacement for state libraries. Use Context for shared app values (theme, auth, locale). For complex app-wide state with many update paths (large forms, caching server data, complex workflows), Redux Toolkit or React Query can offer cleaner patterns and better debugging.

Custom hooks

Custom hooks encapsulate reusable stateful logic in standalone functions, promoting code reuse and separation of concerns. They follow the same rules as built-in hooks, only call hooks at the top level and only from React functions. By extracting patterns into custom hooks, components remain focused on rendering, while business-logic resides in well-tested, shareable utilities.

Creating hooks

Defining a custom hook requires writing a function prefixed with `use` that calls built-in hooks internally and returns the necessary values or callbacks. Custom hooks can manage state, subscriptions, context, or any side-effect logic. They must adhere to hook rules, which are that no calls are allowed inside loops, conditions, or nested functions.

The following demonstrates a window-size hook:

```
import { useState, useEffect } from 'react';

function useWindowSize() {
  const [size, setSize] = useState({ width: window.innerWidth, height: window.innerHeight
  });

  useEffect(() => {
    function handleResize() { setSize({
        width: window.innerWidth, height: window.innerHeight
      });
    }
    window.addEventListener('resize', handleResize);
    return () => {
      window.removeEventListener('resize', handleResize);
    };
  }, []);
  return size;
}

export default useWindowSize;
```

The following table presents custom hook best practices:

Practice	Description
Name prefix use	Ensures React enforces hook rules.
Top-level calls	Avoid conditional or nested calls.
Return a clear API	Provide values and updater functions.
Accept parameters	Make hook behavior configurable.
Handle cleanup	Prevent memory leaks on unmount.

Table 7.8: Custom hook best practices

Reusing logic

Once defined, custom hooks can be imported and used like built-in hooks, allowing multiple components to share logic without duplication. Hooks can return objects or arrays containing state values and action functions, making them flexible for various use cases.

The following demonstrates hook usage:

```
import React from 'react';
import useWindowSize from './useWindowSize';

function DisplayDimensions() {
  const { width, height } = useWindowSize();
  return <p>Window is {width}px by {height}px</p>;
}

function ResponsiveMenu() {
  const { width } = useWindowSize();
  return width < 600 ? <MobileMenu /> : <DesktopMenu />;
}

export { DisplayDimensions, ResponsiveMenu };
```

Performance

Optimizing performance in React involves minimizing unnecessary renders and expensive computations. By leveraging memoization and built-in hooks, applications can maintain responsiveness even as complexity grows. This section covers memoization concepts, the `useMemo` and `useCallback` hooks, and `React.memo` higher-order component, each designed to cache values or functions and prevent redundant work.

Memoization

Memoization caches the result of an expensive function call and returns the cached result when the same inputs occur again. In React, memoization helps avoid recalculating derived data on every render and prevents child components from re-rendering when props remain unchanged. Proper use of memoization can yield significant performance gains for computationally intensive tasks.

The following presents memoization patterns:

- Cache pure function outputs based on input arguments.
- Use referential equality to detect unchanged inputs.
- Apply selectively to avoid over-optimization.
- Combine with profiling to identify bottlenecks.

useMemo hook

The `useMemo` hook returns a memoized value. It has a function that computes a value and an array of dependencies. React only re-evaluates the function when a dependency changes; otherwise, it returns the cached result. `useMemo` is ideal for expensive calculations or deriving data from props/state.

The following presents `useMemo` signature:

```
const memoizedValue = useMemo(() => compute(), [deps]);
```

- Compute runs on initial render and when any deps change.

- Cached between renders if dependencies remain stable.

The following example demonstrates a practical **useMemo** example (list search/filter). Filtering a large list can be repeated on every render, even when the list and the search term do not change. **useMemo** caches the filtered result and recomputes it only when its dependencies change.

```
import React, { useMemo, useState } from "react";

function ProductSearch({ products }) {
    const [query, setQuery] = useState("");
    const [showOnlyInStock, setShowOnlyInStock] = useState(false);

    const filteredProducts = useMemo(() => {
        const q = query.trim().toLowerCase();

        return products
            .filter(p => (showOnlyInStock ? p.inStock : true))
            .filter(p => (q ? p.name.toLowerCase().includes(q) : true));
    }, [products, query, showOnlyInStock]);

    return (
        <div>
            <input
                value={query}
                onChange={e => setQuery(e.target.value)}
                placeholder="Search products..."
            />

            <label style={{ display: "block", marginTop: 8 }}>
                <input
                    type="checkbox"
                    checked={showOnlyInStock}
                    onChange={e => setShowOnlyInStock(e.target.checked)}
                />
                Show only in-stock
            </label>

            <p style={{ marginTop: 12 }}>
                Results: {filteredProducts.length}
            </p>

            <ul>
                {filteredProducts.map(p => (
                    <li key={p.id}>
                        {p.name} {p.inStock ? "" : "(out of stock)"}
                    </li>
                ))}
            </ul>
        </div>
    );
}

export default ProductSearch;
```

Note: useMemo helps most when the derived computation is noticeable (large lists, expensive transforms) or when it prevents unnecessary work during frequent re-renders. If the calculation is cheap, useMemo can be skipped to keep the code simpler.

useCallback hook

The **useCallback** hook returns a memoized callback function. It prevents child components from re-rendering due to new function references on each render. Use **useCallback** when passing callbacks to optimized children or when dependencies determine callback logic.

The following presents **useCallback** signature:

```
const memoizedFn = useCallback(() => doSomething(), [deps]);
```

- Returns the same function instance if deps stay unchanged.
- Useful for stable event handlers and prop callbacks.

The following demonstrates **useCallback** example:

```
import React, { useState, useCallback } from 'react';
import List from './List';
function TodoApp() {
  const [items, setItems] = useState([]);

  const addItem = useCallback(text => { setItems(prev => [...prev, text]);
  }, []);

  return <List items={items} onAdd={addItem} />;
}
```

React.memo

React.memo is a higher-order component that memoizes a functional component. It performs a shallow comparison of props and skips re-rendering if props have not changed. Wrap components that render the same output for identical props to avoid unnecessary renders.

The following presents **React.memo** usage:

- **Wrap export**: Export default **React.memo(Component);**
- Uses shallow prop comparison by default.
- Accepts a custom compare function for deep checks.

The following demonstrates **React.memo** example:

```
import React from 'react';

function Button({ label, onClick }) { console.log('Button render');
  return <button onClick={onClick}>{label}</button>;
}

export default React.memo(Button);
```

The following table compares memo tools:

Method	Purpose	Trigger
useMemo	Cache computed values	Dependency change
useCallback	Cache function references	Dependency change
React.memo	Skip re-render of component	Prop shallow comparison

Table 7.9: Comparison of memoization methods

Forms

Forms collect user input and handle interactions such as text entry, selections, and submissions. React supports both controlled and uncontrolled patterns, offering flexibility for simple inputs or complex form logic. Validation ensures data integrity before processing or sending it to a server.

Controlled forms

Controlled forms manage input values via React state. Each form element's **value** prop links to the state, and **onChange** updates that state. This approach provides full control over the form data, enables instant validation, and simplifies handling complex interactions.

The following presents controlled form steps:

1. Initialize state for each field with **useState**.
2. Bind the value of inputs to state variables.
3. Update state in **onChange** handlers.
4. Handle submission by reading state values.

The following code demonstrates a controlled login form:

```
import React, { useState } from "react";

function LoginForm() {
    const [email, setEmail] = useState("");
    const [password, setPassword] = useState("");

    function handleSubmit(e) {
        e.preventDefault();
        console.log({ email, password });
        alert("Check the console for submitted values.");
    }

    return (
        <form onSubmit={handleSubmit} style={{ display: "grid", gap: 10 }}>
            <label style={{ display: "grid", gap: 6 }}>
                Email
                <input
                    type="email"
                    value={email}
                    onChange={(e) => setEmail(e.target.value)}
                    placeholder="name@example.com"
                    style={{ padding: 10, border: "1px solid #ccc", borderRadius: 6 }}
                />
            </label>

            <label style={{ display: "grid", gap: 6 }}>
                Password
                <input
                    type="password"
                    value={password}
                    onChange={(e) => setPassword(e.target.value)}
```

```
                placeholder="•••••••"
                style={{ padding: 10, border: "1px solid #ccc", borderRadius: 6 }}
            />
        </label>

        <button
            type="submit"
            style={{
                padding: 10,
                borderRadius: 6,
                border: "1px solid #222",
                background: "#f5f5f5",
                cursor: "pointer",
            }}
        >
            Login
        </button>

        <p style={{ margin: 0, color: "#555", fontSize: 13 }}>
            This is a controlled form. Each keystroke updates React state via onChange,
            and the input value stays in sync through the value prop.
        </p>
    </form>
  );
}

export default LoginForm;
```

Render **LoginForm** in the browser to confirm how controlled inputs work. Controlled inputs always display the values stored in state, so typing should instantly update the UI.

Use the form in App.js:

```
// src/App.js
import React from "react";
import LoginForm from "./LoginForm";

export default function App() {
    return (
        <div style={{ padding: 16, maxWidth: 420 }}>
            <h2>Login</h2>
            <LoginForm />
        </div>
    );
}
```

In the browser, type an email and a password and click **Login**. The fields should reflect exactly what is typed, and the submit handler should print the { email, password } object in the console. This confirms the controlled pattern, where the input value comes from React state, and onChange updates that state on every keystroke.

A controlled form keeps every input value inside React state, so the UI always reflects the current state. In this example, the **Email** and **Password** fields bind their value to email and password. Each keystroke triggers **onChange**, which calls **setEmail** or **setPassword**, updates the state, and causes a re-render. However, the input value comes from the state, and the displayed text stays synchronized with React at all times. On submit, the handler prevents the default page reload and prints the current state object to the browser console, which confirms that the submitted values match what appears in the input boxes. Refer to the following figure:

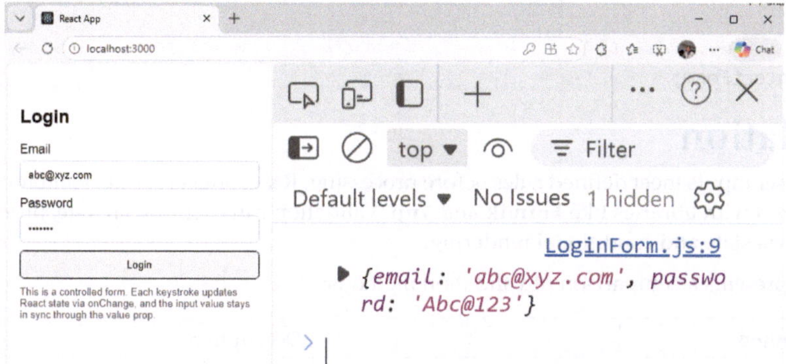

Figure 7.5: Browser view of a controlled LoginForm

Each keystroke updates React state via **onChange**, inputs stay synchronized through the value prop, and form submission logs the current state to the console.

Uncontrolled forms

Uncontrolled forms let the DOM manage input values. React refs access form elements directly, reducing state boilerplate. This pattern suits simple forms or when integrating non-React libraries, but offers less immediate control over data and validation.

The following demonstrates uncontrolled form steps:

1. Create **refs** with **useRef** for each input.
2. Attach refs to form elements via **ref** prop.
3. Read values from **ref.current.value** on submit.

The following demonstrates an uncontrolled contact form:

```
import React, { useRef } from 'react';

function ContactForm() {
  const nameRef = useRef();
  const messageRef = useRef();

  function handleSubmit(e) { e.preventDefault(); console.log({
      name: nameRef.current.value, message: messageRef.current.value
    });
  }

  return (
    <form onSubmit={handleSubmit}>
      <label>Name</label>
      <input type="text" ref={nameRef} />
      <label>Message</label>
      <textarea ref={messageRef} />
      <button type="submit">Send</button>
    </form>
  );
```

```
}

export default ContactForm;
```

Form validation

Validation ensures user inputs meet defined rules before processing. React offers manual validation, HTML5 built-in checks, and integration with libraries like **Formik** and **Yup**. Validation can occur on change, blur, or submit events, providing feedback via state and conditional rendering.

The following table presents a comparison of validation methods:

Method	Description
HTML5	Uses | required, | pattern | and browser messages.
Manual	Custom checks in event handlers, updating state for errors.
Formik+Yup	Declarative schema validation with real-time feedback.
React Hook Form	Performance-optimized | minimal re-renders, integrates with Yup.

Table 7.10: Validation approaches

The following demonstrates a manual validation example:

```
import React, { useState } from 'react';

function SignupForm() {
  const [email, setEmail] = useState('');
  const [error, setError] = useState('');

  function handleSubmit(e) { e.preventDefault();
    if (!/^\S+@\S+\.\S+$/.test(email)) { setError('Enter a valid email');
    } else { setError('');
      console.log('Submitted', email);
    }
  }

  return (
    <form onSubmit={handleSubmit}>
      <label>Email</label>
      <input
        type="email" value={email}
        onChange={e => setEmail(e.target.value)}
      />
      {error && <p className="error">{error}</p>}
      <button type="submit">Sign Up</button>
    </form>
  );
}

export default SignupForm;
```

Testing

Testing ensures React applications work as intended by verifying component behavior, user interactions, and integration between modules. Automated tests catch regressions early, improve code quality, and support refactoring with confidence. Common testing types include unit tests for individual functions or components, integration tests for component interactions, and snapshot tests for UI consistency. A robust testing strategy combines these approaches to cover logic, presentation, and user workflows.

Jest setup

Jest is a JavaScript testing framework designed for simplicity and speed. It provides an integrated test runner, assertion library, and mocking utilities. Setting up Jest in a React project involves installing the Jest package, configuring Babel or TypeScript support, and optionally customizing the **jest.config.js** file for module resolution and coverage thresholds.

The following presents installation commands:

```
# Install Jest and React presets
npm install --save-dev jest babel-jest @babel/preset-env @babel/preset-react

# (Optional) Install React Testing Library
npm install --save-dev @testing-library/react
```

The following demonstrates a basic Jest configuration:

```
/* jest.config.js */
module.exports = { testEnvironment: 'jsdom', transform: {
    '^.+\\.(js|jsx)$': 'babel-jest'
  },
  moduleFileExtensions: ['js', 'jsx'], collectCoverage: true, coverageDirectory: 'coverage'
};
```

Testing library

React Testing Library (**RTL**) builds on Jest to provide utilities for testing UI components by querying the DOM in a way that reflects how users interact. RTL encourages tests that focus on accessibility features and user-centric patterns rather than implementation details. Common query methods include **getBy**, **queryBy**, and **findBy**, each with role, label, or text selectors.

The following presents the installation steps:

```
npm install --save-dev @testing-library/react @testing-library/jest-dom
```

The following table demonstrates common query types:

Query method	Description
getByRole	Select by ARIA role, throws if not found.
queryByText	Select by text returns null if not found.
findByLabelText	Async select by label text.
getAllByTestId	Select elements by data-testid, returns an array.

Table 7.11: Common React testing library queries

The following demonstrates a simple RTL test:

```
import { render, screen, fireEvent } from '@testing-library/react';
import Button from './Button';
```

```
test('calls onClick when clicked', () => {
  const handleClick = jest.fn();
  render(<Button label="Submit" onClick={handleClick} />);

  const button = screen.getByRole('button', { name: /submit/i
  }); fireEvent.click(button);

  expect(handleClick).toHaveBeenCalledTimes(1);
});
```

Async testing and mocking API calls

Many React components fetch data from an API and render different UI states such as loading, success, and error. Testing these components requires waiting for UI updates that happen after the promise resolves or rejects. React Testing Library supports this pattern using async queries like **findBy*** (which automatically waits) and utilities like **waitFor** (which polls until an expectation becomes true).

A key point in async UI testing is isolation. Tests should not depend on real network calls because real APIs can be slow, unstable, or unavailable. Mocking replaces the real API call with a controlled fake response. A clean and common approach is to keep the API logic in a small module (for example, api.js) and then mock that module in tests. This keeps components simple and makes tests predictable. The details are as follows:

- **Component with loading, success, and error UI**: Before writing tests, the component should expose clear UI signals for each state. A loading message confirms the request started. A visible list confirms success. An accessible error message confirms failure. Using **role="alert"** for the error state improves accessibility and also makes testing easier because tests can query by role.

  The following presents a simple component that loads data asynchronously:

```
// api.js
export async function fetchUsers() {
    const res = await fetch("/api/users");
    if (!res.ok) throw new Error("Request failed");
    return res.json();
}

// Users.jsx
import React, { useEffect, useState } from "react";
import { fetchUsers } from "./api";

export default function Users() {
    const [users, setUsers] = useState([]);
    const [status, setStatus] = useState("loading"); // loading | success | error

    useEffect(() => {
        fetchUsers()
            .then(data => {
                setUsers(data);
                setStatus("success");
            })
            .catch(() => setStatus("error"));
    }, []);

    if (status === "loading") return <p>Loading...</p>;
    if (status === "error") return <p role="alert">Failed to load users.</p>;
```

```
    return (
        <ul aria-label="users">
            {users.map(u => (
                <li key={u.id}>{u.name}</li>
            ))}
        </ul>
    );
}
```

- **Testing async success flow (mock resolved value):** A success test checks two things; the component shows the initial loading state, then it updates the UI after the promise resolves. The test should not manually *sleep* or use timeouts. Instead, it should wait in a React Testing Library way.

  `findByText` is ideal here because it waits until the element appears (or fails after a default timeout). Mocking the API module with mockResolvedValue ensures the promise resolves immediately with known data.

  The following demonstrates testing an async success flow by mocking the API module:

```
// Users.test.jsx
import { render, screen } from "@testing-library/react";
import Users from "./Users";
import * as api from "./api";

jest.mock("./api");

test("renders users after successful API call", async () => {
    api.fetchUsers.mockResolvedValue([
        { id: 1, name: "Asha" },
        { id: 2, name: "Ravi" }
    ]);

    render(<Users />);

    // initial state
    expect(screen.getByText(/loading/i)).toBeInTheDocument();

    // wait for async UI update
    expect(await screen.findByText("Asha")).toBeInTheDocument();
    expect(screen.getByText("Ravi")).toBeInTheDocument();
});
```

- **Testing async error flow (mock rejected value**: An error test ensures the component reacts correctly when the promise rejects. The goal is to confirm that the user sees a meaningful error message rather than a blank screen or a crash.

  `findByRole("alert")` works well because the error UI uses **`role="alert"`**. Mocking with mockRejectedValue simulates a failed request without hitting any real endpoint.

  The following demonstrates testing an async error flow:

```
import { render, screen } from "@testing-library/react";
import Users from "./Users";
import * as api from "./api";

jest.mock("./api");

test("shows an error message when API call fails", async () => {
    api.fetchUsers.mockRejectedValue(new Error("Network error"));
```

```
    render(<Users />);

    const alert = await screen.findByRole("alert");
    expect(alert).toHaveTextContent(/failed to load/i);
  });
```

Note: UI-focused assertions produce stronger tests than internal state checks. Tests should verify what the user can see and interact with (loading text, list items, error message). Use `findBy*` when elements appear after async updates, and keep API calls mocked so tests remain fast, stable, and independent of network conditions.

Snapshot testing

Snapshot testing captures the rendered output of a component and saves it to a file. On subsequent runs, Jest compares the current output to the stored snapshot, flagging changes. This approach is useful for detecting unintended UI modifications but should be complemented with more granular tests to validate behavior.

The following demonstrates a snapshot test:

```
import React from 'react';
import renderer from 'react-test-renderer';
import Card from './Card';

test('renders Card correctly', () => {
  const tree = renderer
    .create(<Card title="Hello"><p>World</p></Card>)
    .toJSON();
  expect(tree).toMatchSnapshot();
});
```

Styling

Styling in React encompasses various approaches to apply CSS to components, from modular stylesheets to CSS-in-JS libraries. Each method offers different trade-offs in terms of scoping, dynamic theming, and tooling integration. Choosing the right strategy depends on project size, team preferences, and performance requirements.

Furthermore, Tailwind CSS is also widely used in production React applications. It follows a utility-first approach where developers build UI by composing small class names directly in JSX. This chapter uses CSS Modules in the hands-on examples to keep setup minimal and to show scoped, component-level styling clearly, but the same components can also be styled using Tailwind in real projects.

Tailwind CSS

Tailwind CSS is a utility-first styling framework. Instead of writing many custom CSS selectors, Tailwind encourages composing small utility classes directly in JSX (for example, spacing, typography, border, and layout classes). This approach keeps styling close to the component markup and speeds up building consistent layouts. Tailwind CSS v4 improved performance and targets modern web tooling, but Tailwind CSS v3 remains a common choice for Create React App-based setups. This chapter's hands-on project uses Create React App, so the following steps follow the official Tailwind guide for CRA:

1. **Install Tailwind**:

   ```
   npm install -D tailwindcss
   npx tailwindcss init
   ```

2. **Configure template paths**: Open `tailwind.config.js` and replace the file content with:

```
/** @type {import('tailwindcss').Config} */
module.exports = {
 content: ["./src/**/*.{js,jsx,ts,tsx}"],
 theme: {
  extend: {},
 },
 plugins: [],
};
```

3. **Add Tailwind directives to CSS**: Open **`src/index.css`** and add:

```
@tailwind base;
@tailwind components;
@tailwind utilities;
```

4. **Start the dev server**:

```
npm start
```

5. **Using Tailwind in a component**: The following example styles a button using Tailwind utility classes:

```
function PrimaryButton({ label }) {
 return (
  <button className="rounded-lg bg-blue-600 px-4 py-2 text-white hover:bg-blue-700">
   {label}
  </button>
 );
}
```

CSS Modules

CSS Modules automatically scope class names to a component, preventing global name collisions. When importing a stylesheet as a module, each class is mapped to a unique identifier. This ensures styles apply only to the intended component, while still using familiar CSS syntax.

The following presents the setup steps:

1. Rename stylesheet to **`Component.module.css`**.
2. **Import styles**: **`import styles from './Component.module.css';`**
3. **Apply class**: **`<div className={styles.container}>`**

The following demonstrates a Module example:

```
/* Button.module.css */
.container {
  background-color: #007bff;
  color: white; padding: 0.5rem 1rem; border-radius: 4px;
}
```

The following demonstrates usage in React:

```
import React from 'react';
import styles from './Button.module.css';

function Button({ label }) {
  return <button className={styles.container}>{label}</button>;
}
export default Button;
```

Styled components

Styled components is a CSS-in-JS library that allows writing CSS directly within JavaScript files using tagged template literals. It generates unique class names and injects styles at runtime. This approach supports dynamic styling based on props and theme objects.

The following presents the installation step:

```
npm install styled-components
```

The following demonstrates a styled component:

```
import React from 'react';
import styled from 'styled-components';

const Card = styled.div`
  background: ${props => props.bg ||
  'white'}; border-radius: 8px;
padding: 1rem;box-shadow: 0 2px 4px
                    rgba(0,0,0,0.1);
`;


  function ThemedCard({ bg, children
                                  }) {
    return <Card bg={bg}>{children}</
                                 Card>;
}

export default ThemedCard;
```

CSS in JS

CSS-in-JS refers to a pattern where styles are defined and applied directly in JavaScript, often at the component level. Libraries like Emotion and JSS offer powerful APIs for dynamic theming, critical-path CSS extraction, and runtime style composition.

The following presents CSS-in-JS options:

1. **Emotion**: Similar to Styled Components, with enhanced performance.
2. **JSS**: Uses JavaScript objects to define styles.
3. **Inline styles**: Direct style prop, suitable for small tweaks.

The following demonstrates an Emotion example:

```
/** @jsxImportSource @emotion/react */
import { css } from '@emotion/react';

const headingStyle = css` font-size: 1.5rem; color: hotpink;
`;

function Title({ text }) {
  return <h1 css={headingStyle}>{text}</h1>;
}

export default Title;
```

State libraries

State libraries help manage application-wide data by centralizing state logic, enforcing consistent update patterns, and providing developer tools for debugging. Redux implements a strict unidirectional flow with immutable updates, while Redux Toolkit streamlines Redux setup and reduces boilerplate. MobX adopts an observable/reactive model that automatically tracks dependencies and updates observers when data changes. Choosing the right library depends on project complexity, team preferences, and performance requirements.

Redux basics

Redux uses a single store to hold application state, pure reducer functions to update state based on dispatched actions, and a unidirectional data flow that simplifies reasoning about changes. Components dispatch actions describing events, reducers calculate new state without side effects, and subscribers (usually UI layers) re-render in response.

The following presents Redux core concepts:

- **Store**: Holds the entire state tree.
- **Action**: Plain object with a `type` field describing what happened.
- **Reducer**: Pure function `(state, action) => newState`.
- **Dispatch**: Sends an action to the store.
- **Subscriber**: Function called on every state change.

The following demonstrates a minimal Redux setup:

```
import { createStore } from 'redux';

// Initial state
const initialState = { count: 0 };

// Reducer function
function counterReducer(state = initialState, action) {
      switch
  (action.type)
        {
       case
  'increment':
        return { count: state.count + 1 };
       case
  'decrement':
        return { count: state.count - 1 };
     default:
        return state;
  }
}

// Create store
const store = createStore(counterReducer);

// Subscribe to changes
store.subscribe(() => console.log('State:', store.getState())
);

// Dispatch actions
```

```
store.dispatch({ type: 'increment' }); store.dispatch({ type: 'decrement' });
```

Redux Toolkit

Redux Toolkit (RTK) is the official way to write Redux today. Redux itself is a state management pattern built around a few key ideas. A store holds the global state for the application. An action is a plain object that describes what happened (for example, *counter/increment*). A reducer is a pure function that calculates the next state from the current state and an action. A slice groups state + reducers + action creators for one feature (for example, a counter feature). RTK keeps these ideas but removes most of the manual wiring that makes classic Redux feel verbose.

RTK is usually preferred over *regular Redux* for practical reasons. In classic Redux, developers often write multiple files for constants, action creators, switch-based reducers, and immutable update logic. This repetition increases boilerplate and makes mistakes more likely (especially with immutable updates). RTK simplifies store setup with **configureStore**, generates actions and reducers together with **createSlice**, and uses Immer internally so reducers can be written in a clean *mutating* style while still producing immutable state safely. RTK also enables Redux DevTools by default and encourages a consistent, modern project structure.

Before the code, it helps to understand what the code will show. The following example creates a small counter slice that owns one piece of state (value) and three reducers (increment, decrement, **addByAmount**). RTK automatically generates action creators with the same names as these reducers. Then **configureStore** creates the Redux store and registers the slice reducer under a key (counter). Finally, a React component reads state using **useSelector** and updates state using **useDispatch**.

The following demonstrates a simple RTK setup using **createSlice** and **configureStore**:

```
// store.js
import { configureStore, createSlice } from "@reduxjs/toolkit";

// 1) Create a slice (state + reducers + auto-generated actions)
const counterSlice = createSlice({
    name: "counter",
    initialState: { value: 0 },
    reducers: {
        increment(state) {
            state.value += 1; // safe: Immer handles immutable update
        },
        decrement(state) {
            state.value -= 1;
        },
        addByAmount(state, action) {
            state.value += action.payload; // payload carries extra data
        }
    }
});

// 2) Export the auto-generated action creators
export const { increment, decrement, addByAmount } = counterSlice.actions;

// 3) Create the store (Redux DevTools enabled by default)
export const store = configureStore({
    reducer: {
        counter: counterSlice.reducer
    }
});

// Counter.jsx
import React from "react";
```

```
import { useDispatch, useSelector } from "react-redux";
import { increment, decrement, addByAmount } from "./store";

export default function Counter() {
    const value = useSelector((state) => state.counter.value);
    const dispatch = useDispatch();

    return (
        <div>
            <h3>Counter: {value}</h3>

            <button onClick={() => dispatch(decrement())}>-</button>
            <button onClick={() => dispatch(increment())}>+</button>

            <button onClick={() => dispatch(addByAmount(5))}>
                Add 5
            </button>
        </div>
    );
}

// main.jsx (Vite) or index.js (CRA)
import React from "react";
import ReactDOM from "react-dom/client";
import { Provider } from "react-redux";
import { store } from "./store";
import Counter from "./Counter";

ReactDOM.createRoot(document.getElementById("root")).render(
    <Provider store={store}>
        <Counter />
    </Provider>
);
```

In this example, **createSlice** creates three things at once: the slice reducer, the action creators, and the action types behind the scenes. **configureStore** replaces the older **createStore** API and sets up helpful defaults (good middleware defaults and DevTools support). **useSelector** reads from the Redux store, and **useDispatch** sends actions to update the store. This small example shows the core workflow used in real applications, just with a simple state shape.

Note: RTK is preferred because it reduces boilerplate, prevents common immutable-update mistakes, and provides a standard, modern setup that matches current Redux best practices.

MobX overview

MobX uses observable state and reactive programming to automatically track dependencies and propagate changes. State is made observable, actions modify state, and observers re-render when the observed state changes. This model offers fine-grained updates and minimal boilerplate for simple to complex applications.

The following presents MobX building blocks:

- **Observable**: Marks state objects or values as reactive.
- **Action**: Wraps functions that modify observable state.
- **Observer**: Higher-order component or hook that re-renders on state changes.

The following demonstrates a MobX counter example:

```
import { makeAutoObservable } from 'mobx'; import { observer } from 'mobx-react-lite'; import
```

```
React from 'react';
// Store definition
class CounterStore { count = 0;

  constructor() { makeAutoObservable(this);
  }

  increment() {
    this.count += 1;
  }

  decrement() {
    this.count -= 1;
  }
}

const counterStore = new CounterStore();

// Observer component
const CounterView = observer(() => (
  <div>
    <p>Count: {counterStore.count}</p>
    <button onClick={() => counterStore.increment()}>+</button>
    <button onClick={() => counterStore.decrement()}>-</button>
  </div>
));

export { counterStore, CounterView };
```

Build and deploy

After development, React applications must be optimized and served in production. This involves creating a production-ready build, minified, tree-shaken, and free of development overhead, and then deploying the static files to a hosting platform. A well-configured build improves load times and user experience, while choosing the right deployment option ensures scalability, reliability, and ease of updates.

Production build

Creating a production build transforms source code into optimized static assets. The build process minifies JavaScript, extracts and hashes CSS, splits code into chunks for lazy loading, and inlines critical resources. Environment variables (e.g., **NODE_ENV=production**) enable the removal of development code. The result is a **build/** folder containing all files ready for hosting.

The following presents the **build** command:

```
# Using Create React App
npm run build

# With Vite
npm run build
```

The following presents typical build artifacts:

File/Folder	Description
`build/index.html`	Entry HTML file linking hashed assets.
`build/static/js/*.js`	Minified JavaScript bundles with content hashes.
`build/static/css/*.css`	Minified CSS files with content hashes.
`build/asset-manifest.json`	Mapping of original filenames to hashed outputs.
`build/robots.txt`	Default robots' instructions.

Table 7.12: Production build output files

Deployment options

Several platforms and methods can serve React's static build. Choices range from specialized static hosts with built-in **content delivery networks (CDNs)** to general cloud storage or containerized servers. Key factors include ease of setup, building automation, **Secure Sockets Layer (SSL)** support, and global distribution.

The following table presents popular deployment services:

Platform	Deployment type	Key features
Netlify	Git-based CI/CD	Instant I deploy I previews, functions, CDN, redirects
Vercel	Git-based CI/CD	Zero-config, Serverless Functions, analytics
GitHub Pages	Branch deploy	Free, custom domain support, limited to static sites
AWS S3 + CDN	Static I hosting I cloudfront	Highly I scalable, I custom cache rules, pay-as-you-go
Firebase Hosting	Static hosting + CDN	SSL, rewrites, callable functions, integrated with Firebase

Table 7.13: Deployment platform comparison

The following demonstrates Netlify deploy:

```
# Install Netlify CLI
npm install -g netlify-cli

# Run from project root
netlify deploy --prod --dir=build
```

The following flowchart illustrates a CI/CD pipeline:

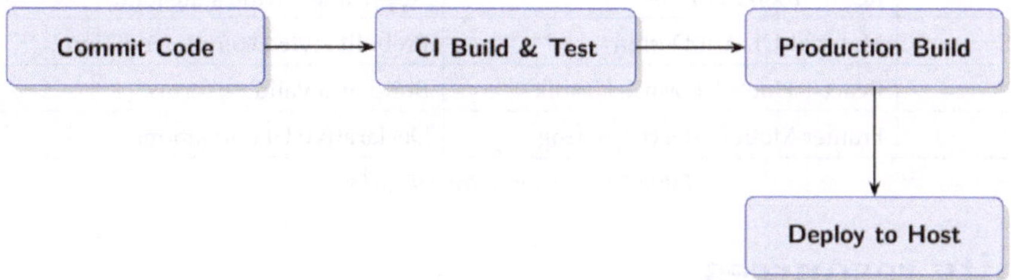

Figure 7.6: Automated CI/CD pipeline for React deployment

Ecosystem

The React ecosystem comprises a rich set of tools, libraries, and community resources that support development, debugging, styling, and learning. While the core library handles rendering and state, surrounding technologies address needs such as code quality, performance analysis, UI components, and collaboration. Leveraging this ecosystem efficiently accelerates development and fosters best practices.

Tooling overview

Tooling in React projects automates tasks like bundling, transpiling, linting, formatting, testing, and debugging. A coherent toolchain ensures consistent code style, catches errors early, and provides insights into performance. Modern setups often combine multiple tools via a central configuration or a zero-config framework.

The following table presents key tooling categories:

Category	Tool	Purpose
Bundler	Webpack, Vite	Module bundling, hot reload, code splitting.
Transpiler	Babel	Transform JSX and modern JavaScript into browser-compatible JavaScript.
Linter	ESLint	Enforce code style and catch errors.
Formatter	Prettier	Consistent code formatting.
Tester	Jest	Unit and integration testing.
DevTools	React DevTools	Inspect the component tree and the hooks state.

***Table 7.14**: Core React tooling*

The following demonstrates installing DevTools:

```
npm install --global react-devtools
```

Popular libraries

Beyond core React, numerous libraries address common needs, such as routing, state management, UI components, animation, and data fetching. Selecting well-maintained, widely adopted libraries reduces boilerplate and accelerates feature development.

The following presents widely used libraries:

Category	Library	Role
Routing	React Router	Declarative client-side routing
Data Fetching	React Query, SWR	Server state management and caching
State	Redux Toolkit, MobX	Application-wide state logic
UI Kit	Material-UI, Ant Design	Prebuilt styled components sign
Forms	React I Hook I Form I Formik	Build and validate forms
Animation	Framer Motion, React I Spring	Declarative UI animations

***Table 7.15**: Common React libraries*

Community resources

A vibrant community underpins React's growth. Official documentation, tutorials, forums, and conference talks provide guidance and best practices. Engaging with these resources helps developers stay current, solve issues, and contribute back.

The following presents key community resources:

- **React official docs (reactjs.org/docs)**: Authoritative guide and API reference.

- **GitHub issues and discussions**: Report bugs and join development conversations.
- **Stack Overflow**: Q and A for common problems.
- **DEV community, medium**: Articles and tutorials by practitioners.
- **Reactiflux Discord, Reddit (r/reactjs)**: Real-time chat and community support.
- **Conference talks (React Conf, JSConf)**: Deep dives and roadmaps.

Advanced patterns

Advanced patterns enable code reuse and separation of concerns by abstracting component logic. Techniques such as higher-order components, render props, and portals address cross-cutting concerns like data fetching, layout management, and DOM placement. These patterns promote composability and maintainable architectures in large React applications.

Higher order components

Higher-order components (**HOCs**) are functions that take a component and return a new component with extended behavior. HOCs wrap the original component in another component, injecting props or logic. They enable the reuse of stateful logic across multiple components without modifying their implementation.

The following presents the HOC structure:

- Accepts a component as input.
- Returns an enhanced component.
- Shares logic via props injection.
- Maintains the original component's display name.

The following demonstrates a `withLoading` HOC:

```
import React from 'react';
function withLoading(Component) {
return function Wrapped(props) {
    const { isLoading, ...rest } = props;
    if (isLoading) {
    return <p>Loading...</p>;
    }
    return <Component {...rest} />;
  };
}

// Usage
function DataList({ items }) {
 return (
   <ul>
     {items.map(i => <li key={i.id}>{i.name}</li>)}
   </ul>
  );
}
export default withLoading(DataList);
```

Render props

Render props is a pattern where a component accepts a function as a prop and calls it to render content. This allows components to share logic by delegating rendering to consumers. The render prop function receives data or callbacks, enabling flexible composition.

The following presents a render prop pattern

- Parent component holds logic or state.
- Child prop is a function that returns UI.
- Provides data via function arguments.
- Encourages clear separation of concerns.

The following demonstrates a **MouseTracker** component:

```
import React, { useState, useEffect } from 'react';
function MouseTracker({ render }) {
  const [pos, setPos] = useState({ x: 0, y: 0 });

  useEffect(() => {
    const handleMove = e => setPos({ x: e.clientX, y: e.clientY }); window.
    addEventListener('mousemove', handleMove);
    return () => window.removeEventListener('mousemove', handleMove);
  }, []);

  return render(pos);
}

// Usage
function App() {
  return (
    <MouseTracker
      render={({ x, y }) => (
        <p>Mouse at ({x}, {y})</p>
      )}
    />
  );
}

export default App;
```

Portals

Portals allow rendering children into a DOM node outside the parent component's hierarchy. This is useful for modals, tooltips, and overlays that need to escape CSS overflow or stacking context. React's **createPortal** API handles this seamlessly while preserving event bubbling.

The following presents portal basics:

- Renders content into a specified DOM node.
- Maintains React event propagation.
- Circumvents parent CSS constraints.

The following demonstrates creating a modal portal:

```
import React from 'react';
import { createPortal } from 'react-dom';

function Modal({ children }) {
  const modalRoot = document.getElementById('modal-root');
  return createPortal(
    <div className="modal-overlay">
      <div className="modal-content">{children}</div>
    </div>, modalRoot
  );
}

// Usage in App
function App() {
  return (
    <>
      <h1>Main App</h1>
      <Modal>
        <h2>Modal Title</h2>
        <p>Modal body text goes here.</p>
      </Modal>
    </>
  );
}
```

The following figure illustrates portal placement:

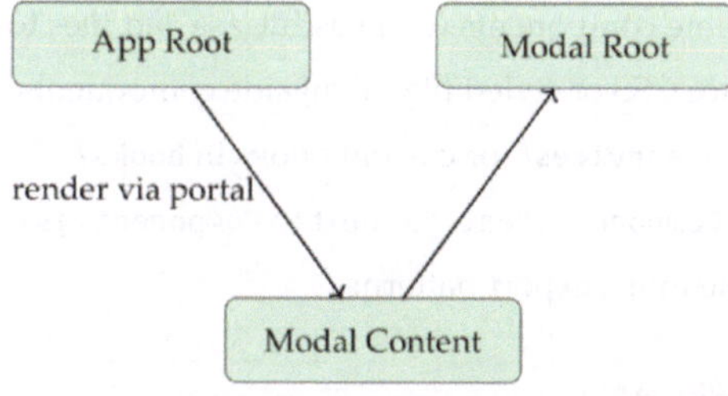

Figure 7.7: React portal rendering outside component tree

Best practices

Adhering to best practices in React development ensures code is maintainable, scalable, and performant. Consistent folder layouts, clear organization of files, and targeted performance optimizations reduce technical debt and improve collaboration. This section covers recommended folder structure, code organization guidelines, and practical performance tips to apply across projects of any size.

Folder structure

A logical folder structure groups related files by feature or function, making it easier to navigate and scale the codebase. Keeping components, hooks, utilities, and assets in dedicated directories reduces cognitive load and supports modular development. Organize folders to reflect project complexity and team workflows.

The following table presents a recommended layout:

Path	Purpose
`src/`	Root of the application source.
`src/components/`	Reusable UI components.
`src/hooks/`	Custom React hooks.
`src/features/`	Feature-specific modules (state and UI).
`src/services/`	API calls and business-logic.
`src/utils/`	Utility functions and helpers.
`src/assets/`	Images, fonts, and static files.
`src/styles/`	Global CSS or styled themes.
`src/tests/`	Unit and integration tests.
`public/`	Static HTML and favicon.

Table 7.16: *Recommended folder structure*

Code organization

Organizing code by feature rather than by file type improves modularity and encapsulation. Each feature folder can include its components, styles, tests, and hooks. Naming conventions and index files simplify imports and enable consistent patterns across the codebase.

The following list outlines the organization guidelines:

- **Group by feature**: Keep related files together under **features/FeatureName/**.
- **Use index files**: Export components or utilities from an **`index.js`** for cleaner imports.
- **Name with PascalCase**: Name components with PascalCase and files to match (e.g., **`Button/Button.jsx`**).
- **Keep styles co-located**: Place CSS or styled files alongside components.
- **Separate business-logic**: use **`services/`** or custom hooks in **`hooks/`**.
- **Write tests adjacent**: Place **`Component.test.js`** next to **`Component.jsx`**.

The following script demonstrates the index export pattern:

```
// components/Button/index.js
export { default } from './Button.jsx';

// Usage elsewhere
import Button from 'components/Button';
```

Performance tips

Improving performance involves minimizing re-renders, reducing bundle size, and deferring non-critical resources. Apply targeted optimizations such as code splitting, lazy loading, and memoization only where they yield measurable benefits. Profiling tools help identify hotspots before investing effort.

The following table presents common performance strategies:

Technique	Description
Code splitting	Split bundles with dynamic **import()** and React lazy.
Lazy loading	Defer components or images until needed.
Memoization	Cache I values/functions I with use Memo/useCallback.
Virtualization	Render only visible list items (e.g., react-window.
Avoid inline objects	Define handlers and objects outside JSX to prevent prop changes.
Tree shaking	Remove unused code via proper imports and production build.
HTTP caching	Leverage service workers or HTTP headers for static assets.

Table 7.17: Key performance optimizations

The following code snippet demonstrates a lazy loading example:

```
import React, { Suspense, lazy } from 'react';

const Chart = lazy(() => import('./Chart'));

function Dashboard() {
  return (
    <Suspense fallback={<p>Loading chart...</p>}>
    <Chart />
   </Suspense>
  );
}

export default Dashboard;
```

Hands-on project

This project builds a complete Todo application with React. The implementation demonstrates component composition, local state management with hooks, reusable custom hooks, persistent storage using the browser's localStorage, and basic styling. The finished project includes all core features (add, toggle, delete, filter) and extends the application with practical enhancements that appear in real products (clear completed tasks, delete all tasks, and persistent UI preferences).

Overview

The todo app enables users to create tasks, mark tasks complete, delete tasks, and filter the visible list by status. The main application component stores the todo list state and the current filter state. The user interface is composed of small, focused components: a form for input, a list for rendering, and an item component for each task. Persistence is handled using a reusable useLocalStorage hook so that both todos and UI settings remain available after refresh. This design keeps rendering logic inside components and keeps persistence logic inside a dedicated hook.

Setup

Create React App (**CRA**) scaffolds a working project with a development server, bundler, and build pipeline. The following commands create the project folder, install dependencies, and start the development server.

The following presents setup commands:

```
npx create-react-app todo-app cd todo-app
npm start
```

Folder structure

A clear folder structure improves readability and helps locate code quickly. Custom hooks belong in **src/hooks** because they provide reusable logic without UI rendering. Components belong in **src/components** because they focus on rendering and user interactions. Styles are kept in a separate folder to keep component files readable.

The following table demonstrates the folder layout:

Path	Description
src/hooks/	Custom hooks (**useLocalStorage**)
src/components/	UI I components I (**TodoApp** I **TodoForm**, **TodoList**, **TodoItem**)
src/styles/	CSS files (global CSS or modules)
src/App.js	Main application component (state + composition)
src/index.js	Entry point that renders **App**

Table 7.18: Project folder structure

Implementation

The following steps present the implementation:

1. **Persistence with a custom hook (use LocalStorage)**: localStorage is a browser storage mechanism that saves key-value pairs as strings. It is useful for small client-side persistence because values remain available even after a refresh. A custom hook wraps **useState** and **useEffect** to provide a clean interface that behaves like **useState**, but automatically syncs data to **localStorage**. The following hook supports lazy initialization (read once on first render), safe JSON parsing, and removal when a value is set to **null**:

```
// src/hooks/useLocalStorage.js
import { useEffect, useState } from "react";

function safeParse(raw, fallback) {
    try {
        return raw ? JSON.parse(raw) : fallback;
    } catch {
        return fallback;
    }
}

export default function useLocalStorage(key, initialValue) {
    const [value, setValue] = useState(() => {
        const stored = localStorage.getItem(key);
        return safeParse(stored, initialValue);
    });

    useEffect(() => {
        if (value === null) {
            localStorage.removeItem(key);
            return;
        }
        localStorage.setItem(key, JSON.stringify(value));
    }, [key, value]);

    return [value, setValue];
}
```

2. **Input component (TodoForm):** Forms in React often use controlled inputs, where the input value lives in state and updates on each keystroke. Controlled inputs make validation and reset logic straightforward. **TodoForm** accepts an **onAdd** callback from the parent component and calls it with cleaned input. This keeps the form focused on input handling rather than state ownership.

```
// src/components/TodoForm.jsx
import React, { useState } from "react";

function TodoForm({ onAdd }) {
    const [text, setText] = useState("");

    function handleSubmit(e) {
        e.preventDefault();
        const cleaned = text.trim();
        if (!cleaned) return;
        onAdd(cleaned);
        setText("");
    }

    return (
        <form onSubmit={handleSubmit} className="todo-form">
            <input
                value={text}
                onChange={(e) => setText(e.target.value)}
                placeholder="Add new todo"
                aria-label="todo input"
            />
            <button type="submit">Add</button>
        </form>
    );
}

export default TodoForm;
```

3. **Item component (TodoItem):** A todo item displays the task text, visual status, and actions. The item component receives the todo data and callback props from its parent. Clicking the task text toggles completion, and the delete button removes the task. This keeps item logic simple and ensures all state updates occur in one place (the main component). Refer to the following code:

```
// src/components/TodoItem.jsx
import React from "react";

function TodoItem({ todo, onToggle, onDelete }) {
    return (
        <li className={`todo-item ${todo.completed ? "done" : ""}`}>
            <button
                className="todo-toggle"
                onClick={() => onToggle(todo.id)}
                aria-label={todo.completed ? "mark as active" : "mark as completed"}
                type="button"
            >
                {todo.completed ? "✓" : "o"}
            </button>

            <span
                className="todo-text"
                onClick={() => onToggle(todo.id)}
```

```
                role="button"
                tabIndex={0}
                onKeyDown={(e) => (e.key === "Enter" ? onToggle(todo.id) : null)}
            >
            {todo.text}
        </span>

            <button
                className="todo-delete"
                onClick={() => onDelete(todo.id)}
                aria-label="delete todo"
                type="button"
            >
                ×
            </button>
        </li>
    );
}

export default TodoItem;
```

4. **List component (TodoList)**: Rendering arrays in React typically uses **`map`**. A stable **`key`** helps React update list items efficiently. **`TodoList`** receives the list and forwards callbacks to each **`TodoItem`**. Refer to the following code:

```
// src/components/TodoList.jsx
import React from "react";
import TodoItem from "./TodoItem";

function TodoList({ todos, onToggle, onDelete }) {
    if (todos.length === 0) {
        return <p className="empty">No tasks to show.</p>;
    }

    return (
        <ul className="todo-list" aria-label="todos">
            {todos.map((todo) => (
                <TodoItem
                    key={todo.id}
                    todo={todo}
                    onToggle={onToggle}
                    onDelete={onDelete}
                />
            ))}
        </ul>
    );
}

export default TodoList;
```

5. **Main component (App.js)**: **`App.js`** coordinates the entire feature. It stores todo and UI preferences using **`useLocalStorage`** so the application persists across refresh. It also stores the current filter and exposes all update functions (add, toggle, delete, clear completed, and delete all). Filtering stays derived from the state rather than being stored separately. This design keeps state consistent and avoids duplicate sources of truth, as shown in the following code:

```
// src/App.js
import React, { useMemo, useState } from "react";
import useLocalStorage from "./hooks/useLocalStorage";
import TodoForm from "./components/TodoForm";
import TodoList from "./components/TodoList";
import "./styles/todo.css";

function App() {
    // Persistent state (saved across reloads)
    const [todos, setTodos] = useLocalStorage("todos", []);
    const [savedFilter, setSavedFilter] = useLocalStorage("todo_filter", "all");

    // In-memory UI state (but initialized from persistent value)
    const [filter, setFilter] = useState(savedFilter);

    function addTodo(text) {
        const newTodo = {
            id: Date.now(),
            text,
            completed: false,
            createdAt: new Date().toISOString()
        };
        setTodos([...todos, newTodo]);
    }

    function toggleTodo(id) {
        setTodos(
            todos.map((t) =>
                t.id === id ? { ...t, completed: !t.completed } : t
            )
        );
    }

    function deleteTodo(id) {
        setTodos(todos.filter((t) => t.id !== id));
    }

    function clearCompleted() {
        setTodos(todos.filter((t) => !t.completed));
    }

    function deleteAll() {
        setTodos([]);
    }

    function updateFilter(next) {
        setFilter(next);
        setSavedFilter(next); // persists the user's last selected filter
    }

    const filteredTodos = useMemo(() => {
        if (filter === "active") return todos.filter((t) => !t.completed);
        if (filter === "completed") return todos.filter((t) => t.completed);
        return todos;
    }, [todos, filter]);
```

```
    const stats = useMemo(() => {
        const total = todos.length;
        const completed = todos.filter((t) => t.completed).length;
        const active = total - completed;
        return { total, active, completed };
    }, [todos]);
```

The following is the continuation of the code:

```
    return (
        <div className="container">
            <header className="header">
                <h1>Todo App</h1>
                <p className="subtitle">
                    Total: {stats.total} | Active: {stats.active} | Done: {stats.
completed}
                </p>
            </header>

            <TodoForm onAdd={addTodo} />

            <div className="toolbar">
                <div className="filters" role="group" aria-label="filters">
                    <button
                        className={filter === "all" ? "active" : ""}
                        onClick={() => updateFilter("all")}
                        type="button"
                    >
                        All
                    </button>
                    <button
                        className={filter === "active" ? "active" : ""}
                        onClick={() => updateFilter("active")}
                        type="button"
                    >
                        Active
                    </button>
                    <button
                        className={filter === "completed" ? "active" : ""}
                        onClick={() => updateFilter("completed")}
                        type="button"
                    >
                        Done
                    </button>
                </div>

                <div className="actions">
                    <button onClick={clearCompleted} type="button">
                        Clear Completed
                    </button>
                    <button onClick={deleteAll} type="button" className="danger">
                        Delete All
                    </button>
                </div>
            </div>
```

```
            <TodoList todos={filteredTodos} onToggle={toggleTodo} onDelete={deleteTodo} />
        </div>
    );
}

export default App;
```

6. **Entry point (index.js)**: The entry point renders the root component into the HTML mount node. CRA provides **`public/index.html`** with a **`<div id="root"></div>`** container:

```
// src/index.js
import React from "react";
import ReactDOM from "react-dom/client";
import App from "./App";

const root = ReactDOM.createRoot(document.getElementById("root"));
root.render(<App />);
```

7. **Basic styling (todo.css)**: Basic styling improves readability and makes state changes visible (for example, completed items appear with a line-through). The following styles keep the UI simple and consistent without extra libraries:

```
/* src/styles/todo.css */
.container {
    max-width: 720px;
    margin: 40px auto;
    padding: 16px;
    font-family: Arial, Helvetica, sans-serif;
}

.header h1 {
    margin: 0 0 6px 0;
}

.subtitle {
    margin: 0 0 16px 0;
    color: #555;
}

.todo-form {
    display: flex;
    gap: 10px;
    margin-bottom: 14px;
}

.todo-form input {
    flex: 1;
    padding: 10px;
}

.todo-form button {
    padding: 10px 14px;
}

.toolbar {
    display: flex;
    justify-content: space-between;
    align-items: center;
```

```
    gap: 14px;
    margin-bottom: 12px;
    flex-wrap: wrap;
}

.filters button {
    margin-right: 8px;
    padding: 8px 12px;
}

.filters .active {
    font-weight: bold;
    border-bottom: 2px solid #222;
}
```

The following is the continuation of the code:

```
.actions button {
    margin-left: 8px;
    padding: 8px 12px;
}

.actions .danger {
    background: #ffe2e2;
    border: 1px solid #ffb3b3;
}

.todo-list {
    list-style: none;
    padding-left: 0;
    margin: 0;
}

.todo-item {
    display: grid;
    grid-template-columns: 32px 1fr 32px;
    align-items: center;
    gap: 10px;
    padding: 10px 8px;
    border-bottom: 1px solid #eee;
}

.todo-item.done .todo-text {
    text-decoration: line-through;
    color: #777;
}

.todo-toggle,
.todo-delete {
    cursor: pointer;
    border: 1px solid #ddd;
    background: #fafafa;
    width: 32px;
    height: 32px;
}

.todo-text {
```

```
        cursor: pointer;
    }

    .empty {
        color: #666;
        padding: 10px 0;
    }
```

Demo

Running **npm start** launches the development server. A user can add tasks through the input, toggle completion by clicking the circle icon or the text, delete tasks with the × button, and switch between filters. The todo list persists across reloads because the state is stored in **localStorage** through the **useLocalStorage** hook. The selected filter also persists, so the application opens in the last used view.

The following figure illustrates the component hierarchy:

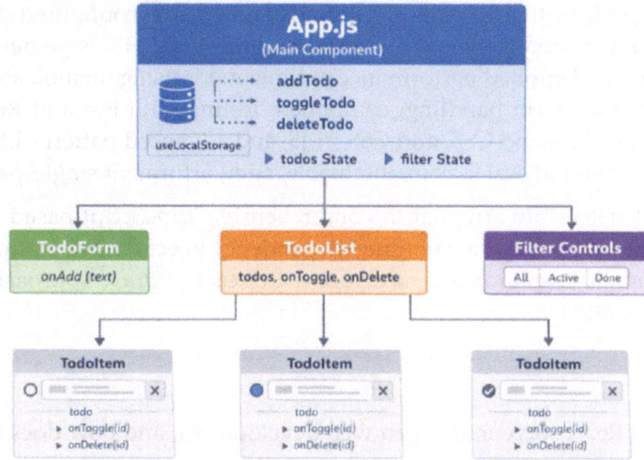

Figure 7.8: Component hierarchy for Todo App

The output of the project is as follows:

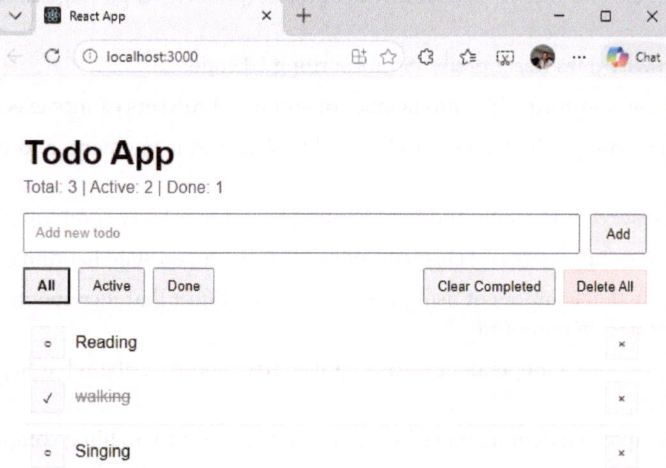

Figure 7.9: Todo list project output

Summary

This hands-on project demonstrated a complete React feature built with component composition and predictable state flow. The main component owned the application state and passed data and callbacks into smaller components using props. User actions triggered state updates through event handlers, which produced consistent UI updates. Persistent storage was integrated through a reusable custom hook that syncs state to localStorage, ensuring that todos and UI preferences remain available after page refresh. The final application serves as a clean reference for structuring larger React features using hooks, reusable components, and practical persistence.

Conclusion

In this chapter, we examined React's core principles and workflows. We began by setting up a React environment, scaffolding a project, and structuring its directories. We then learned to author dynamic UIs with JSX and Babel, and create both functional and class components utilizing props, children, and defaultProps. We explored state management strategies with useState and useReducer, and orchestrated side effects using the useEffect hook. We implemented event handling with synthetic events and bound handlers, and configured client-side routing with React Router to support dynamic and nested routes. We introduced global state management through the Context API, crafted reusable custom hooks, and applied performance optimizations using memoization, useMemo, useCallback, and React.memo. We also covered form handling, component testing with Jest and React Testing Library, styling options including CSS Modules, Tailwind CSS, and CSS-in-JS, and advanced patterns like HOCs, render props, and portals. These tools equip you to build scalable, maintainable, and performant single-page applications.

In the next chapter, we will delve into Angular, a comprehensive TypeScript-based framework. You will learn Angular's modular architecture, two-way data binding, dependency injection, templating syntax, and powerful CLI tooling. We will compare Angular's opinionated structure with React's library approach and explore best practices for enterprise-scale development.

Exercises

1. What problem does React solve in modern web development, and how does its component-based model help build large user interfaces?
2. Explain the difference between Create React App and Vite in terms of development server speed, build tooling, and typical use cases.
3. List the main folders and files in a default React project (public, src, package.json) and state the purpose of each.
4. What is JSX, and why does React prefer JSX for writing UI code?
5. Describe how Babel transforms JSX into JavaScript and why browsers cannot execute JSX directly.
6. Write a simple JSX snippet that uses className, htmlFor, and a fragment, and explain why these rules exist.
7. Explain what a React component is and how UI composition works by combining smaller components.
8. Compare function components and class components, focusing on state handling and side effects.
9. Create a Timer function component using useState and useEffect that increments seconds every 1 second and stops the interval on unmount.
10. Explain the purpose of the dependency array in useEffect and describe what happens for [], [x], and no dependency array.
11. Build a small example that demonstrates lifting state up between two sibling components using a common parent.

12. Explain React synthetic events and show how preventDefault works in a form submit handler.
13. Set up React Router with two normal routes and one dynamic route (for example, /users/:id) and read the parameter using useParams.
14. Demonstrate nested routing using a layout component and Outlet, and explain why nested routes reduce repeated layout code.
15. Create a ThemeContext with a Provider and consume it using useContext to toggle between light and dark theme values.
16. Write a custom hook (useWindowSize or useLocalStorage) and show how two different components can reuse it.
17. Explain memoization in React and write a useMemo example that filters a product list only when dependencies change.
18. Explain useCallback and write an example where a memoized callback prevents unnecessary re-renders in a child component.
19. Create a controlled LoginForm where input values stay synchronized with React state and log the submitted email and password to the console.
20. Write a basic Jest + React Testing Library test that renders a component, triggers a click, and asserts that a handler function was called.

Join our Discord space

Join our Discord workspace for latest updates, offers, tech happenings around the world, new releases, and sessions with the authors:

https://discord.bpbonline.com

CHAPTER 8
Angular Framework

Introduction

Angular is a powerful, full-featured frontend framework maintained by Google, built with TypeScript to deliver scalable, high-performance single-page applications by using efficient change detection, **ahead-of-time** (**AOT**) compilation, and route-based lazy loading to reduce runtime overhead and initial bundle size. Its opinionated architecture enforces modular design through NgModules, enabling developers to encapsulate functionality into self-contained feature sets. Angular's declarative templates combine **Hypertext Markup Language** (**HTML**) with data-binding directives—interpolation, property, event, and two-way binding—to synchronize views and models seamlessly. Component, attribute, and structural directives allow dynamic **Document Object Model** (**DOM**) manipulation, while a robust dependency-injection system supplies services throughout the application, promoting testability and loose coupling. The Angular Router manages client-side navigation with nested routes, guards, and resolvers. Forms can be handled via template-driven or reactive approaches with built-in validation. The HttpClient module simplifies **Create, Read, Update, and Delete** (**CRUD**) operations and integrates interceptors for cross-cutting concerns. Additional features such as pipes, lifecycle hooks, change-detection strategies, lazy loading, and Ahead-of-Time compilation ensure responsive user experiences. This chapter guides you through setting up an Angular environment, structuring a project, and mastering these core features to build maintainable, enterprise-grade applications.

Structure

This chapter covers the following topics:

- Getting started
- Architecture
- Data binding
- Directives
- Services
- Routing
- Router setup
- Forms
- HTTP client
- Pipes
- Lifecycle
- Testing
- Performance
- Deployment
- Hands-on project

Objectives

By the end of this chapter, the readers will be able to set up an Angular development environment and scaffold projects using the Angular **command line interface** (**CLI**), explain the purpose and configuration of NgModules, and define components with associated templates and styles. They will be able to connect the data model to the view using interpolation, property binding, event binding, and two-way binding, and apply pipes for common data transformations. They will also be able to create reusable services, inject them using Angular's dependency injection framework, and explain the injector hierarchy and service scope. Readers will develop capabilities to configure client-side routing with parameters and nested routes, and use guards and resolvers to manage access and data loading, and will be able to implement template-driven and reactive forms with validation, and perform HTTP CRUD operations using the HttpClient module and interceptors. Finally, they will be able to use lifecycle hooks and change-detection strategies, write unit and end-to-end tests, apply lazy loading and AOT compilation, and build, optimize, and deploy a production-ready Angular application.

Getting started

This section covers the initial steps to begin Angular development, including installing the Angular CLI, creating a new project, and understanding the default folder layout. These foundations ensure a smooth start and consistent structure for building applications.

Environment setup

Angular requires Node.js, a package manager such as npm (included with Node.js) or alternatives like Yarn and pnpm, and the Angular CLI. Node.js provides the JavaScript runtime, while npm (or another package manager) installs and manages project dependencies. The Angular CLI handles project scaffolding, building, serving, and generating code. Installing compatible versions of Node.js, the package manager, the Angular CLI, and verifying the installation using version commands, helps avoid dependency and tooling conflicts later.

The following presents installation steps:

```
# Install Node.js (v22+)
brew install node

# Install Angular CLI globally
npm install -g @angular/cli

# Verify installations
node --version          # e.g. v22.12.0
ng version
```

Project creation

The Angular CLI's `ng new` command generates a project with default configurations: TypeScript setup, testing tools, and a development server. Options allow routing and style sheet formats. Creating with strict mode enforces best practices.

The following demonstrates project creation:

```
ng new my-angular-app \
  --routing true \
  --style css \
  --strict
cd my-angular-app
```

The following table presents a CLI output example:

Step	Sample output
Creating project	CREATE my-angular-app/README.md
Installing deps	npm install –save
Initial build	Bundle complete in 3.5s

Table 8.1: *ng new command output*

Folder layout

Angular projects follow a modular folder layout. The **src/app** folder contains feature modules, components, and services. Configuration files reside at the root. A consistent layout simplifies navigation and scaling.

The following figure demonstrates the default structure:

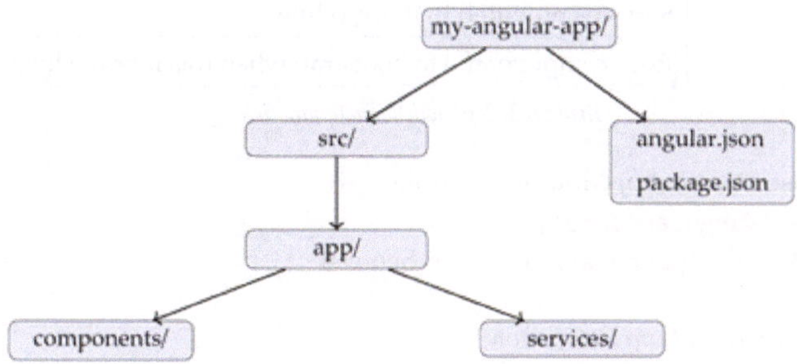

***Figure 8.1:** Angular project folder layout*

The following table presents key folders and files:

Path	Purpose
angular.json	CLI configuration (build, serve)
tsconfig.json	TypeScript compiler settings
src/app/	Application modules and code
src/index.html	Main HTML file
src/main.ts	Application bootstrap file
src/styles.css	Global styles

***Table 8.2:** Angular project files*

Architecture

Angular architecture relies on the modular organization of code into NgModules, reusable components, and declarative templates. NgModules group related features and dependencies, components encapsulate **user interface** (**UI**) and logic, and templates define the view layer with data binding and directives. This layered structure promotes scalability, maintainability, and clear separation of concerns in large applications. Compared with lightweight libraries such as React, which focus mainly on the view layer and let developers choose additional tools for routing and state management, Angular provides a more complete, opinionated structure out of the box. In contrast to frameworks like Vue, which can be adopted gradually and often stay flexible in project organization, Angular encourages a consistent project layout and patterns that fit well for large teams and enterprise applications.

NgModules

NgModules organize application functionality into cohesive blocks. Each NgModule declares the components, directives, and pipes it owns, imports external modules, and exports features for use in other modules. The root module can bootstrap the application, and modularization can support lazy loading and improve compile times. In modern Angular, NgModules are not mandatory for all use cases because standalone components, directives, and pipes can be used and imported without defining an NgModule, which reduces boilerplate in new projects. NgModules still appear frequently in existing codebases and remain useful for understanding legacy structure and some module-based patterns.

The following table presents core NgModule fields:

Field	Description
`declarations`	Components, directives, and pipes owned by this module
`imports`	External modules used by this module
`providers`	Services provided in this module
`bootstrap`	Root component(s) to bootstrap when this module loads

Table 8.3: NgModule metadata fields

The following script demonstrates an AppModule example:

```
import { NgModule } from '@angular/core';
import { BrowserModule } from '@angular/platform-browser';

import { AppComponent } from './app.component';
import { TodoModule } from './todo/todo.module';

@NgModule({
  declarations: [AppComponent],
  imports: [BrowserModule,
  TodoModule], providers: [],
  bootstrap: [AppComponent]
})
export class AppModule { }
```

The following figure illustrates module relationships:

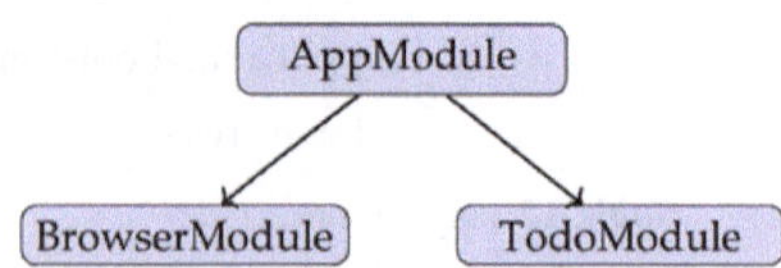

Figure 8.2: NgModule import hierarchy

Components

Components are the basic UI building blocks. Each component consists of a TypeScript class with decorators that specify metadata, including the selector, template, and styles. The class contains data properties and methods, while the template defines the view with data binding. Components are declared in NgModules and instantiated via selectors in templates.

The following table presents component decorator fields:

Field	Description
`selector`	CSS selector to insert this component.
`templateUrl`	External HTML template file path.
`template`	Inline HTML template string.
`styleUrls`	External CSS file paths.
`styles`	Inline CSS styles.

Table 8.4: Component metadata fields

The following demonstrates a component example:

```
// hello.component.ts
@Component({
  selector: ‹app-hello›,
  templateUrl: ‹./hello.html›,
  styleUrls: [‹./hello.css›]
})
export class HelloComponent {
  name = ‹Angular›;

  greet() {
    alert(`Hello, ${this.name}!`);
  }
}
```

```
<!-- hello.html -->
<div class="hello">
  <h2>Hello, {{ name }}</h2>
  <button (click)="greet()">Greet</button>
</div>
```

The following demonstrates rendered output:

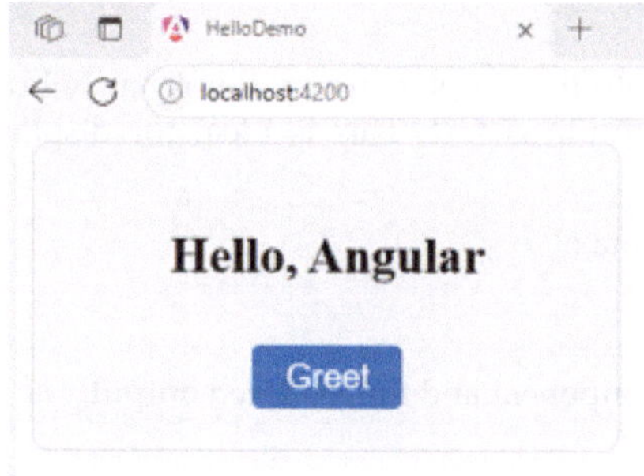

Figure 8.3: Rendered HelloComponent output

Templates

Templates define the component view using HTML enhanced with Angular binding syntax and directives. Interpolation, property binding, and event binding connect the view to component data and methods. Structural directives like **`ngIf`** and **`ngFor`** control the DOM structure, while attribute directives modify element behavior.

The following presents template binding types:

- **Interpolation:** **`{{ expression }}`** for data display.
- **Property binding**: **`[src]="imageUrl"`** for setting DOM properties.
- **Event binding**: **`(click)="onClick()"`** for handling events.
- **Two-way binding**: **`[(ngModel)]="value"`** for sync data.

The following list demonstrates a template example:

```
<div *ngIf="items.length; else noItems">
 <ul>
    <li *ngFor="let item of items">{{ item }}</li>
 </ul>
</div>
<ng-template #noItems>
  <p>No items available</p>
</ng-template>
```

The following figure illustrates template rendering:

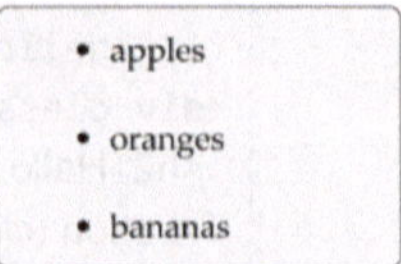

***Figure 8.4:** Rendered list via *ngFor directive*

Data binding

Angular's data binding synchronizes data between the component class and the template view. Binding types include interpolation and property binding, which are **one-way bindings** that flow from the component to the view, and event binding, which sends user actions from the view back to the component. Two-way binding combines property binding and event binding, so changes stay synchronized in both directions between the view and the component model. Each mechanism uses distinct syntax and fits specific use cases in templates.

Interpolation

Interpolation inserts component data into the template using double curly braces. Angular evaluates expressions inside interpolation and renders the result as text. This is ideal for displaying strings, numbers, and simple expressions.

The following presents interpolation syntax:

```
<h2>Hello, {{ userName }}</h2>
<p>Sum: {{ 2 + 3 }}</p>
```

The following code demonstrates the component and the rendered output:

```
@Component({
  selector: 'app-welcome',
  templateUrl: './welcome.component.html'
})
export class
  WelcomeComponent {
  userName = 'Alice';
}
```

The following figure illustrates the use of Angular's interpolation feature, where the component property **userName** is bound to the template and rendered dynamically in the browser output:

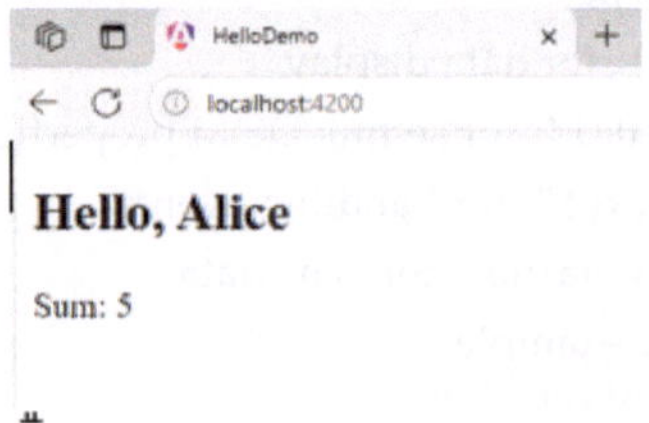

***Figure 8.5:** Interpolation code (left) and output (right)*

Property binding

Property binding sets DOM element properties to component values. It uses square brackets around the property name. This ensures safe assignment to elements or directives and prevents unwanted HTML injection.

The following code presents property binding syntax:

```
<img [src]="imageUrl" [alt]="imageAlt" />
<input [value]="defaultText" />
```

The following code demonstrates a binding example:

```
@Component({
  selector: ‘app-avatar’,
  template: `<img [src]=”url”                    \
   \ alt="Avatar">`
})
export class
  AvatarComponent { url
  = 'avatar.png';
}
```

The following figure demonstrates Angular's property binding, where the **url** property defined in the component is bound to the **src** attribute of the **<img>** tag in the template, resulting in the rendered avatar image.

Figure 8.6: Property binding code (left) and rendered image (right)

Event binding

Event binding listens for and responds to user events such as clicks, input, or key presses. The syntax uses parentheses around the event name. The handler method in the component receives a **$event** object for further processing.

The following presents event binding syntax:

```
<button (click)="onSave()">Save</button>
<input (input)="onInput($event)" />
```

Figure 8.7 illustrates Angular's event binding mechanism, where the **(click)** event of a button is bound to the **onSave()** method in the component, triggering a console log message when the button is clicked:

```
@Component({
  selector: 'app-save',
  template: `<button (click)="onSave(    \
   \ )">Save</button>`
})
export class SaveComponent {
  onSave() {
    console.log('Saved');
  }
}
```

[Save]

(Console: Saved)

Figure 8.7: Event binding code (left) and console output (right)

Two-way binding

Two-way binding combines property and event binding using the `[(ngModel)]` syntax. It synchronizes a property in the component with an input element's value, updating on user input and programmatic changes. `ngModel` is primarily intended for simple inputs and template-driven forms, while reactive forms typically use `FormControl` and `formControlName` instead of `ngModel`. `FormsModule` must be imported to use `ngModel`.

The following list presents a two-way binding setup:

- Import `FormsModule` in the NgModule's `imports`.
- Use `[(ngModel)]` in the template to bind a field.

The following demonstrates a two-way binding example:

```
<input [(ngModel)]="name" placeholder="Enter name">
<p>Hello, {{ name }}</p>
```

The following presents the module configuration:

```
@NgModule({
  imports: [ BrowserModule,
  FormsModule ], declarations: [
  AppComponent ], bootstrap: [
  AppComponent ]
})
export class AppModule { }
```

Directives

Directives in Angular add behavior to DOM elements or components. Components themselves are special directives with templates. Attribute directives modify element appearance or behavior, while structural directives change the DOM layout by adding or removing elements. Understanding these categories enables building rich, reusable UI patterns.

Component directives

Component directives encapsulate UI and behavior in a reusable element with its own template and styles. They are declared with the `@Component` decorator and used via their selector in templates. Components manage their own data, handle events, and can host child components.

The following presents the component directive steps:

1. Define class with `@Component` metadata.
2. Specify `selector`, `template`, or `templateUrl`, and styles.
3. Declare the component in an NgModule.
4. Use the selector as a custom element in templates.

The following demonstrates a simple panel component:

```
@Component({
  selector:
  'app-panel',
  template: `
    <div class="panel">
      <h3>{{ title }}</h3>
      <ng-content></ng-content>
    </div>
```

```
  `,
  styles: [`.panel { border: 1px solid #ccc; padding: 1rem; }`]
})
export class PanelComponent {
  @Input() title = 'Panel';
}
```

Attribute directives

Attribute directives change the appearance or behavior of an existing element without changing the overall DOM structure. They are defined using the **@Directive** decorator and typically work by binding to the host element's properties, classes, styles, or events. Angular provides built-in attribute directives such as **ngClass** for adding or removing CSS classes dynamically and **ngStyle** for applying inline styles based on expressions.

The following table presents built-in attribute directives:

Directive	Purpose
ngClass	Adds or removes CSS classes dynamically
ngStyle	Sets inline styles based on expressions
[hidden]	Toggles element visibility via CSS

***Table 8.5:** Common attribute directives*

The following code demonstrates a custom highlight directive:

```
@Directive({
  selector: '[appHighlight]'
})
export class HighlightDirective
  { @Input('appHighlight') color
  = 'yellow'; constructor(el:
  ElementRef) {}
  @HostListener('mouseenter') onEnter() {
    this.el.nativeElement.style.backgroundColor = this.color;
  }
  @HostListener('mouseleave') onLeave() {
    this.el.nativeElement.style.backgroundColor = '';
  }
}
```

The following demonstrates usage in template:

```
<p appHighlight="lightblue"> Hover to highlight this text.
</p>
```

Structural directives

Structural directives alter the DOM structure by adding, removing, or manipulating elements. They use the * prefix in templates. Built-in examples are ***ngIf** for conditional rendering and ***ngFor** for list rendering. Custom structural directives control repeated or conditional layouts.

The following table presents common structural directives:

Directive	Purpose
`*ngIf`	Includes element if expression is truthy.
`*ngFor`	Iterates over a collection and creates elements.
`*ngSwitch`	Conditionally displays nested `ngSwitchCase` blocks.

Table 8.6: Common structural directives

The following demonstrates a custom repeat directive:

```
@Directive({
  selector: '[appRepeat]'
})
export class RepeatDirective {
  constructor(
    private tpl:
    TemplateRef<any>,
    private vc:
    ViewContainerRef
  ) {}
  @Input('appRepeat') set repeat(count: number) {
    this.vc.clear();
    for (let i = 0; i < count; i++) {
      this.vc.createEmbeddedView(this.tpl, { index: i });
    }
  }
}
```

The following demonstrates repeat usage:

```
<ul>
  <li *appRepeat="3; let i =
    index"> Item {{ i + 1 }}
  </li>
</ul>
```

Services

Services in Angular encapsulate business logic, data access, and utility functions in reusable classes. Decorated with **@Injectable**, services are instantiated and shared via Angular's dependency injection system. This promotes separation of concerns and makes it easy to mock or replace services during testing.

Creating services

A service is a class decorated with **@Injectable** that declares how it should be provided in the application. The **providedIn** metadata determines the injector scope (e.g., root or a specific module). The following presents service creation steps:

1. Generate a service with Angular CLI or manually create a file.
2. Add **@Injectable(providedIn: 'root')** decorator.
3. Implement methods for data retrieval or business logic.

The following demonstrates a data service example:

```
import { Injectable } from '@angular/core';
import { HttpClient } from '@angular/common/http';
import { Observable } from 'rxjs';

@Injectable({ providedIn: 'root' })
export class TodoService {
  private apiUrl = 'https://api.example.com/todos';

  constructor(private http: HttpClient) {}

  fetchTodos(): Observable<Todo[]> {
    return this.http.get<Todo[]>(this.apiUrl);
  }

  addTodo(todo: Todo): Observable<Todo> {
    return this.http.post<Todo>(this.apiUrl, todo);
  }
}
```

Dependency injection

Dependency injection (**DI**) supplies service instances to components and other services. Angular resolves constructor parameters by matching types (or injection tokens) to providers registered in injectors, so classes do not need to create their own dependencies. This approach improves decoupling because classes depend on abstractions rather than concrete instantiation logic, and it improves testability because mock or stub services can be injected easily during unit testing.

The following presents the DI workflow:

- Component declares dependencies in its constructor.
- Angular injector locates or creates service instances.
- Service is passed to the component automatically.

The following demonstrates injecting a service into a component:

```
import { Component, OnInit } from '@angular/core';
import { TodoService } from './todo.service';
@Component({
  selector: 'app-todo-list',
  templateUrl: './todo-list.component.html'
})
export class TodoListComponent implements
  OnInit { todos: Todo[] = [];

  constructor(private todoService: TodoService) {}

  ngOnInit() {
    this.todoService.fetchTodos()
      .subscribe(data => this.todos = data);
  }
}
```

Injector hierarchy

Angular maintains a tree of injectors matching the component tree. The root injector provides application-wide singletons. Child injectors created for modules or components can override providers, enabling scoped instances.

The following table presents injector levels:

Injector	Scope
Root injector	App-wide singletons (`providedIn: 'root'`)
Module injector	Providers declared in `@NgModule.providers`
Component injector	Providers in `@Component.providers` (scoped to component subtree)

***Table** 8.7: Injector levels and scope*

The following illustrates the injector tree:

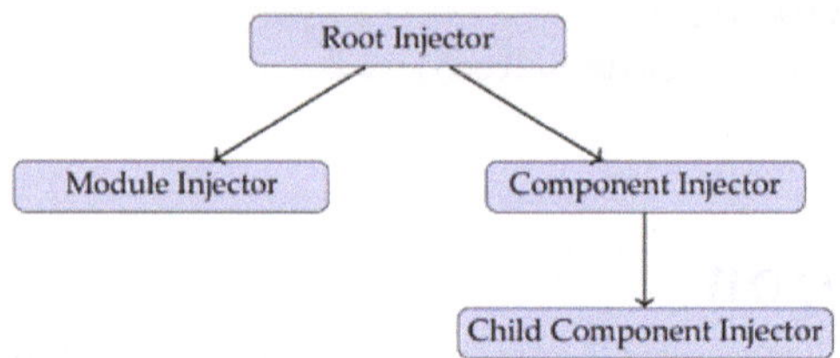

***Figure** 8.8: Angular injector hierarchy aligned with the component tree*

Routing

Routing in Angular enables navigation between views by mapping URLs to components, which allows a single-page application to feel like a multi-page website without full page reloads. The RouterModule listens to URL changes, renders the matching component inside a `<router-outlet>`, and manages browser history so back and forward buttons work as expected. In a real application, routing drives commonly flow, such as authentication and dashboards. For example, an app can expose `/login` for sign-in, redirect authenticated users to `/dashboard`, and protect routes like `/dashboard/reports or /dashboard/settings` using guards so only logged-in users can access them. Dynamic parameters support detail pages such as `/users/42 or /orders/1005`, where the route ID is used to fetch and display the correct record. Nested routes help build layouts where a parent page (Dashboard) stays visible while child views (Overview, Reports, Settings) change inside it. Resolvers can fetch required data before the page loads, so the component starts with ready-to-use data rather than showing an empty screen and loading later.

Router setup

The router is configured by importing `RouterModule` in a routing module, defining an array of routes, and adding the routing module to the root module's imports. This establishes the route table and enables router outlets in templates.

The following presents setup steps:

1. Generate a routing module: `ng generate module app-routing --flat --module=app`.
2. Define routes in `AppRoutingModule`.
3. Import `AppRoutingModule` into `AppModule`.

The following demonstrates routing module code `import { NgModule } from '@angular/core'`:

```
import { RouterModule, Routes } from '@angular/router';
```

```
import { HomeComponent } from './home/home.component';
import { AboutComponent } from './about/about.component';
const routes: Routes = [
  { path: '', component: HomeComponent },
  { path: 'about', component: AboutComponent },
  { path: '**', redirectTo: '' }
];

@NgModule({
  imports: [RouterModule.
  forRoot(routes)], exports:
  [RouterModule]
})
export class AppRoutingModule { }
```

The following illustrates router outlet usage:

```
<!-- app.component.html -->
<nav>
  <a routerLink="">Home</a>
  <a routerLink="about">About</a>
</nav>
<router-outlet></router-outlet>
```

Route parameters

Route parameters capture dynamic values from the URL, such as IDs. Define parameters with **`:param`** in the path. Components use **`ActivatedRoute`** to read parameters and fetch or display corresponding data.

The following presents a parameterized route definition:

```
const routes: Routes = [
  { path: 'user/:id', component: UserComponent }
];
```

The following demonstrates accessing parameters:

```
import { Component, OnInit } from '@angular/core';
import { ActivatedRoute } from '@angular/router';

@Component({ /* ... */ })
export class UserComponent implements OnInit {
  userId!: string;
  constructor(private route: ActivatedRoute) {}
  ngOnInit() {
    this.userId = this.route.snapshot.paramMap.get('id')!;
  }
}
```

The following table presents the URL and extracted parameter:

URL	Extracted id
`/user/42`	`"42"`
`/user/alpha "alpha"`	`/user/alpha "alpha"`

Table 8.8: Route parameter example

Nested routes

Nested routes allow child components to render within parent component layouts. Define children in the route configuration and place a secondary `<router-outlet>` in the parent template to render child routes.

The following presents a nested route configuration:

```
const routes: Routes = [
  {
    path: 'dashboard', component: DashboardComponent, children: [
      { path: '', component: OverviewComponent },
      { path: 'stats', component: StatsComponent },
      { path: 'settings', component: SettingsComponent }
    ]
      }
     ];
```

The following demonstrates a parent template:

```
<!-- dashboard.component.html -->
<h2>Dashboard</h2>
<nav>
  <a routerLink="">Overview</a>
  <a routerLink="stats">Stats</a>
  <a routerLink="settings">Settings</a>
</nav>
<router-outlet></router-outlet>
```

The following flowchart demonstrates a nested route tree:

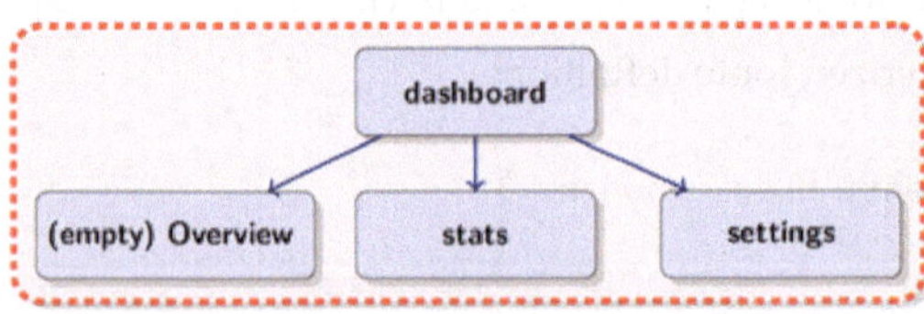

Figure 8.9: Nested routes under /dashboard with fit highlighting

Guards and resolvers

Guards control navigation by allowing or preventing route activation, deactivation, or children loading. Resolvers fetch data before route activation, ensuring components have the required data on initialization. Implement guard interfaces (`CanActivate`, `CanDeactivate`) and resolver (`Resolve`) to enforce logic.

The following table presents guard and resolver types:

Interface	Purpose
`CanActivate`	Allow or block navigation to a route.
`CanDeactivate`	Prevent leaving a route.
`CanLoad`	Block lazy-loaded module loading.
`Resolve`	Pre-fetch data before route activation.

Table 8.9: Route guard and resolver interfaces

The following demonstrates a simple auth guard:

```
@Injectable({ providedIn: 'root' })
export class AuthGuard implements CanActivate {
  constructor(private auth: AuthService, private router:
  Router) {} canActivate(): boolean {
    if (this.auth.isLoggedIn()) return true; this.router.
    navigate(['login']);
    return false;
  }
}
```

The following demonstrates a data resolver:

```
@Injectable({ providedIn: 'root' })
export class UserResolver implements Resolve<User>
  { constructor(private service: UserService)
  {} resolve(route: ActivatedRouteSnapshot):
  Observable<User> {
    return this.service.fetchUser(route.paramMap.get('id')!);
  }
}
```

The following presents guard and resolver usage:

```
const routes: Routes = [
  {
    path: 'profile/:id', component: ProfileComponent, canActivate: [AuthGuard],
    resolve: { user: UserResolver }
  }
];
```

Forms

Angular offers two primary form handling approaches, template-driven and reactive, each suited to different complexity levels. Both integrate validation seamlessly, ensuring data integrity before submission. Selecting the right approach depends on form complexity, dynamic behavior, and test requirements.

Template driven

Template-driven forms rely on directives in the template to create and manage form controls. Angular parses the template at runtime to build a **FormGroup**. This approach is intuitive for simple forms, using **ngModel** for two-way binding and built-in validators via attributes.

The following presents key directives:

- **ngForm**: Container for all controls.
- **ngModel**: Binds input to model property.
- **Validation attributes**: required, minlength, etc.
- **ngModelGroup**: Groups controls logically.

The following demonstrates a login form:

```
<form #loginForm="ngForm" (ngSubmit)="onSubmit(loginForm)">
  <label>Email</label>
  <input
    name="email" ngModel required email
    #emailCtrl="ngModel" />
```

```
  <div *ngIf="emailCtrl.invalid && emailCtrl.touched">
    <small *ngIf="emailCtrl.errors?.required">Email is required</small>
    <small *ngIf="emailCtrl.errors?.email">Invalid email format</small>
  </div>
  <label>Password</label>
  <input
    name="password" type="password" ngModel required minlength="6"
    #pwCtrl="ngModel" />
  <div *ngIf="pwCtrl.invalid && pwCtrl.touched">
    <small *ngIf="pwCtrl.errors?.required">Password is required</small>
    <small *ngIf="pwCtrl.errors?.minlength"> Minimum 6 characters
    </small>
  </div>

  <button [disabled]="loginForm.invalid">Login</button>
</form>
```

Reactive forms

Reactive forms use explicit **FormGroup** and **FormControl** instances in the component class. This model-driven approach allows full control over form state, dynamic validation, and syncing with observables. Reactive forms are ideal for complex, dynamic forms requiring conditional controls or programmatic updates.

The following presents the setup steps:

1. Import **ReactiveFormsModule** in NgModule.
2. Define **FormGroup** and **FormControl** in the component.
3. Bind template to form controls via **formGroup** and **formControlName**.

The following code demonstrates the component and template side by side:

```
import { Component } from '@angular/core';
import { FormGroup, FormControl,                    \
<form [formGroup]="profileForm"                     \
 \ (ngSubmit)="onSubmit()">
 \ Validators } from
 \ '@angular/forms';

@Component({ /* ... */ })
export class ProfileComponent {
\               <label>First Name</label>
                <input formControlName="firstName" />
                <div *ngIf="profileForm.get('firstN ┘          \
                 \ ame')?.invalid">
                  <small *ngIf="profileForm.get('fi ┘          \
  profileForm = new FormGroup({ firstName: new FormControl('', \
     \ Validators.required), age: new FormControl(null, [
      Validators.required, Validators.min(18)
    ])
  });
     \ rstName')?.errors?.required"> Required
    </small>
```

```
    </div>

    <label>Age</label>
    <input type="number"                              \
     \ formControlName="age" /><div *ngIf="profileForm.get('age')? ⌋     \
    onSubmit() { console.log(this.profileForm.value);
    \ .invalid">
     <small *ngIf="profileForm.get('ag ⌋          \
    }\ e')?.errors?.required">
  }Required
  </small>
  <small *ngIf="profileForm.get('ag ⌋
  \
   \ e')?.errors?.min"> Minimum age 18
                                          </small>
                                           </div>

 <button [disabled]="profileForm.inv ⌋
 \
  \ alid">Submit</button>
</form>
```

Validation

Validation ensures form data meets business rules before processing. Both template-driven and reactive forms support built-in validators (required, min/max, pattern) and custom validators. Reactive forms allow synchronous or asynchronous validators defined in the component class.

The following table presents validator options:

Validator	Description
`Validators.required`	Field must have a non-empty value
`Validators.min(length)`	Minimum numeric value or string length
`Validators.max(length)`	Maximum numeric value or string length
`Validators.email`	Validates email format
`Validators.pattern(regex)`	Matches input against regex

Table 8.10: Built-in validators

The following code demonstrates a custom validator:

```
import { AbstractControl, ValidationErrors } from '@angular/forms';

export function noSpaceValidator(control: AbstractControl):
  ValidationErrors | null {
  return (control.value as string).includes(' ')
    ? { noSpace: true }
    : null;
}

// Usage in reactive form
new FormControl('', [Validators.required, noSpaceValidator])
```

HTTP client

Angular's HTTP Client provides a streamlined API for interacting with backend services. Built on RxJS observables, it supports request and response interception, typed responses, and error handling. Proper setup and use of CRUD operations and interceptors ensure clean, maintainable data access layers.

Setup

Before making HTTP calls, import **`HttpClientModule`** into the root or feature NgModule. Then inject **`HttpClient`** into services or components to perform requests. This configuration wires Angular's HTTP infrastructure and enables dependency injection.

The following presents the module setup:

```
import { BrowserModule } from '@angular/platform-browser';
import { NgModule } from '@angular/core';
import { HttpClientModule } from '@angular/common/http';
import { AppComponent } from './app.component';

@NgModule({
  declarations:
  [AppComponent],
  imports: [
    BrowserModule,
    HttpClientModule           // Enables HttpClient throughout app
  ],
  bootstrap: [AppComponent]
})
export class AppModule {}
```

The following example demonstrates client injection and a basic request:

```
import { Component, OnInit } from        \
 \  '@angular/core';
import { HttpClient } from               \
 \  '@angular/common/http';

@Component({ selector: 'app-root',       \
 \ template: '' })
export class AppComponent implements     \
 \ OnInit {
  constructor(private http: HttpClient) {}

  ngOnInit() {
    this.http.get('/api/status')
      .subscribe(status =>               \
       \ console.log(status));
  }
}
```

```
{"status":"OK"}
```

(Logged in console)

Figure 8.10: HttpClient injection (left) and sample excpected response (right)

CRUD operations

Implementing CRUD operations is straightforward with **HttpClient**. Each method returns an **Observable<T>** for the response type. Use RxJS operators for transformation and error handling.

The following table depicts the CRUD method mapping:

Operation	Method	Description
Create	**http.post<T>(url, body)**	Send new resource to the server
Read	**http.get<T>(url)**	Retrieve resource(s)
Update	**http.put<T>(url, body)**	Replace existing resource
Delete	**http.delete<T>(url)**	Remove resource
Patch	**http.patch<T>(url, body)**	Partial update

Table 8.11: *CRUD operations with HttpClient*

The following figure demonstrates Service CRUD methods and a sample GET response:

```
// In DataService
getItems() {
  return this.http.get<Item[]>('/api/  \
  \ items');
}
addItem(item: Item) {
  return this.http.post<Item>('/api/i  \
  \ tems', item);
}
updateItem(item: Item) {
  return this.http.put<Item>(`/api/it  \
  \ ems/${item.id}`, item);
}
deleteItem(id: number) {
  return this.http.delete<void>(`/api  \
  \ /items/${id}`);
}
```

```
[
{"id":1,"name":"Item
A"},
{"id":2,"name":"Item
B"}
]
```

Figure 8.11: *Service CRUD methods (left) and sample GET response (right)*

Interceptors

Interceptors allow inspection and transformation of HTTP requests or responses. They implement the **HttpInterceptor** interface, enabling tasks such as adding authentication headers, logging, or handling errors globally. Register interceptors in the provider array with multi-token configuration.

The following presents an interceptor skeleton:

```
import { Injectable } from '@angular/core';
import { HttpInterceptor, HttpRequest, HttpHandler, HttpEvent
} from '@angular/common/http';
import { Observable } from 'rxjs';

@Injectable()
export class AuthInterceptor implements HttpInterceptor { intercept(req: HttpRequest<any>,
```

```
        next: HttpHandler):
          Observable<HttpEvent<any>> {
          const authReq = req.clone({
            setHeaders: { Authorization: 'Bearer TOKEN' }
          });
          return next.handle(authReq);
        }
    }
```

The following demonstrates provider registration:

```
@NgModule({ providers: [
    {
      provide: HTTP_INTERCEPTORS, useClass: AuthInterceptor,
      multi: true          // Allows multiple interceptors
    }
      ]
    })
export class AppModule {}
```

The following process diagram illustrates the interceptor flow:

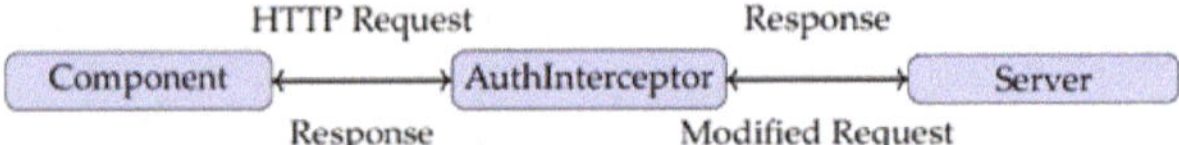

Figure 8.12: Request/response flow through interceptor

Pipes

Pipes transform data in templates, allowing formatting, filtering, and transformation without altering component logic. They take input values, apply a transformation, and return formatted output. Angular includes built-in pipes for common tasks and supports custom pipes for application-specific needs.

Built-in pipes

Built-in pipes cover common formatting needs, such as dates, numbers, text case, and JSON serialization. They accept arguments for customization and can be chained. Using built-in pipes keeps templates concise and leverages optimized implementations.

The following table presents common built-in pipes:

Pipe	Description
`date`	Formats dates (e.g., `'shortDate'`)
`currency`	Formats numbers as currency (e.g., `'USD'`)
`percent`	Formats numbers as percentages
`uppercase`	Converts text to uppercase
`lowercase`	Converts text to lowercase
`json`	Serializes objects to JSON strings

Table 8.12: Common built-in pipes

The following example demonstrates pipe usage and output:

```
<p>Today is {{ today | date:'fullDate' }}</p>
<p>Price: {{ price |                        \
 \ currency:'EUR':'symbol' }}</p>
<p>Progress: {{ percent | percent:'1.0-0'   \
 \ }}</p>
<p>{{ message | uppercase }}</p>
```

HelloDemo
localhost:4200
Today is Wednesday, June 18, 2025
Price: €123.45
Progress: 75%
HELLO WORLD

***Figure 8.13:** Built-in pipes code (left) and rendered output (right)*

Custom pipes

Custom pipes encapsulate application-specific transformations. To create one, implement the **`PipeTransform`** interface, decorate the class with **`@Pipe`**, and register it in an NgModule. Custom pipes can accept arguments and be pure or impure depending on change detection needs.

The following table presents custom pipe metadata:

Field	Description
`name`	Pipe name used in templates
`pure`	**`true`** for pure (default) or **`false`** for impure pipes

***Table 8.13:** Custom pipe metadata*

The following code demonstrates a truncated pipe:

```
import { Pipe, PipeTransform } from '@angular/core';
@Pipe({ name: 'truncate' })
export class TruncatePipe implements PipeTransform {
  transform(value: string, limit = 20): string {
    return value.length > limit
      ? value.substring(0, limit) + '…'
      : value;
  }
}
```

The following presents registration in the module:

```
@NgModule({
  declarations: [TruncatePipe, /* other components
  */], imports: [BrowserModule],
  bootstrap: [AppComponent]
})
export class AppModule {}
```

Lifecycle

Angular components and directives follow a clear sequence of lifecycle hooks, which provide defined points for running code during initialization, updates, and destruction. These hooks support practical tasks such as setting initial values, reacting to input changes, and cleaning up resources (for example, unsubscribing from observables, removing event listeners, or clearing timers) so components behave predictably and avoid memory leaks in real applications.

Lifecycle hooks

Lifecycle hooks are methods a component can implement to respond to specific phases. Hooks such as **`ngOnInit`** and **`ngOnDestroy`** provide entry points for initialization and cleanup. Understanding the order and purpose of each hook is essential for orchestrating complex component behavior.

The following table presents common lifecycle hooks:

Hook	Purpose
`ngOnChanges`	Called when input properties change; receives SimpleChanges.
`ngOnInit`	Called once after first ngOnChanges; ideal for initialization.
`ngDoCheck`	Called during every change detection cycle for custom checks.
`ngAfterContentInit`	After projecting content into a component.
`ngAfterContentChecked`	After each content check.
`ngAfterViewInit`	After the component's view and child views are initialized
`ngAfterViewChecked`	After each view check.
`ngOnDestroy`	Just before Angular destroys the component, cleanup here.

Table 8.14: Lifecycle hook sequence

The following demonstrates hooks in a component:

```
@Component({ selector: 'app-timer', template: '{{count}}' })
export class TimerComponent implements OnInit, OnDestroy { count = 0;
  private intervalId!: any;

  ngOnInit() {
    this.intervalId = setInterval(() => this.count++, 1000);
  }

  ngOnDestroy() { clearInterval(this.intervalId);
  }
}
```

Change detection

Angular's change detection monitors component data and updates the DOM when values change. The default strategy checks the entire component tree each cycle, while the OnPush strategy limits checks to components with changed inputs or events. Choosing the right strategy optimizes performance.

The following table presents change detection strategies:

Strategy	Behavior
Default	Checks all components every cycle.
OnPush	Checks only when @Input references change, or events occur.

Table 8.15: Change detection strategies

The following demonstrates the OnPush configuration:

```
@Component({
  selector: 'app-item',
  template: '<p>{{item.name}}</
  p>', changeDetection:
  ChangeDetectionStrategy.OnPush
})
export class ItemComponent {
  @Input() item!: { name: string };
}
```

The flowpath illustrates detection flow:

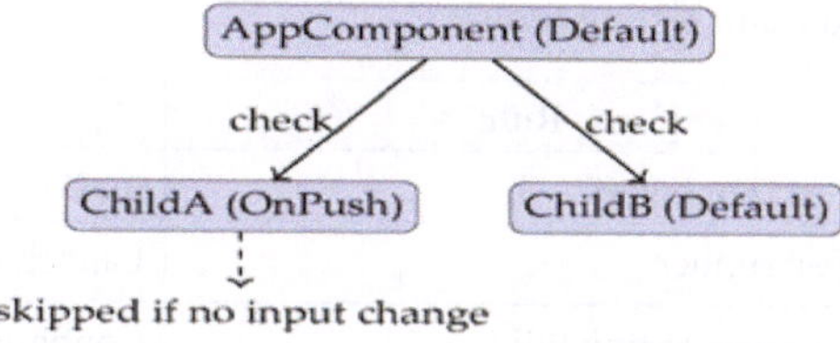

Figure 8.14: Change detection with Default and OnPush

Testing

Testing in Angular ensures application reliability by validating individual units and user workflows. Unit tests verify component logic, services, and pipes in isolation using Jasmine and Karma. **End-to-end** (**E2E**) tests simulate real user interactions against a running application, commonly with Cypress. A balanced strategy combines fast unit tests with comprehensive E2E tests to catch both code defects and integration issues.

Unit testing

Unit tests exercise small pieces of code—components, services, and pipes, without launching a browser. Angular's TestBed utility configures a testing module that mimics the NgModule environment. Tests use Jasmine's `describe/it` structure and assertions via `expect`. Karma runs tests in real browsers or headless environments.

The following presents the TestBed setup:

```
import { TestBed } from '@angular/core/testing';
import { HelloComponent } from './hello.component';

describe('HelloComponent', ()
  => { beforeEach(async () => {
    await TestBed.
      configureTestingModule({
      declarations:
      [HelloComponent]
    }).compileComponents();
  });
});
```

The following figure demonstrates component test side by side:

```
// hello.component.spec.ts
it('should display greeting', () => {
  const fixture = TestBed.createCompo    \
   \ nent(HelloComponent);
  fixture.detectChanges();
  const el: HTMLElement =                \
   \ fixture.nativeElement;
  expect(el.querySelector('h2')!.text    \
   \ Content)
    .toContain('Hello, Angular');
});
```

Figure 8.15: Unit test code (left) and sample output (right)

The following table presents common unit testing tools:

Tool	Role	Notes
Jasmine	Test framework	BDD syntax (describe, it)
Karma	Test runner	Launches tests in browsers
TestBed	Angular testing util	Configures NgModule for tests
HttpTestingController	HTTP mocking	Intercepts HttpClient calls

Table 8.16: *Unit testing tools overview*

End-to-end testing

E2E tests validate the complete application flow in a real browser. Cypress offers a modern, developer-friendly API for writing and running tests, with live reloading and time-travel debugging. Tests navigate the app, interact with elements, and assert on UI and network behavior.

The following presents the Cypress installation:

```
npm install --save-dev cypress npx cypress open
```

The following demonstrates a login E2E test:

```
// cypress/integration/login.spec.js
describe('Login flow',
  () => { it('logs in
  successfully', () => {
    cy.visit('/login'); cy.get('input[name=email]').
    type('user@example.com');
    cy.get('input[name=password]').type('password123');
    cy.get('button[type=submit]').click();
    cy.url().should('include', '/dashboard');
    cy.contains('Welcome, user');
  });
});
```

The following table presents the E2E testing comparison:

Tool	Language/API	Highlights
Protractor	TypeScript/Jasmine	Angular-specific, deprecated
Cypress	JavaScript/BDD	Fast, real-time reload, debug UI
TestCafe	JavaScript	No browser plugin needed

Table 8.17: *E2E testing tools comparison*

Performance

Optimizing Angular applications helps achieve fast initial load times and smooth, responsive interactions as an application grows. This chapter has already introduced building blocks that directly affect performance, such as routing, lazy loading, and change-detection strategies, and this section connects them into a practical optimization view. Lazy loading works through the router to split the application into smaller bundles and load a feature only when a user navigates to it, which reduces the initial JavaScript download for the first screen. AOT compilation precompiles templates during the build so the browser does not need to compile Angular templates at runtime, which improves startup time and catches template errors earlier. Change detection also plays a key role after the app loads: Default change detection checks a wider portion of the component tree, while OnPush limits checks to specific triggers (input reference changes and events), which keeps large views responsive. In a real scenario, such as an admin dashboard, lazy loading can keep heavy areas like *Reports* or *User Management* out of the initial bundle, AOT can speed up first render, and OnPush can reduce unnecessary UI updates when large tables and charts refresh. Combined, these techniques reduce initial bundle size, lower runtime overhead, and improve both perceived and measured performance.

Lazy loading

Lazy loading defers the loading of feature modules until the user navigates to routes that require them. This splits the application into smaller bundles, improving initial load performance. The router's **`loadChildren`** property specifies the module path and its class. Angular CLI automatically generates separate chunks for each lazy module.

The following presents a lazy route definition:

```
const routes: Routes = [
  { path: '', component: HomeComponent },
  {
    path: 'admin', loadChildren: () =>
      import('./admin/admin.module')
        .then(m => m.AdminModule)
          }
          ];
@NgModule({
  imports: [RouterModule.forRoot(routes)], exports: [RouterModule]
})
export class AppRoutingModule {}
```

The following figure illustrates the bundle loading flow:

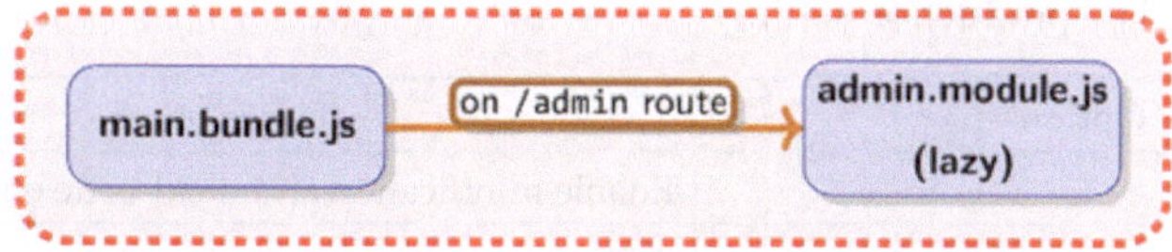

***Figure 8.16:** Lazy loading of* AdminModule *chunk with route-based loading*

Ahead Of Time

AOT compilation transforms templates and components into efficient JavaScript during build time, removing the need for the browser to compile Angular code at runtime. This results in smaller bundles, faster rendering, and earlier detection of template errors. The Angular CLI's production build uses AOT by default.

The following presents build commands:

```
# Production build with AOT (default)
ng build --configuration production
# Explicit AOT flag (for older CLI)
ng build --aot
```

The following table presents JIT versus AOT comparison:

Aspect	JIT	AOT
Compilation time	In the browser at runtime	During the build process

Bundle size	Larger (compiler included)	Smaller (no compiler)
Startup speed	Slower (compile on load)	Faster (precompiled)
Error detection	Runtime template errors	Compile-time template errors

Table 8.18: JIT versus AOT compilation

The following demonstrates a compiled output snippet:

```
// AOT generated code fragment
ɵɵdefineComponent({ type: HelloComponent,
  factory: function HelloComponent_Factory(t) { return new (t || HelloComponent)(); },
  template: function HelloComponent_Template(rf, ctx) {
    if (rf & 1) { ɵɵelementStart(0, "h1"); ɵɵtext(1, "Hello, AOT!"); ɵɵelementEnd();
    }
  }
});
```

Deployment

Deploying an Angular application involves configuring the build for production and choosing a hosting environment. Production builds optimize bundle size and performance, while hosting options determine scalability, SSL, and CDN integration. This section covers building configuration in **angular.json** and compares popular hosting platforms.

Build configuration

Angular's build system uses the **angular.json** file to define development and production settings. Production configurations enable AOT compilation, minification, and file hashing. Adjusting options like **baseHref** or **polyfills** ensures correct asset loading and browser support.

The following table presents key production settings:

Option	Description
optimization	Enable minification and dead-code elimination.
aot	AOT compilation of templates.
outputHashing	Append content hash to filenames.
sourceMap	Generate source maps for debugging.
baseHref	Set the base URL for the application.

Table 8.19: Production build settings

The following example demonstrates **angular.json** snippet and its output:

```
"configurations": {
  "production": {
    "optimization": true,
    "aot": true,
    "outputHashing": "all",
    "sourceMap": false,
    "extractCss": true,
    "namedChunks": false,
    "buildOptimizer": true,
    "baseHref": "/my-app/"
  }
}
```

```
ng build –prod
✓ Compiled successfully.
✓ Budgets passed.
Initial Chunk Files | Names | Raw Size
main.js | main | 150 KB
polyfills.js | polyfills | 45 KB
```

Figure 8.17: Production configuration (left) and build output summary (right)

Hosting options

Choosing a hosting platform involves evaluating ease of deployment, CDN support, and custom domain configuration. Static hosting services and cloud storage both serve Angular's generated files. Key factors include automated deploys, SSL, and global distribution.

The following presents hosting platforms:

Platform	Type	Key features
Netlify	Git CI/CD	Instant previews, functions, and free SSL.
Vercel	Git CI/CD	Zero-config, serverless, analytics.
Firebase	Static + CDN	Integrated auth, SSR, CLI deploy.
AWS S3 + CF	Storage + CDN	Highly scalable, custom caching.
GitHub Pages	Branch deploy	Free, custom domain, limited to static

Table 8.19: Hosting platform comparison

The following demonstrates Firebase deploy:

```
npm install -g firebase-tools
firebase login
firebase init hosting
firebase deploy
```

The following illustrates the deployment flow:

Figure 8.18: Angular deployment workflow with build, deploy, and hosting steps

Hands-on project

1. Build an Angular application that fetches a list of posts from **https://jsonplaceholder. typicode.com/posts** using HttpClient. Display the posts in a paginated list and implement navigation between pages via the Angular Router.
2. Create a user-registration reactive form in Angular with custom validators enforcing password strength and email format. Display validation feedback and submit the data to a mock service.

Conclusion

In this chapter, we established a comprehensive foundation in Angular development. Starting with environment setup and project scaffolding via the Angular CLI, we explored NgModules, components, and declarative templates. We mastered data binding, interpolation, property, event, and two-way, and applied built-in and custom directives for dynamic DOM manipulation. We created services and utilized Angular's hierarchical dependency injection to share logic, then configured client-side routing with parameters, nested routes, and guards. We built both template-driven and reactive forms with validation, performed HTTP CRUD operations using the Http-Client module and interceptors, and applied pipes for data transformation. We examined lifecycle hooks, change-detection strategies, unit, and end-to-end testing, and implemented performance optimizations like lazy loading and AOT compilation.

In the next chapter, we will extend this knowledge through hands-on projects and a side-by-side comparison of React and Angular. You will develop complete applications in each framework, reinforce best practices, and evaluate trade-offs in architecture, development workflow, and performance, enabling you to select the most appropriate tool for diverse web-development scenarios.

Exercises

1. Which decorator defines an Angular module?
   a. @Component
   b. @NgModule
   c. @Injectable
   d. @Directive
2. What syntax enables two-way binding in template-driven forms?
   a. (ngModelChange)
   b. [(ngModel)]
   c. {ngModel}
3. Which service class handles HTTP requests?
   a. HttpService
   b. HttpClient
   c. HttpModule
   d. HttpController
4. Define Angular's dependency injection pattern and explain two benefits.
5. Explain the difference between template-driven and reactive forms.
6. Describe structural versus attribute directives, giving one example of each.
7. Compare and contrast Angular modules and components. How do they collaborate to structure an application?
8. Describe Angular's change detection mechanism and the OnPush strategy. When and why would you use OnPush?

CHAPTER 9
Hands-on Projects and Frameworks Comparison

Introduction

Hands-on experience is essential for internalizing theoretical concepts and gaining confidence in real-world development. In this chapter, we build two complete frontend applications—first in React, then in Angular, to reinforce the principles covered earlier. The React project walks you through scaffolding with **Create React App** (**CRA**), component design, state management with hooks, event handling, list rendering, conditional rendering, and deployment options. You will implement a todo list application that supports adding, completing, and deleting tasks, and learn how to structure components for reusability and maintainability. Next, the Angular project guides you through Angular **command line interface** (**CLI**) setup, module and component creation, template-driven and reactive forms, dependency-injected services, routing with guards and resolvers, and **Hypertext Transfer Protocol** (**HTTP**) based **create, read, update, delete** (**CRUD**) operations against a simulated backend. Finally, we compare React and Angular across architecture, data binding, performance, scalability, and ecosystem to help you make informed framework choices. By the end of this chapter, you will have built full-featured applications in both frameworks and understand their relative strengths and trade-offs.

Structure

This chapter covers the following topics:

- Hands-on React project
- Hands-on Angular project
- React vs. Angular comparison
- Case studies
- Summary and practices

Objectives

By the end of this chapter, the readers will have taken a React application from zero to production; initializing with CRA, breaking the UI into functional components, managing local state with useState and useEffect, handling events and forms, rendering lists conditionally, and deploying to platforms like GitHub Pages or Netlify. They will then scaffold an Angular project using the Angular CLI, define NgModules and components, implement template-driven and reactive forms with validation, consume RESTful services via HttpClient, and configure client-side routing with parameters and guards. Finally, they will evaluate React and Angular across key dimensions, architecture, data binding, performance optimization, tooling, and community, to articulate when each framework is most appropriate for a given project. This hands-on approach cements the reader's understanding and equips them to choose and apply the right framework in real-world scenarios.

Hands-on React project

Building a hands-on project is one of the best ways to understand how React works in real-world scenarios. In this section, a complete React application is developed from scratch to apply the core concepts covered earlier, including components, props, state, and event handling, along with component lifecycle behavior using hooks such as `useEffect` for side effects and cleanup.

The project chosen is a simple but practical todo list application. This type of app helps reinforce concepts like list rendering, conditional rendering, form handling, event handling, and state management. By the end of this project, learners will be comfortable with building and organizing components, handling user interactions, and managing application state effectively.

Project overview

The application will allow users to:

- Add tasks to a list.
- Mark tasks as completed.
- Delete tasks from the list.
- View the list of current tasks.

The project will follow these major steps:

1. Project setup using CRA.
2. Creating and styling components (Input, Task List, Task Item).
3. Managing state and handling user events.
4. Deploying the React app to a web server.

Technologies and tools

The following tools and technologies are used:

- **React**: For building the user interface.
- **JavaScript (ES6+)**: Core programming logic.
- **CSS**: For styling components.
- **Node.js and npm**: Environment and package management.
- **CRA**: Toolchain for bootstrapping the project.

Directory structure

Once the project is created using CRA, the structure will resemble:

```
todo-app/
│
├── public/
│   └── index.html
├── src/
│   ├── components/
│   │   ├── TodoInput.js
│   │   ├── TodoList.js
│   │   └── TodoItem.js
│   ├── App.js
│   ├── App.css
│   └── index.js
├── package.json
└── README.md
```

Each component will be created in **the `src/components/` directory** and imported into **`App.js`**, which serves as the root component.

Learning outcomes

Upon completing this hands-on project, learners will:

- Understand the structure of a real React application.
- Learn how to divide UI into reusable components.
- Gain proficiency in managing React state and handling events.
- Apply conditional rendering and list mapping.
- Be ready to build and deploy basic React applications.

Note: In the following subsections, each stage of the todo list application will be explored in detail, from project setup to deployment.

Todo list application with React

In this subsection, a complete implementation of a todo list application using React is presented. The goal is to understand how to structure a React project, create and organize components, manage state, handle user input, and render data dynamically in the user interface.

Application requirements

The application will allow users to:

- Enter a task in an input field and add it to a list.
- Mark tasks as complete/incomplete.
- Delete individual tasks.
- Maintain an updated view without reloading the page.

This application demonstrates real-world concepts, including:

- Component hierarchy and reusability.
- Form handling in React.
- State lifting and props passing.
- Dynamic rendering using array mapping.

Component structure

The todo app will consist of the following components:

- **App**: Root component that manages state and renders all others.
- **TodoInput**: Component with an input field and submit button.
- **TodoList**: Component that renders the list of tasks.
- **TodoItem**: Component that renders each individual task.

The following figure depicts the component hierarchy of the project:

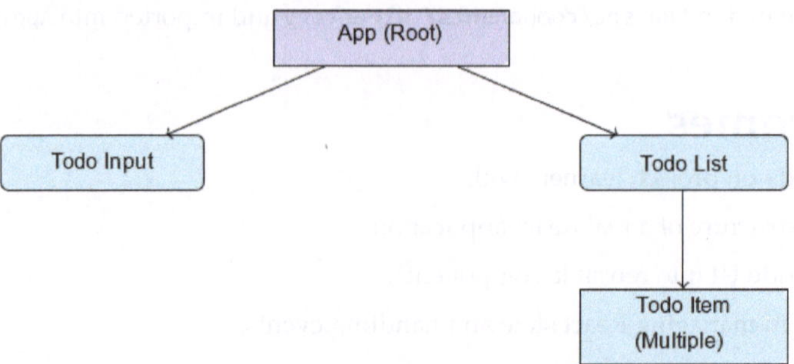

***Figure 9.1:** Component hierarchy of the todo list app*

Functional goals

This section outlines the key objectives for the hands-on project, guiding the development step by step. By following these goals, you will gain practical experience in setting up a React application, building and composing components, managing state, and handling user interactions. Completing each goal will reinforce core React concepts and prepare you for more advanced tasks.

The following presents the project goals:

1. Setting up the React project environment.
2. Building reusable **user interface (UI)** components.
3. Managing state with `useState` hook.
4. Passing data via props to child components.
5. Handling user events and callbacks.
6. Applying styles and CSS modules.

Tools required

A reliable set of tools ensures a smooth development workflow. You will need a JavaScript runtime, a package manager, and an environment for editing and testing code. These tools are industry standard and support features like linting, formatting, and live reloading to streamline your work.

The following table presents the required tools:

Tool	Purpose
Node.js and npm	Run development server, install packages.
Code editor (VS Code)	Edit code with syntax highlighting and extensions.
Modern web browser	Test and debug the application (Chrome).
Internet connection	Download dependencies and documentation.

***Table 9.1:** Development tools overview*

Initial setup preview

Before understanding the code, the project structure must be generated. This project uses CRA for simplicity and learning because it bootstraps a React application with sensible defaults, including bundling, transpilation, and a development server. In modern production work, many teams prefer Vite for faster startup and builds during development, or Next.js when **server-side rendering (SSR)**, file-based routing, and built-in performance features are required. This preview shows the setup commands and the resulting folder layout, giving a clear roadmap before implementation.

The following demonstrates project initialization using CRA:

```
npx create-react-app todo-app
cd todo-app
npm start
```

The following figure presents the generated structure:

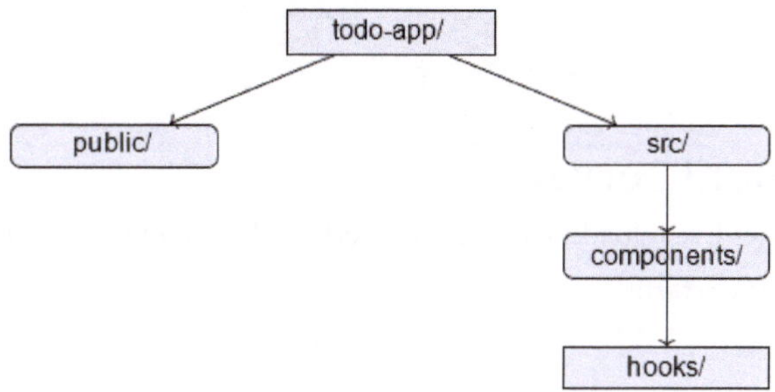

***Figure 9.2:** Preview of CRA folder layout*

Project setup

This section guides you through initializing a new React project using CRA. CRA provides a zero-configuration setup including Webpack, Babel, and a development server. Following these steps ensures a standardized project structure and efficient workflow.

Install Node and npm

React development requires a JavaScript runtime and package manager. Node.js supplies the runtime, and `npm` installs and manages dependencies. Verifying their installation prevents issues during project creation.

The following demonstrates version checks:

```
node --version
npm --version
```

If missing, install from the official site: **https://nodejs.org/**.

Create React App

CRA bootstraps the project with a standardized folder layout and build scripts. It installs dependencies and configures the development server.

The following demonstrates a CLI command:

```
npx create-react-app todo-app
```

Review folder layout

After CRA completes, inspect the generated directories and files. Understanding this structure helps organize code and assets.

The following presents the generated structure:

```
todo-app/
├── node_modules/
```

```
├── public/
│   └── index.html
├── src/
│   ├── App.css
│   ├── App.js
│   ├── App.test.js
│   ├── index.css
│   ├── index.js
│   └── logo.svg
├── package.json
└── README.md
```

Start the development server

The development server provides live reloading and error overlays. Launching it confirms the project runs correctly.

The following demonstrates server start:

```
cd todo-app
npm start
```

The app opens at **http://localhost:3000,** showing the default React welcome page.

Clean up boilerplate

Removing unused files and code reduces clutter before adding new features. Retain only essential entry points and styles.

The following presents cleanup steps:

1. Delete **App.test.js**, **logo.svg**, and **reportWebVitals.js**.
2. In **src/**, keep only **App.js**, **index.js**, and **App.css**.
3. Replace **App.js** content with minimal structure.

The following demonstrates minimal **App.js**:

```
import React from 'react';

function App() {
 return (
   <div>
       <h1>Todo List App</h1>
     </div>
   );
}

export default App;
```

Organize the source folder

For a scalable codebase, group related files into feature directories. This organization promotes modularity and simplifies navigation.

Recommended layout is as follows:

```
src/
├── components/
```

```
│       ├── TodoInput.js
│       ├── TodoList.js
│       └── TodoItem.js
├── hooks/
│       └── useLocalStorage.js
├── App.js
├── index.js
└── App.css
```

Having completed these steps, the project is ready for building components, managing state, and implementing the todo list functionality.

Component development

Developing components involves creating modular, reusable units that encapsulate their own logic and UI. Each component in the todo list app has a single responsibility, communicates via props and callbacks, and can be styled independently. This approach makes the codebase easier to maintain and extend.

The following table presents component roles:

Component	Responsibility
TodoInput	Capture and submit new todo text.
TodoList	Render list of TodoItem components.
TodoItem	Display a single todo with a delete action.

Table 9.2: Component roles overview

TodoInput

TodoInput uses React's **useState** hook to track the input value. It validates that text is non-empty on form submission, calls the **addTodo** callback provided by the parent, and then clears its input state.

The following demonstrates the **TodoInput** code:

```
import React, { useState } from 'react';

function TodoInput({ addTodo }) {
  const [text, setText] = useState('');

  const handleSubmit = e => { e.preventDefault();
    const value = text.trim(); if (!value) return; addTodo(value); setText('');
  };
  return (
    <form onSubmit={handleSubmit}>
      <input
        value={text}
        onChange={e => setText(e.
        target.value)}
        placeholder="Add todo item"
      />
      <button type="submit">Add</button>
    </form>
  );
```

```
}

export default TodoInput;
```

TodoItem

TodoItem receives a todo string and its index. It displays the text and offers a delete button that invokes the **removeTodo** callback with the item's index, enabling the parent to update state.

The following demonstrates **TodoItem** code:

```
import React from 'react';

function TodoItem({ todo, index, removeTodo }) {
  return (
    <div className="todo-item">
      <span>{todo}</span>
      <button onClick={() => removeTodo(index)}>Delete</button>
    </div>
  );
}

export default TodoItem;
```

TodoList

TodoList maps over an array of todos, rendering a **TodoItem** for each. It passes down the text, index, and **removeTodo** callback. This separation keeps list logic in one place and delegates item rendering.

The following demonstrates **TodoList** code:

```
import React from 'react';
import TodoItem from './TodoItem';

function TodoList({ todos, removeTodo }) {
 return (
  <div className="todo-list">
   {todos.map((todo, index) => (
    <TodoItem
     key={index}
     todo={todo}
     index={index}
     removeTodo={removeTodo}
    />
   ))}
  </div>
 );
}

export default TodoList;
```

Integrate in app

The **App** component holds the todo array state using **useState**. It defines **addTodo** and **removeTodo** functions, passes them as props to **TodoInput** and **TodoList**, and renders the overall layout.

The following demonstrates **App.js** code:

```
import React, { useState } from 'react';
import TodoInput from './components/
TodoInput'; import TodoList from './
components/TodoList'; import './App.
css';

function App() {
  const [todos, setTodos] = useState([]);

  const addTodo = text => setTodos([...todos, text]);
  const removeTodo = idx => { const list = [...todos]; list.splice(idx, 1); setTodos(list);
  };

  return (
    <div className="app-container">
      <h1>Todo List</h1>
      <TodoInput addTodo={addTodo} />
      <TodoList todos={todos} removeTodo={removeTodo} />
    </div>
  );
}

export default App;
```

The following figure illustrates the output of the project with a sample task added:

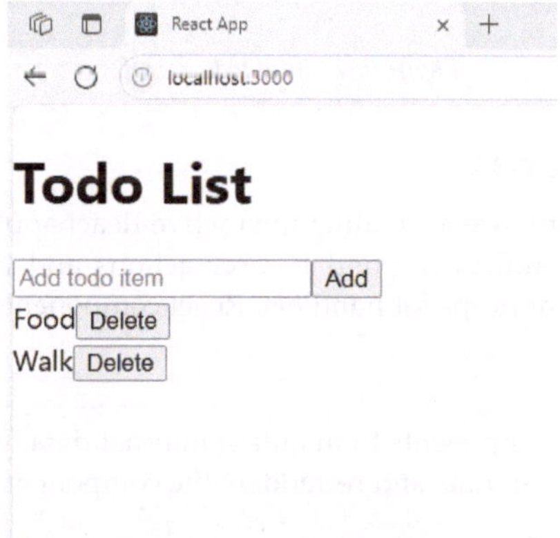

Figure 9.3: Output of the todo list project

Styling components

Styling enhances usability and clarity. We use a **cascading style sheets** (**CSS**) file with classes for layout, spacing, and basic theming. Classes are applied to containers, forms, and buttons to achieve a consistent look.

The following demonstrates **App.css**:

```
/* App.css */
.app-container { max-width: 400px; margin: auto;
  text-align: center;
```

```
    font-family: Arial, sans-serif;
  }
  .todo-list {
    margin-top: 20px;
    text-align: left;
  }
  .todo-item {
    display: flex;
    justify-content: space-between; margin-bottom: 8px;
  }
  input { padding: 8px; width: 70%;
    margin-right: 8px;
  }
  button {
    padding: 8px 12px;
    cursor: pointer;
  }
```

The following figure illustrates the output of the project with a sample task added with styled UI:

Figure 9.4: Styled todo list UI

Managing state and events

Managing state and handling events are core to creating interactive React applications. State holds data that drives component rendering, while event handlers respond to user actions and trigger state updates. By combining **`useState`** for state and camelCase event props for handlers, React components remain declarative and predictable.

State hook

The **`useState`** hook enables function components to maintain internal data. It returns a state variable and a setter function. Calling the setter enqueues an update and re-renders the component with the new value.

The following presents **`useState`** usage:

- **Import**: **`import { useState } from 'react';`**
- **Initialize**: **`const [value, setValue] = useState(initial);`**
- **Update**: **`setValue(newValue)`** triggers re-render.

The following demonstrates todo list state:

```
const [todos, setTodos] = useState([]);
// Add a todo:
setTodos([...todos, 'New task']);
```

The following figure illustrates the state change flow:

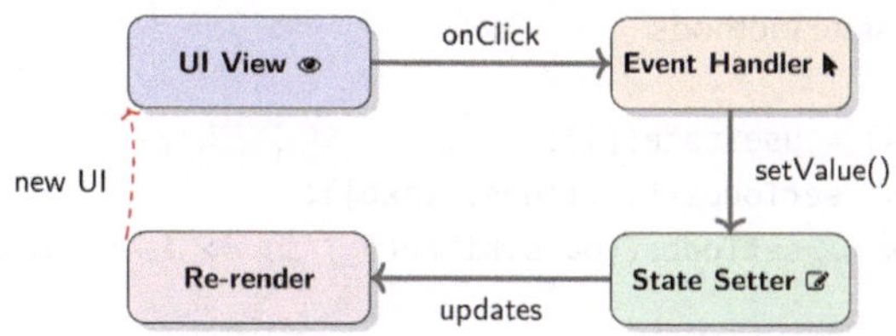

Figure 9.5: Sequence of state update and re-render in a component

Event handling

Event handling in React uses camelCase props to attach callbacks to elements. Handlers receive a SyntheticEvent, allowing the prevention of default behavior and access to event details.

The following table presents common events:

Event	Description
`onClick`	Mouse clicks on the element
`onChange`	Input value change
`onSubmit`	Form submission
`onKeyDown`	Key press in input

Table 9.3: Typical React events

The following demonstrates add and delete events:

```
<button onClick={() => addTodo(text)}>Add</button>
<button onClick={() => removeTodo(idx)}>Delete</button>
```

The following figure illustrates event to state update:

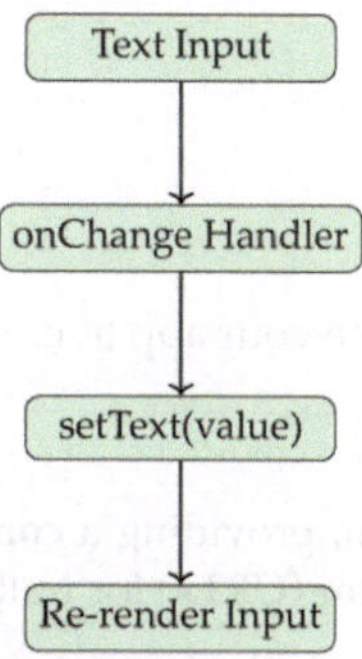

Figure 9.6: Flow of input event updating state

Parent state updates

The parent component holds the master state and passes setter functions down as props. Child components call these props to request state changes, keeping state management centralized.

The following presents prop drilling:

```
<TodoInput addTodo={addTodo} />
<TodoList todos={todos} removeTodo={removeTodo} />
```

The following demonstrates **App** state methods:

```
function App() {
  const [todos, setTodos] = useState([]);
  const addTodo = text => setTodos([...todos, text]);
  const removeTodo = idx => setTodos(todos.filter((_, i) => i !== idx));
  // ...
}
```

Deploying a React application

Deploying a React application packages the static assets produced by the build process and serves them from a hosting environment. A successful deployment pipeline automates building, testing, and publishing, ensuring that users always see the latest version. This section covers four popular hosting options and general best practices.

GitHub Pages

GitHub Pages hosts static sites directly from a GitHub repository. By publishing the **build/** folder via the **gh-pages** branch, you can serve your React app under your username's domain.

The following presents GitHub Pages steps:

1. Install the deployment package:

   ```
   npm install --save gh-pages
   ```

2. Add a homepage field to **package.json**:

   ```
   "homepage": "https://your-username.github.io/your-repo-name"
   ```

3. Configure deploy scripts:

   ```
   "scripts": {
     "predeploy": "npm run build",
     "deploy": "gh-pages -d build"
   }
   ```

4. Push your code and run:

   ```
   git push origin main
   npm run deploy
   ```

5. Visit the URL in the **homepage** field to see your app live.

Netlify hosting

Netlify automates deployment via Git integration, providing a **content delivery network** (**CDN**), **Secure Sockets Layer** (**SSL**), and preview **uniform resource locator** (**URLs**) for pull requests. It detects the build command and the publish directory automatically for CRA.

The following presents Netlify steps:

1. Build the production bundle:

   ```
   npm run build
   ```

2. Log in to Netlify and choose **New site from Git**.
3. Connect your GitHub repository and set:
   a. Build command: **npm run build**
   b. Publish directory: **build/**

4. Click **Deploy site** and wait for the URL to become available.

Vercel hosting

Vercel provides instant deployments with zero configuration for React apps. It supports previews, serverless functions, and analytics out of the box.

The following presents Vercel steps:

1. Sign in to Vercel and select **New Project**.
2. Import your GitHub repository containing the React app.
3. Accept the detected settings (`npm run build, build/`).
4. Click **Deploy** and note the generated URL for your application.

Firebase hosting

Firebase hosting delivers static files over a global CDN and integrates with other Firebase services. It supports single-page apps with automatic rewrites.

The following presents Firebase steps:

1. Install the Firebase CLI:

   ```
   npm install -g firebase-tools
   ```

2. Log in and initialize hosting:

   ```
   firebase login firebase init hosting
   ```

   a. When prompted, select your project and set the public directory to `build/`, answering *yes* to **single-page application** (**SPA**) rewrites.

3. Build and deploy:

   ```
   npm run build firebase deploy
   ```

4. Access your app via the Firebase-provided URL.

Deployment practices

Following best practices ensures reliable and secure deployments. These guidelines apply across hosting platforms and improve maintainability.

The following presents best practices:

- Test the production build locally:

  ```
  npm run build
  npx serve -s build
  ```

- Exclude the `build/` folder from version control with `.gitignore`.
- Store secrets and API keys in environment variables, not in source code.
- Automate deployment with **continuous integration** (**CI**) pipelines for consistency.
- Monitor site uptime and errors using analytics or logging services.

The following flowpath illustrates a generic **continuous integration and continuous deployment** (**CI/CD**) flow:

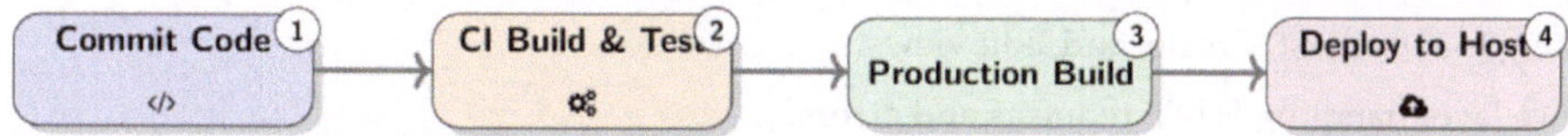

Figure 9.7: Automated deployment pipeline with four key stages

Hands-on Angular project

This project guides you through building a complete user management system using Angular. It demonstrates setting up the Angular environment, creating components, services, routing, and deploying a CRUD application. By following each step, you will apply core Angular concepts in a cohesive, real-world scenario.

Project overview

The user management system allows administrators to manage user records through a web interface. Users can be created, viewed in a list, updated, and deleted. This end-to-end exercise reinforces component architecture, data binding, and interaction with a REST-style **application programming interface** (**API**).

The following presents key features:

- Add new users with name and email fields.
- Display existing users in a paginated table.
- Edit user details in a pre-populated form.
- Delete users with a confirmation dialog.

Technologies used

Angular and its ecosystem provide the framework, language support, and tooling required for rapid development. A mock backend is simulated using JSON Server to focus on frontend functionality.

The following presents the technology stack:

Technology	Role
Angular CLI	Project scaffolding, build, serve.
TypeScript	Strongly-typed application code.
HyperText Markup Language (**HTML**) / CSS	Templates and styling.
Bootstrap	UI layout and components.
JavaScript Object Notation (**JSON**) Server	Mock REST API for CRUD operations.
RxJS	Reactive data handling.

Table 9.4: *Project technology stack*

Functional requirements

The application must fulfill the following requirements to be considered complete. These ensure full CRUD support and seamless navigation.

The following presents a requirements list:

- Form to create and validate new users.
- Table view listing users with pagination.
- Edit form populated with selected user data.
- Delete action with confirmation prompt.
- Routing for User List, Create, and Edit views.
- Service layer handling HTTP requests and errors.

Application structure

A clear folder and module layout promotes maintainability. Feature modules group related components and services, while a routing module centralizes navigation logic.

The following figure demonstrates the folder layout:

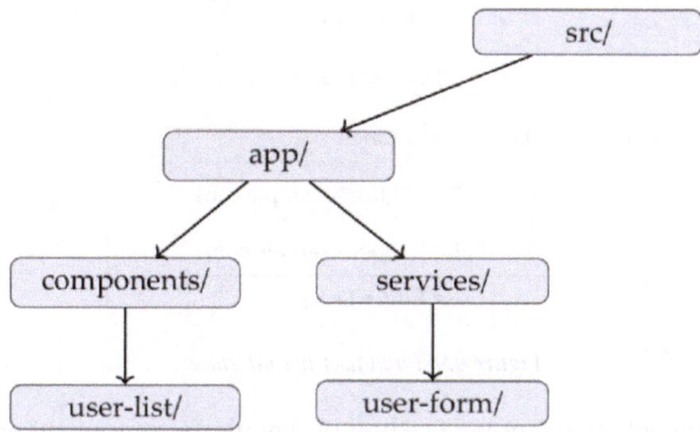

***Figure 9.8:** Angular project folder structure*

The following table shows module files:

File name	Purpose/Description
`app.module.ts`	Root module declaring components and imports.
`app-routing.module.ts`	Defines application routes.
`user.service.ts`	Service for HTTP CRUD operations.
`user-list.component.ts`	List view of users.
`user-form.component.ts`	Create/Edit form for users.

***Table 9.5:** Key application files*

Development steps

The project is implemented in stages. Each stage builds on the previous, gradually adding functionality and complexity.

The following steps presents a development roadmap:

1. Initialize Angular project with CLI (routing and styling).
2. Generate components and services using Angular CLI.
3. Configure routing for List, Create, and Edit views.
4. Implement `UserService` with HTTP CRUD methods.
5. Build `UserListComponent` to fetch and display users.
6. Build `UserFormComponent` with a reactive form and validation.
7. Add edit and delete functionality via routes and dialogs.
8. Style UI with Bootstrap classes and custom CSS.
9. Test the application locally and fix issues.
10. Deploy to a hosting platform of choice.

Expected output

Upon completion, the application provides a responsive UI for managing users. It demonstrates data flow from service to components, navigation via router, and error handling.

The following presents the final interface:

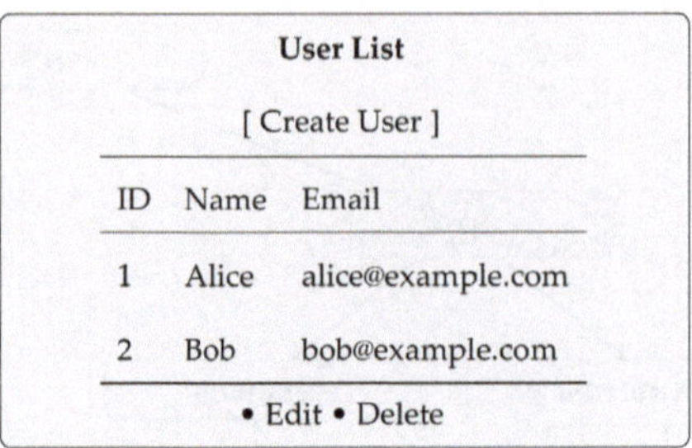

Figure 9.9: Final user list interface

This comprehensive exercise cements your understanding of Angular's component architecture, service injection, routing, and deployment, providing a solid foundation for real-world application development.

React vs Angular comparison

React and Angular are leading solutions for building interactive web applications. React is a lightweight library focused on UI components, whereas Angular is a comprehensive framework with built-in features. This comparison examines their differences across architecture, tooling, performance, and scalability to guide technology selection.

The following table presents a feature comparison:

Feature	React	Angular
Framework type	UI library	Full framework
Language	JavaScript with JSX	TypeScript
Component model	Function and class components	Decorator-based components
Data binding	One-way via props and state	Two-way with `[(ngModel)]`
Routing	External (React Router)	Built-in router
State management	External libraries (Redux, Zustand)	Services or NgRx
Change detection	Virtual DOM	Zone.js-based
CLI tooling	CRA, Vite	Angular CLI
Learning curve	Gentle entry with optional complexity	Steeper initial learning due to integrated features
Bundle optimization	Code-splitting with **`React.lazy`** and Suspense	Lazy loading modules, AOT compilation

Table 9.6: Comparison of React and Angular

Learning curve

The ease of adoption impacts developer productivity. React's minimal core API allows quick onboarding, but complex apps require learning additional libraries. Angular's all-in-one approach demands understanding TypeScript, decorators, dependency injection, and RxJS upfront, offering consistency in return.

The following list presents React learning points:

- JSX syntax combining JavaScript and HTML.
- Functional components and hooks (**useState**, **useEffect**).
- Props for one-way data flow.
- Ecosystem choices for routing, state, and data fetching.

The following code demonstrates a React component:

```
import React from 'react';

function Welcome({ name }) {
  return <h1>Hello, {name}</h1>;
}
```

The following list presents Angular learning points:

- TypeScript classes and decorators (**@Component, @NgModule**).
- Templates with interpolation and directives.
- Dependency injection for services.
- RxJS observables for asynchronous data.

The following code demonstrates an Angular component:

```
// welcome.component.ts
import { Component, Input } from '@angular/core';

@Component({
  selector: 'app-welcome',
  template: `<h1>Hello, {{ name }}</h1>`
})
export class WelcomeComponent {
  @Input() name = '';
}
```

Performance efficiency

Rendering speed and bundle size determine application responsiveness. React's Virtual **Document Object Model** (**DOM**) and memoization offer fine-grained update control. Angular's change detection and AOT compilation provide automatic optimizations but require strategy configuration for large trees.

The following list presents React optimizations:

- Virtual DOM reconciliation to minimize real DOM updates.
- **React.memo** is used to cache functional components and prevents re-rendering only when the component's props remain unchanged, helping reduce unnecessary renders in performance-sensitive parts of an application.
- **useMemo** and **useCallback** to cache values and handlers.
- Code-splitting via **React.lazy** and **Suspense**.

The following demonstrates **React.memo** use:

```
const Greeting = React.memo(({ name }) => { console.
  log('Rendering Greeting');
  return <h2>Hello, {name}</h2>;
});
```

The following list presents Angular optimizations:

- OnPush change detection to skip unchanged components.
- `trackBy` functions in `*ngFor` loops.
- Lazy loading feature modules.
- **Ahead-of-time** (AOT) compilation to precompile templates.

The following demonstrates the OnPush strategy:

```
import { Component, Input, ChangeDetectionStrategy } from '@angular/core';

@Component({
  selector: 'app-profile',
  template: `<p>{{ user.name
  }}</p>`, changeDetection:
  ChangeDetectionStrategy.OnPush
})
export class ProfileComponent {
  @Input() user!: { name: string };
}
```

The following figure illustrates the rendering flow:

React Virtual DOM → Diff & Patch → Real DOM Update

Figure 9.10: React rendering optimization

Scalability practices

Large applications demand clear structure and conventions. React's flexibility allows custom architectures using feature folders and services, while Angular enforces modularity with NgModules, services, and CLI-generated scaffolding for consistent organization.

The following presents a scalable React layout:

```
src/
├── components/
│   ├── Header.js
│   └── TodoItem.js
├── hooks/
│   └── useLocalStorage.js
├── pages/
│   ├── HomePage.js
│   └── SettingsPage.js
├── services/
│   └── api.js
└── App.js
```

The following presents a scalable Angular layout:

```
src/
├── app/
│   ├── core/
│   │   └── services/
│   ├── features/
```

```
│   │       ├── user-management/
│   │       │   ├── user-list/
│   │       │   └── user-form/
│   ├── shared/
│   │       └── components/
│   └── app.module.ts
└── index.html
```

The following table presents a tooling comparison:

Aspect	React	Angular
Project setup	Flexible (CRA, Vite)	Structured (Angular CLI)
Module boundaries	Developer-defined	NgModule enforced
Dependency injection	Context API or libraries	Built-in DI
Code generation	Manual or schematics	CLI generators (components, services)
Long-term consistency	Team conventions	Framework conventions

Table 9.7: *Scalability and maintainability*

Case studies

This section presents real-world examples of React and Angular in production. Each case study describes the application context, objectives, technical implementation, and outcomes. These examples illustrate how to apply framework features in large-scale scenarios and highlight best practices.

Facebook platform

Facebook created React to power its dynamic social interface. The platform required real-time updates, modular components, and high performance under heavy user interaction. React's Virtual DOM and component model enabled Facebook to build a scalable, maintainable UI across multiple products.

The following presents objectives and implementation:

- Deliver responsive updates without full page reloads.
- Manage local and global state with hooks and context.
- Reuse UI components across news feed, messenger, and notifications.

The following presents technical highlights:

- Virtual DOM diffing to minimize real DOM changes.
- `useState` and custom hooks for component logic.
- Context API and Redux for application-wide state.
- **Server-side rendering** (**SSR**) for **search engine optimization** (**SEO**) and first-load speed.

Outcomes are as follows:

- Modular architecture reduced code duplication.
- Faster development through reusable components.
- Smooth real-time updates improved user experience.

Gmail clone

A community-built Gmail clone using Angular showcases how to structure a complex email client. The app features inbox routing, message threads, and form-driven compose, demonstrating Angular's tooling for SPAs.

The following presents objectives and implementation:

- Implement Gmail-style navigation between mailbox views.
- Sync compose and search forms with two-way binding.
- Organize code into feature modules and services.

The following presents technical highlights:

- `@angular/router` for client-side routing.
- `ngModel` for two-way form binding.
- Angular Material for consistent UI components.
- Lazy loading modules to improve initial load time.

The following presents the outcomes:

- Clear module boundaries enhanced maintainability.
- Seamless navigation without page reloads.
- Consistent theming and responsive design.

Netflix UI

Netflix uses React for its streaming interface, where performance and scalability are critical. By combining Virtual DOM updates with code-splitting and SSR, Netflix delivers a fast, responsive experience across devices.

The following presents objectives and implementation:

- Achieve high performance under heavy multimedia loads.
- Dynamically load personalized content on demand.
- Minimize initial bundle size for quick startup.

The following presents technical highlights:

- `React.lazy` and `Suspense` for code-splitting
- Redux for centralized state management
- Server-side rendering for faster first-page loads.

The following list presents outcomes:

- Reduced latency on low-powered devices.
- Reusable component library across platforms.
- Improved load times via SSR and dynamic imports.

Forbes migration

Forbes migrated its content platform to Angular to improve maintainability and SEO. Angular's CLI, dependency injection, and Universal SSR enabled a modular, high-performance architecture for a global news site.

The following presents objectives and implementation:

- Refactor legacy pages into an Angular application.

- Improve SEO with Angular Universal for SSR.
- Use lazy loading and feature modules for speed.

The following presents technical highlights:

- Angular Universal for server-side rendering.
- Feature modules and shared services for structure.
- Custom pipes and directives for dynamic content.

The following presents outcomes:

- Faster page loads and better SEO rankings.
- Streamlined content updates via service layer.
- Consistent development patterns reduced cycle time.

Summary and practices

This chapter compared React and Angular across architecture, performance, and development workflows. It highlighted real-world use cases and distilled best practices to guide developers in building scalable, maintainable applications. The following sections summarize framework-specific guidance and offer criteria for selecting the appropriate tool for your project.

React practices

React emphasizes flexibility and composability through small, focused components. Adopting a consistent approach to state, side effects, and styling ensures your application remains maintainable as it grows.

The following presents recommended React practices:

- Break UI into reusable function components.
- Manage state with hooks (`useState`, `useReducer`).
- Lift state up and pass data via props.
- Use Context or state libraries (Redux, Zustand) for global data.
- Optimize rendering with `React.memo`, `useMemo`, `useCallback`.
- Code-split with `React.lazy` and `Suspense`.
- Organize styles with CSS modules or styled components.
- Write tests using Jest and React testing library.

Angular practices

Angular provides a structured, turnkey framework with dependency injection and a powerful CLI. Following the official style guide and leveraging built-in features leads to consistent and scalable code.

The following presents recommended Angular practices:

- Scaffold and generate with Angular CLI for consistency.
- Structure features into modules for lazy loading.
- Use Reactive Forms for complex validation logic.
- Encapsulate HTTP logic in injectable services.
- Manage async data with RxJS and async pipe.

- Secure routes with guards and preload with resolvers.
- Enable OnPush change detection where possible.
- Test with Jasmine/Karma and Cypress for E2E.

Framework selection

Choosing between React and Angular depends on project size, team expertise, and long-term goals. Consider flexibility versus convention, ecosystem maturity, and performance requirements.

The following table presents the selection criteria:

Criterion	React	Angular
Learning curve	Gentle start, add libraries as needed	Steep initial, all-in-one solution
Architecture	Unopinionated, flexible	Opinionated, modular structure
Tooling	CRA, Vite, manual setup	Angular I CLI I built-in schematics
State management	External (Redux, Context)	Services/NgRx built-in
Performance tuning	Virtual DOM, custom memoization	OnPush, AOT, lazy modules
Community support	Vast open-source ecosystem	Enterprise focus, official updates

Table 9.8: *Framework selection criteria*

Further resources

Continuous learning and experimentation accelerate mastery. The official guides and hands-on projects below will deepen your understanding of each framework's advanced concepts.

The following presents recommended resources:

- **React documentation**: **https://reactjs.org/docs/getting-started.html**.
- **Angular documentation**: **https://angular.io/docs**.
- **React tutorial**: Build a Tic-Tac-Toe game on the official site.
- Angular Tour of Heroes tutorial for CRUD operations.
- Explore SSR with Next.js (React) and Angular Universal.
- **Practice with small apps**: Dashboards, forms, media viewers.

Conclusion

In this chapter, you applied core React and Angular concepts in two end-to-end projects. With React, you mastered functional components, hooks, state and effect management, list and conditional rendering, and deployment workflows. In Angular, you learned modular architecture with NgModules, component templating, data binding, dependency-injected services, reactive and template-driven forms, routing with guards, and HTTP-based CRUD operations. The comparative analysis highlighted React's flexibility, virtual DOM, and ecosystem extensibility against Angular's opinionated structure, two-way binding, and built-in tooling. The sample implementations in this chapter were developed and tested using React 18 (with CRA/Vite as the tooling option) and Angular 17+ with the Angular CLI, so the code and commands align with these versions. Equipped with practical experience and a clear view of each framework's strengths and trade-offs, you can now select the most suitable tool for your next project.

In the next chapter, we turn to backend development with Node.js and Express.js: you will set up a server-side JavaScript environment, implement RESTful APIs, handle middleware and routing, and secure endpoints with JWT authentication, completing your full-stack development skill set.

Exercises

1. Initialize a React project with CRA named todo-app, start the dev server, and confirm the app runs on http://localhost:3000. Write the exact terminal commands in order.
2. Clean the default CRA boilerplate: list the files to delete, and provide a minimal replacement for App.js that renders the heading todo list app.
3. **Implement TodoInput**: a controlled input with useState that adds a non-empty trimmed task on form submit, then clears the input. Write the full component.
4. **Implement TodoItem**: render the task text and a Delete button; call removeTodo(index) when clicked. Write the full component.
5. **Implement TodoList**: map an array of todos to TodoItem, passing todo text, index, and removeTodo. Write the full component and one usage line in a parent.
6. **Integrate in App.js**: hold todos in state, implement addTodo(text) and removeTodo(index), and compose TodoInput and TodoList. Write the full App.js (imports included).
7. **Extend the model to support completion**: store todos as objects { text, done }, add a toggleDone(index) handler, and render completed items with a completed class. Show the updated components and the minimal CSS class for styling.
8. Persist todos between reloads using a custom hook useLocalStorage(key, initialValue). Implement the hook and replace useState in App.js to load/save todos automatically.
9. **Deploy the React app to GitHub Pages**: add the homepage field and predeploy/deploy scripts in package.json, then write the exact git and npm commands to publish. Include the expected final URL format.
10. Scaffold an Angular project named user-mgr with routing enabled and CSS styling; start the dev server. Then add JSON Server as a dev dependency and write the command to run a mock API on port 3000 with a db.json file. Provide all commands.
11. Create UserService that performs CRUD against http://localhost:3000/users using HttpClient. Write methods: getUsers(), getUser(id), addUser(user), updateUser(user), deleteUser(id). Include basic error handling with catchError.
12. Configure routes for User List (/users), Create (/users/new), and Edit (/users/:id/edit). Add a resolver that preloads a user for the Edit route. Provide the routes array and the resolver skeleton.
13. Build UserFormComponent using Reactive Forms with controls name (required, minlength 2) and email (required, email). Show template snippets that display validation errors and disable the Submit button when invalid.
14. Protect the /users routes with an AuthGuard: allow navigation only if AuthService.isLoggedIn() returns true; otherwise redirect to /login. Provide the guard code and the route configuration that uses it.
15. Write a concise framework comparison (5–7 bullets) covering architecture, data binding, performance optimization, tooling/CLI, learning curve, and ecosystem. Then cite one case study per framework (from this chapter) and state in one sentence how each framework's feature set helped that product meet its goals.

CHAPTER 10
Backend Development with Express.js

Introduction

Backend development has evolved rapidly in recent years, and at the forefront of this evolution is Node.js: a JavaScript runtime built on Chrome's V8 engine that brings event-driven, non-blocking **input/output** (**I/O**) to the server side. By unifying frontend and backend languages, Node.js empowers developers to build fast, scalable network applications, and everything from real-time chat and collaborative tools to streaming services, all without the overhead of managing multiple runtimes. On top of Node.js sits Express.js, a minimalist web framework that abstracts boilerplate **Hypertext Transfer Protocol** (**HTTP**) handling into a clean, middleware-driven **application programming interface** (**API**). Together, Node.js and Express.js form a powerful duo for crafting RESTful APIs, implementing authentication and authorization, and enforcing best practices such as modular code organization, error handling, and security hardening. In this chapter, you will learn how to set up your development environment, leverage the event loop for concurrency, build routes and middleware in Express, secure endpoints with **JSON Web Tokens** (**JWT**) and OAuth, and apply industry-standard patterns to create maintainable, production-ready backends.

Structure

This chapter covers the following topics:

- Introduction to Node.js
- Express.js framework
- Authentication and authorization
- Best practices in backend development
- Creating a RESTful API server

Objectives

By the end of this chapter, the readers will confidently navigate the Node.js runtime and its event-driven, non-blocking I/O model to build high-performance servers using a single language across both client and server. They will master setting up a development environment, writing and running their first HTTP server, and layering in Express.js to define clean, modular routes and middleware. They will design and implement complete **create, read, update, and delete** (**CRUD**) operations in RESTful APIs, handling JSON payloads and **uniform resource locator** (**URL**) parameters with ease. They will also secure those endpoints by integrating JWTs for stateless authentication and, where required, delegate authentication to third-party providers via OAuth. Along the way, they will apply industry-standard best practices—managing sensitive configuration with environment variables, centralizing error handling, validating input, logging requests, and hardening their application with security headers. Finally, readers will consolidate their learning by building and deploying a fully functional, token-protected API server and analyzing strategies for scaling a real-world Node.js application.

Introduction to Node.js

Node.js is an open-source, cross-platform runtime that executes JavaScript code outside the browser. Built on *Google's V8 engine*, it compiles JavaScript into native machine code for high performance. Its event-driven, non-blocking I/O model makes it ideal for real-time applications, APIs, and microservices.

Node.js features

Node.js provides a set of characteristics that streamline modern backend development. By using a single language across the stack and leveraging an extensive package ecosystem, teams can build scalable, maintainable systems efficiently.

The following table presents core Node.js features:

Features	Description
Asynchronous APIs	Non-blocking operations for file, network, and database I/O.
Single language	JavaScript on both the frontend and backend.
High performance	V8 engine compiles JS to optimized machine code.
Scalable architecture	Event loop handles thousands of connections on one thread.
npm ecosystem	Vast registry of reusable packages and CLI tools.

Table 10.1: *Core Node.js features*

Event-driven I/O

Node.js uses a single-threaded event loop to manage concurrent connections without spawning multiple OS threads. When an I/O operation is initiated, Node.js registers a callback and continues processing other events. Once the I/O completes, the callback is queued in the event loop, ensuring high throughput and low latency.

The following figure presents the event loop flow, which manages callback execution, enabling asynchronous operations:

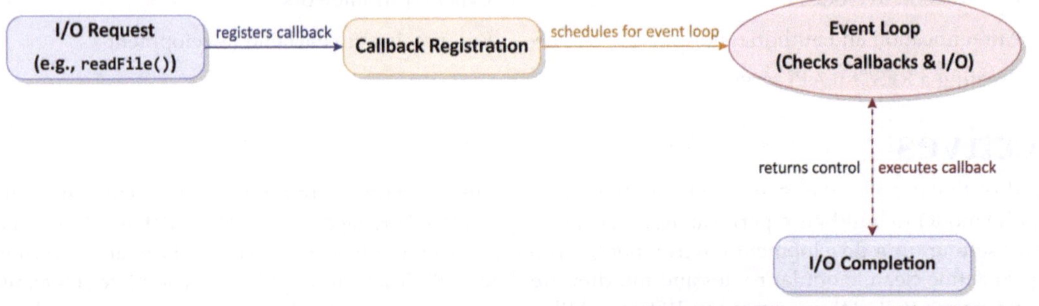

Figure 10.1: *Node.js event-driven, non-blocking I/O model*

The following demonstrates non-blocking I/O:

```
// Asynchronous (non-blocking) I/O
const fs = require('fs');
fs.readFile('data.txt', 'utf8', (err, content) => {
  if (err) throw err;
```

```
    console.log('File contents:', content);
  });
  console.log('This runs before file is read');
```

Environment setup

Setting up Node.js involves installing the runtime and its package manager, **npm**. On Windows and macOS, use the official installer. On Linux, install via distribution packages or **nvm** for version control.

The following presents installation steps:

1. Download the installer from **https://nodejs.org/** and follow the prompts.
2. Or on Linux, use **nvm**:

   ```
   curl -o- https://raw.githubusercontent.com/nvm-sh/nvm/v0.39.3/install.sh
   | bash
   # restart shell (or source ~/.nvm/nvm.sh), then:
   nvm install -lts
   ```

3. Verify installation.
4. The following demonstrates version check:

   ```
   node --version # e.g. v20.1.0
   npm --version  # e.g. 9.6.0
   ```

First application

Creating a minimal HTTP server showcases how Node.js handles requests and responses without external web servers. This example uses the built-in **http** module to listen on a port and serve text.

The following script demonstrates server code:

```
const http = require('http');

const server = http.createServer((req, res) => {
    res.writeHead(200, {
        'Content-Type': 'text/plain'
    });
    res.end('Hello from Node.js!');
});

server.listen(3000, () => {
    console.log('Server running at http://localhost:3000');
});
```

The following presents runtime steps:

1. Save code to **app.js**.
2. Run **node app.js** in the terminal.
3. Open **http://localhost:3000** in a browser to see the message.

Express.js framework

Express.js is a minimal, unopinionated web framework for Node.js that simplifies HTTP server development. It abstracts the core HTTP module, provides a clean routing API, middleware support, and integrates easily with template engines. This enables developers to build scalable, maintainable applications with concise code.

Express overview

Express provides essential features for web and API development, including flexible routing, middleware composition, and HTTP utility methods. Its middleware architecture allows inserting custom logic at each request stage, facilitating tasks like logging, authentication, and error handling without cluttering business code.

The following list presents key Express features:

- Simplified routing for HTTP methods and URL patterns.
- Middleware functions for request preprocessing and postprocessing.
- HTTP utilities (status, headers, JSON responses).
- Template engine integration (EJS, Pug, Handlebars).
- Static file serving via built-in middleware.

Installing express

To use Express in a Node.js project, initialize **npm** and install the package. This setup creates a **package.json** and fetches Express and its dependencies.

The following demonstrates installation commands:

```
npm init -y             # create package.json with defaults
npm install express     # install Express.js
```

Basic server

A minimal Express server handles HTTP GET requests at the root path. The following code shows creating an application instance, defining routes, and starting the listener, and demonstrates server code:

```
const express = require('express');
const app = express();

// route for GET /
app.get('/', (req, res) =>
  { res.send('Welcome to
  Express.js!');
});

// start server on port 3000
app.listen(3000, () => {
  console.log('Server running at http://localhost:3000');
});
```

The following table presents HTTP method mappings:

Method	Description
`app.get(path, handler)`	Handle HTTP GET requests.
`app.post(path, handler)`	Handle HTTP POST request.
`app.put(path, handler)`	Handle HTTP PUT requests.
`app.delete(path, handler)`	Handle HTTP DELETE requests.
`app.use(middleware)`	Register middleware for all routes.

Table 10.2: *Express route methods*

Middleware usage

Middleware functions in Express intercept requests before they reach route handlers. They can modify **req** and **res**, perform logging, authentication, or terminate the cycle by sending a response. The following demonstrates simple middleware:

```
// request logger middleware
app.use((req, res, next) => {
  console.log(`${req.method}
  ${req.url}`); next(); //
  pass control to next handler
});


// JSON body parser
app.use(express.json());
```

Project structure

Organizing an Express application into directories improves maintainability as the codebase grows. Separating routes, middleware, views, and static assets keeps concerns clearly defined.

The following presents a typical layout:

myapp/

├─	app.js	# main application entry point
├─	package.json	
├─	routes/	
│	└─ index.js	# route definitions
├─	middleware/	
│	└─ logger.js	# custom middleware
├─	public/	
│	├─ css/	
│	├─ js/	
│	└─ images/	# static assets
└─	views/	
	└─ index.ejs	# template files

E-commerce API example

This example shows how to build a simple RESTful API for an e-commerce site using Express.js. It demonstrates JSON body parsing, route handlers for retrieving and creating products, proper HTTP status codes, and response formatting. Such an API can serve as the backend for a storefront or inventory management system.

The following script demonstrates the API:

```
const express = require('express');
const app = express();
// parse JSON bodies
app.use(express.json());
```

```
// GET /products returns product list
app.get('/products', (req, res) => {
  const products = [
    { id: 1, name: 'Laptop', price: 999 },
    { id: 2, name: 'Phone', price: 499 }
  ];
  res.json(products);
});

// POST /products creates a new product
app.post('/products', (req, res) => {
  const newProduct = req.body;
  // In a real app, save to database here
  res.status(201).json({
    message: 'Product created
    successfully', product: newProduct
  });
});

// start server
app.listen(4000, () => {
  console.log('E-commerce API running at http://localhost:4000');
});
```

The output of the preceding server created is depicted in the following figure:

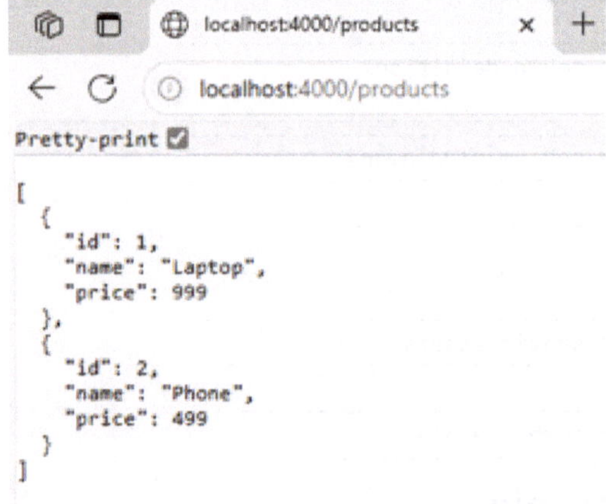

Figure 10.2: The output of the e-commerce API

Express use cases

Express.js is versatile and powers many server-side tasks in modern web development. Its middleware architecture and routing capabilities make it suitable for a wide range of applications, from APIs to full-stack rendering.

The following presents common Express use cases:

- RESTful API development for single-page applications and mobile clients.
- Server-side rendering with template engines (EJS, Pug, Handlebars).

- Handling form submissions, file uploads, and multipart data.
- Integrating third-party services such as OAuth, payment gateways, and social logins.
- Implementing microservices and proxying requests to other APIs.
- Real-time features via WebSocket or libraries like Socket.io.

Middleware and routing

Middleware and routing are core to Express's extensibility and modularity. Middleware functions intercept requests for logging, authentication, parsing, and error handling before they reach route handlers. Routing directs requests to specific handlers based on HTTP method and URL, enabling RESTful API design and clean code organization.

Middleware functions

Middleware functions have access to the request (`req`), response (`res`), and a `next` callback to pass control. They can execute arbitrary code, modify `req`/`res`, end the cycle, or delegate to downstream middleware.

The following list presents middleware capabilities:

- Execute custom logic (logging, authentication).
- Parse or validate request data.
- Modify `req` or `res` objects.
- Terminate the request by sending a response.
- Call `next()` to continue the chain.

The following script demonstrates application-level logging:

```
app.use((req, res, next) => {
  console.log(`[${new Date().toISOString()}] ${req.method}
  ${req.url}`); next();
});
```

Route handlers

Routes map HTTP methods and URL paths to handler functions. Express's `app.METHOD(path, handler)` API covers common verbs and supports pattern matching.

The following presents basic routing:

```
app.get('/', (req, res)
  => { res.send('Home
  Page');
});


app.post('/submit', (req,
  res) => { res.send('Form
  Submitted');
});
```

Dynamic segments

Route parameters and query strings enable dynamic request handling. Parameters are part of the path, while queries follow a `?` in the URL.

The following presents route parameters:

```
app.get('/users/:id',
  (req, res) => { const
  id = req.params.id;
  res.send(`User ID is
  ${id}`);
});
```

The following presents query string access:

```
app.get('/search', (req,
  res) => { const q =
  req.query.q; res.
  send(`Search for
  ${q}`);
});
```

Router modules

To organize routes, use **express.Router()** in separate modules. This keeps the main file concise and groups related endpoints.

The following presents a router module (**routes/users.js**):

```
// routes/users.js
const router = require('express').Router();

router.get('/', (req, res) => res.send('Users home')); router.
get('/:id', (req, res) => res.send(`User ${req.params.id}`));

module.exports = router;
```

The following script integrates the router in **app.js**:

```
// app.js
const express = require('express');
const userRoutes = require('./routes/users');
const app = express();

app.use('/users', userRoutes);
```

Protected API example

This example demonstrates JSON parsing middleware, a simple API-key check, and product routes to show a typical API flow. Do not hard-code API keys in real applications. Store secrets in environment variables (or a secret manager) and validate them at runtime.

The following script demonstrates the protected product API using an environment-based API key:

```
const express = require('express');
require('dotenv').config();

const app = express();
app.use(express.json());

// Educational example:
// Store the expected API key in an environment variable (do not hard-code secrets).
const EXPECTED_API_KEY = process.env.API_KEY;

// API key validation middleware
```

```
app.use((req, res, next) => {
    const key = req.headers['x-api-key'];

    if (!EXPECTED_API_KEY) {
        return res.status(500).send('Server misconfigured: API key not set');
    }

    if (key !== EXPECTED_API_KEY) {
        return res.status(403).send('Forbidden: Invalid API key');
    }

    next();
});

app.get('/products', (req, res) => {
    res.json([
        { id: 1, name: 'Phone' },
        { id: 2, name: 'Tablet' }
    ]);
});

app.post('/products', (req, res) => {
    const prod = req.body;

    res.status(201).json({
        message: 'Created',
        product: prod
    });
});

app.listen(3000, () => {
    console.log('Server on port 3000');
});
```

Express routing

Routing in Express directs incoming HTTP requests to appropriate handlers based on method and URL path. A clear routing strategy improves maintainability and enables RESTful API design. Express uses a simple **app.METHOD(path, handler)** syntax and supports dynamic segments, query parameters, middleware chaining, and modular routers.

Basic routing

Basic routes match static paths and HTTP verbs. Handlers receive **req** and **res** objects to process input and send responses.

The following demonstrates basic routes:

```
app.get('/', (req, res) => {
  res.send('Home Page');
});

app.post('/submit', (req,
  res) => { res.send('Form
  submitted successfully');
});
```

Route parameters

Route parameters capture dynamic values in the URL. They appear in **req.params** and enable resource-specific endpoints.

The following demonstrates route params:

```
app.get('/users/:userId',
  (req, res) => { const userId
  = req.params.userId; res.
  send(`User ID: ${userId}`);
});
```

Query parameters

Query parameters follow a **?** in the URL and are parsed into **req.query**. They support optional filters and searches.

The following demonstrates query params:

```
app.get('/search', (req,
  res) => { const term
  = req.query.q; res.
  send(`Search for
  ${term}`);
});
```

Multiple handlers

Routes can invoke multiple middleware or handler functions in sequence. Each must call **next()** to continue the chain.

The following demonstrates chained handlers:

```
const logRequest = (req, res, next) => {
  console.log(`${req.method}
  ${req.url}`); next();
};

app.get('/info', logRequest, (req, res) => {
  res.send('Information page');
});
```

Router modules

Modular routers group related routes in separate files, keeping **app.js** uncluttered and improving organization.

The following presents a router module (**routes/users.js**):

```
// routes/users.js
const router = require('express').Router();

router.get('/', (req, res) =>
  { res.send('Users home');
});

router.get('/:id',
  (req, res) => { res.
  send(`User ${req.
```

```
  params.id}`);
});

module.exports = router;
```

The following integrates the router in **app.js**:

```
// app.js
const express = require('express');
const userRoutes = require('./routes/users');
const app = express();

app.use('/users', userRoutes);
```

Product routes example

This example combines JSON parsing, API-key validation middleware, and product CRUD routes to illustrate a realistic routing setup.

The following presents the product API:

```
require('dotenv').config();

const express = require('express');
const app = express();

app.use(express.json());

// API key validation
app.use((req, res, next) => {
      if (req.headers['x-api-key'] !== process.env.API_KEY) {

    return res.status(403).send('Forbidden: Invalid API key');
  }
  next();
});

let products = [
  { id: 1, name: 'Laptop' },
  { id: 2, name: 'Phone' }
];

app.get('/products',
  (req, res) => { res.
  json(products);
});

app.get('/products/:id', (req, res) => {
  const p = products.find(x => x.id === +req.
  params.id); if (!p) return res.status(404).
  send('Not found'); res.json(p);
});
app.post('/products', (req, res) => {
```

```
    const newP = { id: products.length+1, name: req.body.name };
    products.push(newP);
    res.status(201).json(newP);
});

app.listen(3000, () => console.log('Server on port 3000'));
```

The following figures demonstrate the output of the Product API when accessed via the browser. The first subfigure displays the list of all products retrieved using the **/products** endpoint. The second subfigure shows the output for a single product queried using its ID via the **/products/1** endpoint.

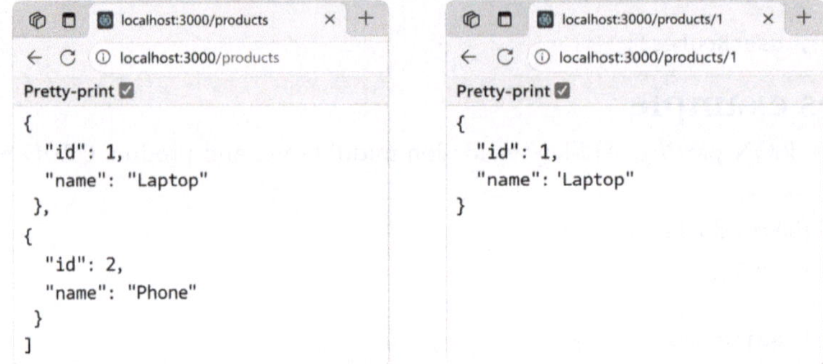

***Figure 10.3:** Product API outputs*

Figure 10.3 illustrates Product API outputs in the browser showing the response of the GET /products endpoint for all products and the GET /products/1 endpoint for a single product by ID.

The following figure illustrates the complete routing flow:

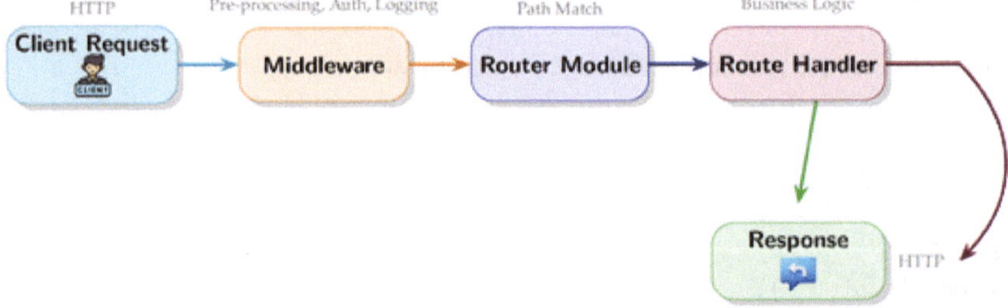

***Figure 10.4:** Express.js routing and middleware sequence*

RESTful APIs

This section covers designing and implementing RESTful APIs with Express.js. It explains the core REST principles, shows how to define CRUD endpoints, details server startup, and demonstrates testing methods. Express's routing and middleware features make it straightforward to build scalable, stateless services.

Principles

RESTful APIs adhere to a set of architectural constraints that enable interoperability, scalability, and simplicity. Understanding these principles ensures your API follows best practices for web services.

The following presents key REST constraints:

- **Stateless requests**: Each request contains all necessary information.

- **Resource-based URIs**: Each endpoint identifies a resource.
- **Standard HTTP methods**: Use GET, POST, PUT, DELETE for CRUD.
- **Uniform responses**: Typically return JSON with appropriate status codes.

Endpoints

Defining clear, consistent endpoints is critical for a maintainable API. Each route corresponds to a CRUD operation on a resource, and Express maps these routes to handler functions.

The following script demonstrates CRUD routes:

```
// Initialize Express and sample data
const express = require('express');
const app = express();

app.use(express.json());

let books = [
    { id: 1, title: 'Atomic Habits', author: 'James Clear' },
    { id: 2, title: 'The Alchemist', author: 'Paulo Coelho' }
];

// GET all books
app.get('/books', (req, res) => {
    res.json(books);
});

// GET a book by ID
app.get('/books/:id', (req, res) => {
    const book = books.find(b => b.id === +req.params.id);
    if (!book) return res.status(404).json({ error: 'Not found' });
    res.json(book);
});

// POST a new book
app.post('/books', (req, res) => {
    const newBook = { id: books.length + 1, ...req.body };
    books.push(newBook);
    res.status(201).json(newBook);
});

// PUT to update a book
app.put('/books/:id', (req, res) => {
    const book = books.find(b => b.id === +req.params.id);
    if (!book) return res.status(404).json({ error: 'Not found' });
    Object.assign(book, req.body);
    res.json(book);
});

// DELETE a book
app.delete('/books/:id', (req, res) => {
    const index = books.findIndex(b => b.id === +req.params.id);
    if (index === -1) return res.status(404).json({ error: 'Not found' });
    const [deleted] = books.splice(index, 1);
    res.json(deleted);
});
```

The following table summarizes these routes:

Method	Path	Action
GET	`/books`	Retrieve all books
GET	`/books/:id`	Retrieve a specific book
POST	`/books`	Create a new book
PUT	`/books/:id`	Update an existing book
DELETE	`/books/:id`	Delete a book

Table 10.3: Book resource endpoints

Server start

Once routes are defined, start the server to listen for incoming requests. Proper error handling and logging can be added as middleware before or after route definitions.

The following script starts the server:

```
const PORT = 3000; app.listen(PORT, () => {
  console.log(`RESTful API server running on port ${PORT}`);
});
```

API testing

Testing your API ensures endpoints behave as expected. Tools like curl, Postman, and Thunder Client in VS Code can exercise each route, verify response bodies, status codes, and error handling.

The following presents example **curl** commands:

```
# Get all books
curl http://localhost:3000/books

# Get a single book
curl http://localhost:3000/books/1
# Create a book
curl -X POST -H "Content-Type: application/json" \
  -d '{"title":"New Book","author":"Jane Doe"}' \
  http://localhost:3000/books

# Update a book
curl -X PUT -H "Content-Type: application/json" \
  -d '{"title":"Updated","author":"John Doe"}' \
  http://localhost:3000/books/1

# Delete a book
curl -X DELETE http://localhost:3000/books/1
```

The following demonstrates testing with Thunder Client in VS Code:

- Install the Thunder Client extension and open its sidebar.
- Create a new request and set the method to GET with URL **http://localhost:3000/books**.
- Click **Send** and inspect the JSON array and status code.
- Repeat for other endpoints (POST, PUT, DELETE), configuring the **Body** tab to send JSON payloads.

The following figure shows a sample Thunder Client response for the GET /books request:

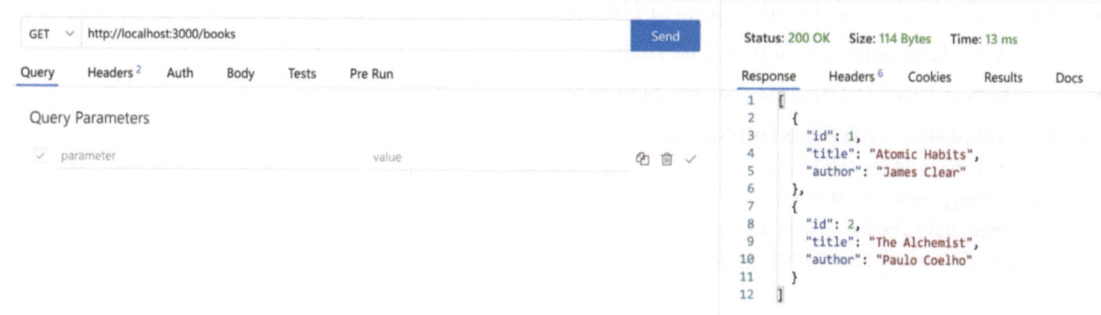

***Figure 10.5:** Thunder Client response for GET /books*

Authentication and authorization

Authentication and authorization secure web applications by verifying user identity and enforcing access control. This section explains each concept, highlights its differences, and demonstrates implementation in a Node.js/ Express environment using bcrypt, JWTs, and middleware.

Authentication versus authorization

Authentication and authorization serve distinct roles in security. Authentication confirms who the user is, while authorization determines what they can do. Both are essential to protect resources and enforce business rules.

Authentication

Authentication verifies user identity by validating credentials. Secure implementations hash passwords and issue tokens to avoid storing sensitive data in plaintext.

The following presents authentication details:

- Confirms identity via credentials (passwords, tokens, biometrics).
- Typically occurs at login and issues a session or token.
- Protects against credential theft by hashing (**bcrypt**).

The following script shows password hashing with **bcrypt**:

```
const bcrypt = require('bcrypt');

async function hashPassword(plain) { const salt = await bcrypt.genSalt(10); return await
  bcrypt.hash(plain, salt);
}

// Usage
hashPassword('MySecret123').then(hash => console.log('Hashed password:', hash)
);
```

Authorization

Authorization checks permissions after authentication. It ensures that authenticated users can only access resources and actions they are allowed to.

The following presents authorization details:

- Grants or denies access based on roles or policies.
- Enforced via middleware on protected routes.
- Can be role-based (admin, user) or attribute-based.

The following script shows role-based middleware:

```
function authorizeRole(role) {
  return (req, res, next) => {
    if (req.user.role !== role) {
      return res.status(403).json({ error: 'Forbidden' });
    }
    next();
  };
}

// Usage
app.get('/admin', authenticate, authorizeRole('admin'), (req, res) => { res.send('Admin
  content');
});
```

The following table presents a comparison of authentication and authorization:

Authentication	Authorization
Verifies user identity	Determines user permissions.
Occurs at login	Occurs on each protected request.
Uses credentials (password, token)	Uses roles or policies.
Results in a session or token	Results in access grants or denials.

Table 10.4: *Authentication vs. authorization*

Implementation overview

Implementing secure authentication and authorization in Express involves hashing, token issuance, and middleware for protected routes. Common libraries include **`bcrypt`** for hashing, JWT for tokens, and Passport for strategies.

JWT workflow

JWT enables stateless authentication. After verifying credentials, the server issues a signed token that clients include in future requests. The server validates the token's signature and extracts user data without storing session state.

The following figure illustrates the JWT flow:

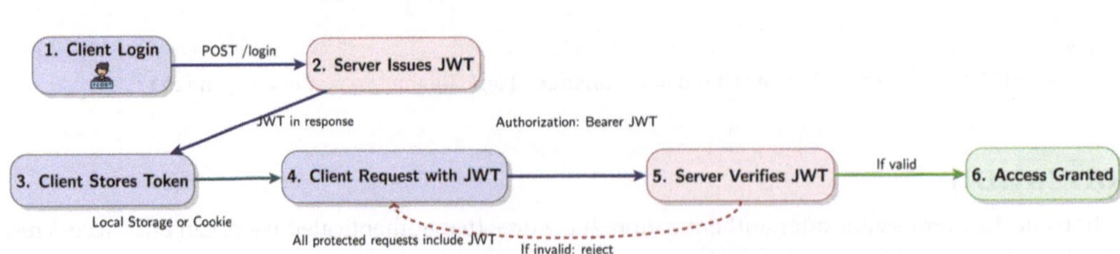

Figure 10.6: *JWT authentication flow: After login, the server issues a token*

Auth routes example

This script illustrates user registration, login (issuing JWT), and middleware to protect routes.

The following script demonstrates auth routes:

```
const express = require('express');
const bcrypt = require('bcrypt');
const jwt = require('jsonwebtoken');

const app = express();
app.use(express.json());

const users = []; // in-memory store (demo only)

// Register
app.post('/register', async (req, res) => {
    const { username, password } = req.body;

    const hash = await bcrypt.hash(password, 10);
    users.push({
        id: users.length + 1,
        username,
        password: hash,
        role: 'user'
    });

    res.status(201).send('User registered');
});

// Login
app.post('/login', async (req, res) => {
    const { username, password } = req.body;

    const user = users.find(u => u.username === username);
    if (!user || !(await bcrypt.compare(password, user.password))) {
        return res.status(401).json({ error: 'Invalid credentials' });
    }

    const token = jwt.sign(
        { id: user.id, role: user.role },
        'secretKey',
        { expiresIn: '1h' }
    );

    res.json({ token });
});

// Middleware to authenticate JWT
function authenticate(req, res, next) {
    const auth = req.headers['authorization'];
    if (!auth) return res.status(401).json({ error: 'No token' });

    const token = auth.split(' ')[1];

    try {
        req.user = jwt.verify(token, 'secretKey');
```

```
        next();
    } catch (err) {
        res.status(403).json({ error: 'Invalid token' });
    }
}

// Protected route
app.get('/profile', authenticate, (req, res) => {
    res.json({ message: `Hello user ${req.user.id}`, role: req.user.role });
});

app.listen(3000, () => console.log('Auth server on port 3000'));
```

Testing auth

Testing authentication involves obtaining a token and using it to access protected endpoints. Thunder Client or Postman can automate this workflow by chaining requests.

The following presents Thunder Client setup:

- Send POST /login with JSON body **{ "username": "...", "password": "..." }**.
- Extract **token** from response.
- In subsequent requests, add header **Authorization: Bearer <token>**.

The following figure shows the authentication workflow tested using Thunder Client. The first subfigure demonstrates the user registration process with a JSON body, resulting in a successful registration response.

Figure 10.7: User registration via POST /register endpoint

The following displays a protected profile request, where the user includes the JWT in the authorization header to receive a personalized response:

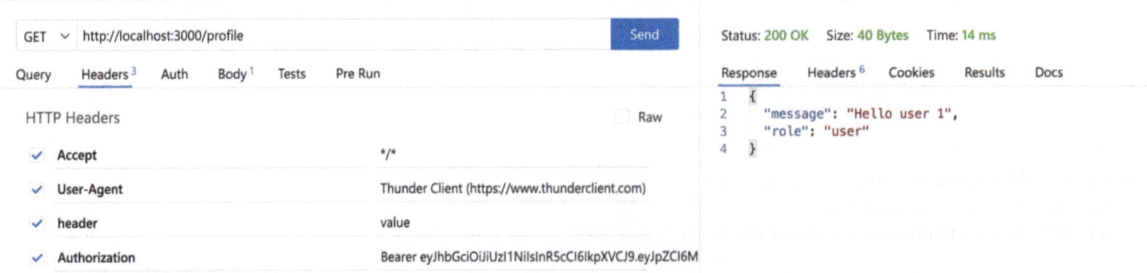

Figure 10.8: Thunder Client authentication workflow—User registration, and protected profile access using JWT

Figure 10.8 demonstrates profile access via GET /profile with JWT Authorization header.

JSON Web Token

JWT provides a stateless and widely used approach for authenticating client–server communication. In a JWT-based system, the server does not store session data for each logged-in user. Instead, the server issues a token after successful authentication, and the client includes that token with every subsequent request to protected resources. This design improves scalability because multiple backend instances can validate the same token without sharing session state, which fits well in distributed systems and microservice architectures.

A JWT is a compact string made of three parts separated by dots, which consists of a header, payload, and signature. The header describes the token type and the signing algorithm (for example, HS256). The payload contains claims, which are pieces of information about the user and the token itself, such as user ID, role, issued-at time, and expiry time. The signature is generated by applying a cryptographic signing process to the header and payload using a secret key (or a private key in asymmetric signing). The signature ensures integrity, meaning that any tampering with the token can be detected during verification.

JWT offers authentication through verification, not through encryption. In most common cases, the payload is Base64URL encoded, so it can be read if someone gets the token. For this reason, a JWT should not contain sensitive data such as passwords, personal identifiers, or confidential information. Security relies on signing (to prevent modification) and transport protection such as HTTPS (to prevent interception in transit). When a request arrives, the server validates the token by checking the signature, confirming that the token has not expired, and optionally verifying additional constraints such as issuer and audience. After successful validation, the server treats the decoded claims as the authenticated identity context and uses them for authorization decisions, such as role-based access control.

JWT usage becomes stronger when combined with good practices. Short token lifetimes reduce risk if a token is leaked. Refresh tokens (stored securely) can be used to obtain new access tokens without forcing users to log in repeatedly. Secrets or private keys should be stored outside source code using environment variables or secret managers, and rotation policies should be defined for long-term security. Proper validation, secure storage on the client side, and consistent use of HTTPS collectively make JWT a practical and robust method for building secure, scalable web APIs.

JWT overview

A JWT consists of three Base64URL-encoded parts: header, payload, and signature. The header declares the token type and signing algorithm. The payload carries user claims and metadata. The signature, generated with a secret key, ensures token integrity.

The following presents the JWT structure:

Part	Content	Purpose
Header	`{"alg":"HS256","typ":"JWT"}`	Specifies algorithm and token type
Payload	User claims (e.g., ID, role)	Carries data for authentication
Signature	**`HMACSHA256(header.payload, secret)`**	Verifies token authenticity

Table 10.5: *JWT components*

The following figure illustrates the token flow:

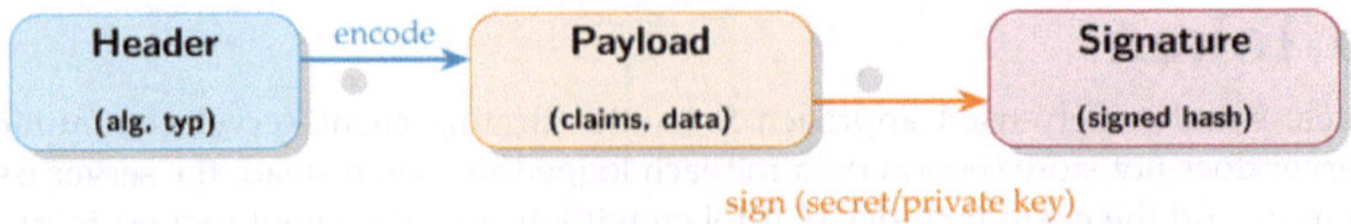

***Figure 10.9:** JWT structure: A JWT contains a header, payload, and signature*

Installation and setup

To implement JWT in Express, install core libraries and load environment variables. Use **bcryptjs** for password hashing and **jsonwebtoken** for token operations.

The following demonstrates installation:

```
npm install express jsonwebtoken bcryptjs dotenv
```

Then create a **.env** file with a secret key:

```
JWT_SECRET=yourStrongSecretKey
```

Login and token creation

Upon user login, verify credentials and issue a JWT containing the user ID and role. Set a reasonable expiration time to limit token lifetime.

The following script shows the login route:

```
const express = require('express'); const bcrypt = require('bcryptjs'); const jwt =
require('jsonwebtoken'); require('dotenv').config();

const app = express(); app.
use(express.json());

const users = [
{ id:1, username:'admin', passwordHash:'<bcrypt-hash-here>'}
];

app.post('/login', async (req, res) => {
  const { username, password } = req.body;
  const user = users.find(u => u.username === username);
  if (!user || !(await bcrypt.compare(password, user.password))) {
    return res.status(401).json({ message:'Invalid credentials' });
  }
  const token = jwt.sign(
    { id:user.id, username:user.username },
    process.env.JWT_SECRET,
    { expiresIn:'1h' }
  );
  res.json({ token });
});
```

Token verification

Protected routes require validating the JWT. The middleware extracts the token from the Authorization header, verifies its signature and expiration, and attaches the decoded user data to **req.user**.

The following script shows verification middleware:

```
function authenticateToken(req, res, next) {
  const auth = req.headers['authorization'];
  const token = auth && auth.split(' ')[1];
  if (!token) return res.sendStatus(401);
  jwt.verify(token, process.env.JWT_SECRET, (err, user) => {
    if (err) return res.
    sendStatus(403); req.user
    = user;
    next();
  });
}
```

Protecting routes

Apply the authentication middleware to any route that requires a valid token. This ensures only authorized requests reach the handler.

The following script shows a protected endpoint:

```
app.get('/dashboard', authenticateToken, (req, res) => {
  res.json({ message:`Welcome ${req.user.username}`, user:req.user });
});
```

Best practices

Secure JWT usage by following industry standards. Protect the token in transit and storage, enforce short expirations, and rotate secrets regularly.

The following presents JWT best practices:

- Use HTTPS to encrypt tokens in transit.
- Store tokens in HttpOnly, secure cookies to prevent XSS.
- Set short **expiresIn** and implement refresh tokens.
- Avoid sensitive data in the payload.
- Rotate **JWT_SECRET** and handle token revocation.

OAuth integration

OAuth enables secure delegated access by issuing tokens instead of handling user credentials directly. It separates authentication from resource access, allowing third-party apps to obtain limited permissions without exposing passwords.

OAuth overview

OAuth defines a protocol for authorization using tokens. Clients redirect users to an authorization server, receive a code, exchange it for an access token, and use that token to call protected APIs. This flow ensures credentials stay with the provider.

The following list presents the OAuth benefits:

- Secure delegation without sharing passwords.
- Clear separation between client and resource server.
- Scalable stateless access via expiring tokens.

Core terminology

Understanding OAuth requires knowing key roles and artifacts in the protocol.

The following presents the OAuth terms:

- **Resource owner**: User granting access
- **Client**: application requesting access
- **Authorization server**: Issues authorization codes and tokens
- **Resource server**: Hosts protected APIs
- **Access token**: Credential for API access
- **Refresh token**: Used to obtain new access tokens

Auth code flow

The authorization code flow provides secure token exchange. It involves five steps:

1. User login.
2. Consent.
3. Code issuance.
4. Token exchange.
5. API calls with the token.

The following figure presents the flow:

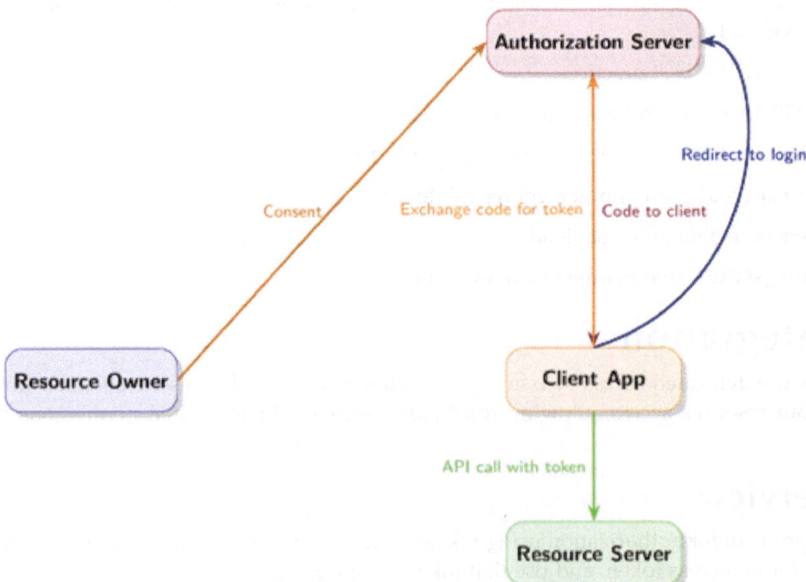

***Figure 10.10**: OAuth2 authorization code flow*

The client app redirects the user to login and consent, receives a code, exchanges it for a token, and accesses the resource server with that token.

Google OAuth setup

Integrate Google OAuth2 in Express using Passport. Install packages, configure the environment, define routes, and secure sessions.

The following presents the package installation:

```
npm install express passport passport-google-oauth20 express-session dotenv
```

The following presents Passport configuration:

```
require('dotenv').config();
const express = require('express');
const passport = require('passport');
const session = require('express-session');
const GoogleStrategy = require('passport-google-oauth20').Strategy;

passport.use(new GoogleStrategy({ clientID: process.env.GOOGLE_CLIENT_ID,
    clientSecret: process.env.GOOGLE_CLIENT_SECRET, callbackURL: process.env.GOOGLE_CALLBACK_URL
}, (accessToken, refreshToken, profile, done) => { done(null, profile);
}));

passport.serializeUser((user, done) => done(null, user)); passport.deserializeUser((obj, done) =>
done(null, obj));

const app = express();
app.use(session({
    secret: process.env.SESSION_SECRET,
    resave: false,
    saveUninitialized: true
}));

app.use(passport.initialize());
app.use(passport.session());
```

The following figure illustrates the Google sign-in prompt that appears when authentication is initiated:

Sign in with Google

Google Logo <Your Google Email Address> [Password field, Sign in button, etc.]

Figure 10.11: Google OAuth sign-in prompt

The following presents auth routes:

```
// Initiate OAuth flow
app.get('/auth/google', passport.authenticate('google', { scope:['profile','email'] }));

// Callback URL
app.get('/auth/google/callback',
  passport.authenticate('google',{ failureRedirect:'/'
  }), (req,res) => { res.redirect('/profile'); }
);
```

```
// Protected profile
app.get('/profile', (req,res) => { if(!req.
  isAuthenticated()) return res.redirect('/');
  res.json(req.user);
});

app.get('/logout', (req,res) => { req.logout(() => res.redirect('/')); });
```

The following figure demonstrates the profile output returned after successful authentication:


```
{
    "id": "11234...",
    "displayName": "Rupesh Kumar",
    "emails": [{"value": "rupesh@example.com"}]
}
```


Figure 10.12: JSON response for user profile after Google OAuth login

The following figure presents the overall Google OAuth authentication flow:

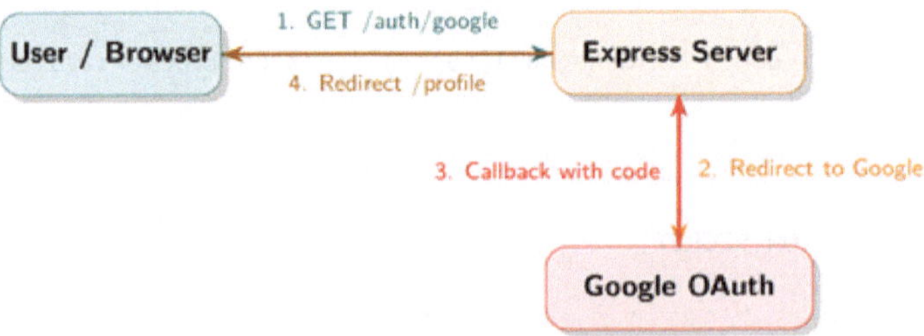

Figure 10.13: Google OAuth workflow

Advanced topics

Enhance OAuth security with best practices: use HTTPS, implement **Proof Key for Code Exchange** (**PKCE**) for public clients, manage refresh tokens securely, and handle token revocation.

The following presents advanced enhancements:

- Enable PKCE to prevent code interception.
- Store refresh tokens in HttpOnly cookies.
- Rotate client secrets and enforce short token lifespans.
- Validate scopes and audience in access tokens.

Best practices in backend development

Writing maintainable, secure, and efficient backend code requires adhering to proven patterns and conventions. The best practices cover project organization, configuration management, error handling, security, and testing.

Project structure

A clear directory layout improves readability and collaboration. Group related files by functionality—controllers, routes, models, middleware, and services—so each layer's purpose is obvious.

The following demonstrates a typical structure:

```
project/
│
├── controllers/
│     └── userController.js
├── routes/
│     └── userRoutes.js
├── models/
│     └── userModel.js
├── services/
│     └── emailService.js
├── middleware/
│     └── authMiddleware.js
├── config/
│     └── dbConfig.js
├── app.js
└── server.js
```

Environment variables

Storing credentials and configuration in code risks leaks. Use environment variables loaded via **dotenv** to separate secrets from source. The following demonstrates usage:

```
require('dotenv').config();

const dbUrl  = process.env.DB_URL;
const port   = process.env.PORT || 3000;
```

Error handling

Centralized error handling ensures consistent responses and hides internal details. Express error middleware catches thrown or passed errors.

The following demonstrates an error handler:

```
app.use((err, req, res, next)
  => { console.error(err.
  stack); res.status(err.
  status || 500)
     .json({ error: 'Internal server error' });
});
```

Input validation

Validating and sanitizing user input prevents injections and XSS. Libraries like **express-validator** or **joi** enforce schemas and cleanse data.

The following demonstrates **express-validator**:

```
const { body, validationResult } = require('express-validator');

   app.post('/register', [ body('email').isEmail().normalizeEmail(), body('password').isLength({
     min: 6 }).escape()
   ], (req, res) => {
     const errors = validationResult(req);
```

```
  if (!errors.isEmpty()) {
                return res.status(400).json({ errors: errors.array() });
  }
  // proceed
});
```

Asynchronous code

Use **async/await** for non-blocking operations and wrap them in **try/catch** to handle errors cleanly.

The following demonstrates an async route:

```
app.get('/data', async (req, res) => {
  try {
    const items = await fetchFromDatabase();
    res.json(items);
  } catch (err) {
    res.status(500).json({ message: 'Fetch error' });
              }
          });
```

Logging and monitoring

Comprehensive logs aid debugging and performance tracking. Use middleware like **morgan** for request logs and **winston** for app events.

The following demonstrates **morgan** setup:

```
const morgan = require('morgan'); app.
use(morgan('combined'));
```

Security

Harden your app by securing headers, enforcing rate limits, and hashing sensitive data. Use **helmet** for HTTP headers, **express-rate-limit** for throttling, and **bcrypt** for passwords.

The following demonstrates security middleware:

```
const helmet = require('helmet');
const rateLimit = require('express-rate-
limit'); app.use(helmet());

const limiter = rateLimit({ windowMs:15*60*1000, max:100 });
app.use(limiter);
```

Database practices

Efficient data access and integrity rely on proper indexing, schema definitions, and connection management. Use **object-relational mapping/object-document mapping** (**ORMs/ODMs**) (Mongoose, Sequelize) for validation and transaction support.

The following demonstrates Mongoose schema indexing:

```
const userSchema = new mongoose.Schema({
  email: { type:String, unique:true,
  index:true }, name: String
});
```

Version control and documentation

Maintain history and enable collaboration with Git. Document your API using Swagger or Postman collections so consumers understand endpoints, payloads, and response formats.

The following presents a minimal Swagger setup:

```
openapi: 3.0.0
info:
  title: Book API
  version: 1.0.0
paths:
  /books:
    get:
      summary: List books
      responses:
        '200':
          description: OK
```

Testing

Automated testing ensures each API endpoint behaves correctly and prevents regressions. Unit tests validate individual functions in isolation, while integration tests verify how components interact, for example, routes, middleware, and database layers together. Using frameworks like Jest or Mocha for assertions and Supertest for HTTP requests allows comprehensive coverage of controller logic and server responses.

The following demonstrates a Supertest integration test:

```
const request = require('supertest');
const app     = require('../app');

describe('Books API', () => {
  test('GET /books returns JSON array', async
    () => { const res = await request(app).
    get('/books'); expect(res.statusCode).
    toBe(200); expect(Array.isArray(res.
    body)).toBe(true);
  });

  test('POST /books creates a new book', async () => {
    const newBook = { title:'Test Book', author:'Jane Doe' };
    const res = await request(app)
      .post('/books')
      .send(newBook); expect(res.
    statusCode).toBe(201); expect(res.
    body).toMatchObject(newBook);
  });
});
```

Security considerations

A robust security posture relies on multiple layers of defense, from validating user input to securing communication channels and managing third-party dependencies. Adhering to industry standards and conducting regular audits helps prevent common vulnerabilities and ensures your application remains resilient against evolving threats.

Input sanitization

Preventing injection attacks and cross-site scripting begins with rigorous input handling. Validation ensures data matches expected formats, while sanitization removes or encodes dangerous characters.

The following demonstrates input validation and sanitization best practices:

- Validate against strict schemas using a whitelist approach rather than blacklists.
- Normalize input (e.g., trim whitespace, enforce canonical forms).
- Escape or strip HTML in text fields to block XSS payloads.
- Reject or sanitize special characters in database queries to prevent injections.

The following script shows express-validator in action:

```
const { body, validationResult } = require('express-validator');

app.post('/submit', [
  // Validate and sanitize
  body('username')
    .trim()
    .isAlphanumeric().withMessage('Username must be letters and numbers')
    .escape(),
  body('email')
    .isEmail().withMessage('Must be a valid email')
    .normalizeEmail(), body('comment')
    .trim()
    .escape()
], (req,
res) => {
  const errors = validationResult(req);
  if (!errors.isEmpty()) {
    return res.status(400).json({ errors: errors.array() });
  }
  // proceed with safe data
});
```

HTTPS enforcement

Encrypting all traffic thwarts eavesdropping and tampering. TLS (HTTPS) should be non-negotiable in production environments, with secure configurations to guard against protocol and cipher vulnerabilities.

The following presents HTTPS best practices:

- Obtain certificates from trusted authorities (e.g., Let's Encrypt).
- Redirect all HTTP requests to HTTPS using middleware or server configuration.
- Enable HSTS (HTTP Strict Transport Security) to prevent protocol downgrades.
- Disable outdated TLS versions (TLS 1.0/1.1) and weak ciphers.
- Renew certificates automatically and monitor expiration.

Dependency hygiene

Keeping third-party code secure requires ongoing vigilance. Unpatched vulnerabilities in dependencies can compromise your entire application, so integrate automated tools and policies to manage risk.

The following demonstrates dependency management practices:

- Lock versions in **`package.json`** and **`package-lock.json`** to ensure reproducible installs.
- Run **`npm audit`** regularly and address high-severity findings promptly.
- Use tools like **`Dependabot`** or Snyk to receive automated pull requests for updated packages.
- Remove unused dependencies and verify package provenance to avoid supply-chain attacks.
- Review security advisories for major frameworks and update core modules (e.g., Express, Mongoose).

Code organization

A modular codebase enhances readability, reuse, and testing. Separate concerns into distinct layers, routing, controllers, models, services, and middleware, so each file has a clear responsibility.

The following demonstrates the central app setup:

```
// app.js
const express      = require('express');
const userRoutes  = require('./routes/userRoutes');
const errorHandler = require('./middleware/errorHandler');

const app = express(); app.use(express.json()); app.use('/api/users', userRoutes); app.
use(errorHandler);

module.exports = app;

// server.js
const app = require('./app');
const PORT = process.env.PORT || 3000; app.listen(PORT, () => {
  console.log(`Server running on port ${PORT}`);
});
```

Creating a RESTful API server

This project walks through building a secure, modular RESTful API server with Node.js, Express, MongoDB, and JWT authentication. It covers requirements, project setup, CRUD operations, authentication, and testing/deployment.

Overview and requirements

A clear understanding of functional and technical needs guides API design and implementation. This API will manage user accounts with registration, login, and CRUD operations, and secure routes using JWT tokens.

The following presents functional requirements:

- User registration (create account)
- User login (obtain JWT)
- Read, update, delete user data (CRUD)
- Protect routes via token-based authentication

The following presents the technical stack:

- **Runtime**: Node.js with Express.js
- **Database**: MongoDB via Mongoose
- **Authentication**: JWT
- **Utilities**: dotenv, bcryptjs, cors

Structure and initialization

Modular project layout improves maintainability and scalability. Organize code by responsibility.

The following presents the project layout:

```
project-rest-api/
├── controllers/
│   └── userController.js
├── models/
│   └── userModel.js
├── routes/
│   └── userRoutes.js
├── middleware/
│   └── authMiddleware.js
├── .env
├── server.js
├── package.json
└── README.md
```

Install dependencies and scaffold the package. The following demonstrates initialization commands:

```
mkdir project-rest-api cd project-rest-api npm init -y
npm install express mongoose dotenv jsonwebtoken bcryptjs cors
```

Create the entry point, and the following code presents **server.js**:

```
const express = require('express'); const mongoose = require('mongoose'); require('dotenv').
config();

const app = express(); app.use(express.json()); app.use(require('cors')());

const PORT = process.env.PORT || 5000;

mongoose.connect(process.env.MONGO_URI, { useNewUrlParser:true, useUnifiedTopology:true })
  .then(() => app.listen(PORT, () => console.log(`Server running on port ${PORT}`)
  ))
  .catch(err => console.error(err));
```

CRUD implementation

Define a Mongoose schema, controller functions, and route handlers to manage user data.

The following presents the user schema:

```
const mongoose = require('mongoose');

const userSchema = new mongoose.Schema({
    name: { type: String, required: true, trim: true },
    email: { type: String, required: true, unique: true, lowercase: true, trim: true, index:
true },
    passwordHash: { type: String, required: true, select: false }
});

module.exports = mongoose.model('User', userSchema);
```

The following demonstrates controller logic **(controllers/userController.js)**:

```
const User = require('../models/userModel');

exports.getAllUsers = async (req, res) => {
    const users = await User.find().select('-passwordHash');
```

```
        res.json(users);
    };

    exports.getUserById = async (req, res) => {
        const user = await User.findById(req.params.id).select('-passwordHash');
        if (!user) return res.status(404).send('User not found');
        res.json(user);
    };

    exports.createUser = async (req, res) => {
        const { name, email } = req.body;
        const newUser = await User.create({ name, email, passwordHash: 'TEMP_NOT_ALLOWED' });
        res.status(201).json({ id: newUser._id, name: newUser.name, email: newUser.email });
    };

    exports.updateUser = async (req, res) => {
        const { name, email } = req.body;
        const updated = await User.findByIdAndUpdate(
            req.params.id,
            { name, email },
            { new: true, runValidators: true }
        ).select('-passwordHash');

        if (!updated) return res.status(404).send('User not found');
        res.json(updated);
    };

        exports.deleteUser = async (req, res) => {
            const deleted = await User.findByIdAndDelete(req.params.id);
            if (!deleted) return res.status(404).send('User not found');
            res.send('User deleted');
        };
```

The following demonstrates route definitions (**routes/userRoutes.js**):

```
const express = require('express');
const router = express.Router();

const ctrl = require('../controllers/userController');
const authCtrl = require('../controllers/authController');
const auth = require('../middleware/authMiddleware');

// Auth
router.post('/register', authCtrl.register);
router.post('/login', authCtrl.login);

// Protected CRUD (example)
router.get('/', auth, ctrl.getAllUsers);
router.get('/:id', auth, ctrl.getUserById);
router.put('/:id', auth, ctrl.updateUser);
router.delete('/:id', auth, ctrl.deleteUser);

module.exports = router;
```

The following demonstrates route **authController** (**controllers/authController.js**):

```
// controllers/authController.js
const bcrypt = require('bcryptjs');
const jwt = require('jsonwebtoken');
```

```
const User = require('../models/userModel');

exports.register = async (req, res) => {
    const { name, email, password } = req.body;

    const existing = await User.findOne({ email });
    if (existing) return res.status(409).json({ message: 'Email already exists' });

    const passwordHash = await bcrypt.hash(password, 10);
    const user = await User.create({ name, email, passwordHash });

    res.status(201).json({ id: user._id, name: user.name, email: user.email });
};

exports.login = async (req, res) => {
    const { email, password } = req.body;

    // passwordHash is select:false, so explicitly select it
    const user = await User.findOne({ email }).select('+passwordHash');
    if (!user) return res.status(401).json({ message: 'Invalid credentials' });

    const ok = await bcrypt.compare(password, user.passwordHash);
    if (!ok) return res.status(401).json({ message: 'Invalid credentials' });

    const token = jwt.sign(
        { id: user._id },
        process.env.JWT_SECRET,
        { expiresIn: '1h' }
    );

    res.json({ token });
};
```

Attach routes in **server.js** and the following script integrates routes:

```
const userRoutes = require('./routes/userRoutes');
app.use('/api/users', userRoutes);
```

JWT authentication

Secure protected endpoints by issuing and validating JWT upon login.

The following demonstrates the auth controller additions:

```
const bcrypt = require('bcryptjs');
const jwt    = require('jsonwebtoken');
const User   = require('../models/userModel');

exports.register = async (req, res) => {
  const { name, email, password } = req.body;
  const hash = await bcrypt.hash(password, 10);
  await User.create({ name, email, password:hash });
  res.status(201).json({ message:'Registered' });
};

exports.login = async (req, res) => {
  const { email, password } = req.body;
```

```
    const user = await User.findOne({ email });
    if (!user || !(await bcrypt.compare(password, user.password))) {
      return res.status(401).send('Invalid credentials');
    }
    const token = jwt.sign(
      { id:user._id }, process.env.JWT_SECRET, { expiresIn:'1h' }
    );
    res.json({ token });
  };
```

The following demonstrates auth middleware (**`middleware/authMiddleware.js`**):

```
const jwt = require('jsonwebtoken');

module.exports = (req, res, next) => {
  const auth = req.headers['authorization'];
  if (!auth) return res.status(403).send('Token required');
  const token = auth.split(' ')[1];
  try {
    req.user = jwt.verify(token, process.env.JWT_SECRET); next();
  } catch {
    res.status(401).send('Invalid token');
        }
      };
```

Protect routes by applying middleware. The following demonstrates protected routes:

```
const auth = require('../middleware/authMiddleware'); router.get('/', auth, ctrl.getAllUsers);
```

Testing and deployment

Validate functionality locally, then deploy to a cloud service with secure configuration. The following presents API testing steps:

1. **Register user**: POST **`/api/users/register`** with JSON **`{ "name": "...", "email": "...", "password": "..." }`**.
2. **Login**: POST **`/api/users/login`** uses the same body to receive a token.
3. **Access protected**: GET **`/api/users`** with header **`Authorization: Bearer <token>`**.

The following presents deployment tips:

- Store secrets in environment variables (**`.env`**).
- Use managed MongoDB (Atlas) for production.
- Deploy to platforms like Heroku, Railway, or Render.
- Disable detailed errors and enable HTTPS in production.

Conclusion

In this chapter, we built an understanding of the fundamentals, advanced uses of Node.js, and Express.js for backend development. The chapter explained how Node's single-threaded, event-loop architecture and V8 performance combine to handle thousands of concurrent connections without blocking. With Express.js, you learned to abstract core HTTP functionality into middleware, define clean routing patterns, and build modular, maintainable applications. We walked through creating RESTful APIs, implementing authentication via JWT and OAuth, and enforcing best practices—such as environment configuration, centralized error handling, input validation, and security hardening. The hands-on project guided through building and deploying a complete CRUD API server with user registration, login, and protected routes, while the case study highlighted strategies for scaling a real-world task management system.

In the next chapter, we will explore how to persist and manage data by integrating both **structured query language (SQL)** and NoSQL databases into your Node.js applications. You will learn to model data with MongoDB (using Mongoose) and PostgreSQL (using Sequelize), perform transactions, optimize performance with indexing, and secure your data layer—culminating in a project that brings together polyglot persistence for maximum flexibility and scalability.

Exercises

1. Install Node.js using nvm (Linux/macOS): write the exact commands to install the latest LTS version, set it as default, and verify Node and npm versions; also note the official installer step for Windows/macOS.
2. Create a minimal HTTP server with Node's built-in http module that responds with Hello from Node.js!. Show the complete code, the file name you use, the terminal command to run it, and the URL to open in a browser.
3. Demonstrate the event loop: write a small script that uses setTimeout(..., 0), a Promise (microtask), and a synchronous console.log. Predict the exact output order and explain why in one sentence.
4. Initialize a new project (npm init -y) and install Express. Write a minimal Express server on port 3000 with a request-logging middleware (method and URL) and a GET / route that returns Welcome to Express.js!.
5. Add JSON body parsing to the Express app and create a global error-handling middleware that returns status 500 with { "error": "Internal server error" }. Show where you register it and one example route that throws an error to test it.
6. Design RESTful CRUD endpoints for a books resource. List the five endpoints (GET /books, GET /books/:id, POST /books, PUT /books/:id, DELETE /books/:id) with expected success and not-found status codes, and write concise handler skeletons for each.
7. Implement route and query parameters: add GET /books/:id to return one book by numeric ID and GET /search?q=term to echo the query. Show the two handler functions that read from req.params and req.query.
8. Validate and sanitize input for POST /books using express-validator: require a non-empty title and author. Return HTTP 400 with the validation errors when invalid; show the middleware chain and one valid and one invalid curl example.
9. Implement password hashing with bcryptjs and a login route that issues a JWT signed with process.env.JWT_SECRET. Provide (a) the /register route that stores { name, email, passwordHash }, (b) the /login route that returns { token }, and (c) an authenticateToken middleware that protects GET /books.
10. Add role-based authorization: write an authorizeRole(role) middleware and protect DELETE /books/:id so only admin can delete. Show how you attach the user's role to req.user (decoded from JWT) and the route that uses the middleware chain.
11. Outline OAuth2 Authorization Code with PKCE in Express: list the required routes (for example, /auth/login, /auth/callback), the IDs/secrets needed in .env, and write pseudocode for creating the code verifier/challenge and performing the token exchange (no SDK required).
12. Harden the app: add helmet for security headers, express-rate-limit with a 15-minute window and max 100 requests per IP, and CORS with a specific origin. Write the exact app.use(...) lines and one short reason for each.
13. Refactor into layers: write the folder tree for controllers/, routes/, models/, services/, middleware/, config/, app.js, and server.js. For the books API, state which file defines handlers, which file defines routes, and which file wires the app.
14. Integrate MongoDB with Mongoose: (a) connect using MONGO_URI from .env in server startup, (b) define a User schema with { name, email (unique, indexed), passwordHash } and a unique index on email, and (c) show a simple pre-save check that rejects passwords shorter than 6 before hashing (or validate length before hashing).
15. Write two Supertest integration tests (Jest): one confirms GET /books returns status 200 and a JSON array, and another confirms POST /books with a valid body returns 201 and echoes the title. Include the npm test script and the command to run the tests.

Chapter 11
Databases and Integration

Introduction

In today's data-driven world, databases lie at the heart of virtually every web and mobile application. Whether you are tracking user profiles, managing product catalogs, or logging high-volume events, choosing the right database and integrating it seamlessly into your backend is paramount. This chapter begins by contrasting the two dominant paradigms, such as **structured query language** (**SQL**) and NoSQL, highlighting their data models, consistency guarantees, and scaling strategies. You will then learn how to connect a Node.js server to both MongoDB (via Mongoose) and PostgreSQL (via Sequelize), defining schemas/models, performing **create, read, update, and delete** (**CRUD**) operations, and enforcing data validation. Building on these foundations, we explore advanced topics such as indexing for query performance, transaction management for atomic operations, and security best practices to protect sensitive data. To cement your understanding, you will undertake a hands-on project—a student course registration **application programming interface** (**API**) that combines authentication, relational modeling, and many-to-many associations. Finally, we pose a series of exercises and a case study on polyglot persistence that challenge you to apply these concepts in realistic scenarios.

Structure

This chapter covers the following topics:

- Database fundamentals SQL vs. NoSQL
- Database integration with Node.js
- Building a data-driven application

Objectives

By the end of this chapter, readers will be able to evaluate and select appropriate database technologies for different application scenarios, comparing the strengths and limitations of SQL and NoSQL paradigms. They will configure and establish connections between a Node.js backend and MongoDB using Mongoose, and with PostgreSQL using Sequelize, applying schema definitions, model associations, and query operations. Learners will implement complete CRUD functionality, enforce schema validation, and handle errors in both environments. Additionally, they will apply advanced techniques such as index creation for query optimization, transaction management to guarantee atomic operations, and robust security measures, including encrypted connections, parameterized queries, and role-based access control. Through a comprehensive hands-on project, students will design and deploy a student course registration API featuring many-to-many relationships and **JSON Web Tokens** (**JWT**) based authentication. This chapter also emphasizes best practices for environment configuration, testing, and deployment, preparing learners to build production-ready, maintainable backends with real-world requirements.

Database fundamentals SQL vs. NoSQL

Databases underpin all data-driven applications, providing mechanisms to store, query, and update information reliably. Choosing between SQL (relational) and NoSQL (non-relational) systems hinges on data structure, consistency needs, scalability requirements, and development agility. This section explores both paradigms in depth, covering models, guarantees, tradeoffs, and real-world use cases.

SQL relational

Relational databases enforce a predefined schema of tables, columns, and data types. They excel at complex queries and transactional integrity.

The following list presents relational model features:

- **Schema enforcement**: Tables define column names and types up front.
- **ACID transactions**: Atomicity, consistency, isolation, and durability ensure reliable multi-step operations.
- **Joins and subqueries**: Combine data across tables with powerful SQL.
- **Normalization**: Reduces redundancy by splitting data into related tables.
- **Indexes**: B-tree or hash structures accelerate lookups on key columns.

The following code presents a sample schema and query:

```
-- Schema
CREATE TABLE users (
  id SERIAL PRIMARY KEY,
  name VARCHAR(100) NOT NULL,
  email VARCHAR(100) UNIQUE NOT NULL,
  created_at TIMESTAMP DEFAULT now()
);

CREATE TABLE orders (
  id SERIAL PRIMARY KEY,
  user_id INT REFERENCES
  users(id), total
  NUMERIC(10,2) NOT NULL,
  status
  VARCHAR(20),
  order_date DATE
  NOT NULL
);

-- Query: recent shipped orders with user info
SELECT u.name, u.email, o.total, o.order_date
  FROM users AS u
  JOIN orders AS o
 ON u.id = o.user_
       id
 WHERE o.status =
    'shipped'
   AND o.order_date > current_date - INTERVAL '30 days'
 ORDER BY o.order_date DESC;
```

NoSQL non-relational

NoSQL covers diverse models, such as document, key-value, columnar, and graph, and each is optimized for specific patterns and scale.

Document stores

Document databases (e.g., MongoDB, CouchDB) store JSON-like documents. Each document can have a different structure, enabling flexible schemas and easy horizontal scaling.

The following list presents document features:

- **Schema flexibility**: Documents in the same collection need not share fields.
- **Nested structures**: Arrays and subdocuments enable denormalized data for faster reads.
- **MapReduce and aggregation**: Built-in pipelines process documents on the server.

The following code presents a MongoDB example:

```
// Insert a user document
db.users.
  insertOne({
  name:
  "Alice",
  email: "alice@example.com",
  preferences: { newsletter:
  true }, orders: [
    { id: 1, total: 99.99, status: "shipped" },
    { id: 2, total: 49.50, status: "pending" }
]
}
)
;

// Query shipped orders for Alice
db.users.find(
  { "orders.status": "shipped" },
  { name:1, "orders.$":1 }
);
```

Key-value stores

Key-value databases (e.g., Redis, DynamoDB) store opaque values indexed by a unique key. They provide extremely low-latency lookups for simple data access patterns.

The following list presents key-value features:

- **Simplicity and speed**: Direct access by key.
- **In-memory variants**: Redis offers microsecond responses for caching.
- **TTL and eviction**: Automatic expiration policies for cache data.

Wide-column stores

Columnar databases (e.g., Cassandra, HBase) organize data by column families rather than rows, optimizing for high throughput on large datasets.

The following presents column-store features:

- **Sparse storage**: Only store non-empty columns per row.
- **Partitioning and clustering**: Automatic data distribution across nodes.
- **Tunable consistency**: Choose per-query consistency levels.

Graph databases

Graph systems (e.g., Neo4j, JanusGraph) model entities as nodes and relationships as edges, enabling efficient traversal of highly connected data.

The following list presents graph features:

- **Relationship focus**: Edges carry properties and support deep joins cheaply.
- **Cypher/Gremlin queries**: Expressive languages for pattern matching.
- **Use cases**: Social networks, recommendation engines, fraud detection.

Choosing between SQL and NoSQL

Selecting a database requires balancing **consistency, availability, partition tolerance** (**CAP**), and application needs. The details are as follows:

- **ACID vs. BASE**: Relational systems guarantee ACID. NoSQL often provides **basically available, soft state, eventual consistency** (**BASE**), relaxing strict consistency for scalability.
- **CAP theorem**: Distributed systems cannot simultaneously guarantee consistency, availability, and partition tolerance. SQL excels in C/A within a single replica but may sacrifice availability under a network fault. NoSQL systems often favor A/P with eventual consistency.

The following section presents CAP tradeoffs.

Scalability and performance

Relational databases scale vertically by adding **Central Processing Unit** (**CPU**), **random access memory** (**RAM**), and **solid state drive** (**SSD**), while **Not Only SQL** (**NoSQL**), which often scales horizontally by adding commodity servers.

The following figure illustrates the CAP trade-offs flow path, highlighting how scalability and performance decisions differ across database architectures:

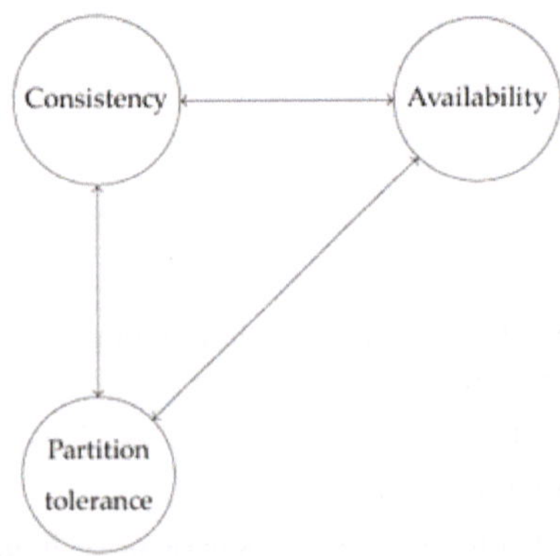

Figure 11.1: *CAP tradeoffs flow path overview*

The following strategies demonstrate key approaches for achieving distributed scalability and reliability in modern database systems:

- **Sharding**: Partition data across nodes by key range or hash (MongoDB, Cassandra).
- **Replication**: Maintain copies for high availability and read scaling.
- **Caching**: Use in-memory engines (Redis, Memcached) to offload database reads.

The following table presents a summary of SQL and NoSQL databases:

Feature	SQL	NoSQL
Schema	Fixed, structured	Flexible, evolving
Transactions	Strong ACID support	Often eventual consistency
Relationships	Complex joins	Denormalized or graph queries

Scale	Vertical scaling	Horizontal sharding
Examples	Financial, ERP systems	Big data, real-time analytics

***Table 11.1**: When to choose SQL vs. NoSQL*

Modern applications often combine both, using SQL for transactional data and NoSQL for high-velocity or semi-structured data, to leverage each paradigm's strengths.

NoSQL databases

NoSQL databases eschew fixed schemas in favor of flexible, scalable storage models that suit modern applications handling large volumes of unstructured or semi-structured data. They distribute data across clusters, allow rapid iteration of data structures, and optimize horizontal scaling and high throughput.

Document stores

Document databases store data as self-contained **JavaScript Object Notation** (**JSON**) or **Binary JavaScript Object Notation** (**BSON**) documents, allowing nested structures and arrays that mirror application objects. This denormalized approach reduces the need for joins and speeds up read operations.

The following list presents key traits of document stores:

- **Flexible schema**: Each document can include different fields.
- **Nested data**: Embed arrays and subdocuments for related data in one record.
- **Rich queries**: Support filtering, projections, and aggregation pipelines.

The following example shows a MongoDB document insert and query:

```
/* =============================================================
   MongoDB Shell Example: Document Store (Insert + Query)
   Run in: mongosh
   ============================================================= */

// 1) Select (or create) a database
use storeDB;

// 2) Clean the collection so results are predictable in a demo
db.products.deleteMany({});

// 3) Insert one product document (JSON-like structure with nested fields + arrays)
db.products.insertOne({
    name: "Wireless Mouse",
    price: 29.99,
    status: "active",
    specs: { dpi: 1600, wireless: true },
    tags: ["electronics", "accessory"]
});

// 4) Insert a second document (helps show filtering)
db.products.insertOne({
    name: "USB Keyboard",
    price: 45.00,
    status: "active",
    specs: { layout: "QWERTY", wireless: false },
    tags: ["electronics", "accessory"]
});
```

```
// 5) Query: active products under $50
//    - Filter: status must be "active" and price < 50
//    - Projection: return only name and price (hide _id)
// Convert cursor output to an array (easier to read)
db.products.find(
    { status: "active", price: { $lt: 50 } },
    { name: 1, price: 1, _id: 0 }
).toArray();
```

Key-value stores

Key-value databases treat each record as an opaque value accessible by a unique key. They excel at caching, session storage, and simple lookup scenarios, often providing in-memory performance. The following presents key traits of key-value stores:

- **Simple API**: GET, SET, DELETE operations by key.
- **Extreme performance**: In-memory engines like Redis deliver microsecond latency.
- **Expiry and eviction**: Native TTL support for automatic data expiration.

The following example shows Redis commands:

```
# Store and retrieve user session
SET session:12345 '{"user":"alice","role":"admin"}' EX 3600
GET session:12345
```

Column-family stores

Column-family databases organize data into tables of rows and dynamic columns grouped into families. They shine when writing and reading large datasets across distributed nodes, supporting wide tables and sparse data.

The following list presents key traits of column-family stores:

- **Wide rows**: Store thousands of columns per key without penalty.
- **Tunable consistency**: Choose the consistency level per operation.
- **Automatic partitioning**: Data shards by row key for horizontal scale.

The following example shows Cassandra CQL:

```
CREATE TABLE metrics ( device_id text,
  ts timestamp, temperature float, humidity float,
  PRIMARY KEY (device_id, ts)
) WITH CLUSTERING ORDER BY (ts DESC);

SELECT * FROM metrics
  WHERE device_id='sensorA' AND ts > '2025-01-01';
```

Graph databases

Graph databases model data as nodes and edges, making them ideal for highly connected datasets. They support efficient traversals and complex relationship queries.

The following presents key traits of graph databases:

- **Native relationships**: Store edges with properties linking nodes.
- **Traversal queries**: Use graph-specific languages (Cypher, Gremlin).
- **Use cases**: Social networks, recommendation engines, fraud detection.

The following example shows a Neo4j Cypher query:

```
// Find friends of friends for user Alice
MATCH (a:User {name:"Alice"})-[:FRIEND]->(f)-[:FRIEND]->(fof)
RETURN fof.name AS friendOfFriend;
```

Comparing NoSQL models

Different NoSQL types suit different needs. The table below contrasts their strengths and typical use cases.

The following table presents a comparison of NoSQL models:

Model	Strengths	Use cases	Examples
Document	Flexible schema, rich queries.	Content management, catalogues.	MongoDB, CouchDB
Key-value	Ultra-fast lookups, TTL support.	Caching, sessions	Redis, DynamoDB
Column-family	High write throughput, sparse data.	Time-series, IoT metrics	Cassandra, HBase
Graph	Efficient relationship traversal.	Social graphs, fraud detection.	Neo4j, JanusGraph

Table 11.2: *NoSQL database model comparison*

Choosing a NoSQL database

Selecting the right NoSQL system depends on data access patterns, consistency needs, and scaling strategy. Document stores suit apps with evolving schemas; key-value excels for caching; column-family handles large-scale analytics; graph databases resolve complex relationship queries efficiently.

Comparison of SQL vs. NoSQL

Relational and non-relational databases serve different application needs by trading off between structure and flexibility, strong consistency, and scale. This comparison highlights their core differences to guide technology selection.

The following table presents a comparison table:

Aspect	SQL (Relational)	NoSQL (Non-relational)
Data model	Rigid tables with rows and columns, normalised schemas	Collections of documents, key–value pairs, wide columns, or graph nodes.
Schema	Strongly typed, predefined **data definition language (DDL)**.	A schema-less or dynamic schema can evolve per record.
Query	Declarative SQL with JOINs and subqueries.	Varies by type: document queries, key lookups, CQL, Cypher, etc.
Transactions	Full ACID support across multiple operations.	Limited or tunable consistency (BASE), multi-document transactions in some systems.
Consistency	Immediate consistency within a single database instance	Eventual consistency is the default, configurable per operation in many systems.
Scalability	Vertical scaling (scale-up hardware)	Horizontal scaling (shard or replicate across many nodes).
Performance	Strong for complex joins and analytics; can degrade under heavy write load.	Optimized for high-volume reads or writes, denormalised access patterns.
Tooling	Mature ecosystem: backup, replication, reporting, stored procedures	Rapid adoption tools, but the ecosystem varies; it may require custom integrations.

Use cases	Financial systems, **enterprise resource planning (ERP)**, **customer relationship management (CRM)**, structured data with relations.	Real-time analytics, content management, **Internet of Things (IoT)**, social graphs.
Examples	MySQL I PostgreSQL I SQL Server, Oracle.	MongoDB, Cassandra, Redis, Neo4j.

Table 11.3: *Comparison of SQL and NoSQL databases*

The following list outlines the major dimensions that differentiate SQL (relational) and NoSQL (non-relational) database systems, highlighting how they vary in structure, query mechanisms, transaction guarantees, scalability approaches, ecosystem maturity, and use-case suitability:

- **Data model and schema**: Relational databases enforce a strict schema defined by DDL. Every table row must conform, ensuring predictable structure and referential integrity via foreign keys. NoSQL systems allow each record to differ, supporting rapid iteration of application data shapes without migrations.
- **Query capabilities**: SQL's expressive declarative language excels at complex queries involving joins, subqueries, aggregations, and window functions. NoSQL queries depend on the model: document stores use JSON-style filters and aggregation pipelines, key–value stores provide simple GET/SET operations, columnar databases offer CQL for wide-row scans, and graph databases use pattern-matching languages like Cypher.
- **Transactions and consistency**: Relational systems guarantee ACID for multi-step transactions, critical in financial and inventory contexts. Most NoSQL databases prioritize availability and partition tolerance, offering eventual consistency or tunable consistency levels. Some newer NoSQL engines provide multi-document ACID transactions, but often with performance tradeoffs.
- **Scalability and performance**: Scaling a relational database typically involves adding resources to a single instance (scale-up), eventually encountering hardware limits. NoSQL databases are designed for horizontal scaling, sharding data across clusters, allowing near-linear performance gains. Denormalized data layouts in NoSQL minimize joins, resulting in faster read/write performance for large datasets.
- **Ecosystem and tooling**: SQL databases benefit from decades of tooling, graphical clients, reporting systems, and mature backup/replication frameworks. NoSQL tooling is newer and more heterogeneous; some projects provide built-in clustering and monitoring, while others rely on third-party or custom solutions.
- **Selecting the right database**: Choose SQL when you need strong consistency, complex relational queries, and mature transactional support. Opt for NoSQL when your application demands flexible schemas, massive horizontal scale, or specialized models such as document, key–value, or graph to match data access patterns.

Introduction to MongoDB

MongoDB is a leading document-oriented NoSQL database designed for high performance, horizontal scalability, and flexible schema. Rather than rows and tables, MongoDB stores JSON-like documents in collections, making it ideal for evolving data models, real-time analytics, and distributed systems.

The following list presents core MongoDB concepts:

- **Database**: A namespace for collections, analogous to an SQL database.
- **Collection**: A group of related documents, similar to a table.
- **Document**: A BSON-encoded JSON object, equivalent to a row, supporting nested fields and arrays.
- **Field**: A key-value pair within a document; values can be primitives or nested documents/arrays.
- **Index**: Data structure for efficient query execution on one or more fields.
- **Replica Set**: A group of mongod instances providing redundancy and automatic failover.
- **Sharding**: Distributes data across multiple shards (servers) for horizontal scale.

The following code demonstrates a typical MongoDB document:

```
{
  "_id": ObjectId("60d5f483f9a7c8b4e5c3d1a2"),
  "username": "alice",
  "email": "alice@example.com",
  "profile": {
    "age": 29,
    "interests": ["reading", "hiking"]
  },
  "status": "active",
  "createdAt": ISODate("2025-06-25T12:34:56Z")
}
```

Connecting and CRUD basics

Applications interact with MongoDB via official drivers. The following is a Node.js example using the MongoDB driver. The following script demonstrates connecting and basic CRUD:

```
const { MongoClient } = require('mongodb');

async function run() {
    const client = new MongoClient(process.env.MONGO_URI, {
        // Small safety options for demos; production often tunes these
        serverSelectionTimeoutMS: 5000
    });

    try {
        await client.connect();

        const db = client.db('appDB');
        const users = db.collection('users');

        // Create
        await users.insertOne({ username: 'bob', email: 'bob@example.com', status: 'active' });

        // Read
        const active = await users.find({ status: 'active' }).toArray();
        console.log('Active users:', active);

        // Update
        await users.updateOne(
            { username: 'bob' },
            { $set: { status: 'inactive' } }
        );

        // Delete
        await users.deleteOne({ username: 'bob' });
    } catch (err) {
        console.error('MongoDB operation failed:', err.message);
    } finally {
        // Ensure the connection is closed even if an error occurs
        await client.close();
    }
}

run();
```

Indexing for performance

Indexes dramatically speed up queries at the cost of additional write overhead. MongoDB supports single-field, compound, text, geospatial, and **time-to-live** (TTL) indexes.

The following presents an index creation example:

```
const users = db.collection('users');
// Single-field index
await users.createIndex({ email: 1 }, { unique: true });
// Compound index
await users.createIndex({ status:1, createdAt:-1 });
// TTL index for automatic document expiration
await users.createIndex({ createdAt:1 }, { expireAfterSeconds:3600 });
```

Replication architecture

Replica Sets ensure high availability and data redundancy by maintaining multiple copies of data. A primary node handles writes; secondaries replicate operations and can become primary upon failure.

The following presents the Replica Set architecture:

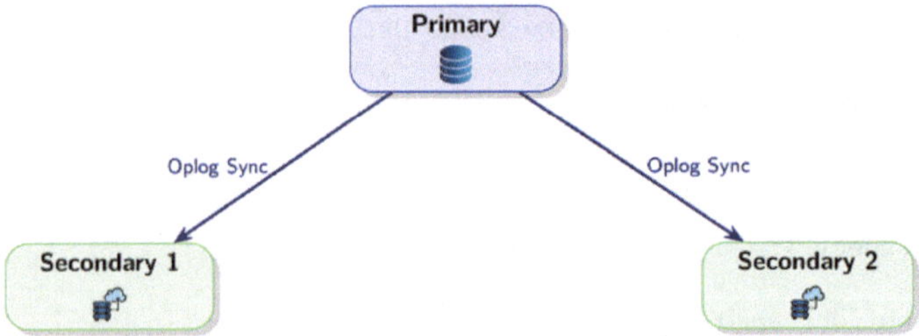

***Figure 11.2:** MongoDB Replica Set*

The primary node replicates data to secondaries via the oplog, ensuring redundancy and high availability, as shown in *Figure 11.2*.

Sharding for scale

Sharding partitions data across shards by a shard key, supporting massive horizontal scale. A config server tracks metadata; mongos routers direct queries.

The following figure presents a sharded cluster overview:

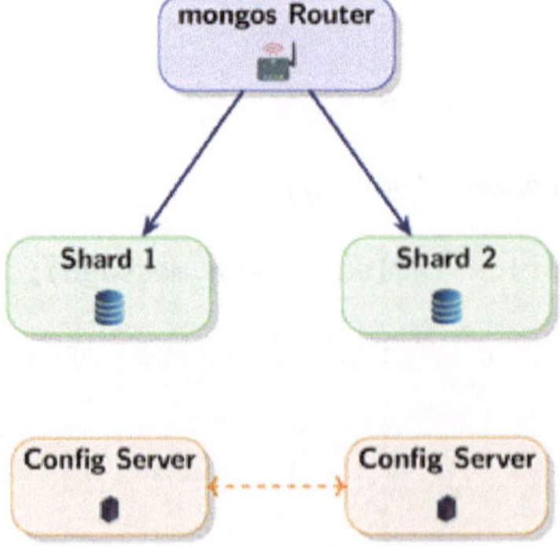

***Figure 11.3:** MongoDB sharded cluster*

Mongos routers direct queries to shards, while config servers store cluster metadata and synchronize configuration, as illustrated in the preceding figure.

Aggregation framework

MongoDB's aggregation pipeline processes data through stages, **$match**, **$group**, **$project**, **$sort**, etc., enabling complex data transformations server-side.

The following demonstrates an aggregation example:

```
db.orders.aggregate([
  { $match: { status:'shipped' } },
  { $group: {
      _id: '$customerId',
      totalSpent: {
      $sum:'$amount' }, count:
      { $sum:1 }
    }
  },
  { $sort: { totalSpent:-1 } },
  { $limit: 5 }
]);
```

Backup and monitoring

MongoDB provides **mongodump/mongorestore** for backups and cloud manager or Ops manager for monitoring, alerting, and automation of operational tasks.

The following sections explores the use cases where MongoDB suits content management, real-time analytics, mobile backends, and IoT, where schema flexibility, distributed data, and rapid development are paramount.

PostgreSQL overview

PostgreSQL is a powerful, open-source relational database celebrated for its standards compliance, extensibility, and rich feature set. It supports advanced data types, robust transaction guarantees, and a modular architecture that allows custom extensions. Commonly used in enterprise and analytics workloads, PostgreSQL balances performance with data integrity.

The following list presents core PostgreSQL features:

- **ACID transactions**: Full support for atomic, consistent, isolated, durable operations.
- **Advanced types**: Built-in JSON/JSONB, arrays, hstore, UUID, and geometric types.
- **Indexing**: B-tree, hash, GIN, GiST, BRIN indexes for varied query patterns.
- **Extensibility**: Custom functions, operators, procedural languages (PL/pgSQL, PL/Python).
- **Replication**: Streaming replication and logical replication for high availability.
- **Security**: Row-level security, SSL/TLS encryption, and robust authentication methods.

Defining tables

Relational structure in PostgreSQL relies on tables with columns, types, and constraints. Proper schema design enforces data quality and query performance.

The following presents a user table example:

```
CREATE TABLE users (
  id SERIAL PRIMARY KEY,
  name VARCHAR(100) NOT NULL,
  email VARCHAR(255) UNIQUE NOT NULL,
  status VARCHAR(20) DEFAULT 'active',
  created_at TIMESTAMP WITH TIME ZONE DEFAULT now()
);
```

Advanced data types

PostgreSQL's type system supports complex and flexible data representations, enabling JSON document storage alongside traditional columns.

The following presents JSON and array usage:

```
-- JSONB column for profile details
ALTER TABLE users
  ADD COLUMN profile JSONB;

-- Array column for user roles
ALTER TABLE users
  ADD COLUMN roles TEXT[] DEFAULT ARRAY['user'];

-- Insert sample data
INSERT INTO users (name,email,profile,roles)
VALUES (
  'Alice', 'alice@example.com', '{"age":30,"city":"London"}', ARRAY['admin','editor']
);
```

Index strategies

Indexes accelerate lookups but add write overhead. PostgreSQL offers multiple index types to optimize different query patterns.

The following presents index examples:

```
-- B-tree on email for fast equality lookups
CREATE INDEX idx_users_email ON users(email);

-- GIN index on JSONB for key existence
CREATE INDEX idx_users_profile ON users USING GIN (profile);

-- BRIN index on created_at for large time-series
CREATE INDEX idx_users_created_at ON users USING BRIN (created_at);
```

Querying JSON data

PostgreSQL allows filtering and extracting JSON fields using operators and functions in SQL queries.

The following presents a JSON query example:

```
SELECT name, profile->>'city' AS city
  FROM users
 WHERE profile->>'age' > '25';
```

Transactions and concurrency

PostgreSQL uses **multi-version concurrency control** (MVCC) to provide consistent snapshots and reduce locking.

The following presents a transactional example:

```
BEGIN;
  UPDATE users SET status='inactive' WHERE created_at < now() - INTERVAL '1 year';
  DELETE FROM sessions WHERE user_id NOT IN (SELECT id FROM users);
COMMIT;
```

Replication setup

High availability is achieved via streaming replication. A primary sends **write ahead log** (WAL) to replicas for failover.

The following presents the replication topology:

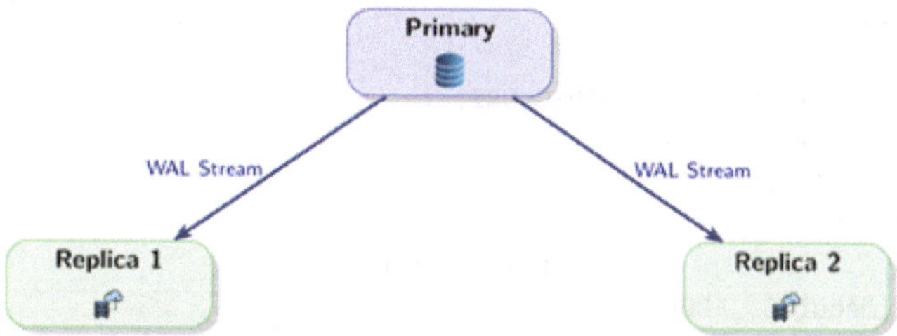

***Figure 11.4**: Streaming replication architecture*

The primary PostgreSQL server streams WAL changes to replicas for synchronous or asynchronous data redundancy, as illustrated in *Figure 11.4*.

Extensibility with extensions

PostgreSQL can be enhanced via extensions that add functions, types, or index methods without rebuilding the core database.

The following presents popular extensions:

- **`uuid-ossp`** for UUID generation.
- **`postgis`** for geospatial support.
- **`pgcrypto`** for cryptographic functions.
- **`timescaledb`** for time-series capabilities.

The following shows enabling PostGIS:

```
CREATE EXTENSION IF NOT EXISTS postgis;
```

Backup and monitoring

Regular backups and performance monitoring are critical. Tools like **`pg_dump`**, **`pg_restore`**, and **`pg_stat_statements`** helps maintain health and recoverability.

The following presents a backup command:

```
pg_dump -U dbuser -h localhost -F c -b -v -f backup.dump mydatabase
```

The following section provides use cases where PostgreSQL is ideal for transactional applications, complex reporting, geospatial workloads, and any scenario requiring advanced SQL features and reliability.

Database integration with Node.js

Node.js enables seamless database integration with both SQL and NoSQL systems. In this section, we will explore how to use MongoDB with Mongoose and PostgreSQL with Sequelize. This integration is essential for building real-world backend applications that persist and retrieve data efficiently.

Connecting with Mongoose

Mongoose provides a promise-based API to manage MongoDB connections, handle connection events, and apply global options. Properly establishing the connection ensures your application can retry on failure and close connections gracefully on shutdown.

The following presents the database connection setup:

```
const mongoose = require('mongoose');

async function connectDB() {
  try {
    await mongoose.connect(process.env.MONGO_URI, {
      useNewUrlParser: true,
      useUnifiedTopology: true,
      // Optional settings
      autoIndex: false,                // Disable in production
      serverSelectionTimeoutMS: 5000
    });
    console.log('✓ MongoDB connected');
  } catch (err) {
    console.error('MongoDB connection error:', err.message); process.
    exit(1);
  }
}

module.exports = connectDB;
```

The following demonstrates using the connection in Express:

```
const express = require('express');
const connectDB = require('./db');

const app = express(); app.
use(express.json());

connectDB();

app.get('/', (req, res) => {
  res.send('API is running');
});

const PORT = process.env.PORT
|| 3000; app.listen(PORT, () =>
  console.log(`Server listening on port ${PORT}`)
);
```

Defining schemas and models

Schemas in Mongoose enforce document structure, apply validation, and define static or instance methods. Models compiled from schemas provide an interface for CRUD and query operations on a specific collection.

The following presents a user schema definition:

```
const mongoose = require('mongoose');

const UserSchema = new mongoose.Schema({
  name: { type: String, required: true, trim: true }, email: {
    type: String,
    required: true, unique: true, lowercase: true,
    match: /^\S+@\S+\.\S+$/
  },
  status: {
    type: String,
    enum: ['active','inactive','pending'],
    default: 'pending'
  },
  createdAt: { type: Date, default: Date.now }
}, {
  timestamps: true // adds createdAt and updatedAt
});

// Instance method example
UserSchema.methods.isActive = function() {
  return this.status === 'active';
};

// Static method example
UserSchema.statics.findByStatus = function(status) {
  return this.find({ status });
};

module.exports = mongoose.model('User', UserSchema);
```

Basic CRUD operations

CRUD operations form the backbone of data handling. Mongoose models expose methods for creating, reading, updating, and deleting documents, returning promises that can be awaited.

The following presents CRUD examples:

```
// Create user
const user = await User.create({ name:'Bob', email:'bob@example.com' });
// Read users
const allUsers = await User.find();
const activeUsers = await User.find({ status:'active' });

// Update user
const updated = await User.findByIdAndUpdate(
  user._id,
```

```
  { status:'active' },
  { new:true, runValidators:true }
);

// Delete user
await User.findByIdAndDelete(user._id);
```

Advanced queries

Mongoose supports query chaining, pagination, projection, sorting, and population for relationships. These features enable efficient data retrieval and complex filters.

The following demonstrates pagination and sorting:

```
// Pagination parameters
const page = parseInt(req.query.page) || 1;
const limit = parseInt(req.query.limit) || 10;

// Query with skip, limit, sort and projection
const users = await User.find({ status:'active' })
  .sort({ createdAt:-1 })
  .skip((page-1)*limit)
  .limit(limit)
  .select('name email status');
```

Aggregation and indexing

Aggregation pipelines allow server-side data transformations (filter, group, project). Indexes improve performance; define them in schemas or create them manually.

The following presents an aggregation example:

```
const stats = await User.aggregate([
{ $match: { status:'active' } },
  { $group: {
      _id: '$status', count: { $sum:1 }
    }
  },
  { $project: {
      _id:0, status:'$_id', total:'$count'
    }
}
]
)
;
```

The following presents index creation in the schema:

```
UserSchema.index({ email:1 }); UserSchema.index({ status:1, createdAt:-1 });
```

The following presents manual index creation:

```
await User.collection.createIndex(
  { status:1 },
  { name:'idx_status', background:true }
);
```

CRUD with Mongoose

Mongoose models expose a rich set of methods to perform CRUD operations on MongoDB documents. Proper use of these methods with async/await and error handling ensures reliable data persistence and validation in your Node.js application.

The following examples demonstrate how Mongoose facilitates essential CRUD operations within a Node.js application, providing schema validation, query helpers, and robust error handling for reliable interaction with MongoDB collections:

- **Create document**: To insert a new document, use `Model.create()` or instantiate and `save()`. Mongoose applies schema validations before writing to the database.
    - The following demonstrates document creation:

```
app.post('/users', async (req, res) => {
  try {
    const user = await User.create(req.body); res.status(201).json(user);
  } catch (err) {
    res.status(400).json({ error: err.message });
}
}
)
;
```

- **Read documents**: Reading data involves `find()` for multiple documents or `findById()` for a single record. You can chain query helpers for filtering, sorting, and projection.
    - The following demonstrates fetching documents:

```
// Fetch all users
app.get('/users', async (req, res) => {
  try {
    const users = await User.find().
    sort({ createdAt: -1 }); res.
    json(users);
  } catch (err) {
    res.status(500).json({ error: err.message });
}
}
)
;

// Fetch one user by ID
app.get('/users/:id', async (req, res) => {
  try {
    const user = await User.findById(req.params.id);
    if (!user) return res.status(404).json({ error: 'Not found' }); res.
    json(user);
  } catch (err) {
    res.status(500).json({ error: err.message });
}
)
;
```

Update Document

Updating uses **findByIdAndUpdate()** or **save()** on a fetched document. Always enable **runValidators** and request the updated document with **new:true**. Following demonstrates updating a document

```
app.put('/users/:id', async (req, res) => {
  try {
    const updated = await User.
      findByIdAndUpdate( req.params.id,
      req.body,
      { new: true, runValidators: true }
    );
    if (!updated) return res.status(404).json({ error: 'Not found' }); res.
    json(updated);
  } catch (err) {
    res.status(400).json({ error: err.message });
}
}
)
;
```

- **Delete document**: Removing documents can be done with **findByIdAndDelete()** or **deleteOne()**. Verify existence before deletion to handle not-found cases.
  - The following demonstrates document deletion:

```
app.delete('/users/:id', async (req, res) => {
  try {
    const deleted = await User.findByIdAndDelete(req.params.id);
    if (!deleted) return res.status(404).json({ error: 'Not found' }); res.json({
    message: 'Deleted successfully' });
  } catch (err) {
    res.status(500).json({ error: err.message });
}
}
)
;
```

Some key methods are as follows:

- **create()** and **save()** for insertion with schema validation.
- **find()**, **findById()**, and query chaining for flexible retrieval.
- **findByIdAndUpdate()** with **new:true** and **runValidators** for in-place updates.
- **findByIdAndDelete()** or **deleteOne()** for removal, handling missing documents.
- All operations return Promises; use async/await with try/catch for clean error handling.

PostgreSQL with Sequelize

Sequelize is an **object-relational mapping** (**ORM**) that maps JavaScript objects to PostgreSQL tables, simplifying database interactions. It handles model definitions, associations, querying, and migrations, enabling clean, maintainable code in Node.js applications.

Configuring Sequelize

Before defining models, Sequelize must connect to a PostgreSQL database. This setup handles authentication, pooling, and dialect-specific options.

The following demonstrates connection setup:

```
const { Sequelize } = require('sequelize');

const sequelize = new
  Sequelize( process.env.
  DB_NAME, process.env.DB_USER,
  process.env.DB_PASS,
  {
    host: process.env.DB_HOST, dialect: 'postgres',
    logging: false,              // Disable SQL logging
    pool: { max: 10, min: 0 } // Connection pool settings
}
)
;

(async () => {
  try {
    await sequelize.authenticate();
    console.log('PostgreSQL connected');
  } catch (err) {
    console.error('Connection error:', err); process.exit(1);
  }
})();

module.exports = sequelize;
```

Defining models

Models in Sequelize represent tables. Each model maps fields to columns and supports validations, default values, and hooks.

The following demonstrates a **User** model:

```
const { DataTypes } = require('sequelize');
const sequelize = require('./db');

const User = sequelize.define('User', { username: {
    type: DataTypes.STRING, allowNull: false, unique: true,
    validate: { len: [3, 30] }
  },
  email: {
    type: DataTypes.STRING, allowNull: false, unique: true,
    validate: { isEmail: true }
}
}
,
{
  timestamps: true,              // adds createdAt and updatedAt
  tableName: 'users'
}
)
```

```
;

module.exports = User;
```

Model associations

Defining relationships lets Sequelize generate joins and eager loading. Common patterns include one-to-many and many-to-many.

The following demonstrates a one-to-many association:

```
const Task = sequelize.define('Task', {
  title: { type: DataTypes.STRING, allowNull: false }, completed: { type: DataTypes.BOOLEAN,
  defaultValue: false }
});

User.hasMany(Task, { foreignKey: 'userId', onDelete: 'CASCADE' }); Task.belongsTo(User, {
foreignKey: 'userId' });
```

The following figure demonstrates the relationship between the user and task:

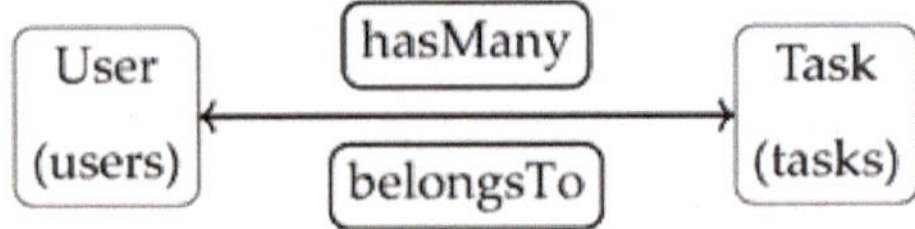

Figure 11.5: One-to-many between user and task

CRUD operations

Sequelize provides promise-based methods for CRUD. Proper error handling ensures robust APIs.

The following demonstrates basic CRUD:

```
// Create
await User.create({ username: 'alice', email: 'alice@example.com' });

// Read
const allUsers = await User.findAll();
const singleUser = await User.findByPk(1);

// Update
await User.update(
  { email: 'new@mail.com' },
  { where: { id: 1 } }
);

// Delete
await User.destroy({ where: { id: 1 } });
```

Managing transactions

Transactions group multiple operations into an atomic unit, ensuring all succeed or none apply. Sequelize's transaction API supports managed and unmanaged patterns.

The following demonstrates a managed transaction:

```
const result = await sequelize.transaction(async (t) => {
  const user = await User.create({ username: 'bob' }, { transaction: t });
  await Task.create(
    { title: 'Initial Task', userId: user.id },
    { transaction: t }
  );
  return user;
});
```

The following list summarizes key concepts:

- Use **`authenticate()`** to test the connection.
- Define models with fields, validations, and options.
- Establish associations before syncing with **`sync()`**.
- Perform CRUD via built-in methods returning Promises.
- Wrap multi-step operations in transactions for atomicity.

Indexing and query optimization

Indexing is a critical technique that accelerates data retrieval by creating auxiliary data structures. These structures, commonly B-trees or hash maps, allow the database engine to locate rows matching query predicates without scanning entire tables or collections. Proper indexing dramatically improves performance for large datasets, but over-indexing can increase storage needs and slow write operations.

The following presents key indexing concepts and examples:

- **Single-column indexes** optimize queries filtering on one field.
- **Compound indexes** support queries on multiple fields in a specified order.
- **Unique indexes** enforce uniqueness constraints (e.g., unique email per user).
- **Full-text indexes** enable text search capabilities.

The following demonstrates creating indexes in SQL and NoSQL:

```
-- PostgreSQL: single-column and compound indexes
CREATE INDEX idx_users_email ON users(email);
CREATE INDEX idx_users_status_created ON users(status, created_at);

// MongoDB: single-field and compound indexes db.users.
createIndex({ email: 1 });                              //
ascending db.users.createIndex({ status: 1, createdAt: -1
}); // compound
```

Overuse of indexes can degrade write performance, so index only columns frequently used in **`WHERE`**, **`JOIN`**, **`SORT`**, or **`GROUP BY`** clauses.

Transactions and consistency

Transactions group multiple operations into a single unit that either fully succeeds or fully rolls back, preserving database integrity. They follow the ACID properties—atomicity, consistency, isolation, durability—which ensure reliable behavior under concurrent access and failures.

The following summarizes ACID properties:

- **Atomicity**: All-or-nothing execution.

- **Consistency**: Database moves from one valid state to another.
- **Isolation**: Concurrent transactions do not interfere.
- **Durability**: Committed changes persist despite crashes.

The following presents a PostgreSQL transaction example:

```
BEGIN;
UPDATE accounts SET balance = balance - 100 WHERE
id = 1; UPDATE accounts SET balance = balance + 100
WHERE id = 2; COMMIT;
```

The following shows a Sequelize managed transaction:

```
const result = await sequelize.transaction(async (t) => {
  const user = await User.create({ name: 'Bob' }, { transaction: t });
  await Task.create({ title: 'New Task', userId: user.id }, { transaction: t });
  return user;
});
```

Use **ROLLBACK** in SQL or rollback methods in ORMs to revert on errors.

Security best practices

Securing database systems involves enforcing strong authentication, encrypting data, and minimizing exposure to injection attacks. Adhering to best practices prevents unauthorized access and data breaches and maintains compliance.

The following presents core security measures:

- **Least privilege**: Grant applications only the minimum database permissions needed.
- **Encrypted connections**: Use **Secure Sockets Layer/Transport Layer Security** (**SSL/TLS**) for all client-server communications.
- **Data encryption**: Encrypt sensitive columns at rest (e.g., using PostgreSQL's **pgcrypto**).
- **Input sanitization**: Validate and sanitize inputs to prevent SQL/NoSQL injection.
- **Prepared statements**: Always use parameterized queries or ORM methods.
- **Regular patching**: Keep database engines and drivers up to date.
- **Monitoring and auditing**: Log access and changes; review regularly.

The following demonstrates a parameterized query in Sequelize:

```
const user = await User.findOne({
  where: { username: req.body.username }
});
```

The following shows enabling SSL in a PostgreSQL connection:

```
const sequelize = new Sequelize('db', 'user', 'pass',
  { host: 'db.host.com',
  dialect: 'postgres', dialectOptions: {
    ssl: { require: true, rejectUnauthorized: false }
}
}
)
;
```

The following table demonstrates isolation levels and effects:

Level	Behavior
Read Uncommitted	Dirty reads allowed.
Read Committed	Prevents dirty reads.
Repeatable Read	Prevents non-repeatable reads.
Serializable	Fully isolated, highest consistency.

***Table 11.4:** Transaction isolation levels*

Adopt these practices to build secure, reliable, and performant database-backed applications.

Building a data-driven application

This hands-on project guides you through building a complete backend application for student course registration. You will initialize a Node.js and Express.js server, connect to PostgreSQL via Sequelize, define models and relations, implement CRUD APIs, add JWT authentication, test endpoints, and prepare for deployment. Each step is explained in detail with examples.

Requirements overview

The following presents project goals and features:

- Student signup, login, and JWT issuance.
- Course creation, listing, updating, and deletion.
- Enrollment of students in courses via a many-to-many relation.
- Protected routes for authenticated access.
- API testing with Postman or Thunder Client.

Aim: Create a Node.js and Express.js application with PostgreSQL as the backend to manage students and course registrations. The application should support user authentication, course CRUD operations, and enrollment functionality.

The tools and technologies required are as follows:

- Node.js and Express.js
- PostgreSQL with Sequelize ORM
- JWT for authentication
- dotenv for environment configuration
- Postman for API testing

Key features are as follows:

- Student registration and login.
- Add, edit, and delete courses.
- Enroll students in courses.
- View all students and their enrollments.
- Secure access with JWT-based protected routes.

Backend setup and database connection

Before building the application logic, it is essential to set up the backend environment and establish a connection to the database. This ensures that the server can handle API requests, authenticate users, and perform data operations reliably. The following steps outline how to initialize the backend project, configure environment variables, and connect a PostgreSQL database using Express and Sequelize ORM:

1. **Initialize the project**: Begin by creating a new Node.js project folder and installing the required dependencies for backend development. These include Express for server setup, Sequelize as the ORM, **pg** and **pg-hstore** for PostgreSQL integration, **jsonwebtoken** and **bcrypt** for authentication, **dotenv** for environment configuration, and CORS for secure cross-origin communication:

```
mkdir student-registration-api cd student-registration-api npm init -y
npm install express sequelize pg pg-hstore jsonwebtoken bcrypt dotenv cors
```

2. **Configure the environment**: Create a **.env** file: Store sensitive information such as database credentials, port numbers, and secret keys in an **.env** file. This keeps the configuration secure and separate from the source code:

```
PORT=3000
DB_NAME=registration_db
DB_USER=postgres
DB_PASS=yourpassword
DB_HOST=localhost
JWT_SECRET=supersecretkey
```

3. **Create Sequelize config and connect database**: The following code sets up Sequelize to manage the PostgreSQL connection using the environment variables defined earlier. The **config/database.js** file initializes a Sequelize instance that handles all communication with the database:

```
// config/database.js
const { Sequelize } = require('sequelize');require('dotenv').config();

const sequelize = new Sequelize( process.env.DB_NAME, process.env.DB_USER, process.env.
  DB_PASS,
  {
    host: process.env.DB_HOST, dialect: 'postgres',
  }
);

module.exports = sequelize;
```

4. **Test database connection**: Once the configuration is complete, test the connection to ensure that the backend can communicate with the database successfully. The following code snippet uses Sequelize's **authenticate()** method to verify connectivity and log the result to the console:

```
// test-db.js
const sequelize = require('./config/database');

sequelize.authenticate()
  .then(() => console.log('Database connected successfully!'))
  .catch((err) => console.error('Database connection failed:', err));
```

API development and CRUD logic

This section describes how to implement the core API routes and business logic for managing students and courses, including CRUD functionality using Express.js and Sequelize.

Let us begin by defining Sequelize models. After successfully connecting the backend to the database, the next step is to define Sequelize models. Models in Sequelize act as blueprints for database tables—each model corresponds to a specific table, and each model property maps to a table column. By defining models, the application can perform structured CRUD operations while maintaining consistency and validation rules across the database.

In this step, model definitions specify data types, constraints, and relationships among entities. For example, a Student model can define fields like name, email, and course, while Sequelize automatically handles table creation, validations, and associations with other models.

The following code demonstrates how to define a simple model in Sequelize that represents a student registration table in PostgreSQL.

First step is to define Sequelize model:

```
// models/Student.js
const { DataTypes } = require('sequelize');
const sequelize = require('../config/database');

const Student = sequelize.define('Student', { name: {
        type: DataTypes.STRING, allowNull: false
    },
    email: {
        type: DataTypes.STRING, unique: true, allowNull: false
    },
    password: {
        type: DataTypes.STRING, allowNull: false
    }
});

module.exports = Student;

// models/Course.js
const { DataTypes } = require('sequelize');
const sequelize = require('../config/database');

const Course = sequelize.define('Course', {
    title: {
        type: DataTypes.STRING, allowNull: false
    },
    description: {
        type: DataTypes.TEXT, allowNull: true
    }
});
```

The following is the continuation of the code:

```
module.exports = Course;

// models/Enrollment.js
const { DataTypes } = require('sequelize'); const sequelize = require('../config/database'); const
Student = require('./Student');
const Course = require('./Course');

const Enrollment = sequelize.define('Enrollment', {});

Student.belongsToMany(Course, { through: Enrollment }); Course.belongsToMany(Student, { through:
Enrollment });

module.exports = Enrollment;
```

Sync database and create tables

Once the Sequelize models are defined, the next crucial step is to synchronize them with the database. Synchronization ensures that Sequelize creates the necessary tables and columns in the PostgreSQL database according to the model definitions. This process establishes the actual database structure that your backend application will use to store and retrieve data.

Sequelize provides a convenient **sync()** method to automatically generate or update tables based on your model schema. It reads the model definitions and translates them into appropriate SQL commands for table creation, constraints, and indexes. Refer to the following code:

```
// sync.js
const sequelize = require('./config/
database'); const Student = require('./
models/Student'); const Course =
require('./models/Course');
const Enrollment = require('./models/Enrollment');

// ⚠ note:
// Use force: true ONLY in development because it drops and recreates tables (data loss).
// In production, avoid force.
// Prefer migrations (sequelize-cli) or use sync({ alter: true }) carefully.
sequelize.sync({ force: true })
    .then(() => console.log('Database & tables created!'))
    .catch(err => console.error(err));
```

Build API routes

After defining models and synchronizing the database, the next step is to build API routes to allow communication between the frontend and backend. These routes define how the application handles HTTP requests such as creating, reading, updating, or deleting records. In this case, the API will manage student registration data by exposing endpoints that interact with the Student model through Express.js routes.

Each route corresponds to a specific operation and ensures that data is correctly validated, processed, and returned as JSON responses. Express provides a simple and modular way to organize these routes in separate files, making the backend easier to maintain and scale. The details are as follows:

- **Create student router**: To organize backend logic efficiently, define a dedicated router that manages all student-related API endpoints. This router handles HTTP POST requests to add new student records and GET requests to retrieve existing records from the database. The following code demonstrates how to implement these routes using Express.js and the previously defined student model:

```
// routes/students.js
const express = require('express');
const router = express.Router();
const Student = require('../models/Student');

router.post('/', async (req, res) => {
    try {
        const student = await Student.create(req.body); res.status(201).json(student);
    } catch (error) {
        res.status(400).json({ error: error.message });
    }
});
```

```
router.get('/', async (req, res) => {
    const students = await Student.findAll(); res.json(students);
});

module.exports = router;
```

- **Create course router**: To manage operations related to courses, define a separate router that handles all course-specific API endpoints. This modular structure keeps the backend organized and makes it easier to maintain and expand later. The course router allows adding new courses through POST requests and retrieving all available courses using GET requests. The following code demonstrates how to implement these routes using Express.js and the defined Course model:

```
// routes/courses.js
const express = require('express');
const router = express.Router();
const Course = require('../models/Course');

router.post('/', async (req, res) => {
    try {
        const course = await Course.create(req.body);
        res.status(201).json(course);
    } catch (error) {
        res.status(400).json({ error: error.message });
    }
});

router.get('/', async (req, res) => {
    const courses = await Course.
    findAll(); res.json(courses);
});

module.exports = router;
```

Register API routes in the main app

Register the API routes for all the routes in the main application using the following code:

```
// app.js
const express = require('express');
const cors = require('cors');
require('dotenv').config();

const sequelize = require('./config/database');
const studentRoutes = require('./routes/students');
const courseRoutes = require('./routes/courses');

const app = express();

// Middleware
app.use(cors());
app.use(express.json());

// Routes
```

```
app.use('/api/students', studentRoutes);
app.use('/api/courses', courseRoutes);

const PORT = process.env.PORT || 3000;

// Start server only after DB sync
sequelize.sync()
    .then(() => {
        app.listen(PORT, () => {
            console.log(`Server running on port ${PORT}`);
        });
    })
    .catch((err) => {
        console.error('Database sync failed:', err);
    });
```

With this setup, the server supports basic CRUD operations for both students and courses. In the next section, user authentication and protected routes will be implemented.

Authentication and protected routes

To ensure secure access to the API, this section implements user authentication using JWT. It allows only authenticated users to perform sensitive operations such as creating, updating, or deleting resources.

The given list outlines the process of implementing authentication and securing API routes in the backend application. Authentication ensures that only verified users can access or modify sensitive data, preventing unauthorized operations. By integrating JWT for session handling and bcrypt for password encryption, the system provides both confidentiality and integrity in user management. The sequence explains how to install the necessary packages, hash passwords, create login routes, and protect critical API endpoints using middleware authentication:

- **Install required packages**: Install the necessary packages for password hashing and JWT handling:

  ```
  npm install bcryptjs jsonwebtoken
  ```

- **Update the student model for hashing password**: Use a Sequelize hook to hash the user's password before saving it to the database:

  ```
  // models/Student.js
  const bcrypt = require('bcryptjs');

  // Add hook inside model definition
  Student.beforeCreate(async (student) => {
       const salt = await bcrypt.genSalt(10);
       student.password = await bcrypt.hash(student.password, salt);
  });
  ```

- **Create authentication controller**: Create a new route for user login and JWT generation:

  ```
  // routes/auth.js
  const express = require('express'); const jwt = require('jsonwebtoken'); const bcrypt =
  require('bcryptjs');
  const Student = require('../models/Student');

  const router = express.Router();

  // Login route
  router.post('/login', async (req, res) => { const { email, password } = req.body; try {
            const user = await Student.findOne({ where: { email } });
  ```

```
        if (!user) return res.status(400).json({ error: 'Invalid credentials' });

        const isMatch = await bcrypt.compare(password, user.password);
        if (!isMatch) return res.status(400).json({ error: 'Invalid credentials' });

        const token = jwt.sign({ id: user.id }, process.env.JWT_SECRET, { expiresIn: '1h'
        }); res.json({ token });
    } catch (err) {
        res.status(500).json({ error: 'Server error' });
    }
});

module.exports = router;
```

- **Create middleware to protect routes**: Create middleware to validate the JWT token in protected routes:

```
// middleware/auth.js
const jwt = require('jsonwebtoken');

const authenticate = (req, res, next) => {
    const token = req.header('Authorization');
    if (!token) return res.status(401).json({ error: 'No token provided' });
    try {
        const decoded = jwt.verify(token, process.env.JWT_
        SECRET); req.user = decoded;
        next();
    } catch (err) {
        res.status(401).json({ error: 'Invalid token' });
    }
};

module.exports = authenticate;
```

- **Protect sensitive API routes**: Apply the middleware to sensitive operations such as creating a student or course:

```
// routes/students.js
const authenticate = require('../middleware/auth');

router.post('/', authenticate, async (req, res) => {
    try {
        const student = await Student.
        create(req.body); res.status(201).
        json(student);
    } catch (error) {
        res.status(400).json({ error: error.message });
    }
});

// app.js
const authRoutes = require('./routes/auth');
app.use('/api/auth', authRoutes);
```

- **Test authentication flow**: Use tools like Postman or curl to test:
  - Create a new student (user).
  - Log in using the credentials.
  - Use the JWT token in the Authorization header (e.g., `Bearer <token>`) to access protected routes.

With this authentication layer, the application is now secure against unauthorized access and can maintain user-specific sessions across protected endpoints.

Deployment and testing

Once the API server has been implemented and authentication has been secured, the final steps include thorough testing and deploying the application to a production environment. This section provides best practices and steps for deployment and testing.

Local testing

Use tools like Postman, Insomnia, or curl to test the API endpoints:

- Ensure that all CRUD operations work correctly for students and courses.
- Validate the authentication mechanism using JWT.
- Test protected routes by including the JWT token in the request headers:

```
curl -X GET http://localhost:3000/api/students \
-H "Authorization: Bearer <JWT_TOKEN>"
```

Environment configuration

Ensure all environment variables are stored securely in a `.env` file. Common variables include:

```
PORT=3000
DATABASE_URL=postgres://username:password@host:port/
dbname JWT_SECRET=your_jwt_secret
```

Use the `dotenv` package to load environment variables:

```
require('dotenv').config();
```

Production deployment options

Several platforms support Node.js deployments. Some popular options include:

- **Render**: Offers simple deployments and PostgreSQL integration.
- **Railway**: Developer-friendly and great for hosting Node.js and PostgreSQL apps.
- **Heroku**: Easy deployment with **command line interface** (**CLI**) and PostgreSQL support.
- **Vercel/Netlify**: Primarily for frontend, but supports backend functions via serverless APIs.
- **Docker**: For containerizing and deploying anywhere (cloud or local server).

Deployment on Render is as follows:

1. Push your code to a Git repository (GitHub or GitLab).
2. Create a new Web Service on Render.
3. Link the repository and set the environment variables under the **Environment** tab.
4. Define build and start commands:
   - **Build command**: `npm install`

- **Start command:** `node app.js`

5. Deploy and verify the public endpoint.

Testing in production

After deployment, test all endpoints via public URLs. Use tools like:

- Postman for manual testing.
- Jest or Mocha/Chai for writing unit and integration tests.
- Swagger UI or Postman Docs to generate API documentation.

Monitoring and logging

Set up basic monitoring and logging:

- Use `morgan` for HTTP logging in Express.
- Add logging libraries like `winston` for more advanced logging.
- Enable application performance monitoring with tools like LogRocket, New Relic, or Datadog.

The final checklist is as follows:

- All environment variables are secured.
- Production database is configured and separated from development.
- CORS policies are appropriately defined.
- Sensitive routes are protected.
- All API routes are tested.

This completes the hands-on project of building and deploying a secure, scalable, and data-driven API server using Node.js, Express, PostgreSQL, and Sequelize.

Conclusion

In this chapter, we surveyed the landscape of SQL and NoSQL databases, understanding their respective strengths: SQL's robust ACID guarantees, complex joins, and mature tooling versus NoSQL's flexible schemas, horizontal scalability, and specialized data models. We then demonstrated how to integrate these databases with Node.js, using Mongoose for MongoDB and Sequelize for PostgreSQL, establishing connections, defining schemas/models, and executing CRUD operations. Advanced topics such as indexing strategies, transaction handling, and security best practices equipped you to build performant and resilient backends. The hands-on project guided you through designing a student course registration system with JWT-based authentication and many-to-many enrollments. Finally, exercises and the polyglot persistence case study illustrated how to leverage multiple database technologies within a single application to optimize different workloads.

In the next chapter, we shift focus from data storage to data exchange and user interaction. You will explore JSON and AJAX for asynchronous client-server communication, learn to consume and secure third-party APIs, master Git and GitHub for collaborative development, and deploy applications on modern cloud platforms. Security considerations, such as **Cross-Site Scripting** (**XSS**), **Cross-Site Request Forgery** (**CSRF**), and API protection, will be integrated throughout, preparing you to develop comprehensive, end-to-end web services.

Exercises

1. Contrast SQL and NoSQL for three applications: banking ledger, social media feed, and IoT telemetry. For each, pick one primary database family, justify the choice in 5–6 sentences, and list key risks or tradeoffs.

2. Design a PostgreSQL schema for Student, Course, and Enrollment (many-to-many). Enforce a unique student email, a course capacity, and a UNIQUE(student_id, course_id). Provide complete CREATE TABLE statements with keys, types, and CHECK constraints.
3. Write SQL to: (a) list all students enrolled in 'CS101' using joins, (b) count enrollments per course ordered by count (desc), and (c) return courses with zero enrollments.
4. Model the same domain in MongoDB with two designs: embedded enrollments in student documents vs. separate collections (students, courses, enrollments). For the separate-collection design, write one aggregation pipeline that returns each student's total enrolled courses.
5. Pick indexes for common queries: Lookup by student email, list courses sorted by created_at, and fetch enrollment by (student_id, course_id). Write exact PostgreSQL CREATE INDEX commands and MongoDB createIndex calls. Justify each index in one sentence.
6. Explain Read Committed vs. Repeatable Read with a short enrollment scenario. Then write a two-session PostgreSQL demo that shows a non-repeatable read at Read Committed but not at Repeatable Read.
7. Define a Mongoose Student model { name, email, passwordHash, status } with validations (email pattern, status ∈ {active,inactive,pending}), unique index on email, timestamps, an instance method isActive(), and a static findByStatus(status).
8. Define Sequelize models Student, Course, Enrollment with belongsToMany associations (through Enrollment). Show association code and call sync({ alter: true }). Explain what alter does.
9. Connect one Express server to both MongoDB (Mongoose) and PostgreSQL (Sequelize). Expose GET / health/ dbs that returns JSON reporting each connection's status.
10. Implement enroll(studentId, courseId) in Sequelize using a managed transaction: check capacity, insert Enrollment, increment a course.enrolled counter, and rollback on overflow. Provide complete function code.
11. Using Mongoose transactions, insert a student profile and an audit log atomically. Show startSession(), withTransaction(async session => {...}), and proper cleanup.
12. Show parameterized queries in Sequelize (e.g., findOne({ where: { email } })) and input sanitization in Mongoose. Add production SSL/TLS options for both connections (Sequelize dialectOptions.ssl, MongoDB TLS).
13. Write backup and restore commands for PostgreSQL (pg_dump / pg_restore) and MongoDB (mongodump/ mongorestore). Then write a Sequelize migration that adds a capacity INT CHECK (capacity >= 0) column to Course, and the CLI commands to run it.
14. Run EXPLAIN ANALYZE on the count enrollments per course query. Paste a sample plan and point out two issues (e.g., seq scan, missing index). Propose specific index or query changes.
15. Write two Jest + Supertest tests for /api/courses: GET returns 200 and an array; POST with valid body returns 201 and echoes fields. Add one unit test that mocks a Mongoose static findByStatus and asserts return handling.
16. Add express-validator to POST /students: Require non-empty name and valid email. On invalid input, return 400 with error details; on success, create via Sequelize and return 201. Include route code.
17. Propose a Redis cache for GET /courses with a 60-second TTL. Define key naming, GET/SET EX flow, and invalidation after POST/PUT/DELETE. Explain cache stampede avoidance briefly.
18. Add observability: Morgan for HTTP logs and winston for app logs. Log Sequelize queries over 300 ms with correlation IDs per request. Show minimal setup and one example slow-query log line.
19. Polyglot persistence case study: Keep relational data (students, courses, enrollments) in PostgreSQL; store activity logs and notifications in MongoDB. Describe ID mapping, idempotent keys for at-least-once delivery, and failure recovery steps.
20. Write a minimal Docker Compose file that starts Postgres, Mongo, and the Node API with environment variables, depends_on, and healthchecks. Provide the commands to build, run, view logs, and tear down the stack.

Chapter 12
Web Services and APIs

Introduction

In modern web development, the ability to exchange data asynchronously and integrate with external services is paramount for building responsive, feature-rich applications. This chapter begins by exploring JSON and AJAX, the foundational technologies that enable web pages to fetch and render data from servers without full-page reloads. We then examine techniques for consuming third-party **application programming interfaces** (**APIs**), ranging from simple REST endpoints to OAuth-protected services, using both browser-based tools like `fetch` and server-side libraries such as Axios and node-fetch. Next, we turn to version control and collaboration, introducing Git workflows, branching strategies, and pull requests on GitHub. With a stable codebase in place, we discuss deployment strategies for both frontend and backend applications, covering platforms like Vercel, Netlify, Render, and Heroku, as well as best practices for environment configuration and monitoring. Finally, we address web application security fundamentals, mitigating threats like XSS, CSRF, and injection attacks, and conclude with a hands-on project that ties together asynchronous data fetching, secure API usage, and cloud deployment.

Furthermore, **JavaScript Object Notation** (**JSON**) and **Asynchronous JavaScript and XML** (**AJAX**) remain essential today because most modern web communication still depends on the same core idea: exchange structured data over **Hypertext Transfer Protocol** (**HTTP**) without refreshing the page. JSON acts as the common data format across REST APIs, GraphQL responses, configuration files, and even messages sent through WebSockets or streaming endpoints. AJAX refers to the request pattern rather than a single tool, so it still applies when using fetch(), Axios, or any client that sends asynchronous HTTP calls. Newer approaches such as GraphQL and streaming often build on top of these fundamentals instead of replacing them, since they still rely on JSON-like payloads and asynchronous request handling. In many real applications, simple request–response calls remain the easiest and most reliable option for forms, dashboards, search, and partial page updates, while WebSockets or streaming get added only when true real-time behavior becomes necessary.

Structure

This chapter covers the following topics:

- JSON and AJAX
- Consuming third-party APIs
- Version control with Git and collaboration with GitHub
- Deployment strategies
- Web application security fundamentals
- Hands-on API integration and deployment
- Real-world API integration and security practices

Objectives

After completing this chapter, it becomes possible to structure and parse JSON data and implement AJAX requests that fetch and update content dynamically without reloading the page. The chapter explains how to integrate external services in both frontend and backend code using the Fetch API, Axios, or native Node.js modules, and how to select a suitable authentication method, such as API keys, OAuth 2.0 flows, or **JSON Web Tokens (JWT)**, for a third-party API. It also develops practical skills in Git and GitHub collaboration, including branching, pull requests, and issue management. In addition, the chapter covers deployment on common cloud platforms, secure environment configuration, and basic logging and uptime monitoring. Security concepts such as input validation, HTTPS, secure headers, and role-based access control are applied to reduce risks from XSS, CSRF, SQL injection, and related vulnerabilities, culminating in a hands-on project that brings these practices together in a production-ready workflow.

JSON and AJAX

JSON and AJAX together enable web pages to exchange data with servers asynchronously, updating parts of the **user interface (UI)** without full page reloads. JSON is a lightweight data-interchange format based on key–value pairs, while AJAX refers to the technique of using JavaScript (via **`fetch()`** or **`XMLHttpRequest`**) to send and receive data.

JSON structure

JSON represents data using objects and arrays. A JSON object stores key–value pairs, where each key must be a string enclosed in double quotes, and each value can be a string, number, Boolean, null, array, or another object. A JSON array stores an ordered list of values.

The following code demonstrates a typical JSON object structure:

```
{
  "name":       "Alice",
  "age":        25,
  "isStudent": false,
  "skills":     ["JavaScript", "HTML", "CSS"],
  "address": {
    "city": "New York",
    "zip": "10001"
  }
}
```

In this example:

- **`"name"`** is a string.
- **`"age"`** is a number.
- **`"isStudent"`** is a Boolean.
- **`"skills"`** is an array.
- **`"address"`** is a nested object.

Note: Unlike JavaScript objects, JSON does not allow unquoted keys, single-quoted strings, functions, or trailing commas.

AJAX requests

AJAX allows JavaScript to communicate with the server without reloading the page. Modern implementations use the Fetch API, while legacy systems may still use **`XMLHttpRequest`**. Both typically exchange data in JSON format.

Fetch API usage

The Fetch API provides a promise-based interface for HTTP requests. The following demonstrates basic Fetch usage to retrieve JSON data:

```
fetch('https://api.example.com/users')
    .then((response) => {
        if (!response.ok) {
            throw new Error(`HTTP ${response.status} ${response.statusText}`);
        }
        return response.json();
    })
    .then((data) => {
        console.log('User Data:', data);
        // Update DOM elements here
    })
    .catch((error) => {
        console.error('Fetch error:', error.message);
    });
```

Key points are as follows:

- **`fetch()`** returns a promise that resolves to a response.
- **`response.json()`** parses the body as JSON and returns a promise, because JSON parsing is asynchronous; use return **`response.json()`** inside **`.then()`** or await **`response.json()`** in async/await code.
- **`catch()`** handles network or parsing errors.

XHR usage

`XMLHttpRequest` (**XHR**) is the traditional API for AJAX requests.

The following demonstrates a basic XHR GET request:

```
var xhr = new XMLHttpRequest();
xhr.open("GET", "https://api.example.com/users", true); xhr.onreadystatechange = function () {
if (xhr.readyState === 4 && xhr.status === 200) { var data = JSON.parse(xhr.responseText);
console.log("User Data:", data);
}
};
xhr.send();
```

The following list provides notes:

- **`readyState === 4`** indicates the request is done.
- **`status === 200`** indicates a successful HTTP response.
- **`JSON.parse()`** converts the response text to an object.

Dynamic user loading

This example fetches and displays a list of users on page load without reloading the page, and the following demonstrates fetching and rendering the user list dynamically:

```
<!DOCTYPE html>
<html>
<head><title>AJAX Example</title></head>
<body>
  <h2>User List</h2>
```

```
  <ul id="userList"></ul>
  <script> fetch('https://jsonplaceholder.
    typicode.com/users')
      .then(res => res.json())
      .then(users => {
        const ul = document.getElementById('userList'); users.
        forEach(u => {
          const li = document.
          createElement('li'); li.textContent
          = `${u.name} - ${u.email}`;
          ul.appendChild(li);
        });
      })
      .catch(err => console.error('Error:', err));
  </script>
</body>
</html>
```

AJAX use cases

AJAX and JSON power many dynamic web features.

The following presents common use cases:

- Infinite scrolling to load additional content.
- Live search suggestions as the user types.
- Submitting forms and displaying results without reload.
- Periodic polling or WebSocket fallbacks for real-time dashboards.

Polling repeatedly sends requests at fixed intervals (for example, every 5–10 seconds) to check for updates. Polling is simple to implement and works everywhere, but it can waste bandwidth and server resources because many requests return no change, and it may feel less responsive between intervals. On the other hand, WebSockets keep a single long-lived connection open so the server can push updates instantly to the client. This gives near real-time responsiveness and reduces repeated request overhead, but it adds complexity because the connection must be managed (reconnects, timeouts, scaling, and authentication over a persistent channel). Polling suits occasional updates such as notifications or status checks, while WebSockets suit frequent, real-time updates such as chat, live dashboards, and multiplayer interactions.

Using the Fetch API, build a web page that retrieves and displays a list of posts from **https://jsonplaceholder.typicode.com/posts**. It shows each post's title and body in an unordered list.

Refer to the following steps:

1. **Initialize the fetch request**: Use the `fetch()` method to send an HTTP GET request to the API endpoint `https://jsonplaceholder.typicode.com/posts`.
2. **Handle the response**: When the server responds, convert the raw response into JSON format using the `.json()` method.
3. **Process and render the data**: Once the JSON data is available, iterate through the list of posts using a loop (e.g., `forEach()`).
4. **Create and append elements dynamically**: For each post, create new DOM elements (`<li>`, `<h3>`, and `<p>`) using `document.createElement()`.
    - Set the text content of the `<h3>` element to the post title.

- Set the text content of the `<p>` element to the post body.
- Append both elements inside the `<li>` and then append the `<li>` to an existing `<ul>` element in the HTML.

5. **Error handling**: Use `.catch()` to handle any network or parsing errors gracefully by logging them to the console or displaying an error message on the page.

The following code represents the core JavaScript logic:

```
// Fetch posts from API
fetch('https://jsonplaceholder.typicode.com/posts')
  .then(response => response.json()) // Convert response to JSON
  .then(posts => {
    const list = document.getElementById('postList'); // Target <ul> element

    posts.forEach(post => {
      const li = document.createElement('li');
      const title = document.createElement('h3');
      const body = document.createElement('p');

      title.textContent = post.title;
      body.textContent = post.body;

      li.appendChild(title);
      li.appendChild(body);
      list.appendChild(li);
    });
  })
  .catch(error => console.error('Error fetching posts:', error));
```

Consuming third-party APIs

Modern web applications frequently leverage external services, such as payment gateways, social media platforms, and data providers, via third-party APIs. These APIs expose endpoints over HTTP, allowing clients to perform operations like retrieving data, creating resources, or triggering actions without reinventing core functionality. Integrating such APIs requires handling request methods, response parsing, error conditions, and authentication securely and efficiently.

Integration techniques

API calls can be made from the frontend or backend, using built-in or third-party libraries. Each approach has its advantages in terms of simplicity, security, and control.

Frontend with Fetch

The following demonstrates Fetch usage for a weather API:

```
fetch('https://api.openweathermap.org/data/2.5/weather'
    + '?q=London&appid=YOUR_API_KEY')
  .then(res => {
    if (!res.ok) throw new Error('Network response was not ok');
    return res.json();
  })
```

```
  .then(data => {
    console.log('Weather Data:', data);
  })
  .catch(err => console.error('Fetch error:', err));
```

Frontend/Backend with Axios

The following demonstrates Axios in either environment:

```
import axios from 'axios';

axios.get('https://api.github.com/users/octocat')
  .then(resp => console.log('GitHub User:', resp.data))
  .catch(err => console.error('Axios error:', err));
```

Backend with Node.js

The following demonstrates Node.js Fetch for crypto prices:

```
const fetch = require('node-fetch');

async function getBitcoinPrice() {
try {
    const res = await fetch( 'https://api.coindesk.com/v1/bpi/
      currentprice.json'
    );
    const json = await res.json();
    console.log('BTC Price (USD):', json.bpi.USD.rate);
  } catch (error) {
    console.error('Error fetching price:', error);
  }
}
getBitcoinPrice();
```

Authentication methods

Securing API access prevents unauthorized use and protects data integrity. Common methods are discussed in the following section.

API keys

The following demonstrates sending an API key in headers:

```
axios.get('https://api.example.com/data', {
  headers: { 'Authorization': 'ApiKey YOUR_API_KEY' }
});
```

OAuth 2.0

OAuth 2.0 allows users to grant third-party apps access without sharing credentials. The typical authorization code flow involves:

- Redirecting the user to the provider's consent page.
- User authenticates and authorizes the app.
- Provider returns an authorization code.

- App exchanges the code for an access token.
- App uses the token for subsequent API calls.

Bearer tokens with JSON Web Tokens

Bearer tokens are a common way to call protected APIs after login. The server issues a signed JWT, and the client sends that token on every request in the **Authorization** header using the **Bearer** scheme. The server validates the token signature and checks claims such as expiry (**exp**) before returning the resource. This approach stays stateless because the server does not need to store a session on each request.

The following demonstrates using a JWT in Fetch:

```
const token = 'YOUR_JWT_TOKEN';

fetch('https://api.example.com/profile', {
    method: 'GET',
    headers: {
        Authorization: `Bearer ${token}`,
        Accept: 'application/json',
    },
})
    .then((res) => {
        if (!res.ok) throw new Error(`HTTP ${res.status}`);
        return res.json();
    })
    .then((profile) => console.log('Profile:', profile))
    .catch((err) => console.error('Profile fetch failed:', err));
```

Basic authentication

Basic authentication is the simplest HTTP authentication scheme. The client sends a username and password in the **Authorization** header as **Basic <base64(username:password)>**. Base64 is only an encoding, not encryption, so this method must be used only over HTTPS. Basic authentication fits internal tools, quick demos, or legacy APIs, but token-based authentication is usually safer and more flexible for modern apps.

The following demonstrates Basic auth (use HTTPS):

```
// Basic authentication example: send username/password in Authorization header
// Use HTTPS only. Base64 is encoding, not encryption.
const username = 'YOUR_USERNAME';
const password = 'YOUR_PASSWORD';

const basicToken = btoa(`${username}:${password}`);

fetch('https://api.example.com/login', {
    method: 'GET', // some APIs use POST; follow the provider docs
    headers: {
        Authorization: `Basic ${basicToken}`,
        Accept: 'application/json',
    },
})
    .then((res) => {
        if (!res.ok) throw new Error(`HTTP ${res.status}`);
        return res.json();
    })
    .then((data) => console.log('Login response:', data))
    .catch((err) => console.error('Basic auth request failed:', err));
```

Best practices

The following presents key guidelines:

- Always use HTTPS to encrypt traffic and protect credentials.
- Store API keys and tokens in environment variables, never in source code.
- Handle network and API errors gracefully, with retries or fallbacks.
- Honor provider rate limits and implement exponential backoff on failures.
- Validate and sanitize all responses before use.
- Rotate and revoke credentials periodically.
- Cache responses where appropriate to reduce redundant calls.

Select a public API (e.g., OpenWeatherMap, GitHub REST API). Write a small script using Fetch or Axios to fetch data, handle errors, and display selected fields in the console or on a webpage.

The following outlines core Fetch logic for OpenWeatherMap:

```
async function showTemperature(city) {
try {
const res = await fetch(
`https://api.openweathermap.org/data/2.5/weather`
+ `?q=${city}&appid=YOUR_API_KEY&units=metric`
);
if (!res.ok) throw new Error(‹City not found›);
const { main } = await res.json();
console.log(`Temperature in ${city}: ${main.temp}°C`);
} catch (err) {
console.error(err.message);
}
}
showTemperature(‹London›);
```

Version control with Git and collaboration with GitHub

Version control is the backbone of modern software development, enabling teams to track code history, collaborate safely, and roll back changes when needed. Git is a distributed version control system that manages snapshots of your code locally and remotely. GitHub builds on Git by providing a web-based interface, collaboration tools such as pull requests, issues, and automation via Actions.

Git fundamentals

Git stores three main areas, which consist of the working directory (your files), the staging area (index), and the repository (history of commits). Understanding these zones is key to effective version control.

The following presents core Git commands:

```
# Initialize a new repository
git init

# Stage all changes for commit
```

```
git add .

# Commit staged changes
git commit -m "Describe your changes"

# View status of working directory
git status

# Show commit history in one-line format
git log --oneline

# Clone a remote repository
git clone https://github.com/username/repo.git
```

The following presents additional useful commands:

- `git diff` to view unstaged changes.
- `git reset HEAD <file>` to unstage a file.
- `git revert <commit>` to create a new commit that undoes an earlier one.
- `git rm <file>` to remove files and stage the removal.
- `git stash` to temporarily save uncommitted changes.

Branching strategies

Branches allow parallel development without affecting the main codebase. Common strategies include feature branches, release branches, and hotfix branches (Gitflow).

The following presents branch operations:

```
# Create and switch to a new feature branch
git checkout -b feature/login

# Switch back to main branch
git checkout main

# Merge feature into main
git merge feature/login

# Delete a local branch after merging
git branch -d feature/login
```

Merge conflicts occur when changes overlap. Git marks conflicts in files, resolves them manually, and then adds and commits the resolved files. The following presents conflict resolution:

```
# After editing conflicts:
git add <file>
git commit      # completes the merge
```

The following flowpath presents a branching diagram:

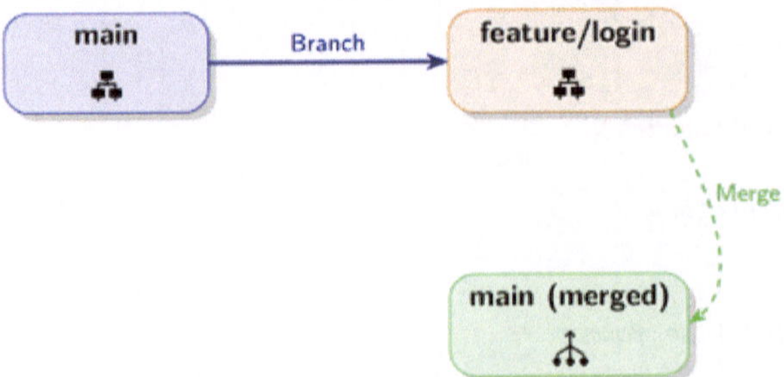

Figure 12.1: Feature branch workflow

Figure 12.1 illustrates a feature branch workflow where the new features are developed in separate branches and then merged back into the main branch.

GitHub collaboration

GitHub extends Git with hosted repositories, **pull requests** (**PRs**), issue tracking, and project boards.

The following presents the repository setup:

1. Create a new repository on GitHub via the web interface.
2. In your local project:
   ```
   git remote add origin https://github.com/username/repo.git
   git push -u origin main
   ```
3. Subsequent pushes:
   ```
   git push
   ```

The following presents a typical pull request workflow:

- Fork a repository (if you lack write access).
- Create a feature branch and commit changes.
- Push the branch to GitHub.
- Open a pull request, assign reviewers, and discuss changes.
- After approval, merge the PR via the GitHub UI.
- Optionally delete the branch post-merge.

GitHub issues and projects help track tasks and bugs following the project board usage:

- Create columns (To Do, In Progress, Done).
- Link issues or PRs to the board.
- Move cards as work progresses.

GitHub Actions enables CI/CD automation. The following presents a simple workflow file:

```
# .github/workflows/ci.yml
name: CI
on: [push, pull_request]

jobs:
  build:
    runs-on: ubuntu-latest
```

```
steps:
  - uses: actions/checkout@v3
  - name: Install Dependencies
    run: npm install
  - name: Run Tests
    run: npm test
```

Deployment strategies

Deployment is the process of publishing your application to a production environment where users can access it. A robust deployment strategy considers hosting platform selection, environment configuration, security, and monitoring. In this section, we cover popular cloud platforms, best practices for managing environment variables, and techniques for keeping your app healthy post-launch.

Cloud deployment platforms

Cloud platforms abstract away server management and provide scaling, logging, and CI/CD integrations. Choosing the right service depends on your stack, team expertise, and budget.

The following presents a comparison of platforms:

Platform	Strengths	Use cases
Vercel	Instant frontend builds, preview deployments	Static sites, Next.js apps
Netlify	Built-in CMS, edge functions	JAMstack sites, forms handling
Render	Full-stack support, auto-deploy from Git	Node.js backends, cron jobs
Heroku	Easy dyno scaling, buildpacks	Small to medium apps, prototypes
AWS Elastic Beanstalk	Deep AWS integration, customizable	Enterprise services, microservices
Azure App Service	Windows/.NET support, DevOps pipelines	Microsoft-centric stacks
GCP App Engine	Auto-scaling, Cloud Functions	Serverless and containerized apps

Table 12.1: Cloud platform comparison

The following demonstrates deploying a Node.js app to Render:

1. Push your code to GitHub.
2. Sign in at **https://render.com** and link your repository.
3. Set build command:
   ```
   npm install
   ```
4. Set start command:
   ```
   node server.js
   ```
5. Add environment variables (e.g., `DATABASE_URL`, `JWT_SECRET`) in the Render dashboard.
6. Click **Create Service** to trigger the first deployment.

Environment configuration

Separating configuration from code ensures that sensitive values are not checked into version control and can vary by environment (development, staging, production).

The following presents environment variable usage:

- Store secrets in a **.env** file or in cloud provider settings.
- Load variables at startup with the **dotenv** package.
- Never commit **.env** to Git—add it to **.gitignore**.

The following demonstrates **dotenv** setup:

```
# .env
PORT=4000
DATABASE_URL=postgres://user:pass@host:5432/dbname JWT_
SECRET=somesecretkey

// index.js
require('dotenv').config();
const express = require('express');
const app = express();
const port = process.env.PORT || 3000;

app.listen(port, () => {
  console.log(`Server listening on port ${port}`);
});
```

Monitoring and logging

Once deployed, continuous monitoring and logging are essential to detect issues, analyze performance, and ensure uptime.

The following presents common monitoring tools:

- UptimeRobot or Pingdom for basic availability checks.
- LogRocket or Sentry for frontend error tracking.
- Prometheus + Grafana for metrics and dashboards.
- New Relic or Datadog for full-stack APM.

The following demonstrates HTTP logging with Morgan:

```
const morgan = require('morgan');
app.use(morgan('combined')); // logs requests in Apache combined format
```

The following presents a basic health check endpoint:

```
app.get('/health', (req, res) => {
  res.json({ status: 'OK', uptime: process.uptime() });
});
```

The following presents a simple metrics exporter using the Prometheus client:

```
// metrics.js
const client = require('prom-client');
const collectDefaultMetrics = client.collectDefaultMetrics;
collectDefaultMetrics({ timeout: 5000 });

// In your app:
app.get('/metrics', async (req, res) => {
 res.set('Content-Type', client.register.contentType);
 res.end(await client.register.metrics());
});
```

Web application security fundamentals

Web applications face numerous security risks due to their exposure on the internet. Protecting user data, maintaining integrity, and ensuring trust require understanding common attack vectors and applying robust defenses throughout the development lifecycle. This section covers the major threats and outlines best practices to secure both client-side and server-side components.

Common security threats

Web applications must be designed to resist malicious inputs, unauthorized actions, and data leaks. Recognizing the primary threat types enables developers to proactively guard against them.

The following presents common threats:

- **XSS**: Attackers inject malicious scripts into pages viewed by other users, enabling session hijacking or data theft. The following demonstrates an XSS payload:

```
<script>fetch('/steal?cookie='+document.cookie)</script>
```

- **CSRF**: Unauthorized commands are transmitted from a user that the web application trusts, exploiting active sessions.
- **SQL injection (SQLi)**: Malicious SQL fragments alter database queries, exposing or corrupting data. The following demonstrates a classic SQLi input:

```
' OR '1'='1
```

- **Broken access control**: Users gain privileges beyond their intended scope, accessing or modifying protected resources.
- **Insecure authentication**: Weak password storage or session handling allows attackers to hijack accounts or impersonate users.
- **Insecure APIs**: Poorly protected endpoints expose internal services and data to unauthorized clients.

Securing web applications

A layered defense, combining secure coding, configuration, and monitoring, is essential to mitigate the threats outlined in the preceding section.

The following list outlines the key security best practices:

- **Input validation and sanitization**: Always validate the type, length, and format of user inputs. Sanitize to remove harmful content. The following demonstrates express-validator usage:

```
const { body } = require('express-validator'); app.
post('/submit', [
  body('email').isEmail().normalizeEmail(), body('name').
  trim().escape()
], (req, res) => {
  // handle request
});
```

- **HTTPS everywhere**: Encrypt data in transit using **Transport Layer Security** (**TLS**) certificates. Redirect all HTTP traffic to HTTPS.
- **Secure authentication**: Hash passwords with **bcrypt**, enforce strong policies, and protect against brute-force with rate limiting. The following demonstrates **bcrypt** hashing:

```
const bcrypt = require('bcrypt');
const hash = await bcrypt.hash(password, 12);
```

- **Cookie and session hardening**: Set cookies with `HttpOnly`, `Secure`, and `SameSite` attributes to prevent theft.
- **Secure headers with Helmet**: Use the `helmet` middleware to configure HTTP headers that block common attacks. The following demonstrates Helmet setup:

```
const helmet = require('helmet'); app.use(helmet());
```

Escape output in HTML to prevent XSS by encoding user input before display. The details are as follows:

- **Role-based access control (RBAC)**: Define and enforce permissions based on user roles to protect sensitive routes and operations.
- **Anti-CSRF tokens**: Embed unique tokens in forms and verify them on submission to block CSRF attacks.
- **Dependency hygiene**: Regularly run `npm audit` and update libraries. Employ automated tools like Dependabot to track vulnerabilities.
- **Monitoring and logging**: Log security-relevant events with tools like `winston` or `morgan` and monitor for anomalies.

Hands-on API integration and deployment

This project guides you through building a React frontend that consumes a third-party weather API, secures sensitive credentials, and deploys the finished application to a cloud platform. You will learn how to fetch and render data asynchronously, manage environment variables securely, and configure continuous deployment.

Project overview and tools

This application fetches current weather information for a user-selected city from the OpenWeatherMap API. It demonstrates asynchronous data fetching, error handling, and deployment workflows.

The following presents the required tools:

- Node.js and npm for package management and scripts.
- React (bootstrapped with Vite or Create React App).
- Axios or Fetch API for HTTP requests.
- dotenv for local environment variables.
- Netlify **command line interface** (**CLI**) or Vercel CLI for deployment.

Fetching and displaying data

Fetching remote data without blocking the UI is essential for modern web apps. We use React's `useEffect` hook and Axios to issue HTTP GET requests and update state.

The following demonstrates a weather component:

```
import React, { useState, useEffect } from 'react';
import axios from 'axios';
function Weather() {
  const [data, setData] = useState(null);
  const [error, setError] = useState(null);
  const apiKey = import.meta.env.VITE_OPENWEATHER_API_
  KEY; const city = "Delhi";

  useEffect(() => {
    axios.get(
```

```
      `https://api.openweathermap.org/data/2.5/weather`,
      { params: { q: city, appid: apiKey, units: 'metric' } }
    )
    .then(res => setData(res.data))
    .catch(err => setError(err.message));
  }, []);

  if (error) return <p>Error: {error}</p>;
  if (!data) return <p>Loading weather...</p>;

  return (
    <div>
      <h2>Weather in {data.name}</h2>
      <p>{data.weather[0].description}</p>
      <p>Temperature: {data.main.temp} °C</p>
    </div>
  );
}

export default Weather;
```

This component initializes state, fetches data on mount, handles errors, and renders weather details.

Securing API credentials

Storing API keys in source code exposes them publicly. Environment variables keep secrets out of version control and allow safe configuration per environment.

The following demonstrates environment setup:

- Create a **.env** file at the project root:

  ```
  VITE_OPENWEATHER_API_KEY=your_api_key_here
  ```

- Add **.env** to **.gitignore** to prevent commits:

  ```
  # .gitignore
  .env
  ```

- Access the variable in React via:

  ```
  const apiKey = import.meta.env.VITE_OPENWEATHER_API_KEY;
  ```

This approach ensures that API keys remain private and can be changed per deployment without code modifications.

Deployment and monitoring

Deploying to a platform like Netlify or Vercel automates builds and serves your application over HTTPS. Monitoring ensures uptime and catches errors early.

Netlify deployment

The following presents Netlify steps:

1. Push the project to GitHub.
2. In the Netlify dashboard, select **New site from Git**.
3. Set build command:

```
npm run build
```

Publish the directory to `dist/` or `build/`.

4. In **Site Settings | Environment**, add: `VITE_OPENWEATHER_API_KEY` with your key.
5. Click **Deploy site** to publish.

Vercel deployment

The following presents the Vercel deployment steps:

- Install Vercel CLI: `npm install -g vercel`
- Run Vercel in the project folder.
- Link to your GitHub repo when prompted.
- Add environment variable `VITE_OPENWEATHER_API_KEY` in Vercel dashboard.
- Vercel builds and provides a live URL.

Monitoring recommendations

The following list outlines the essential monitoring tools:

- Sentry or LogRocket for frontend error tracking.
- UptimeRobot for availability checks.
- Inspect browser console and network logs for runtime issues.

Extend the weather app by adding a search form. Allow users to type a city name, fetch data on submit, and display the new results dynamically, handling loading and error states.

Real-world API integration and security practices

This section focuses on applying the concepts learned throughout the chapter in real-world contexts. It bridges theory and practice by guiding readers through hands-on exercises, secure integration workflows, and a comprehensive case study. Learners will gain practical experience in connecting frontend and backend systems with third-party APIs, handling authentication tokens securely, and managing data exchange over HTTPS.

The section emphasizes industry-grade security techniques such as secure key storage, environment configuration, and validation of external API responses. It also explores best practices for protecting APIs against common threats like unauthorized access, data tampering, and exposure of sensitive credentials. Readers will learn how to structure API calls efficiently, implement token-based authentication, monitor API usage, and apply rate limiting for stability and safety.

Secure integration of a payment gateway

Aim: Demonstrate how a modern e-commerce frontend can securely integrate with a payment gateway (e.g., Stripe) using best practices in authentication, API management, and frontend/backend separation.

Context: An online bookstore allows users to purchase books online using a credit/debit card. The payment integration must ensure secure transaction flow and data protection. Refer to the following steps:

1. **Selecting a payment gateway**: Stripe is chosen for its developer-friendly APIs and built-in security features. It uses HTTPS, **Payment Card Industry** (**PCI**) compliant encryption, and token-based secure payment handling.
2. **Backend integration**: Install Stripe in Node.js backend:

   ```
   npm install stripe
   ```

a. Create an endpoint to handle payments:

```
const express = require("express");
const Stripe = require("stripe");
const stripe = Stripe(process.env.STRIPE_SECRET_KEY);

const router = express.Router();

router.post("/create-payment-intent", async (req, res) => {
    const { amount, currency } = req.body;
    try {
        const paymentIntent = await stripe.
            paymentIntents.create({ amount,
            currency
        });
        res.send({ clientSecret: paymentIntent.client_secret });
    } catch (error) {
        res.status(500).send({ error: error.message });
    }
});

module.exports = router;
```

3. **Frontend integration (React)**: Install Stripe libraries:

```
npm install @stripe/react-stripe-js @stripe/stripe-js
```

a. Create Stripe checkout component:

```
import { Elements, CardElement, useStripe, useElements } from "@stripe/react-stripe-
js";
import { loadStripe } from "@stripe/stripe-js";

const stripePromise = loadStripe(import.meta.env.VITE_STRIPE_PUBLISHABLE_KEY);

function CheckoutForm() {
    const stripe = useStripe();
    const elements = useElements();

    const handleSubmit = async (event) => { event.preventDefault();
        const card = elements.getElement(CardElement);
        const { error, paymentMethod } = await stripe.createPaymentMethod({ type:
            "card",
            card
        });
        // Send to backend to create payment intent...
    };

    return (
        <form onSubmit={handleSubmit}>
            <CardElement />
            <button type="submit" disabled={!stripe}>Pay</button>
        </form>
```

```
    );
}

function StripeCheckout() {
    return (
        <Elements stripe={stripePromise}>
<CheckoutForm />
        </Elements>
    );
}
export default StripeCheckout;
```

4. **Security considerations**:
   - Always use HTTPS for all frontend-backend communication.
   - Store secret keys securely (never in frontend).
   - Validate request amounts and user sessions on the backend.
   - Monitor usage for fraud detection and anomalies.
5. **Deployment**:
   - Set environment variables in deployment platforms (e.g., Netlify, Vercel, Heroku).
   - Enable logging and real-time monitoring.
   - Test using Stripe's sandbox environment before moving to live mode.

Outcome: The bookstore now supports secure card payments, reduces PCI compliance burdens via tokenization, and separates frontend/backend roles efficiently. This case study illustrates full- cycle API integration with industry-grade security.

Conclusion

This chapter has equipped you with the tools and techniques to build interactive web applications that communicate asynchronously with servers and external services. We began by mastering JSON syntax and AJAX patterns for non-blocking data retrieval, then extended our capabilities to consume and authenticate against third-party APIs using fetch, Axios, and Node.js libraries. Version control fundamentals with Git and GitHub provided the discipline for collaborative development, while our exploration of deployment strategies to Vercel, Netlify, Render, and Heroku demonstrated how to release code securely and monitor health in production. Emphasizing security, we reviewed common web threats—XSS, CSRF, SQLi—and implemented defenses through HTTPS, input sanitization, secure headers, and token-based access control. A hands-on React project solidified these lessons by fetching live data, managing API keys via environment variables, and deploying to a cloud platform.

In the next chapter, we will shift focus to DevOps practices that streamline and automate your development lifecycle. You will learn how to containerize applications with Docker, orchestrate multi-container setups using Kubernetes or Docker Compose, and implement CI/CD pipelines in Jenkins and GitHub Actions. Monitoring and logging with Prometheus, Grafana, and centralized log management will round out your ability to deliver reliable, scalable web services in a professional environment.

Exercises

1. Parse a JSON string, handle bad input with try/catch, and print a friendly error. Add an example that includes nested objects and arrays.

2. Define a JSON schema for a User object (name, email, roles[]). Validate three samples (valid, missing field, wrong type) with a validator like Ajv. Report which rule fails.
3. Use fetch() to load posts from https://jsonplaceholder.typicode.com/posts. Render the first 10 titles to the page. Show a Loading… state and an error message on failure.
4. Wrap a fetch() request with AbortController. Abort after 3 seconds if the server does not respond. Display a clear timeout message.
5. Add an Axios response interceptor that retries on HTTP 429 with exponential backoff using the Retry-After header when present. Limit retries to 3 attempts.
6. Create a small Express API and enable CORS for a single origin with GET, POST and headers Content-Type, Authorization. Demonstrate a successful preflight from a simple HTML page.
7. List the exact steps in the Authorization Code + PKCE flow. Generate a code_verifier and S256 code_challenge in JavaScript. Explain where to store state and why.
8. Decode a JWT payload in the browser, check exp, and handle expiry by showing session expired. Do not store tokens in localStorage; explain safer options briefly.
9. Add Helmet to an Express app. Set CSP that allows scripts from self and a single CDN. Prove CSP works by showing one blocked inline script in the browser console.
10. Implement csurf or a double-submit cookie approach. Show a protected POST route that rejects requests without a valid token. Verify with a failing and a passing request.
11. Use express-validator to validate email, name, and amount (numeric, > 0) on a POST route. Return HTTP 400 with a clear errors array on invalid input.
12. Create a repo, branch feature/search, commit changes with conventional messages (e.g., feat: add search bar), open a Pull Request, and resolve one merge conflict.
13. Add a workflow that runs npm ci, npm run lint, and npm test on pushes and PRs. Cache ~/.npm. Make the job fail on test errors.
14. Deploy a React app that calls a public API. Store the API key as an environment variable. Prove it works by sharing the live URL and a screenshot of the loaded data.
15. Deploy a small Express API with /health and /weather?city=…. Configure environment variables in the dashboard. Add a health check and show a green status.

Join our Discord space

Join our Discord workspace for latest updates, offers, tech happenings around the world, new releases, and sessions with the authors:

https://discord.bpbonline.com

Chapter 13
DevOps for Web Development

Introduction

DevOps has emerged as a cornerstone of modern web development, bridging the gap between coding and operations through automation, collaboration, and continuous feedback. DevOps is a culture and a set of practices and tools that enable teams to build, release, and run software reliably through shared ownership and automation. As applications grow in complexity and scale, manual deployment processes become brittle and error prone. **Continuous integration** and **continuous deployment** (**CI/CD**) pipelines solve this by automatically building, testing, and deploying code whenever changes are committed. Containerization with Docker packages applications and their dependencies into lightweight, portable units, ensuring consistent behavior across development, testing, and production environments. Tools like Docker Compose and Kubernetes take this further, orchestrating multi-container deployments and enabling self-healing, load balancing, and auto-scaling. Additionally, robust monitoring and logging practices, using Prometheus, Grafana, and libraries such as Winston, provide critical visibility into application health and performance. This chapter explores these DevOps practices end-to-end: from defining pipelines in Jenkins and GitHub Actions, to containerizing services, orchestrating clusters, and setting up centralized monitoring. By the end of this chapter, the workflow for automated delivery and reliable operations becomes clear enough to design and implement in real projects.

Structure

This chapter covers the following topics:

- CI/CD pipelines and containerization
- Monitoring and logging
- CI/CD containerization project

Objectives

By the end of this chapter, an introductory understanding of DevOps principles and culture will be in place, including the advantages of CI/CD. The chapter explains how to design and implement CI/CD pipelines using Jenkins and GitHub Actions, using pipeline-as-code through a Jenkinsfile or a GitHub workflow YAML file. It also explains how to create Dockerfiles, build container images, and manage multi-container setups using Docker Compose. The chapter introduces Kubernetes architecture and shows how to deploy applications into a Kubernetes cluster by configuring Deployments, Services, and ConfigMaps. The chapter also covers how to integrate automated testing and deployment stages and how to handle credentials using secrets management. Finally, the chapter introduces monitoring and logging pipelines by exposing application metrics to Prometheus, visualizing them in Grafana, and implementing structured logging with Winston. These skills support faster and more reliable delivery of web applications at a beginner-friendly scale.

CI/CD pipeline and containerization

CI/CD are fundamental practices in modern web development and DevOps. These practices automate the process of building, testing, and deploying applications, enabling developers to deliver features and updates faster with higher confidence and fewer errors.

Introduction to CI/CD and DevOps culture

CI/CD represents a set of best practices that enable rapid development and delivery of software. It is deeply aligned with the DevOps culture, which emphasizes collaboration, automation, and monitoring throughout the software development lifecycle. The details are as follows:

- CI is the practice of automatically integrating code changes from multiple contributors into a shared repository several times a day. Each integration is verified by an automated build and automated tests to detect errors early.
- CD automatically releases every change that passes the full pipeline (build, tests, and quality checks) to the production environment, so updates reach users quickly and consistently without manual release steps.
- DevOps culture focuses on breaking down the barriers between development and operations teams. It emphasizes automation, continuous feedback, rapid iterations, and shared responsibility for software performance and delivery.

The following figure illustrates the key stages in a CI/CD pipeline, showing how code moves from developer commits through automated testing and approval processes to production deployment:

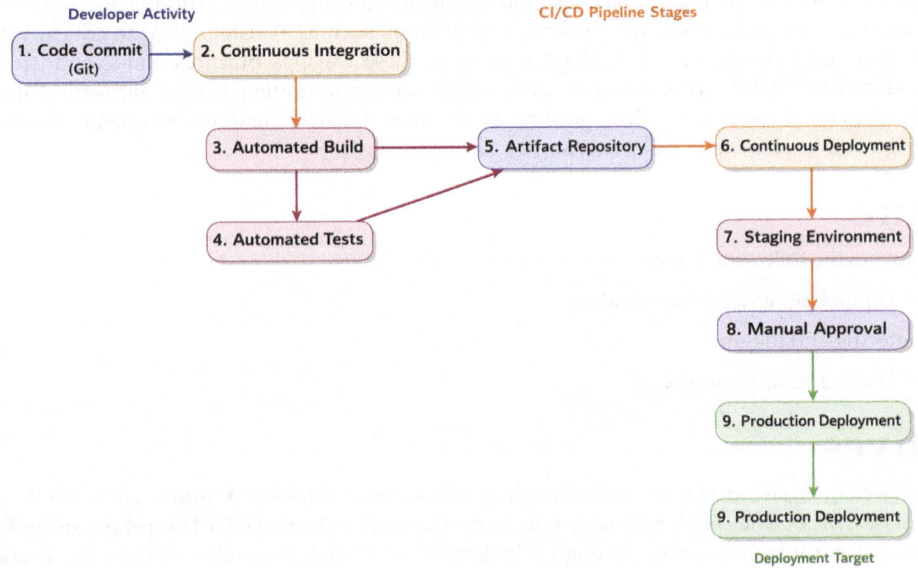

Figure 13.1: CI/CD pipeline workflow

Key benefits of CI/CD and DevOps are as follows:

- Faster time to market.
- Improved code quality and reliability.
- Reduced manual intervention and human errors.
- Greater collaboration between development, testing, and operations.

Introduction to Docker and containerization

Containerization is a technology that packages software code along with its dependencies into isolated environments called **containers**. Docker is the most popular platform used to create, deploy, and manage containers.

Docker allows developers to run applications consistently across different environments (e.g., development, testing, and production). Containers are lightweight and faster to start with compared to traditional virtual machines.

Docker architecture and components

Docker consists of the following main components:

- **Docker Engine**: The core service for creating and managing containers.
- **Docker images**: Read-only templates used to create containers.
- **Docker containers**: Running instances of Docker images.
- **Dockerfile**: A script used to automate the building of Docker images.
- **Docker Hub**: A registry for storing and sharing Docker images.

The following figure illustrates the internal workflow of Docker, showing how client-side tools communicate with the Docker Engine to manage containers, images, and registries efficiently:

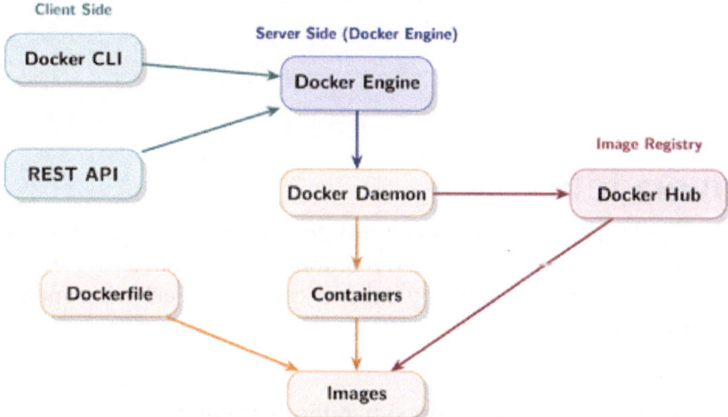

Figure 13.2: CLI/API interaction with Docker Engine managing containers and images

Creating and managing Docker containers

To build and run Docker containers, follow the given steps:

1. **Create a Dockerfile**:

```
# Dockerfile
FROM node:18
WORKDIR /app
COPY package*.json ./
RUN npm install
COPY . .
CMD ["node", "server.js"]
```

2. **Build the Docker image**:

```
docker build -t my-node-app .
```

3. **Run the container:**

```
docker run -p 3000:3000 my-node-app
```

Docker Compose for multi-container applications

Docker Compose is a tool for defining and managing multi-container Docker applications. It uses a `docker-compose.yml` file to configure application services.

Example: Docker Compose file:

```
version: "3"
services:
  web:
    build: .
    ports:
      - "3000:3000"
    depends_on:
      - db
  db:
    image: postgres
    environment:
      POSTGRES_USER: user
      POSTGRES_PASSWORD: pass
      POSTGRES_DB: mydb
```

Run the application using:

```
docker-compose up
```

Kubernetes overview

Kubernetes is a container orchestration system designed to automate the deployment, scaling, and management of containerized applications. It abstracts away the underlying infrastructure, allowing developers to define desired application states declaratively. Kubernetes monitors the cluster continually, ensuring applications run in the correct configuration and scale to meet demand.

The following demonstrates key features:

- Service discovery and load balancing for smooth traffic distribution.
- Automated rollouts and rollbacks to manage updates safely.
- Self-healing via pod restarts and rescheduling on failure.
- Storage orchestration for persistent volumes and dynamic provisioning.

Cluster components

A Kubernetes cluster consists of a control plane and worker nodes, each running essential components to manage and execute workloads.

Control plane components

The control plane maintains the cluster's desired state and exposes the Kubernetes API. The following presents control plane components:

- **Etcd**: A distributed key-value store holding all cluster data.
- **kube-apiserver**: Validates and processes API requests.
- **kube-controller-manager**: Runs controllers for nodes, endpoints, and more.

- **kube-scheduler**: Assigns pods to nodes based on resource availability.

Worker node components

Worker nodes host application workloads and handle networking: The following presents worker node components:

- **kubelet**: Agent that communicates with the API server to manage pods.
- **kube-proxy**: Maintains network rules for services and load balancing.
- **Container runtime**: Runs containers, for example, Docker, containerd.

Workload resources

Applications are packaged into pods and managed by higher-level controllers. The following presents workload resources:

- **Pods**: Atomic deployable units, grouping one or more containers.
- **Deployments**: Declarative updates and scaling of pods.
- **Services**: Stable network endpoints abstracting pods.
- **ConfigMaps** and secrets: Externalize configuration and sensitive data.

The following figure presents the Kubernetes cluster architecture:

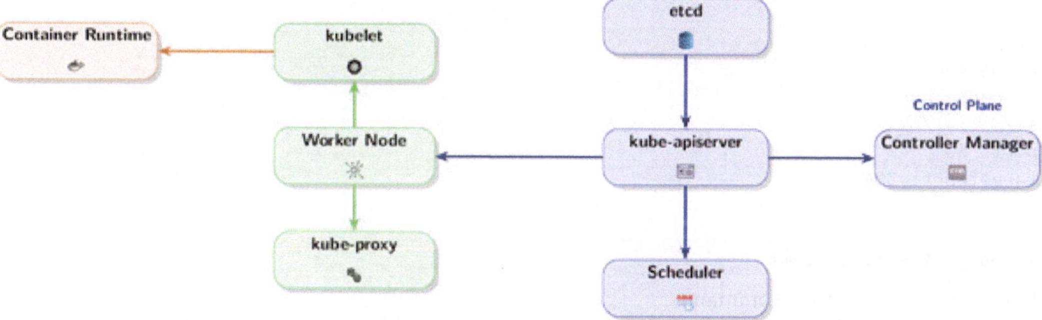

***Figure 13.3:** Kubernetes cluster architecture*

The preceding figure illustrates a cluster architecture where control plane components manage cluster state; worker nodes execute pods and services.

Deploying Kubernetes

Applications are deployed via declarative YAML definitions. Kubernetes continuously reconciles the actual state to match the desired state.

Create a deployment

The following script demonstrates a deployment:

```
apiVersion: apps/v1
kind: Deployment
metadata:
  name: webapp-deployment
spec:
  replicas: 2
  selector:
```

```
    matchLabels:
      app: webapp
  template:
    metadata:
      labels:
        app: webapp
    spec:
      containers:
        - name: webapp
          image: my-node-app:latest
          ports:
            - containerPort: 3000
```

Apply with:

```
kubectl apply -f deployment.yaml
```

Expose via service

The following script demonstrates a service:

```
apiVersion: v1
kind: Service
metadata:
  name: webapp-service
spec:
  selector:
    app: webapp
  type: LoadBalancer
  ports:
    - port: 80
      targetPort: 3000
```

Apply with:

```
kubectl apply -f service.yaml
```

The following presents common commands:

- **kubectl get pods**: List running pods.
- **kubectl get svc**: List services and external IPs.
- **kubectl scale deployment**: Manually adjust replica count.
- **kubectl rollout undo**: Roll back to a previous deployment revision.

This workflow demonstrates how declarative configurations enable repeatable, versioned application deployments with automated scaling and self-healing in Kubernetes.

CI/CD with Jenkins

Jenkins is a self-hosted automation server that orchestrates CI/CD workflows. By defining build, test, and deployment steps as code in pipelines, teams can ensure that every change is verified and released in a consistent, repeatable manner. Jenkins integrates with version control systems, build tools, testing frameworks, and deployment platforms through a rich plugin ecosystem.

Installation and setup

Jenkins requires a Java runtime and can be started via a standalone WAR file or installed as a service. It provides a web UI for configuration and job monitoring.

The following demonstrates installation steps:

1. Install Java (JDK 11 or later) on your server.
2. Following script downloads and launches Jenkins:
   ```
   wget https://get.jenkins.io/war-stable/2.375.3/jenkins.war
   java -jar jenkins.war
   ```
3. Access the UI at **http://localhost:8080** and unlock with the initial admin password found in the Jenkins home directory under **secrets/initialAdminPassword**.
4. Install the suggested plugin set to enable Git, Docker, Pipeline, and popular language integrations.

Defining a pipeline

Jenkins Pipelines allow you to express your CI/CD workflow as code in a **Jenkinsfile**. These pipelines support stages, parallelism, and post-build actions.

The following presents a basic pipeline structure:

```
pipeline { agent any environment {
NODE_ENV = 'production'
}
tools {
nodejs 'Node18'
}
stages { stage('Checkout') {
steps {
git 'https://github.com/user/repo.git'
}
}
stage('Install') { steps {
sh 'npm install'
}
}
stage('Build') { steps {
sh 'npm run build'
}
}
stage('Test') { steps {
sh 'npm test'
}
}
stage('Deploy') { steps {
sh './deploy.sh'
}
}
}
post {
success {
echo 'Pipeline completed successfully'
}
failure {
echo 'Pipeline failed, check logs'
}
}
}
```

GitHub integration

Integrating Jenkins with GitHub enables automated builds on each push or pull request, ensuring code quality and early feedback.

The following demonstrates webhook configuration:

- In GitHub repository settings, under Webhooks, add **`http://<jenkins-server>/github-webhook/`**.
- Install the GitHub integration plugin in Jenkins.
- In the pipeline job configuration, enable **GitHub hook trigger** for GITScm polling.
- Provide GitHub API credentials via Jenkins credentials store to allow secure repository access.

Managing credentials securely

Storing sensitive data such as API keys, **Secure Shell** (**SSH**) tokens, and passwords in Jenkins must be handled securely. Use the Credentials plugin to inject secrets into your pipeline without exposing them in logs.

The following demonstrates credentials usage:

```
pipeline { agent any environment {
DEPLOY_KEY = credentials('deploy-ssh-key')
}
stages { stage('Deploy') {
steps {
sh 'ssh -i $DEPLOY_KEY user@server "deploy script"'
}
}
}
}
```

Pipeline as code benefits

Maintaining the pipeline script within the application repository offers versioned, peer-reviewable CI/CD definitions. This approach ensures that build logic evolves alongside application code.

The advantages are as follows:

- Single source of truth for application and pipeline code.
- Peer reviews of pipeline changes via pull requests.
- Rollback capability to previous pipeline versions.
- Easier onboarding for new team members.
- Monitoring and scaling Jenkins.

As teams grow, Jenkins masters can delegate build execution to distributed agents, improving throughput and isolating workloads.

The scaling strategy is as follows:

- Configure agent nodes via SSH or Kubernetes.
- Use labels to target specific nodes for different build types.
- Monitor build queue and node utilization in the Jenkins dashboard.
- Leverage the **`Blue Ocean`** plugin for enhanced pipeline visualization.

The following table presents key commands:

Command	Description
`java -jar jenkins.war`	Start the Jenkins server.
`jenkins-cli build JOB`	Trigger a job remotely via CLI.
`kubectl scale deployment`	Scale Jenkins on Kubernetes.
`jenkins`	Access Jenkins CLI.

Table 13.1: *Common Jenkins and scaling commands*

This comprehensive setup ensures a robust CI/CD process, from automated testing to secure deployment, providing teams with fast feedback loops and reliable releases.

CI/CD with GitHub Actions

GitHub Actions provides a native CI/CD platform integrated into GitHub repositories. By defining workflows as code in YAML files, teams can automate build, test, and deployment processes in response to repository events. Actions support parallel jobs, matrix configurations, and a marketplace of reusable steps, all versioned alongside the application code.

Workflow triggers

Workflows run in response to specific events in the repository, enabling automation at precisely the right moments.

The following presents common trigger events:

- Push to any branch or tag.
- Creation or update of a pull request.
- Scheduled runs (cron syntax).
- Manual dispatch via the GitHub UI.

Sample workflow

A minimal workflow installs dependencies, runs tests, and builds a Node.js project whenever code lands on **`main`**.

The following code presents a basic workflow file saved under **`.github/workflows/ci.yml`**:

```
name: CI pipeline

on:
  push:
    branches: [main]
  pull_request:
    branches: [main]

jobs:
  build:
    runs-on: ubuntu-latest
    strategy:
      matrix:
        node-version: [18.x]
    steps:
      - uses: actions/checkout@v3
      - uses: actions/setup-node@v3
```

```
      with:
        node-version: ${{ matrix.node-version }}
    - run: npm install
    - run: npm test
    - run: npm run build
```

Workflow components

Each workflow consists of named jobs, which in turn comprise ordered steps executed on specified runner environments.

The following itemizes key workflow elements:

- **name**: A human-readable identifier for the workflow.
- **on**: The event(s) that trigger the workflow (e.g., `push`, `pull_request`).
- **jobs**: Independent units of work; jobs run in parallel by default.
- **runs-on**: Specifies the virtual environment (e.g., `ubuntu-latest`).
- **steps**: Discrete tasks within a job, using actions or shell commands.

Secrets and variables

Sensitive data like API keys and tokens should never be stored in plaintext within workflows. GitHub Actions provides encrypted secrets that can be referenced securely.

The following demonstrates secret usage in a step:

```
- name: Use API key
  run: echo "API key is ${{ secrets.API_KEY }}"
```

Cloud deployment

Workflows can include deployment steps to target platforms, using community actions to simplify the process.

The following presents a Vercel deployment step:

```
- name: Deploy to Vercel
  uses: amondnet/vercel-action@v20
  with:
    vercel-token: ${{ secrets.VERCEL_TOKEN }}
    vercel-org-id: ${{ secrets.VERCEL_ORG_ID }}
    vercel-project-id: ${{ secrets.VERCEL_PROJECT_ID }}
    working-directory: ./
```

Advantages of actions

GitHub Actions offers a streamlined experience for repository-centric automation. The following list presents the core benefits:

- Native integration with GitHub, no external server setup.
- Free minutes for public repositories.
- Matrix builds for testing across environments.
- Extensive marketplace of reusable actions.

Comparison table

Different CI/CD platforms offer unique strengths; the following table highlights key distinctions:

Feature	Jenkins	GitHub Actions
Hosting	Requires a self-hosted or managed setup.	Hosted inside GitHub, no server needed.
Configuration	Plugin-driven, GUI-based setup.	YAML-based in-repo workflows.
Extensibility	Thousands of plugins for any toolchain.	Marketplace with actions and Docker support.
Integration	Connects to any VCS or tool.	Deep GitHub integration (PRs, issues).
Maintenance	Requires OS and plugin updates.	Managed by GitHub, maintenance-free.

Table 13.2: Comparison of Jenkins and GitHub Actions

Monitoring and logging

Monitoring and logging are core DevOps practices that provide visibility into application behavior, performance, and operational health. Monitoring focuses on real-time metrics and alerting, while logging records detailed events and errors. Together they form a feedback loop that helps teams detect, diagnose, and resolve issues quickly, ensuring high availability and reliability.

Application monitoring

Effective monitoring tracks system health, performance, and usage patterns. It enables proactive issue detection and capacity planning.

The following list presents key monitoring dimensions:

- **Uptime and availability**: Monitor service endpoints to ensure they respond within expected parameters.
- **Performance metrics**: Collect CPU, memory, disk I/O, and network latency to detect resource bottlenecks.
- **Error rates**: Track HTTP 5xx/4xx responses to identify spikes in failures.
- **Throughput and load**: Measure requests per second and concurrent connections to understand usage trends.
- **Custom business metrics**: Monitor domain-specific KPIs such as order volume or active sessions.

The following presents popular monitoring tools:

- **Prometheus**: A pull-based time-series database for metrics collection.
- **Grafana**: A dashboard and visualization layer for Prometheus and other data sources.
- **Datadog, New Relic, CloudWatch**: Commercial platforms offering unified logging, metrics, and tracing.

Logging fundamentals

Logs capture discrete events, errors, and state changes within applications. Structured logs enable automated parsing, querying, and alerting.

The following list presents log categories:

- **Access logs**: Record incoming requests, such as timestamp, method, path, and status code.
- **Error logs**: Capture stack traces and error contexts for failed operations.
- **Audit logs**: Track security-relevant actions such as logins or permission changes.
- **Application logs**: Custom diagnostics and debug messages added by developers.

The following presents log levels and their uses:

- **DEBUG**: Detailed output for troubleshooting during development.

- **INFO**: Routine information about application progress.
- **WARN**: Indications of non-critical issues or deprecated usage.
- **ERROR**: Reportable failures that require investigation.
- **FATAL**: Critical errors causing shutdowns or data loss.

Structured logging in Node.js

Structured logging formats records as JSON or key-value pairs, facilitating indexing and search.

`winston` is a popular Node.js library for this purpose.

Setup and configuration

The following demonstrates package installation:

```
npm install winston
```

The following demonstrates logger configuration:

```
const { createLogger, format, transports } = require('winston');

const logger = createLogger({ level: 'info',
format: format.combine( format.timestamp(), format.json()
),
transports: [
new transports.File({ filename: 'logs/error.log', level: 'error' }),
new transports.File({ filename: 'logs/combined.log' }),
new transports.Console({ format: format.simple() })
],
});

module.exports = logger;
```

The following demonstrates usage in application code:

```
const logger = require('./logger');

app.use((req, res, next) => {
  logger.info('Incoming request', { method: req.method, url:
  req.url }); next();
});
app.get('/', (req, res) => {
  logger.debug('Handling root
  route'); res.send('Hello
  World');
});
```

Metrics collection with Prometheus

Prometheus collects numeric metrics via HTTP endpoints called exporters. Applications expose their internal metrics for scraping.

Node.js exporter integration

The following demonstrates package installation:

```
npm install prom-client
```

The following demonstrates metric exposure code:

```
const express = require('express');
const client = require('prom-client');

client.collectDefaultMetrics();

const httpRequestDurationMicroseconds = new client.Histogram({ name: 'http_request_duration_
  ms',
  help: 'Duration of HTTP requests in ms', labelNames: ['method', 'route', 'status_code'],
  buckets: [50, 100, 200, 500, 1000]
});

const app = express();

app.use((req, res, next) => {
  const end = httpRequestDurationMicroseconds.startTimer(); res.on('finish', () => {
    end({ method: req.method, route: req.path, status_code: res.statusCode });
  });
  next();
});

app.get('/metrics', async (req, res) => { res.set('Content-Type', client.register.
  contentType); res.end(await client.register.metrics());
});

app.listen(3000, () => logger.info('Metrics server on port 3000'));
```

The following presents the Prometheus scrape configuration:

```
scrape_configs:
  - job_name: node_app
    metrics_path: /metrics
    static_configs:
      - targets: ['localhost:3000']
```

Grafana dashboard setup

Grafana connects to Prometheus as a data source. Users can create dashboards with panels for metrics such as request latency, error rates, and resource usage.

The following figure depicts metrics flow from application to Grafana:

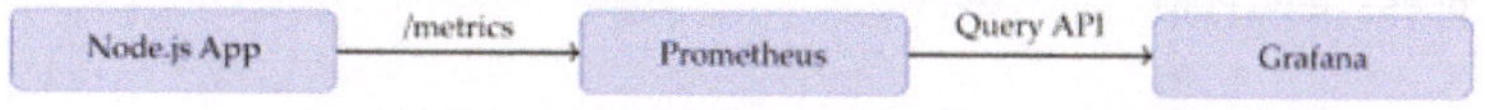

Figure 13.4: *Metrics flow from application to Grafana*

Best practices for monitoring and logging

The following presents recommended practices:

- Centralize logs using systems like **Elasticsearch, Logstash, Kibana** (**ELK**) Stack, or CloudWatch Logs.
- Mask or redact sensitive user data (PII, credentials).

- Correlate logs and metrics with tracing IDs for end-to-end request tracking.
- Define alerts on key thresholds (e.g., error rate > 1%, latency > 500ms).
- Implement log rotation and archival to manage storage.
- Continuously review dashboards and refine metrics for evolving application needs.

CI/CD containerization project

This project walks through the end-to-end DevOps workflow, building a simple Node.js REST API, packaging it in a Docker container, and automating its build, test, and deployment using CI/CD pipelines. You will learn how to integrate with container registries and cloud platforms to achieve repeatable, production-ready deployments.

Project overview

This subsection defines the project goals, required components, and expected outcomes. You will create a RESTful API, containerize it, and implement CI/CD pipelines to push images and deploy to a cloud service.

The following list presents project requirements and stack:

- **Objective**: Build and deploy a Node.js API with automated pipelines.
- **Language**: JavaScript (Node.js, Express).
- **Containerization**: Docker.
- **CI/CD options**: GitHub Actions or Jenkins.
- **Registry**: DockerHub or GitHub Container Registry.
- **Deployment**: Render, Railway, AWS, or Heroku.

Simple Node.js API

This subsection describes how to scaffold a minimal Express.js application that responds to HTTP requests. The API serves as the foundation for containerization and pipeline testing.

The following presents the directory layout:

```
node-api/
|
├── index.js
├── package.json
└── Dockerfile
```

The following code presents API code in **index.js**:

```
const express = require('express');
const app = express();
const PORT = process.env.PORT || 3000;

app.get('/', (req, res) => { res.send('Hello, DevOps World!');
});

app.listen(PORT, () => {
  console.log(`Server is running on port ${PORT}`);
});
```

Dockerfile setup

This subsection explains how to write a Dockerfile to package the Node.js application into a portable container. You will learn best practices for layer caching and minimal image size.

The following presents Dockerfile contents:

```
# Base image with Node.js LTS
FROM node:18

# Create and set working directory
WORKDIR /usr/src/app

# Copy dependency definitions
COPY package*.json ./
# Install dependencies
RUN npm install --production

# Copy application code
COPY . .

# Expose application port
EXPOSE 3000

# Define startup command
CMD ["npm", "start"]
```

The following demonstrates building and running locally:

```
docker build -t node-api .
docker run -d -p 3000:3000 node-api
```

GitHub setup

This subsection covers initializing a Git repository, committing code, and pushing to GitHub. It ensures your pipeline can trigger on repository changes.

The following presents Git commands:

```
git init
git add .
git commit -m "Initial Node.js API"
git remote add origin https://github.com/username/node-api.git
git push -u origin main
```

GitHub Actions CI/CD

This subsection details how to create a GitHub Actions workflow that builds the Docker image, runs tests (placeholder), and pushes the image to a registry upon each push to **`main`**.

The following presents the workflow file **`.github/workflows/ci.yml`**:

```
# .github/workflows/ci.yml
name: CI/CD Pipeline

on:
  push:
```

```
    branches: [main]

jobs:
  build-and-push:
    runs-on: ubuntu-latest

    env:
      IMAGE_NAME: docker.io/${{ secrets.DOCKER_USERNAME }}/node-api

    steps:
      - name: Checkout code
        uses: actions/checkout@v3

      # ---- Tests (placeholder) ----
      # Runs only if package.json exists and the script is present.
      - name: Set up Node.js
        uses: actions/setup-node@v4
        with:
          node-version: "18"
          cache: npm

      - name: Install dependencies
        run: |
          if [ -f package-lock.json ]; then npm ci; else npm install; fi

      - name: Run tests (if present)
        run: npm test --if-present

      # ---- Docker build + push ----
      - name: Set up Docker Buildx
        uses: docker/setup-buildx-action@v2

      - name: Login to Docker Hub
        uses: docker/login-action@v2
        with:
          registry: docker.io
          username: ${{ secrets.DOCKER_USERNAME }}
          password: ${{ secrets.DOCKER_PASSWORD }}

      - name: Build and push image
        uses: docker/build-push-action@v4
        with:
          context: .
          file: ./Dockerfile
          push: true
          tags: |
            ${{ env.IMAGE_NAME }}:latest
            ${{ env.IMAGE_NAME }}:${{ github.sha }}
          cache-from: type=gha
          cache-to: type=gha,mode=max
```

Jenkins CI/CD

As an alternative to GitHub Actions, this subsection shows how to configure a Jenkins pipeline that performs the same build-and-push steps using a `Jenkinsfile`.

The following presents the pipeline script **Jenkinsfile**:

```
pipeline { agent any stages {
stage('Checkout') {
steps { git 'https://github.com/username/node-api.git' }
}
stage('Install') {
steps { sh 'npm install' }
}
stage('Docker Build') {
steps { sh 'docker build -t username/node-api .' }
}
stage('Docker Push') { steps {
withCredentials([usernamePassword( credentialsId: 'docker-hub', usernameVariable: 'DOCKER_USER',
passwordVariable: 'DOCKER_PASS')]) {
sh 'echo $DOCKER_PASS | docker login -u $DOCKER_USER --password-stdin'
sh 'docker push username/node-api'

}
}
}
}
}
```

Cloud deployment

This subsection explains how to deploy the pushed Docker image to a cloud platform for production hosting, covering automatic pulls and environment configuration.

The following presents deployment steps on Render:

1. Create a new Web Service on Render linked to your GitHub repo.
2. Specify Docker deployment; Render will build your container.
3. Add environment variables in the Render dashboard.
4. Deploy; Render manages rolling updates on each push.

Project summary

This project demonstrated the full DevOps lifecycle, which includes writing application code, containerizing with Docker, pushing to a registry, and automating build-and-deploy pipelines via GitHub Actions or Jenkins. You now have a repeatable, production-ready workflow that ensures consistent deployments and rapid iteration.

Company case study

This subsection examines *FinTask,* a fictional global financial platform that employs advanced DevOps to support millions of users. We explore their strategies, tooling, and outcomes to illustrate industry best practices.

FinTask runs on a microservices architecture with continuous delivery and robust observability. CI/CD strategy FinTask uses GitHub Actions for initial builds and Argo CD for GitOps-driven deployments. Every commit triggers automated tests, image builds, and pushes to a private registry. Argo CD continuously reconciles Kubernetes clusters with the Git repository state.

The following points highlight key components of FinTask's DevOps implementation, demonstrating how the company maintains reliability, security, and scalability across its global financial platform through effective monitoring, automation, and deployment strategies:

- **Monitoring and alerts**: Prometheus collects metrics from each service, while Grafana dashboards track latency, error rates, and throughput. Alert manager notifies teams via Slack when key thresholds are breached.
- **Centralized logging**: An ELK Stack ingests logs from all containers. Kibana provides searchable dashboards, and watches detect anomalous patterns, triggering PagerDuty alerts.
- **Security and secrets:** TLS is enforced end-to-end. All secrets are stored in HashiCorp Vault and injected at runtime. CI pipelines include Snyk scans to detect vulnerable dependencies.
- **Deployment strategy**: Blue-green deployments are implemented via Kubernetes services, ensuring zero downtime and easy rollback. Infrastructure-as-code (Terraform) provisions clusters and networking.

The following table presents FinTask impact metrics:

Metric	Improvement
Deployment frequency	From monthly to multiple daily
Mean time to recovery (MTTR)	70% reduction
Incident response time	Under 15 minutes on average
Developer confidence	85% positive feedback

***Table 13.3**: FinTask DevOps outcomes*

To illustrate their blue-green flow, the following figure demonstrates traffic shifting:

***Figure 13.5**: Blue-green deployment traffic shift*

Conclusion

Throughout this chapter, we dissected the full DevOps lifecycle for modern web applications. We began by introducing CI/CD philosophies and demonstrated how Jenkins and GitHub Actions automate build, test, and release processes. Next, we explored containerization with Docker, crafting Docker files to package Node.js services, and orchestrating multi-container stacks via Docker Compose. We then delved into Kubernetes, understanding pods, deployments, services, and how to declaratively deploy scalable, self-healing clusters. Finally, we established monitoring and logging workflows, leveraging Prometheus to collect metrics, Grafana to visualize system health, and Winston to structure logs for effective debugging.

As the culminating chapter of this book, DevOps for web development unifies the skills acquired across all prior chapters—version control, APIs, security, and deployment—into a cohesive, automated workflow. By mastering these practices, you can break down silos between development and operations, accelerate feedback loops, and maintain high availability. Although no further chapters follow, your journey continues, which is to experiment with advanced infrastructure as code tools, service meshes, and chaos engineering to keep evolving your delivery pipelines and ensure robust, scalable web services.

Exercises

1. Define continuous integration, continuous delivery, and continuous deployment in 2–3 lines each. Add one concrete benefit and one risk for each.
2. Create a short commit history that follows conventional commits for a tiny Node.js app. Include at least one feat, one fix, and one chore. Explain why each type matters to release notes.

3. Draw (or describe) a CI pipeline with stages: checkout | install | lint | unit test | build | artifact upload. List clear entry and exit conditions for every stage.
4. Write a Dockerfile for the Node.js API in the chapter. Use a non-root user, pin a Node LTS image, and set a HEALTHCHECK. Explain each instruction in one sentence.
5. Convert the Dockerfile to a multi-stage build that installs dev deps only in the builder stage and copies a minimal production bundle. Compare image sizes before/after and note the percent change.
6. Add build-time labels (org.opencontainers.image.*) with Git commit, build date, and source URL. Show docker inspect output that proves the labels exist.
7. Create a docker-compose.yml that starts the Node app and a PostgreSQL service with a named volume. Prove the app can connect and survive a container restart without data loss.
8. Add a profile: [dev] service for an Adminer or pgAdmin container. Start only the dev profile and confirm other services remain down.
9. Expose /health in the app. Wire Docker HEALTHCHECK, Compose healthcheck, and a simple shell script that curls the endpoint and exits non-zero on failure. Capture one failing run.
10. Create deployment, service (ClusterIP), and ConfigMap YAML for the app. Use kubectl apply and show kubectl get deploy,po,svc proving the rollout.
11. Add readiness and liveness probes with different endpoints/timeouts. Force a failure (e.g., block DB). Observe and explain pod behavior for each probe type.
12. Set CPU and memory requests/limits for the deployment. Use kubectl describe pod to confirm scheduling based on requests. Explain why setting only limits can cause throttling.
13. Perform a rolling update that changes the image tag. Record kubectl rollout status. Then trigger a bad image and roll back. Provide the commands and the final revision.
14. Install NGINX Ingress (or use a managed ingress). Create an Ingress rule for example.local. If possible, add TLS with a self-signed cert or cert-manager in staging. Show a successful HTTPS request.
15. Store a DB password as a Kubernetes Secret (base64). Mount it as an env var. Prove the pod sees it and the value does not appear in pod spec plaintext (kubectl get deploy -o yaml redacts it).

Join our Discord space

APPENDIX A
Resources for Further Reading

This appendix provides curated resources to support a thorough understanding, learning, and continuous improvement in full-stack web development, DevOps, and modern web application security.

Books and documentation

The following are the books and documentation you can refer to:

- **Node.js documentation**: **https://nodejs.org/en/docs**
- **Express.js guide**: **https://expressjs.com**
- **React official documentation**: **https://reactjs.org/docs/getting-started.html**
- **Angular official guide**: **https://angular.io/docs**
- **MongoDB manual**: **https://www.mongodb.com/docs/manual/**
- **PostgreSQL official documentation**: **https://www.postgresql.org/docs/**
- **Docker documentation**: **https://docs.docker.com/**
- **Kubernetes documentation**: **https://kubernetes.io/docs/home/**
- **Git and GitHub guides**: **https://docs.github.com/en/get-started**

Online courses and tutorials

The following are the online courses and tutorials you can refer to:

- **Full stack open (University of Helsinki)**: **https://fullstackopen.com**
- **The Odin Project**: **https://www.theodinproject.com**
- **freeCodeCamp web development curriculum**: **https://www.freecodecamp.org/learn**
- **Coursera**: Full Stack Web Development with React and Node.js
- **Codecademy**: Full-Stack Engineer Path

Communities and forums

The following are the communities and forums you can refer to:

- **Stack Overflow**: **https://stackoverflow.com**
- **Reddit**: r/webdev and r/reactjs
- **Dev.to**: **https://dev.to**
- **Hashnode**: **https://hashnode.com**

Tooling and hosting platforms

The following are the tooling and hosting platforms you can refer to:

- **Vercel**: Hosting and serverless backend for frontend projects: **https://vercel.com**
- **Netlify**: Continuous deployment and frontend hosting: **https://netlify.com**
- **Render**: Full-stack web app hosting: **https://render.com**
- **Heroku**: Cloud platform for app deployment: **https://heroku.com**
- **DigitalOcean app platform**: **https://www.digitalocean.com/products/app-platform**

Note: Learning and staying updated are ongoing processes. Refer to these resources frequently and contribute to open-source communities to solidify your understanding.

Appendix B
Glossary of Terms

This glossary provides the definitions and brief explanations of the essential terms used throughout the book. The following terms are commonly encountered in full-stack development, DevOps, and web technologies:

- **Asynchronous JavaScript and XML (AJAX)**: AJAX and **Extensible Markup Language** (**XML**); A technique for making asynchronous **Hypertext Transfer Protocol** (**HTTP**) requests from the browser without reloading the page.
- **Application programming interface (API)**: An API is a set of rules and protocols that allows different software components to communicate with each other.
- **Authentication**: The process of verifying the identity of a user or system.
- **Authorization**: The process of granting or denying access to resources based on identity.
- **Continuous integration and continuous deployment (CI/CD)**: CI/CD refers to automated practices for testing and deploying code to production environments.
- **Component**: A self-contained and reusable unit of code that manages its own logic and UI in frontend frameworks like React and Angular.
- **Create, read, update, delete (CRUD)**: CRUD is the four basic operations performed on data in a database or application.
- **Docker**: An open-source platform that automates the deployment of applications inside lightweight, portable containers.
- **Express.js**: A minimal and flexible Node.js web application framework that provides a robust set of features for building APIs and web applications.
- **Frontend**: The part of a web application that interacts directly with the user, typically built using **HyperText Markup Language** (**HTML**), **Cascading Style Sheets** (**CSS**), and JavaScript.
- **Git**: A version control system used to track changes in source code during software development.
- **GitHub**: A web-based platform for hosting Git repositories, often used for collaboration and version control in software projects.
- **Hook (React)**: A special function that lets developers hook into React features such as state and lifecycle methods in functional components.
- **JavaScript Object Notation (JSON)**: JSON is a lightweight data format used for storing and exchanging data between client and server.
- **Kubernetes**: An open-source system for automating the deployment, scaling, and management of containerized applications.
- **Middleware**: Functions in Express.js that have access to the request and response objects and can modify them or end the request-response cycle.
- **MongoDB**: A NoSQL, document-oriented database designed for scalability and flexibility.
- **Node.js**: A JavaScript runtime built on Chrome's V8 engine that allows JavaScript to run on the server side.

- **NoSQL**: A class of database systems that are non-relational and often used for large-scale data storage.
- **OAuth**: An open standard for access delegation used to grant third-party applications access to user information without exposing passwords.
- **PostgreSQL**: A powerful, open-source object-relational database system known for reliability and advanced features.
- **Representational State Transfer (REST) API**: An architectural style for designing networked applications using HTTP methods.
- **Routing**: The process of defining **Uniform Resource Locator** (**URL**) paths in a web application and mapping them to specific logic or views.
- **Sequelize**: A promise-based Node.js ORM for relational databases like PostgreSQL, MySQL, and SQLite.
- **State**: In frontend development, a representation of the dynamic data of a component that determines how it renders and behaves.
- **Version control**: A system for tracking changes to source code and managing contributions from multiple developers.
- **Web server**: A software system that handles HTTP requests and serves responses to clients, often used to host websites and APIs.
- **Webpack**: A module bundler used in modern web development to compile and bundle JavaScript files and assets.
- **JSON Web Token (JWT)**: JWT is a compact and secure way to transmit information between parties as a JSON object.

Join our Discord space

Join our Discord workspace for latest updates, offers, tech happenings around the world, new releases, and sessions with the authors:

https://discord.bpbonline.com

Index

A

Absolute Positioning 66
AJAX 388
AJAX, configuring 390, 391
AJAX, terms
- Fetch API Usage 389
- XHR 389

Angular 270
Angular, forms
- Reactive 284
- Template-Driven 283
- Validation 285

Angular, foundations
- Development Server 270
- Environment 270
- Folder Layout 271

Angular, points
- Change Detection 290
- Lifecycle Hooks 289

Angular, sections
- AOT Compilation 294
- Hosting 295

Angular, services
- Dependency Injection (DI) 279
- Injection Hierarchy 280

Angular, techniques
- Ahead Of Time (AOT) 293
- Lazy Loading 293

Angular, terms
- Declarative Templates 273
- NgModules 271
- Reusable Components 272

Angular Test, types
- End-to-End (E2E) 292
- Unit 291

API, concepts
- Package Management 97
- Server Environements 97

API Integration 400
API Integration, illustrating 402-404
API Integration, terms
- Data Fetching 400
- Deployment/Monitoring 401
- Fetching 400
- Securing API 401

Application Monitoring 417
Application Programming Interface (API) 96
Arithmetic Operators 124
Arrays 139
Arrays, configuring 139
Arrays, demonstrating 143
Arrays, elements
- Built-In Utilities 143
- Destructuring 142
- Iteration 140
- Multidimensional Metrics 142
- Sorting 141
- Transformation/Aggregation 141

Assignment Operators 125
Asynchronous Programming 147
Asynchronous Programming, terms
- Async Await 148
- Callbacks 147
- Event Loop 147
- Microtasks 149
- Promises/Chaining 148

Async Testing 242
Async Testing, illustrating 242, 243
Authentication 335
Authentication/Authorization 336
Authentication/Authorization, strategies
- Auth Routes 337
- JWT 336

Authentication/Authorization, terms
- JSON Web Token (JSW) 339
- OAuth 341
- Testing Authentication 338

Authorization 335

B

Backend Development, terms
- Asynchronous Code 346
- Automated Testing 347
- Code Organization 349
- Environment Variables 345
- Error Handling 345
- Input Validation 345
- Logging/Monitoring 346
- Schema Definitions 346
- Sensitive Data 346
- Version Control 347

Backend Development, threats
- Dependency Hygiene 348
- HTTPS Enforcement 348
- Input Sanitization 348

Background Styling 66
BigInt 170
Bitwise Operators 126
Bootstrap 73
Bootstrap, architecture 73

Bootstrap, blocks 74
Bootstrap, terms
  Responsive Breakpoints 74
  Two-Column Layout 74
Branching 395
Bubbling 171

C

Canvas API 178
Canvas API, terms
  Animation 178
  Drawing 178
Capturing 171
CI/CD 408
CI/CD, configuring 408
CI/CD Containerization 420
CI/CD Containerization, terms
  Cloud Deployment 423
  DecOps Lifecycle 423
  Dockerfile 421
Class Components 215
Class Components, integrating 215
Client-Server Architecture 201
Client-Server Architecture, advantages 202
Client-Server Architecture, terms
  Client/Server Roles 201
  Communication 202
  Request Formats 201
  Response Content 202
Comments 116
Comments, architecture 117
Comments, types 117
Comparison Operators 125
Conditional Statements 126
Conditional Statements, types
  If 126
  If Else 126
  If Else If 127
  Switch 127
Containerization 409
Context API 228
Context API, architecture 228
Context API, types
  Consuming Context 229
  Create Context 229
  Provide Context 229
Context Positioning 65
Cookie 200
Cookie, enhancing 200
Cookie, types
  Delete 200
  Read 200
  Set 200
CORS 202
CORS, approaches 203
CORS, configuring 203, 204
CORS, importance 203
CSS Attribute Selectors 54, 55
CSS Box Model 37
CSS Box Model, demonstrating 38
CSS Box Model, dimensions
  Box Size 38
  Margins, collapsing 38
CSS Box Model, parts 37
CSS Box Model, practices 39
CSS Cascade Order 31
CSS Cascade Order, configuring 31
CSS Cascade Order, demonstrating 31, 32
CSS Colors 45
CSS Colors, illustrating 46, 47
CSS Frameworks 72
CSS Frameworks, approaches
  Bootstrap 73
  Bulma 73
  Foundation 73
  Tailwind CSS 73
CSS Frameworks, configuring 72, 73
CSS Frameworks, ensuring 78
CSS Frameworks, factors
  Customization 79
  Ease Use 79
  Performance 79
  Style 80
CSS Frameworks, illustrating 80
CSS Grid 42
CSS Grid, advantages 42
CSS Grid, architecture 42
CSS Grid, configuring 43, 44
CSS Grid, practices 45
CSS Grid, properties
  Grid Container 42
  Grid Item 43
CSS Inheritance 32, 33
CSS Inheritance, illustrating 33
CSS-in-JS 246
CSS Modules 245
CSS Pixels 69
CSS Pixels, terms
  Layout Grids 70
  Media Queries 69
  Responsive Units 69
CSS Positioning 65
CSS Positioning, techniques
  Absolute Positioning 66
  Background Styling 65
  Clearing Floats 68
  Context Positioning 65
  Fixed Positioning 66
  Floating Elements 67
  Overlapping Elements 67
  Relative Positioning 66
  Side-by-Side Columns 68
CSS Selectors 33
CSS Selectors, demonstrating 36
CSS Selectors, elements 34
CSS Selectors, practices 35
CSS Selectors, types 35
CSS Specificity 32
CSS Specificity, illustrating 32

CSS, techniques
- Animations 86
- Transformations 85
- Transitions 85

CSS, terms
- Misaligned Form 59
- Styling Lists 55
- Styling Tables 57

CSS, types
- External 30
- Inline 31
- Internal 30

Custom Events 172
Custom Headers 198
Custom Hooks 233
Custom Hooks, configuring 233

D

Database 355
Database, types
- NoSQL 356
- SQL 356

Data Binding 274
Data Binding, templates
- Event Binding 275
- Interpolation 274
- Property Binding 274
- Two-Way Binding 276

Data-Driven Application 377
Data-Driven Application, concepts
- API Developement 378
- Authentication 382
- Database Connection 377
- Deployment/Testing 384
- Sync Database 380

Data-Driven Application, configuring 377
Data-Driven Application, steps
- Environment Variables 384
- Local Testing 384
- Monitoring/Logging 385
- Production Deployment 384
- URLs Endpoints 385

Data Types 119
Data Types, categories
- Data/Time 120
- Primitive 120
- Reference 120
- Regular Expressions 122

Debouncing 173
Dependency Array 222
Deployment 397
Deployment, concepts
- Monitoring/Logging 398
- Separation Configuration 397
- Server Management 397

Destructuring Objects 169
Development Environment 111
Development Environment, principles
- Automated Testing 113
- Debugging 112
- DOM API 114
- Dynamic Web Applications 114
- Node.js 111
- Package Management 113
- Snippets Testing 112
- Streamline Code 114
- VS Code 111

Directives 276
Directives, types
- Attribute 277
- Component 276
- Structural 277

Docker 409
Docker, components 409
Docker Compose 410
Docker, steps 409
DOM 152
DOM, methods
- Method Comparison 154
- Query Selector 153
- SelectorAll 153

DOM Traversal 160
DOM Update 160
Do While Loop 128
Drag/Drop API 179
Drag/Drop API, terms
- Data Transfer 179
- Events 179

Dynamic Modification 154
Dynamic Modification, capabilities
- Attribute Updates 154
- Class Manipulation 155
- Content Updates 154
- Element Creation 155
- Element Removal 156
- Style Updates 155

Dynamic User Loading 389

E

Effect Hook 221
Effect Hook, configuring 222
Error Handling 135
Error Handling, concepts
- Custom Error Types 135
- Propagation/Logging 136
- Try/Catch Block 135

Error Handling, fundamentals
- Chrome DevTools 165
- Common Errors 164
- Custom Errors 165
- Try/Catch Constructs 164

Event Delegation 157, 172
Event-Driven Programming 171
Event Handling 223
Event Handling, types
- Explicitly Bound 225
- Handlers 223
- Synthetic 224

Event Listeners 156
Expressions 116
Express.js 323

Express.js, architecture 324
Express.js, configuring 324
Express.js, terms
  Dynamic Request Handling 327
  Middleware 327
  Protected API 328
  Route Handlers 327
  Router Modules 328
Express Routing 329
Express Routing, terms
  Multiple Handlers 330
  Product Routes 331
  Query Parameters 330
  Route Parametes 330
  Router Modules 330
  Statis Paths 329
External CSS 30

F

Fetch API 173
Fixed Positioning 66
Flexbox 39
Flexbox, advantages 39
Flexbox, architecture 40
Flexbox, practices 41
Flexbox, propeties
  Flex Container 40
  Flex Item 40
Flexbox, terms
  Content Center 40
  Navigation Bar 41
  Responsive Layout 41
Floating Elements 67
For Loop 128
Forms 237
Forms, categories
  Controlled 237
  Form Validation 240
  Uncontrolled 239
Form Tag 17
Form Tag, attributes 18
Form Tag, demonstrating 19
Form Tag, elements 18
Form Tag, practices 20
Foundation Grids 76
Foundation Grids, terms
  Horizontal Layout 76
  Nested Grids 77
  Rearrange Blocks 77
  Responsive Cells 77
Function Components 213
Function Components, integrating 213, 214

G

Geolocation API 177
Geolocation API, configuring 177
Geolocation API, demonstrating 178
Git 394
GitHub Actions 415
GitHub Actions, concepts
  Cloud Deployment 416
  Minimal Workflow 415
  Sensitive Data 416
  Workflow Elements 416
  Workflow Triggers 415

H

Hand-On Angular Project 310
Hand-On Angular Project, configuring 310
Hand-On Angular Project, steps 311
Hand-On Angular Project, structure 311
Hand-On Angular Project, technologies 310
Hand-On React Project 297
Hand-On React Project, configuring 298
Hand-On React Project, guide
  App Integrate 304
  CRA Bootstraps 301
  Development Server 302
  Event Handling 307
  Firebase Hosting 309
  Generated Directories 301
  GitHub Pages 308
  Netlify Hosting 308
  Node NPM 301
  Parent State Updates 307
  Secure Deployment 309
  Single Responsibility 303
  Source Folder 302
  State Hook 306
  Styling Enhances 305
  TodoItem 304
  TodoList 304
  Todolnput 303
  Unused Files 302
  Vercel Hosting 309
Hand-On React Project, lists
  Application Requirements 299
  Components 299
  Development Workflow 300
  Functional Goals 300
Hand-On React Project, structure 298
Hand-On React Project, tools 298
Header 195
Header, illustrating 196
Heading Tag 3
Heading Tag, configuring 3
Heading Tag, results 4
Higher Order Components (HOCs) 253
HTML 1
HTML, configuring 2
HTML, elements
  Form Tag 17
  Heading Tag 3
  Images Tag 12
  Links Tag 9
  Lists Tag 7
  Paragraphs Tag 5
  Table Tag 15
  Videos Tag 13

HTML, fundamentals
Comments 21
DOCTYPE Declaration 21
Escape Characters 23
ID/Cass Attributes 21
Inline Elements 22
Meta Tag 23
Section Tag 22
HTTP 190
HTTP, architecture 190
HTTP Client 286
HTTP Client, terms
CRUD Operations 287
Interceptors 287
NgModule 286
HTTP, headers
Request 197
Response 197
HTTP Requests 194
HTTP Requests, parts
Cookies 194
Sessions 194
HTTP Requests, steps 195

I

If Else If Statement 127
If Else Statement 126
If Statement 126
Images Tag 12
Images Tag, attributes 12
Images Tag, demonstrating 12
Image/Video Tag, practices 14
Inline CSS 31
Interactive Calculator 182
Interactive Calculator, steps
CSS Styling 184
Error Handling 186
HTML Style 182
Interactive Todo 160
Interactive Todo, concepts
Data Persistence 161
List Container 160
Script Listens 161
Internal CSS 30
Iteration Protocols 129

J

JavaScript 96
JavaScript, architecture 96
JavaScript, arguments
Destructuring 146
Spread/Rest 145
JavaScript, capabilities
Concurrency 106
Content Security Policy (CSP) 108
Cross-Origin Access 107
Cross-Site Request Forgery (CSRF) 108
Dynamic Typing 106
Ecosystem 107
Feature Comparison 105
JIT Compilation 107
Memory/Closures 109
Web Workers 109
JavaScript, functions
Arrow 132
Binding 134
Closures 133
Declaration/Expression 131
Generators 134
Hoisting 134
IIFE 134
Invocation 131
Parameters 132
Recursion 133
JavaScript, fundamentals
ECMAScript 5 99
ES6 100
JS Interpreter 98
Large Integers 101
Module Systems 100
JavaScript, operators
Arithmetic 124
Assignment 125
Bitwise 126
Comparison 125
Logical 125
JavaScript, properties
Classes 138
Constructor 138
Object 137
Prototype Chain 137
JavaScript, syntax 96
JavaScript, terms
DevTools 104
DOM 103
Events 103
Fetch API 103
Performance 104
Storage 104
Timers 104
Jenkins 412
Jenkins, configuring 412, 413
Jenkins, terms
Application Repository 414
Express Pipelines 413
GitHub Integration 414
Secure Shell (SSH) 414
Jest 241
JSDoc Comments 118
JSON 175, 388
JSON, demonstrating 175
JSON Web Token (JWT) 339
JSX 211
JSX, architecture 212
JSX, attributes
Babel 213
Expressions 212
JWT, capabilities
Load Environment 340
Login/Token 340
Protecting Routes 341
Token Verification 341
JWT, configuring 339

K

Kubernetes 410
Kubernetes Cluster, components
Control Plane 410

- Worker Node 411
- Workload Resources 411

Kubernetes, deploying 411

L

Links Tag 9
Links Tag, attributes 10
Links Tag, demonstrating 10
Links Tag, practices 11
Links Tag, results 11
Lists Tag 7
Lists Tag, attributes 7
Lists Tag, demonstrating 7
Lists Tag, practices 9
Lists Tag, results 8
Logging 417
Logical Operators 125
Loop Control 130
Loop Control, statements
- Break 130
- Continue 131

Loops 127
Loops, types
- Do-While 128
- For 128
- While 128

M

Misaligned Form 59
MobX 249
Modules 166
Modules, exports
- Combined 167
- Default 167
- Named 167

MongoDB 362
MongoDB, concepts
- Aggregation Pipeline 365
- Backup/Monitoring 365
- CRUD 363
- Indexing 364
- Replica Sets 364
- Sharding Partitions Data 364

Multi-Line Comments 117

N

Nested Routes 227
Nested Routes, illustrating 227, 228
Node.js 322
Node.js, configuring 322
Node.js, ensuring 323
Node.js, features 322
NoSQL Database, patterns
- Document Store 356
- Graph Systems 357
- Key-Value Stores 357
- Wide-Column Stores 357

Notification API 180
Nullish Coalescing 170

O

OAuth 341
OAuth, configuring 341
OAuth, flow 342
OAuth, illustrating 343, 344
OAuth, terminology 342
Opacity/Transparency 48
Opacity/Transparency, elements 48
Opacity/Transparency, integrating 48, 49
Optional Chaining 170
Overlapping Elements 67

P

Paragraphs Tag 5
Paragraphs Tag, attributes 5
Paragraphs Tag, demonstrating 5
Paragraphs Tag, practices 6
Paragraphs Tag, results 6
Pipes 288
Pipes, types
- Built-In 288
- Custom 289

Polyfills 97, 98
Portals 254
PostgreSQL 365
PostgreSQL, terms
- Data Representations 366
- Extensibility/Extensions 367
- High Availability 367
- Index Accelerate 366
- JSON Data 366
- Regular Backups 367
- Relational Structure 365
- Transactions/Concurrency 367

Prometheus 418
Prometheus, metrics
- Grafana 419
- Node.js 418

Props 216
Props, types
- Children 216
- Default 217

Pseudo-Classes 88
Pseudo-Classes, terms
- Combinators 89
- Dynamic Theming 90
- Negation 89

Pseudo-Elements 89

R

React 210
React/Angular, case studies
- Facebook 315
- Gmail Clone 316
- Netflix UI 316

React/Angular, comparing 312
React/Angular, differences
- Curve Learning 312
- Performance Efficiency 313
- Scalability 314

React Components 213

React Components, properties
Class Components 215
Function Components 213
Props 216
React Development, guidelines
Code Organization 256
Folder Structure 255
Performance Resources 256
React Ecosystem 251
React Ecosystem, terms
Community Resources 252
Numerous Libraries 252
Tooling 252
React, foundation
Development Server 210
Environment 210
Source Code 211
React, patterns
Higher Order Components (HOCs) 253
Portals 254
Render Props 254
React Performance 234
React Performance, concepts
Memorization 234
React.memo 236
useCallback Hook 236
useMemo Hook 234
React Testing Library (RTL) 241
Redux 247
Redux Toolkit 248
Relative Positioning 66
Render Props 254
Request-Response Cycle 191
Request-Response Cycle, mechanisms
Code Classes 192
Performance Bottleneck 191
Request Format 191
Server Response 192
Responsive Design 81
Responsive Design, approaches
Auto Grid 84
Combined Layout 84
Flexbox Layout 84
Grid Layout 83
Responsive Visibility 84
Responsive Design, characteristics
Accessibility/Consistency 82
Fine-Tune Styles 82
High-Density 82
Orientation 82
Standard Breakpoints 81
Responsive Design, steps
CSS, styling 91
Function, navigating 93
HTML File 90
REST APIs 204
REST APIs, architecture 204
REST APIs, guidelines 205
RESTful APIs 332
RESTful API Server 349
RESTful API Server, terms
API Design 349
CRUD 350
Initialization 350
JWT Authentication 352
Validate Functionality 353
RESTful APIs, principles
API Testing 334
Consistent Endpoints 333
Server Start 334
Routing 225, 280
Routing, architecture 226
Routing, concepts
Guards Navigation 282
Nested Routes 282
Route Parameters 281
Routing, configuring 280
Routing, integrating 226

S

Seamless Database Integration 368
Seamless Database Integration, terms
Aggreagation Pipeline 370
CRUD Operations 369
Database Systems 376
Data Retrieval 370
Indexing 375
Mongoose 368
Sequelize 372
Transactions/Consistency 375
User Schema 369
Secure HTTP 192
Secure HTTP, benefits 193
Secure HTTP, terms
Certificate Chain 193
Private Key 193
Redirect Request 193
TLS Handshake 193
Sequelize 372
Sequelize, configuring 373
Sequelize, foundations
Associations 374
Error Handling 374
Models 373
Transactions Groups 374
Side-by-Side Columns 68
Single-Line Comments 117
Snapshot Testing 244
SQL/NoSQL Database, comparing 358
State Management 217
State Management, hooks
Lifting State 220
useReducer 218
useState 217
State Management, libraries
MobX 249
Reduc Toolkit (RTK) 248
Redux 247
Statements 115
Statements/Expressions, comparing 116
Static Website 24
Static Website, steps
About Page 24

Contact Page 25
CSS Stylesheet 26
Homepage 24
Structured Logging 418
Styled Components 246
Styling 244
Styling, approaches
CSS-in-JS 246
CSS Modules 245
Style Components 246
Tailwind CSS 244
Styling Lists 55
Styling Tables 57
Switch Statement 127
Symbols 169

T

Table Tag 15
Table Tag, attributes 15
Table Tag, demonstrating 15
Table Tag, integrating 17
Table Tag, results 16
Tailwind CSS 75, 244
Tailwind CSS, terms
Responsive Grid Utilities 75
Utility-First Philosophy 75
Template Literals 168
Testing 241
Testing, approaches
Jest 241
React Testing Library (RTL) 241
Snapshot 244
Testing Auth 338
Text Alignment 53
Text Alignment, terms
Style First 53
Style Links 53
Third-Party APIs 391
Third-Party Authentication, methods
API Keys 392
Basic Authentication 393
Bearer Tokens 393
OAuth 2.0 392
Third-Party Integration, techniques
Axios 392
Crypto Prices 392
Fetch Usage 391
Throttling 172
Todo Application 257
Todo Application, architecture 257
Todo Application, illustrating 265
Todo Application, implementing 258-263
Type Conversion 122
Type Conversion, categories
Explicit 123
Implicit 123
Typeface 49
Typeface, architecture 50
Typeface, configuring 49, 50
Typeface, elements
Font Face 51
Font Size 50
Font Weight 52
Line Spacing 52

U

User Interactions 162
User Interactions, events
Click 162
Keypress 163
Scroll 163

V

Validation 157
Validation, configuring 157
Validation, types
Basic 158
Custom 158
Real-Time 158
Variables 86, 118
Variables, architecture 86
Variables, configuring 87
Variables, types
Declaration 118
Hoisting 119
Scope 119
Version Control 394
Version Control, approaches
Branching 395
Git 394
Videos Tag 13
Videos Tag, attributes 13
Videos Tag, demonstrating 13

W

Web APIs 173
Web Application 399
Web Application, integrating 399, 400
Web Application, threats 399
Web Developer Toolbar 63, 64
Web Server 206
Web Server, implementing 206
Web Server, steps 206
WebSockets 176
WebSockets, configuring 176
WebSockets, integrating 176
Web Storage 159
Web Storage, types
Local 159
Session 159
While Loop 128

X

XMLHttpRequest (XHR) API 174